GENDER INJUSTICE

To My Mother and Father, and My Uncle Theodore,
for their love and devotion.

Gender Injustice

An International Comparative Analysis of Equality in Employment

ANNE-MARIE MOONEY COTTER

ASHGATE

Published by
Ashgate Publishing Limited
Gower House
Croft Road
Aldershot
Hants GU11 3HR
England

Ashgate Publishing Company
Suite 420
101 Cherry Street
Burlington, VT 05401-4405
USA

Ashgate website: http://www.ashgate.com

British Library Cataloguing in Publication Data
Cotter, Anne-Marie Mooney
Gender injustice : an international comparative analysis of equality in employment
1. Sex discrimination in employment - Law and legislation - Cross-cultural studies 2. Sex discrimination against women - Law and legislation - Cross-cultural studies
I. Title
344' .014133

Library of Congress Cataloging-in-Publication Data
Cotter, Anne-Marie Mooney.
Gender injustice : an international comparative analysis of equality in employment / Anne-Marie Mooney Cotter.
p. cm.
Includes bibliographical references and index.
ISBN 0-7546-2377-7
1. Discrimination in employment--Law and legislation. 2. Discrimination in employment. I.Title.

K1770.C68 2004
344.01'4133--dc22

2004000032

ISBN 0 7546 2377 7

Printed and bound in Great Britain by TJ International Ltd, Padstow, Cornwall

Contents

Biography

Dr. Anne-Marie Mooney Cotter, Esq. is a Montrealer, fluent in both English and French. She earned a Bachelor of Arts degree (McGill University, Montreal) at age 18, a Graduate Diploma in Community Politics and the Law (Concordia University, Montreal), a Master of Arts degree in Public Policy Public Administration (Concordia University, Montreal), a Graduate Certificate in Teaching French as a Second Language to Adults (Concordia University, Montreal), a Juris Doctor law degree (J.D.) (Howard University School of Law, Washington, D.C.) from one of the leading Civil Rights Institutions, and a Doctorate degree (Ph.D.) (Concordia University, Montreal) in Political Economy International Law on the issue of equality. Her work experience has been extensive, acting as Chief Advisor and later Administrative Law Judge appointed by the Prime Minister to the Veterans Review and Appeals Tribunal in Canada; Supervising Attorney for the Legal Services Corporation in the United States and later Executive Director; National Director for an Environmental Network in Canada; and she is now Faculty for Business Law (Banking Corporate Financial Services Law, Information Technology Law, Insolvency Law, Intellectual Property Law, Regulatory Law), Environmental Law, and Discrimination (Human Rights) Law at the Law School, the Law Society of Ireland. She has been extensively published, and has acted as editor/author on numerous legal publications. Dr. Cotter is a gold medallist in figure skating.

Chapter 1

Introduction to Gender Injustice

> So we come here today to dramatise a shameful condition. In a sense we've come to our nation's capital to cash a check. When the architects of our republic wrote the magnificent words of the Constitution and the Declaration of Independence, they were signing a promissory note to which every (human) was to fall heir. This note was the promise that all...would be guaranteed the unalienable rights of life, liberty, and the pursuit of happiness....A check which has come back marked insufficient funds. We refuse to believe that there are insufficient funds in the great vaults of opportunity of this nation. And so we've come to cash this check, a check that will give us upon demand the riches of freedom and the security of justice.[1]

In our universal quest for justice, we may learn from the immortal words of one of the greatest civil rights leaders and human rights activists Dr. Martin Luther King Jr. This book 'Gender Injustice' focuses on the goal of gender equality, and the importance of the law and legislation to combat discrimination. The aim of this book is to better understand the issue of inequality and to improve the likelihood of achieving gender justice in the future and ending gender injustice. Gender Injustice examines the primary role of legislation, which has an impact on the court process, as well as the primary role of the judicial system, which has an impact on the fight for gender equality.

Fundamental rights are rights, which either are inherent in a person by natural law or are instituted in the citizen by the State. The ascending view of the natural law of divine origin over human law involves moral expectations in human beings through a social contract, which includes minimum moral rights of which one may not be deprived by government or society. The competing view is that courts operating under the Constitution can enforce only those guarantees which are expressed. Thus, legislation has an impact on the court system and on society as a whole. Internationally and nationally, attempts have been made to improve the situation of women and outlaw discrimination.

Gender discrimination in the labor market involves the unequal treatment of men and women, affecting remuneration and access to employment. More specifically, the concept of pay equity encompasses the rendering of a salary on an objective basis, based on performance for like work without regard to gender. Discrimination involves the deprivation of a fair reward for effort produced.

In looking at the relationship between gender and the law, the book deals comprehensively with the issues of equal pay and equal access to employment throughout its chapters: Chapter 1 introduces the reader to the core area of gender injustice and inequality; Chapter 2 covers women and employment including a look at the feminist perspective and how it relates to the law and the court; Chapter

3 looks at the United Nations; Chapters 4 and 5 examine gender injustice in Australia and New Zealand, and Africa and South Africa, respectively; Chapters 6 and 7 examine gender injustice in Canada, Mexico and the United States, and the North American situation with the North American Free Trade Agreement as to its impact on women in employment, respectively; Chapters 8 and 9 examine gender injustice in the United Kingdom and Ireland, and the European situation with the European Union Treaty as to its impact on women in employment, respectively; and Chapter 10 concludes this overview of gender injustice.

'Gender Injustice' examines equality in employment for men and women in terms of the law, at both the national and international levels. The globalization process and the various economic agreements have a direct impact on women's lives as key players in the labor market today. This study seeks to comparatively analyze legislation impacting women in various countries internationally. It also examines the two most important trade agreements of our day, namely the North American Free Trade Agreement and the European Union Treaty in a historical and compelling analysis of women and equality. Although an important trade agreement with implications for labor, the North American Free Trade Agreement has a different system from the European system in that it has no overseeing court with jurisdiction over the respective countries. Further, the provisions for non-discrimination in the labor process are contained in a separate document, the North American Agreement on Labor Cooperation. On the other hand, the European Union Treaty takes a different approach, by directly providing for non-discrimination, as well as an overseeing court, the European Court of Justice, and the treaty is made part of the domestic law of every Member State, weakening past discriminatory laws and judgments, including gender discrimination in employment. Further, the European process actively implements equal pay and equal treatment in access to employment for men and women by way of EU Directives.

North America, as the new world with its image of freedom and equality, is considered to have made great strides in civil rights. However, the American philosophy of survival of the fittest and the pursuit of materialism have slowed down the process. With the advent of the European Union, the coming together of Nations has had a very positive influence on the enforcement of human rights, much more so than that of North America, because of the unique European approach.

Around the world, in situations where women have won greater equality, the benefits to development have been enormous.[2] However, in both 'developed' and 'developing' countries, often times women's work is unpaid and taken for granted. Internationally, large companies are starting to accept the need to behave responsibly in countries and communities where they operate. Women are getting to the top more than ever before, succeeding in jobs, and making a difference in local and national governments. However, gender injustice still pervades. Women need to be a central part of the decision-making process in every country and at every level. To ensure women's voices are heard, women need an equal right to access to information, and to freedom of expression and association. All Parties must cooperate, and governments need to work with businesses, trade unions and society as a whole, and together, they can create an environment where women can participate at all levels of political life and decision-making. Indeed, combating gender injustice and achieving gender justice requires a strong gender focus in constitutional, legal, judicial and electoral frameworks for women to be actively involved at the national and international levels.

The Role of Women in Global Society

The world population numbers 5,304 million people, with men accounting for slightly over 50 per cent.[3] In terms of economic status, globally, 61 per cent of females aged 15 to 64 are in the labor force compared to 86 per cent of males, while in Europe, 64 per cent of females are in the labor force compared to 80 per cent of males, and in North America, 70 per cent of females are in the labor force compared to 82 per cent of males.[4] In essence, internationally, men continue to dominate the labor force.

Internationally, average female hourly earnings are below those for males, whether measured for part-time or full-time workers. The average earnings for women are roughly 84 per cent of the average earnings for men. In the European Union, the wage gap in the private sector is larger than that in the public sector, with the average earnings for females at 76 per cent in the private sector compared to just under 89 per cent in the public sector. In many countries around the world, women are more likely than men to hold low paying jobs. In Japan, roughly 37 per cent of working women are in low wage employment, compared to just 6 per cent of men. Similar figures are evident in the United States with 33 per cent of women and 20 per cent of men working in low wage employment.[5]

According to the 1995 Human Development Index produced by the United Nations Development Programme (UNDP), poverty has a woman's face; of the 1.3 billion people living in poverty worldwide, 70 per cent are women. Macroeconomic and social policy amended within the context of economic reform programs and globalization trends have resulted in decreases of public expenditures and social welfare provisions. The consequences impact disproportionately upon women and girls in areas such as education, training, health care and social services, public sector employment and general unemployment, and in basic needs such as food and medicines. Women have fewer opportunities for income generation, yet they are expected to provide economic and social sustenance for their families and communities.

Global market forces and competitiveness are increasingly determining the economic framework and opportunities within every country. A number of opportunities have opened up for female employment both within the informal sector through medium, micro/small enterprise development, and the formal sector including export-processing zones. Despite the generally poor wages and equally poor working conditions compared to international standards and male counterparts, women workers often have the potential to earn higher incomes than in their traditional jobs, and can thus benefit from investments in education and training.

The shift to unregulated global markets has also resulted, however, in dramatic and undesirable consequences for female labor. Women generally tend to be the last to benefit from job expansion and the first to suffer from job contraction. Many of the jobs created in recent agro and tertiary industry expansion involve labor-intensive, low-paid, and informal activities that are sub-contracted to women, often on a casual insecure basis. Protective legislation regarding wages, benefits and working conditions is often undermined while social safety nets are non-existent or disappearing. Economic restructuration and contraction in employment levels within the state boundaries have resulted in the destabilization of the social framework and of families and communities, and the reduction in welfare provisions resulting in hardships.

As we begin a new millennium, interesting research has emerged for women in the world, in the areas of population, women and men in families, and education and communication.[6] Overall, in terms of population: 1. Women are having fewer children on average, but with more women of reproductive age, the world population continues to grow; 2. Women outnumber men in most regions, except for Asia; and 3. Women represent a large proportion of international migrants, an estimated 56 million women out of a total of 118 million.

In terms of families: 1. Women are generally marrying later but more than a quarter of women aged 15 to 19 are married in over twenty 'developing' countries; 2. Informal unions are common in 'developed' regions and in some countries of the 'developing' regions; 3. Birth rates continue to decline in all regions of the world; 4. Births to unmarried women have increased dramatically in 'developed' regions; 5. More people are living alone in the 'developed' regions, the majority being women; and 6. In many countries of the 'developed' regions, more than half of mothers with children under age three are employed.

In terms of education and communication: 1. The gender gap in primary and secondary schooling is closing, but women still lag behind men, especially in some countries of Africa and Southern Asia; 2. Two thirds of the world's 876 million illiterates are women, the number of illiterates not expected to decrease significantly in the next twenty years; 3. Women have made significant gains in higher education enrollment in most regions of the world, and in some regions, women's enrollment now equals or surpasses that of men; 4. More women than men lack the basic literacy and computer skills needed to enter 'new media' professions; and 5. In many countries, women represent a rapidly increasing share of Internet users.[7]

The Rule of Law

According to liberal democracy, the rule of law is the foundation stone for the conduct of institutions. 'Gender Injustice' offers a defence of the notion that social reform is possible and plausible through key institutions, which include the legal system and its use of the law. For liberal democracy, the legislative system is the core for the governance of society in the way it functions toward social equality of opportunity. It is clear that if we reform our legislation and our laws, then there will be a change in the institutions of society and their functioning, which will be a major step forward in societal reform.

The law is of central importance in the debate for change from gender injustice to gender justice. Actionable and enforceable rights are legal norms, which represent social facts demarcating areas of action linked with universalized freedom.[8] Law is a powerful tool, which can and must be used to better society. Associated with command, duty and sanction, and emanating from a determined source, law is a rule of conduct enforced by sanctions, and administered by a determinate locus of power concentrated in a sovereign or a surrogate, the court. Therefore, the justice system and the courts play a vital role in enforcing the law.

Legitimacy has subjective guarantees of internalization with the acceptance and belief in authority, and objective guarantees of enforcement with the expectation of reactions to the behavior.[9] Therefore, law must recognize equally all members of society, including women, in order for it to be effective. Further, in order for a law to be seen as legitimate from society's point of view and accepted by the people in general to be followed, a process of inclusive interaction by all affected must first be realized. When creating laws, this means that input from various groups, including women, is critical.

Thus, laws have two components, namely, facts which stabilize expectations and sustain the order of freedom, and norms which provide a claim of approval by everyone. Law makes possible highly artificial communities whose integration is based simultaneously on the threat of internal sanctions and the supposition of a rationally motivated agreement.[10] Discrimination and injustice can be undercut through the effective use of both the law and the courts.

The facticity of the enforcement of law is intertwined with the legitimacy of a genesis of law that claims to be rational, because it guarantees liberty. Laws can go a long way in forbidding inequality and providing for equality; where one ends the other begins. There are two ranks of law, namely ordinary law of legislation, administration and adjudication, and higher constitutional law affecting rights and liberties, which government must respect and protect. The latter encompasses the Constitutions of the various Nations as interpreted by the Supreme Courts. Law holds its legitimacy and validity by virtue of its coercive potential, its rational claim of acceptance as right. It is procedurally constructed to claim agreement by all citizens in a discursive process purported to be open to all equally for legitimacy and a presumption of fair results. The legitimate legal order is found in its reflexive process. Therefore, we must all believe that equality is a good and necessary thing, which is essential to the very growth of society.

Thus, conflict resolution is a process of reasoned agreement, where 1. members assume the same meanings by the same words; 2. Members are rationally accountable for their actions; and 3. Mutually acceptable resolutions can be reached so that supporting arguments justify the confidence in the notion that the truth in justice will not be proven false.[11] Disenchantment with the law and the legal process only serves to undermine the stabilization of communities. By legitimizing the legal process and holding up the ideals of equality in the fight against gender injustice, the law and the courts can bring about change.

Women have had to fight in the formulation of laws and in the enforcement of equality in the courts. It is important to note that women have invoked gender, race, nationality, class, age, and disability, transcending many barriers, in their fight against discrimination. While class rests on economic determination and historical change, like race, gender has no such association and no unanimity of definition. However, gender inequality and class inequality have been compared, since inequality in the distribution of private property between men and women has been and is just as characteristic of society, as inequality in the distribution of private property among different classes of men. The ruling class loathes that which it is not, that which is foreign to it, and this has traditionally been women and minorities. The patriarchal system has freely fashioned laws and adjusted society to suit those in power, and this has traditionally been men.

Equality in Employment

Gender refers to the social attributes and opportunities associated with being female and male, and the relationships between women and men, and girls and boys, as well as between women and between men. These attributes, opportunities and relationships are socially constructed and are learned through socialization processes. They are context and time-specific but changeable, since gender determines what is expected, allowed and valued in a woman or a man in a given situation. In most societies, there are differences and inequalities between men and women in the assignment of responsibilities, undertaking of activities, access to and control over resources, and decision-making opportunities, with gender part of the broader sociocultural context. Along with gender, there are other important criteria for analysis, including race, poverty and class, age, and disability, and hence all these can, alone or combined, amount to discrimination.

In looking at the issue of equal pay, in terms of equal pay for equal work, male and female workers are protected from discrimination, and one should receive the same pay as a worker of the opposite sex performing the same work, provided that both work for the same employer. However, differences in salary can be justified if they are due to objective factors unconnected with sex, such as qualifications and experience. If one job is equally demanding but is paid less, then the employer must justify the wage differential as being based on grounds other than gender. When jobs with different titles are essentially the same, their remuneration should be the same. The term ‘pay’ covers all benefits provided by the employer in connection with employment. These benefits can be received under contract, statutory or collective provisions, or on a voluntary basis, can be in cash or in kind, that is travel facilities or housing, or in the form of shift premiums or overtime pay, and can encompass future benefits such as redundancy benefits, which will be received when employment has ended.

Further, in terms of equal pay for work of equal value, male and female workers are protected from discrimination, which may occur when they are performing different jobs for the same employer, and one should receive equal pay for work of equal value. In concrete terms, this means that where one undertakes work as demanding as that of the other sex, even though the work is different, one should receive the same pay and benefits, unless there is a nondiscriminatory explanation for the differential. To determine whether the work performed is of equal value, a comparison of work is required, which involves assessing the nature of the tasks and the demands made upon the workers in carrying them out, such as skill, effort and responsibility. Only the nature of the job is relevant to this assessment, so that such a factor as one being part-time and the other being full-time, is not relevant and cannot justify the wage differential. Further, the right to equal pay for equal work and work of equal value should apply both to the public and private sectors, whether the pay has been decided by collective agreements, wage scales, wage agreements or individual contracts.

Finally as to job classification systems, jobs are categorized in order to determine the relative pay in a hierarchy of jobs. When a job classification or evaluation system is used to determine the pay, that system must be based on criteria, which does not discriminate based on gender, and should therefore take into account criteria for which workers of either sex can show aptitude. While the system may contain the criterion of physical strength, it should also take into account other criteria to avoid gender discrimination, so that the system should try to reach a balance between different factors present in the job without penalizing those factors present in jobs typically held by women, such as manual dexterity, human relation skills or caring skills.

There remains a difference between the earnings of women and men in the labor market in all industrialized economies.[12] Part of the gap is attributed to differences in the average characteristics of males and females in the labor market, such as educational attainment and work experience. Another part of the gap, which cannot be explained by individual characteristics, is attributed to other factors, that is direct and indirect discrimination against women. There is significant variation in the extent of the gap across sectors, and sectors which tend to have a high proportion of female employees also tend to be characterized as low wage sectors.

Standard or neo-classical economic theory argues that wages are determined by the interplay of the supply and demand for labor and that the earnings of the individual worker are equated to the marginal productivity of the worker, that is the amount added to output by an additional employee, the standard micro-economic analysis. In looking at individual pay differences, economists argue that earnings differences between individuals reflect the market value of what those individuals produce, that is the output. In periods of fast economic development, average earnings can rise rapidly as people move from 'low productivity/low wage' activities to 'high productivity/high wage' activities. While people attempt to move from low wage to higher wage occupations, there is a limit to this process, which helps explain the persistence of wage differentials.

In order to be highly productive, workers are likely to require skills and knowledge, which may be difficult or expensive to acquire. The theory of Human Capital argues that people can increase their productivity by investing in themselves. The typical means of investment in human capital are formal education and in-work training. Usually, a person with a degree level education will on average have higher earnings during their working lifetime than a person with a secondary level education. However, other factors, such as the amount and quality of a person's work experience, also add to human capital and affect a person's earning potential. Earnings reflect human capital investment so that people with higher earnings tend to have invested more heavily in their human capital. These individuals will generally be found in the higher paid occupations and sectors. However, capital market imperfections limit the ability of people to borrow to invest in themselves so that inherited economic advantages and parental income become important factors. Social class still is a powerful influence on access to education, and hence employment.

Further, some aspects of human capital or ability relate to personal characteristics rather than education, such as intelligence or physical strength, affecting an individual's suitability for certain types of employment. Thus, pay differences reflect productivity differences, but the ability of an individual to exploit his productive potential depends upon being able to access employment. Some social groups suffer from discrimination based on social or cultural factors. Since the economic rationale for legislation depends upon the failure of the market due to discrimination, the 'equal pay for work of equal value' argument implies that wage discrimination at the level of individual jobs is based on the fact that employers are able to pay lower wages in female dominated occupations or positions.

Women's over-representation and under-representation in certain sectors can be explained by human capital investment, nonpecuniary 'benefits', and discrimination. In looking at human capital factors, women are 'channelled' into low paid occupations, because of a lack of skills. The main sources of variation in human capital investment relate to education, training in employment and work experience. Historically, women have been less likely to proceed from compulsory schooling to higher education, and less likely to undertake study in disciplines which would have resulted in higher earnings. However, this situation has changed over the last few years in all 'developed' countries, as there has been a much greater equalization in terms of male and female proportions in further education, and hence an increase in the proportion of females in the labor market who hold higher level qualifications.

In terms of nonpecuniary benefits, women have tended to choose lower paid sectors and occupations for certain nonmonetary attributes. Women tend to have quite different labor market experiences from men, and are more likely to leave the labor market for a period of time, because of childcare responsibilities. Women returning to work after a period away from the labor market have less accumulated work experience than men of the same age, which may affect the acquisition of skills and human capital, broadly impacting on vertical promotion. In balancing work and life, many women are constrained in terms of their labor market participation through caring or family responsibilities, and an inability to access affordable full time childcare of an acceptable quality. This may result in some women working part-time rather than full time, or only being able to access employment opportunities close to home rather than commuting to work. The overall effect is to limit the potential employment opportunities of women, and hence the scope for human capital investment.

In looking at discrimination, female earnings are lower than male earnings as a result of labor market discrimination. Human resource processes have not adapted to changes in the overall position of women in society, and indirectly contribute to discrimination against women. Although many countries now have some form of employment equality legislation that outlaws discrimination based on gender, it must be adequately enforced.[13]

Importantly, in looking at group pay differences, the gender pay gap is a difference between groups and not individuals. Like race or age, gender is a factor in employment, and international data show that on average women earn less than men. The occupational and sectoral structures of female employment is both an explanation and a manifestation of the gender pay gap. In looking at the occupational distribution of female employment, occupations which demonstrate significant levels of female employment also tend to be associated with lower relative earnings. There is also a clear under-representation of female employees in the higher skill and higher earning positions, such as managerial, professional and technical occupations. As well, far more women than men work in the 'informal' sector, where wages are low and no benefits such as safety standards, social security or health insurance are afforded. Even when women work in the same sector as men, wages are typically lower.

For many women, working outside the home may not be viewed as a gain in status, but as an unwelcome economic necessity. In addition, more women are remaining in the workforce during their reproductive years, leading to a dual burden, working outside the home while at the same time doing the large share of work in the home. Further, the proportion of female-headed households is on the rise globally, accounting for one-quarter or more of households in North America and in parts of Europe, and these households are typically poorer than those headed by men. Women-headed households can result from divorce, widowhood, unmarried women who begin childbearing, men's migration for work, and war and other armed conflicts. Elderly women living alone account for a growing proportion of female-headed households.

Women today tend to marry later, choose to have smaller families, and are more likely to use contraception and other health care. Further, the gender gap has closed somewhat in recent years, as primary and secondary school enrollments for both girls and boys have increased in almost all regions of the world. However, girls are more likely than boys to discontinue their schooling, because of household duties, early marriage and childbearing, parents' perceptions that education is more beneficial for sons, and worries about girls' safety at school.

Around the world, women's lack of representation in government, especially high-level ministerial, executive and legislative bodies, limits their influence over governance and public policies. Globally, in 2001, women held only 14 per cent of seats in parliaments, a slight increase from a decade earlier.[14]

United Nations conferences have called on governments to reduce the gender pay gap and other disparities between men and women in the workforce and provide additional support to working women, in the form of maternity leave, childcare assistance and other flexible arrangements. As well, they have called for universal access to and completion of primary education.

Women earn lower wages than men in most occupations in most countries. Women's lower pay is partly attributable to the fact that they have, on average, lower seniority in the occupation and grade than men. This is the case where there is a single salary scale applicable to both men and women, such as in the public service, with increments received solely on the basis of seniority. However, overall, the gender pay gap cannot be explained solely by differences in formal qualifications. While occupational and sectoral employment choice is important with a key factor appearing to be career progression and promotion patterns, the role of discrimination remains a problem. Institutional factors impact on the gender pay gap. Apart from the individual characteristics of the employee, other external factors, such as to what extent provisions are made in legislation to outlaw pay discrimination and whether the participation of women in the labor force is facilitated through family-friendly work policies, play an important role in the gender pay gap.

In examining wage setting policies, the more centralized the wage setting system is in a country, the more equitable the outcome for gender pay equality. In the decentralized bargaining system of the American labor market, there is a varied distribution of pay, while in the more centralized systems of the European labor markets, the pay distributions tend to be more compressed. Policies that compress the wage structure and raise the bottom of the wage distribution indirectly benefit women, who are more likely to be found in low-paying jobs. Countries with systems of centrally-determined pay usually have smaller gender wage differentials; centralized systems that reduce the extent of wage variation across industries and firms are likely to lower the gender differential. Since in all countries the female wage distribution lies below the male distribution, centralized systems that consciously raise minimum pay levels, regardless of gender, will also tend to lower the gender pay gap. The impact of gender-specific policies to raise female wages may be greater under centralized systems, where such policies can be more speedily and effectively implemented.

Controlling for the effect of parental leave, unemployment insurance and job protection policies, collective bargaining tends to reduce the gender pay gap. On the other hand, controlling for the presence of centralized bargaining, the effect of minimum wage legislation on the gender pay gap is small and insignificant, and has been found to have a more benign impact on the gender pay gap than collective bargaining.

Overall, there are vast differences in women's and men's access to and opportunities to exert power over economic structures in their societies. In most parts of the world, women are virtually absent from or are poorly represented in decision-making, including the formulation of financial, monetary, commercial and other economic policies, such as rules governing pay. Since it is often within the framework of such policies that individual men and women make decisions on such issues as how to divide time between remunerated and unremunerated work, the actual development of these economic structures and policies has a direct impact on women's and men's access to economic resources, their economic power and consequently the extent of equality between genders at the individual and family levels as well as in society as a whole. Women's participation and gender concerns are still largely absent from and should be integrated into the policy formulation process of the multilateral institutions that define the terms and set the goals of structural adjustment programs, in cooperation with governments.

In many regions, women's participation in remunerated work in the formal and non-formal labor market has increased in the past decade alone. Women have become increasingly involved in micro, small and medium-sized enterprises and, in some cases, have become more dominant in the expanding informal sector. However, due to difficult economic situations and a lack of bargaining power resulting from gender inequality, many women have been forced to accept low pay and poor working conditions, and thus have often become preferred workers. On the other hand, women have entered the workforce increasingly by choice when they have become aware of and demanded their rights, with some having succeeded in entering and advancing in the workplace, and improving their pay and working conditions. Women though have been particularly affected by the economic restructuring processes, which have changed the nature of employment and, in some cases, have led to a loss of jobs, even for professional and skilled women. In addition, many women have entered the informal sector owing to the lack of other opportunities.

In many countries, women are the majority of workers in non-standard work, such as temporary, casual, multiple part-time, contract and home-based employment. Although there has not been a lightening of responsibility for unremunerated work in the household and community, women's share in the labor force continues to rise. Almost everywhere women are working more outside the household, and women's income is becoming increasingly necessary to households of all types.

Although many women have advanced in economic structures, for the majority of women, however, particularly those who face additional barriers, such as race or disability, continuing obstacles have hindered their ability to achieve economic autonomy, and to ensure sustainable livelihoods for themselves and their dependants. Legal and customary barriers to ownership of or access to land, natural resources, capital, credit, technology, and other means of production, as well as important wage differentials, contribute to impeding the economic progress of women.[15] Moreover, attitudinal obstacles inhibit women's participation in developing economic policy and, in some regions, restrict their access.

Discrimination across the board in terms of education and training, hiring and remuneration, vertical promotion and horizontal mobility practices, inflexible working conditions, lack of access to productive resources, and inadequate sharing of family responsibilities, combined with a lack of services such as childcare, continue to restrict employment, as well as professional and economic opportunities for women.

Conclusion

Though humans are mortal and civilizations come and go, from Biblical times to our days, there has been a fixed pivot for the thoughts of all generations and for men of all continents, namely the equal dignity inherent in the human personality.[16] Even Pope John XXIII described the United Nations Declaration of Human Rights in his 1963 Encyclical Pacem in Terris, as 'one of the most important acts of the United Nations' and as 'a step towards the politico-judicial organization of the world community'; 'In social life, every right conferred on man by nature creates in others (individuals and collectivities) a duty, that of recognizing and respecting that right'.[17] Further, Pope John Paul II described the importance of work and of just remuneration in his 1981 Encyclical Laborem Exercens:

> Work bears a particular mark of...humanity, the mark of a person operating within a community of persons....While work, in all its many senses, is an obligation, that is to say a duty, it is also a source of rights on the part of the worker. These rights must be examined in the broad context of human rights as a whole, which are connatural with man, and many of which are proclaimed by various international organisations and increasingly guaranteed by the individual States for their citizens. Respect for this broad range of human rights constitutes the fundamental condition for peace in the modern world: peace both within individual countries and societies and in international relations....The human rights that flow from work are part of the broader context of those fundamental rights of the person....The key problem of social ethic...is that of just remuneration for work done....Hence, in every case, a just wage is the concrete means of verifying the justice of the whole socio-economic system and, in any case, of checking that it is functioning justly.[18]

The concept of equality is the ignoring of difference between individuals for a particular purpose in a particular context, or the deliberate indifference to specified differences in the acknowledgement of the existence of difference.[19] It is important to note that assimilation is not equality. The notion of rights and of equality should be bound to the notion of justice and fairness. Legal freedom and rights must be seen as relationships not possessions, as doing, not having. While injustice involves a constraint of freedom and a violation of human dignity through a process of oppression and domination, justice involves the institutional conditions necessary for the development and exercise of individual capacities for collective communication and cooperation.[20] Discrimination is the withholding from the oppressed and subordinated what enables them to exercise private and public autonomy.

Today, there is still a need to build the identity of 'woman' in order to give it solid legal meaning, while at the same time having a need to tear down its all too solid history of constraint. A tension exists between needing to act as a woman and needing to act as an individual not overdetermined by gender. While women not long ago were perceived as almost a separate species, today the question of what is a woman is not a given. The dilemma is that women are caught between not being heard because of being different, and not being heard because of being almost invisible. On the one hand, there is the promise of solidarity of women, while on the other hand, there is a rebellion about having to be a woman at all. There are minimizers who undermine the very concept of what it is to be a woman with sexual differences, and maximizers who reclaim the all encompassing being of women with empowerment.

In the past decades, women in the so-called 'First-World' have made huge inroads into the labor market, shaking off assumptions that they should be 'homemakers' or 'part-timers', and have taken their place alongside male colleagues. However, inequality remains. The struggle must be continued to bring about psychological, sociological and institutional changes to allow the two halves of the human race, men and women, to feel equal and to recognize one another as being so. Solidarity and cooperation are required for universal and global equality.

> Sometimes I wish that I could no longer see all the pain, the hurt and the longing of my sisters, my brothers, my children and me as we try to be free. Sometimes I wish that my eyes hadn't been opened, for just one moment how sweet it would be not to be struggling, not to be striving, but just to sleep securely in our slavery. But now that I have seen with my eyes, I can't close them, because deep inside me somehow, I still know the road that you, my sisters, my brothers and I would have to travel. My heart would say yes, and my feet would say go. Still sometimes I wish that my eyes hadn't been opened. But now that they have, I'm determined to see that you, my sisters, you, my brothers, my children and I will be the free people that our God created us to be.[21]

An improvement in equality of opportunity is sought rather than a utopian state of equality. No one should misunderstand this. Clearly, oppression exists for men as for women. Rather, this book 'Gender Injustice' seeks to add to the list of inequalities to be considered, and does not rule out other forms of injustices besides gender discrimination against women. Generalities are not presumed nor are they made here for this would detract from the very purpose of this book, to bring to the forefront of discussion the reality of injustice, not to create further injustice. However, we should note that women overall have tended to be disadvantaged, especially in the sphere of equality and employment.

Notes

1 King Jr., Dr. Martin Luther, *March on Washington*, 1963.
2 UK Government, *Equality in Practice*, 2002.
3 United Nations, *Demographic Yearbook*, 1997.
4 United Nations, *The World's Women 2000: Trends and Statistics*, 2000.
5 Department of Justice, Equality & Law Reform, *Developing Sectoral Strategies to Address Gender Pay Gaps*, 2003.
6 *Supra* note 4.
7 *Ibid.*
8 Habermas, Jurgen, *Between Facts and Norms*, 1998, p.xii.
9 Fried, Morton, *The Evolution of Political Society*, 1967, p.23.
10 *Supra* note 8, at p.8.

[11] *Ibid.*, at p.xv.
[12] *Supra* note 5.
[13] *Ibid.*
[14] Population Reference Bureau, *Women of Our World*, 2002.
[15] *Supra* note 5.
[16] Cassin, René, *From the Ten Commandments to the Rights of Man.*
[17] Pope John XXIII, *Pacem in Terris*, 1963.
[18] Pope John Paul II, *Laborem Exercens*, 1981.
[19] Scott, Joan, *Gender and the Politics of History*, 1998, p.172.
[20] *Supra* note 8, at p.419.
[21] Wyatt, Addie, *Public Policy Today: Its Effect on Poor Women*, p.15.

References

Cassin, René, *From the Ten Commandments to the Rights of Man.*

Department of Justice, Equality & Law Reform (2003), *Developing Sectoral Strategies to Address Gender Pay Gaps.*

Fried, Morton (1967), *The Evolution of Political Society*, Random House, New York.

Habermas, Jurgen (1998), *Between Facts and Norms*, MIT Press, Massachussetts.

King Jr., Dr. Martin Luther, *March on Washington*, Aug. 28, 1963.

Pope John XXIII (1963), *Pacem in Terris.*

Pope John Paul II (1981), *Laborem Exercens.*

Population Reference Bureau (2002), *Women of Our World.*

Scott, Joan (1988), *Gender and the Politics of History*, Columbia University Press, New York.

UK Government (2002), *Equality in Practice.*

United Nations (1997), *Demographic Yearbook.*

United Nations (2000), *The World's Women 2000: Trends and Statistics.*

United Nations Division for the Advancement of Women (2002), *Women 2000.*

Wyatt, Addie, *Public Policy Today: Its Effect on Poor Women.*

Chapter 2

Gender Injustice and Women

Introduction

This chapter will examine Gender Injustice and women. It will initially look at women in theory, and will then go on to examine women in employment. In theory, feminism in its various forms will be outlined, and the feminist legal perspective will be analyzed in terms of its relationship with the law, while stressing its paramount importance in relation to the courts. In employment, women in employment will be outlined, including pay inequality and gender segregation, which lead to sex discrimination in employment, and the equal value and wage solidarity approaches will be analyzed to combat gender discrimination.

Women in Theory

Humanity developed gender and sexual identity, and domination arose out of the inability to recognize, appreciate and nurture differences, not simply out of the failure to see all as same. Society developed the symbolic attributes for classifying people, which grew under patriarchy for several reasons: 1. The allocation of rights and responsibilities; 2. The maintenance of civil order and morality; 3. The identity of members; and 4. The aggregation of demographic statistics in the census.[1] Gender rightly identifies the persistence of asymmetric power relations, rather than natural anatomic differences, with women occupying the lesser of dual pairs between man and woman.[2] Justice encompasses several aspirations: 1. The reconciliation of diversities into a new unity of difference; 2. The reciprocity of shared authority and the mutuality of decisions, precluding domination; 3. The recognition of the legitimacy of others and the identification with others; and 4. The judgment process seeing things from the other's point of view of empathy, logic and objectivity.[3] Though all women are women, no woman is only a woman. Thus, gender can be seen as a dichotomy, since one does not necessarily conform to the ascribed character, and can also be seen as a hierarchy within society whereby one gender rules over the other. In believing that the concepts of equality and difference are manifestations of male dominance, 'gender is an inequality of power....Only derivatively is it a difference'.[4] In all, equality does not mean the elimination of difference, and difference does not preclude equality.

Feminist ideology affirms several concepts: 1. Women's oppression is founded in patriarchy, through male defined assumptions and male dominated institutions; 2. The feminist vision is a metamorphosis of society along female principles, not in a reversal of roles but in a partnership; 3. The struggle is about the female condition; 4. Female politics and laws can only be made through the efforts of women in their struggle; 5. Womanness can only be ascertained and verified by women, free from the chains of definition by others; and 6. Women need to be the initiators not the passive recipients.[5] Feminism is a claim by women for the right to self-determination and personal autonomy, and is a form of protest by women about their exclusion from full citizenship, historically considered male. Therefore, the fight is about inclusion as well as rights, and only through a recognition of a commonality among women can structures be changed. In believing that the slogans of the past, 'the personal is the political' and 'sisterhood is powerful' are still useful today, consciousness raising involves showing women that their experiences are not based on inadequacy but are common to many.

Feminist theory is based on the reality of specific historical experiences of oppression. Three key questions in feminist theory highlight the self: 1. How does paying attention to experiences of women, such as caregiving responsibilities and victimization, affect our understanding of the self?; 2. If institutions of male dominance profoundly influence women's lives and minds, how can women form judgments about their own best interests and responsibilities toward others?; and 3. How can feminist politics survive the recognition that the female experience is diverse and shaped by race, class, ethnic, sexual orientation and gender?[6] The conceptualization of the self makes sense of experiences of interpersonal dependency and interdependency in women's lives, while stressing the need to preserve autonomy and integrity. The early quest for the emancipation of women and their access to participation in the existing world can be combined with the later quest for their participation in the transformation of the world toward human equality. Feminism seeks for women the same opportunities and privileges that society gives to men, and asserts the distinctive value of womanhood against patriarchal denigration, in the protest against women's oppression, as it looks to the individuality of each human soul. There is a tension among and within the various feminist schools, namely liberal, radical, cultural, socialist and post-modernist. However, all have as their aim the improvement of women's lives.

Liberal feminism is concerned with equality between men and women above all else. These equality/sameness proponents put forth that sameness does not mean men and women are identical but rather are alike, and they argue that difference is either nonexistent, the product of a mystique, or existing but must be overcome through various efforts including legal activism.[7] There is seen to be a positive relationship between sameness of the sexes in their possession of certain joint qualities, and equality between the sexes in being treated the same way. Women can be seen as capable of combining a career with family, in true fulfillment and equality, cautioning against the damage of overmothering. The push for equality demands advancement for women in education, partnership in labour and remuneration, and coequality in the formation and administration of laws in legislative assemblies, courts of law and executive offices. With equal rights feminism derived from the politics of liberalism, feminism sees greater gender equality through legislation and policy, with the libertarian ideal being that women must fight for general reforms for the benefit of all people.[8] However, liberal feminism has come under attack, because of its tradition of equality using the old male-defined societal structures, with opponents of it arguing that it creates, recreates and renews inequality, and strengthens the public-private split.

Radical feminism sees 'the personal as political' with the patriarchy of male domination at the root of women's oppression, and with women identifying with the subjugated class as they use their primary energy to combat their aggressors.[9] Men and women are seen as fundamentally different, with the female mode the basis of a future society, in the rejection of marriage and family which act as oppressive psychological factors. Further, radical feminism argues for 'womanhood', as it views women as 'we', believing in commonality and mutual support. Espousing the need to be freed from state control and from the constraining association with the family, strong difference feminists argue that the man-made world must be changed as it hinders women.[10] With the end goal being the elimination of male privilege and sexual distinction in order to break the tyranny of biological and psychological power, radical feminism requires the overthrow of patriarchal systems for equality of the sexes. With the philosophy of 'We cannot use the master's tools to dismantle the master's house',[11] the aim is to lift the 'double curse that man should till the soil by the sweat of his brow, and that woman should bear in pain and travail'.[12] In the pursuit of the eradication of gender discrimination, sexual oppression is thought to be the oppression from which all others spring.

Cultural feminism, instead of emphasizing similarities, looks to the differences between men and women, elevating feminine qualities of personal strength as an alternative to the relationship of marriage and home. Underlying cultural feminism is a matriarchal vision of strong women guided by female concerns and values of pacifism, cooperation, non-violent settlement, and harmonious regulation of public life.[13] Strong cultural feminism believes that only women can say what a 'woman' is, by remaking and reclaiming themselves, abhorring the man-made public realm and turning to the deployment of female values for the public good. Although weak cultural feminism believes that the female character with its values and beliefs can be held equally by men, strong cultural feminism believes that women possess qualities superior to men, feminine qualities which are of better use outside the home for entry into the public world, as it can be seen that the woman's voice has been born into and tainted by oppression.[14]

Socialist feminism strives to regain a true human nature. It has moved from revolutionary socialism to accommodation of the political and social system, focusing on differences between groups, while failing to mention class. 'Identity politics' is emphasized through an appreciation of differences between women.[15] Further, socialist feminism explores racism within the feminist movement through the dissatisfaction with the mainly white heterosexual feminist movement, and looks to show that the equality approach has failed within a legal system unable to enforce the most basic rights.

Post-modernist feminism looks away from the category of woman to that of the fluid self, and challenges both equality and difference as employed so far.[16] A central principle of post-feminism is that women have made it or have the opportunity to make it, having the possibilities to decide on priorities and pursuing them.[17] It is at the heart of the 'superwoman' image and the 'new man' image, with access to promotion and job security assumed. Post-modernist deconstruction seeks to attack hierarchies, fighting against closure and the limiting of options. It espouses pluralism by its abolition of the primacy of class, giving women a greater chance of gaining ground. However, in its pursuit of the self, postmodernism will make it difficult to use the term 'woman'.[18]

Feminists have too often been depicted as eternal victims rather than powerful self-sufficient women, the power feminists. There is the ever present false notion that women are unhappy with their new established status both at home and in the office, as wife, mother and career professional, and feminism has been seen as the culprit pushing women to do more, having become fashionable to criticize feminism for the oppression of men. In the 1980s, there was a backlash against feminism, which aimed to turn back the clock and erode the progress brought about by feminism. However, the 'backlash theory' believes if women were miserable, it was not because of feminism, but rather because of the backlash itself.[19]

Further, some see a commitment to family and marriage as a form of escapism, which can produce the narcissist mother who gives incessant attention to the child, an extension of her, her exclusive possession, exaggerating the importance of her offspring. This need to fulfill one's hopes and dreams through another cannot truly make a person whole, and is a reflection of a lost gender. In general, conversely, men can do tasks and work usually associated with mothering. However, mothering and fathering occur in gendered social worlds where masculinities and femininities are largely distinct as experiences. The larger social relations and the social organizations of mothering and fathering preclude men from being socially accepted as 'mothers'.[20] Feminism has at once disengaged the categorizing of women and has also laid claim to it, torn between over-feminization and under-feminization, with the notion of gender and sisterhood becoming at once devaluing and empowering.

Earlier assumptions of shared oppression uniting women have given way to the recognition of difference and diversity, and the subsequent fragmentation, which feminism has experienced, is linked to the notion of sisterhood having hidden differences. Since the western women's liberation has been based on specific identity, that of white middle class young highly educated and heterosexual females, there is at times a mistrust of feminism as not being the story of 'my life'. Further, it has sometimes been seen as irrelevant to most women's day to day lives, not fitting into the official feminist programs or slogans, showing the complexities and inadequacies of simple solutions. However, cutting through the different labels attached to it, feminism means radically different things to different people while heightening social policies and opportunities, and transforming women's lives.

Historically, women were limited to motherhood, in a state of mindless 'maternity-fecundity', causing the birth of the mother and the disappearance of the woman.[21] However, today, females are mothers for a while, and women always, no more in a quasi-prison invented by men, with the choice of life's options the important element for equality.

The Law, The Courts and Women

In examining the interaction between the law and the courts as concerns women's rights, we see that there are various forms of legal paradigms. The liberal paradigm sees the women's struggle for equal access, but it falls short of its stated goal. Further, the overall feminist perspective has been criticized for being too concerned with formal legal equality and ignoring real inequalities, which stem from contingent social conditions and gender differences. The social welfare paradigm looks at the specific benefits to women, such as maternity leave, aid to women with children and childcare services, but it too falls short as government aid programs often define differences inappropriately and serve to make people dependent.

A viable solution is the dynamic proceduralist paradigm, which sees women as essential to public discussions, adding to the necessary process of valued discourse.[22] With its identity politics and consciousness-raising, feminism can fit within the proceduralist understanding of basic rights, a process which secures the private autonomy of equally entitled citizens in step with the activation of their political autonomy. The feminist movement has undergone a reawakening in its dissatisfaction with the liberal approach, the social welfare approach, and the existing institutional framework contributing to the feminization of poverty, which all lead to the consolidation of stereotypes.

The Feminist Legal Perspective

If the sexes were equal, women would not be subjected, their desperation and marginality cultivated, and their enforced dependence exploited. Law has been constructed to structurally adopt the male point of view, with the notion of gender equality remaining but a dream.[23] The legal mandate of equality is to treat likes alike. The transformative potential of the law is the role it can play in the creation of a society based on an ethic, which responds to needs, honours differences and rejects discriminatory abstractions. Gender equality law is still based on the notion that to be human is to be a man.[24] Women are born degraded and die degraded.[25] With the traditional legal system as it is, law becomes legitimate and social dominance becomes invisible, perpetuating discrimination and male dominance. Male forms of power over women are affirmatively embodied as individual rights in law.

The female experience of social inequality and subordination strictly on the basis of sex needs to be confronted. There needs to be a relationship, an interaction between life and law for there to be adequate change. We must speak to the vital role of the law and the courts. Doctrinally, there have been two alternative paths to gender equality within the mainstream legal approach to gender discrimination, illustrating the sameness/difference tension, namely 1. Be the same as men, the gender neutrality doctrine, the single standard philosophy, the formal equality rule of equal to/same as; and 2. Be different from men, the special benefit special protection doctrine, the double standard philosophy of protective labor laws which serve to reinforce subordination and male preference.[26] The debate over equality and difference, the fight for the rendering of equality or the fight for the protection of difference, still lies at the core of contemporary feminist thought.

The early response by feminism was playing the equality game, insisting on the fundamental sameness of women and men, with the key to legal judgments seen as the concept of similarly situated in order to be treated equally. However, stereotypes and the difficulty in finding strict comparisons between the sexes allowed the courts to find women differently situated. The opposite response was to show women's difference and special needs, not taken into account in a degrading way. In reality, equality requires the recognition of both equal rights and special rights. Both individual and collective experiences of women need to be appreciated and incorporated into a non-patriarchal culture. However, both concepts of equality and difference have been used against women, in that formal equality has been defined in male terms, while appeals to female difference or otherness has justified the inequality of the sexes. Equality and difference beg the questions of equal to whom and different from what. The debate is for a gender neutral society based on equality or a dual world with differences, both sometimes playing into the hands of inequality.

Feminist theory is a clarifying structure of the world and of the way in which gender functions produce and reproduce male domination and female subordination.[27] Our personal identity is socially mediated, the constituent of the self being concomitant with the establishment of relations. Only when the force of a group and of tradition loosens the grip do individuals question the legitimacy of norms and move beyond conventionally justified beliefs and values, and thus beyond prejudicial practices. Feminist legal theory views the western legal system as one of the faces of patriarchal domination. The terms of legal discourse too often project masculinist subjectivity, which men have transformed into false universals by virtue of the traditional power they exert to enforce their views. Legal theory or masculinist jurisprudence is an ideology of male supremacy. When women are the subject matter of legal doctrine, it is concerned with the uses men can make of them. Therefore, only women who meet male defined criteria and who speak in voices acceptable to men are welcome to participate in such legal discourse.

Traditionally, law has been used for the definition, appropriation and exploitation of women, and this often for the benefit of men. Feminist theory of law examines the ways in which law reflects and reinforces the social, economic and political structures that surround women. Certain historically perpetuating features of law have served to maintain women's depressed status: 1. Women were not persons but subject matter; 2. Women were viewed by the courts as things that could not enter into legal relationships, and were thus dominated by the patriarchal culture; 3. Women were not able to participate in social, economic and political processes; 4. Women were strictly seen as the means of human reproduction; and 5. Women were simply viewed as sexualized objects for the benefit of men.[28] Men's historic and absolute monopoly over formal political and legal processes has been the biggest barrier to structural reform. Traditionally, men have controlled the interpretation and enforcement of laws, with their vantage point supreme, and still do to a certain extent. Serious reform is still needed to improve conditions.

In looking at the role of gender justice in the court system, it is important to examine the case of Equal Employment Opportunity Commission v. Sears Roebuck & Company (839 F.2d 301 (1988)), which involved the nation-wide sex discriminatory employment practices of an American corporation failing to hire or promote women for commission sales jobs traditionally seen as male jobs.[29] The case was closely observed by feminist groups. The Sears case brought two fundamental opinions into legal focus. One argued that the fundamental differences between the sexes, a result of culture and a long socialization period, justified unequal institutional practices and the manipulation of employment definitions and standards. This position was used by Rosalind Rosenberg and Sears Roebuck to show women as different from men, and as lacking interest in the positions traditionally held by men. Alternatively, however, Alice Kessler-Harris argued for the diversity of women's work when women were given the opportunity. She endeavored to show that 1. Historically, there was evidence of a large variety of jobs that women actually took; 2. Economic considerations offset the effects of socialization in women's attitudes toward employment, with wage incentives playing a role in taking new demanding atypical positions; and 3. Job segregation by sex was the consequence of employment preferences not employee choices, with the hiring process predetermining outcome and a generalized gender criteria not necessarily being relevant to work (Equal Opportunity Commission v. Sears Roebuck & Company, 839 F.2d 301 (1988)).[30] The debate went beyond equality versus difference to the general ideas of sexual differences in a specific context.

When the Sears case went on appeal, the United States Court of Appeals Seventh Circuit affirmed the decision of the United States District Court for the Northern District of Illinois and decided that 1. The Equal Employment Opportunity Commission (EEOC) failed to establish that the employer Sears discriminated against women in hiring into commission sales positions, in light of the evidence presented by the employer indicating that women were not as interested in commission sales jobs as men; 2. Statistical analyses presented by the EEOC failed to show that the employer discriminated against women in promotions from non-commission sales jobs; 3. The EEOC failed to establish sex discrimination in the wages that the employer paid management, professional and administrative employees; and 4. Conflict of interest arising from the fact that the EEOC attorney and the special assistant were members of a woman's organization which urged litigation against employers did not require dismissal of the suit (Equal Opportunity Commission v. Sears Roebuck & Company, 839 F.2d 301 (1988)).[31] Thus, the court found that the assumption of equal interest between the sexes was unfounded, because of the differences between men and women. This judgment of real and fundamental difference redefined discrimination by a recognition of natural difference synonymous with inequality. Thus, the Sears ruling was seen to essentialize difference and naturalize inequality. However, in order to overcome its negative impact to the cause of gender equality, the Sears case can factually or jurisdictionally be distinguished from other cases at hand. As well, it can be argued that the Sears decision was rendered by a lower court in the United States judicial process and not one that is controlling, such as decisions emanating from the Supreme Court. In fact, United States Supreme Court Justice

Ruth Ginsburg once reiterated that men and women should be treated as individuals, not as members of a sexually determined class.[32]

In essence, legislation and adjudication have become part of the problem, since traditional approaches have failed in their definitions of differences. There is a need for substantial change in the legal paradigm of equality, since courts have too often allowed biology to dictate one's destiny. With the court system traditionally relying heavily on precedent, old prejudices become new prejudices.

Rights should be seen as tools for continuing communal discourse with human responsibility of action and inaction.[33] Public discussions must clarify aspects of sameness and difference, not only between men and women but also among women for gender justice. This requires the affected parties to conduct public discourse to better articulate standards of comparison and justify relevant experiences. Through this process, it is important to interpret rights as relationships, to negotiate a community committed to solve problems, with law newly focused on human responsibility for patterns of relationships. Laws should be predicated on principles of disinterestedness and on the observance of norms of reason not power, rationality not domination, truth not authority. Women have risked disrupting the gendered organization of society and the general opinion that has assigned them a place in the private domestic realm only.

Law has tended to overlook the substantive particularities of women's situations. It presumes neutrality and impartiality by assuming fairness. This ignores substantive inequalities, which exist by virtue of societal, economic and ideological factors. In law, women's injuries are not analogous to men's. However, the debate is still whether to allot to women a different status as a special group with special treatment, or to allot a fair and equal status with existing remedies. Reform of existing law is not by itself enough to improve the status of women, but acts only as a necessary precondition to advancement. With this comes the need to avoid the excesses of cooptation and the threat of a backlash in the law reform process. It is necessary that women act as key players in law, for the achievement of a meaningful reform process of legislation and court judgments. Women have endured struggles in law, in order to bring about two objectives: 1. The repeal of laws, which form the conditions of women's oppression; and 2. The enactment of laws, which mean to improve the status of women.[34]

A new strategy must be undertaken: 1. Women themselves must look at the whole theory of law from an unfettered female perspective; 2. Women must obtain the repeal of all provisions that perpetuate male appropriation of female production, reproduction and sexual capacity; 3. Women must closely scrutinize every aspect of the law for disparate impact, differential application and nonneutralities in the language of legal thought; and 4. Women must develop methods to prevent existing legal provisions from being applied in a discriminatory manner.[35] It is important that legal enforcement mechanisms be revised around the realities of women's experiences with the law.

Utopia is the ideal society envisioned according to one's own perception. There are three classes of feminist utopia: 1. Feminists who emphasize that women and men are basically equal describe the utopian society where both have equal rights and opportunities, expecting to live in the same situations with an equal division of the household responsibilities; 2. Feminists who emphasize differences between men and women formulate the utopian society where women's positions are better than men's in a matriarchy of amazon days where feminine qualities are valued more highly than traditional masculine qualities for emotion over rationality, love over status; and 3. Feminists who neither want equality of the sexes nor female supremacy envision the utopian society where gender is hardly or is of no importance or no longer exists.[36]

Women in Employment

The concept of gender does not have a well-entrenched meaning, and was first used by feminists to denote a difference in the biological sexes and in the social process. However, today, gender is far more. The term gender is used to show the complexity between males and females as a basis for organizing social life, to establish an identity and interpret experiences, and to symbolize the material line dividing work resources, power and honor.[37] Inequality between the sexes has shown itself to be a persistent problem. Since the mid-1960s, gender segregation and the wage gap have only slightly altered, and while there has been improvement for women in some middle class jobs, there has been a persistent standstill in others. Job inequality is so deeply imbedded in societal structures and processes as to be recreated as others are eliminated, so that the differences between the sexes are reconstituted in new guises in the restructuring process. However, efforts must still be undertaken to alleviate inequality, through resort to legislation and the courts.

Gender Segregation in the Labor Market

The division of labor is a fragmentation or a splitting up of work tasks into increasingly narrow and more distinct components, which are fuelled by pressure to increase output and produce more goods and services with limited resources.[38] The result is specialization of the production process. The redistribution of uncertainty is an underlying issue, being a response to worker unrest and a proximate cause of duality in the labor market. The market is separated into a stable component which consists of an extensive division of labor and highly specialized resources, and an unstable component which consists of less articulate or specialized labor.[39] The supply-side argues that women prefer certain occupations, accounting for their overrepresentation in certain jobs.[40] This is because of certain characteristics like caretaking, or because of issues of time training, flexible employment or re-entry possibilities. The demand-side argues that employers prefer women for some jobs and men for other jobs, and that workers and customers have preferences, which would allow for some discrimination.

The concept of dualism looks to the structure of institutions, which have maintained a difference between the modern sector consisting of advanced technology and capital intensive enterprises, and the traditional sector consisting of smaller enterprises, local rather than imported technology and a lack of formal educational requirements. The evidence from developed and developing societies suggests the persistence of the traditional or informal sector, with the processes of industrialization and modernization generating a heterogeneous recast of old moulds.[41] The theory of dual labor markets involves either good jobs with high responsibility, salary and job stability, or bad jobs, the rest that make up the lower echelon. Access to good jobs is controlled by institutional factors and discrimination. Incorrect beliefs become self-fulfilling. Therefore, occupational segregation is a lack of opportunity, which will not be automatically reversed. It requires affirmative action to overcome stereotypes.

The theory of labor market discrimination involves civil rights, the women's movement and anti-discrimination legislation. It postulates that earnings differences are based on race and gender, which are only reduced through effective enforcement of anti-discrimination policies.[42] Discriminatory economic policy defines, explains and measures labor market discrimination in the unequal access to jobs and to education, with the policy used to appraise the effect of anti-discrimination measures. In business, client processing is a highly sexualized operation catering to comforts and prejudices. Race and gender are moral evaluations, which have a consequence on the allocation of goods and services, in terms of quantity and priority, in a discriminatory manner. These are traditional elements of the discipline of queuing in the discriminatory service system. Some groups judged inferior, such as women, are assigned a lower priority. Transformation rules, whether explicit or implicit, formal or informal, enable service systems to infer from one's character the priority category to which one belongs.[43]

The labor market is a labor queue, comprised of ordered elements, with society granting men first choice of jobs which are the most attractive. A queue has three structural properties, namely the order of elements which includes jobs and groups of workers; the shape which includes the size of various elements, the population subgroups in the labor queue and the occupations in the job queue; and the intensity of rankers' preferences.[44] Organizational constraints are expressed through the functionally necessary task hierarchy. A queue is a societal structure, which consists of elements organized in terms of a priority and waiting system.[45] The queue discipline involves the moral rule of first come first served. Queuing for resources is the fundamental process of social organization.

Occupational segregation is created by the fact that the queue governs labor outcomes, with employers hiring workers from as high in the labor queue as possible and the worker accepting the best jobs. If preferred jobs outnumber the high ranked, then the employer will fill them with the lower ranked, and visa versa. A preferred group is often chosen regardless of qualifications on the basis of group membership. Shortages spur occupational composition change to force employers to resort to a lower rank. Therefore, non-white men, white women and non-white women benefit from employment descent and labor shortage. Further, the queue theory notes that the worker from the lowest rank is the last hired and the first fired. Specifically, the gender queue is the system of gender segregation established in most jobs. This has resulted in the fact that the high ranked male workforce has grown the fastest, is paid the best, has more vocational training, requires less strength, and shelters incumbents from competition.

Several conclusions can be drawn: 1. Gender labels of jobs as male or female influence the day to day hiring and job assignments, which affects the employment notion of appropriate workers; 2. Difficulty in identifying productive workers requires the resort to proxies of educational attainment, experience and group membership. Gender stereotyping produces the beliefs that men outproduce and are rationally stronger than women, who are perceived to have higher absenteeism and turnover rates. Where observers can easily judge preferences, the employer will act less on stereotypes; 3. The male worker has a negative response to female interlopers, who are seen as reducing production and raising labor costs by increasing turnover. This leads men to demand higher wages to compensate for working with women, and to organise opposition through strikes, slowdowns and on the job resistance; and 4. Higher wages for men is a reality, since they are often favored in biased rankings.[46] Gender solidarity preserves male sex based privileges, forestalling women in a patriarchal norm of power. Women could move ahead if employers believed that: 1. Production costs between sexes have changed; 2. Aversion to women has declined; 3. Costs for discriminatory preferences have risen, due to legislation limiting employer down-ranking of women; and 4. New rankers do not have a male preference.

However, occupational segregation of the sexes along different lines of work is recognized. Men are usually found in sectors of management, craft and transportation, being the best paid white and blue collar workers, while women are usually found in the service and administrative support jobs, as well as the semi-professional female dominated sectors of nursing, library, social work and teaching. Over the last decades, we have seen the rise of employed married women with children, who have experienced the most growth in the labor force. Only a century ago, the women who worked were young and unmarried. One factor considered to have played a role in the segregation of women is the marital-parental status, which has acted as a limiting force. As well, there has been a change in the gender distribution of certain occupations. In terms of clerical workers, few of whom were women in the late 19th century, they are now predominantly female, due to the fact that women were considered less expensive and well suited for boring manual work. In terms of waiting occupations which were predominantly male until the 1920s, they are now mainly female, with waitressing the sixth largest occupation for women, due to the perceived greater cleanliness of women. While schoolteachers were mostly male at one point, a changeover occurred early on, with women being less costly. However, men likewise have had an increase in numbers in three female occupations, namely cooks, kitchen workers and maids.

Women today, however, have a sense of entitlement to a greater choice in the types of jobs. Education has been a pathway for the advancement of women, who have earned professional degrees in male occupations. In many cases, women have moved into jobs men have left, leaving a choice to employers to hire men who are less qualified or hire women. Economic exigencies should give an advantage to women who are hired at a lower labor price. As well, anti-discrimination legislation has made it costly not to hire women, with the possibility of litigation to enforce the law. There has been some change in social attitudes with some decline in discrimination and in resistance by male workers. However, there is also a resurgence in the movement toward segregation in desegregated occupations. Both the Civil Rights movement and the women's movement have challenged the white man's birthright to first place in the labor queue. These movements have worked tirelessly to transform public attitudes toward the propriety of exclusion based on gender, by way of anti-discrimination legislation.

However, queues still exist through collective gender segregation; such factors in ranking of working conditions as autonomy, social standing, career opportunities, gender compositions, peer pressure and stereotyping; the assumption of gender as to occupational characteristics, with superior rewards for male occupations spurning female entry; and the ghettoizing of women into specific types of jobs.[47] Certain alternatives undermine women, namely the mechanization of jobs, the exportation of jobs, non-documented workers and the employment of youth. The more things change the more they stay the same, with the endurance of internal segregation, men's advancement, and social inequality.

Women have made significant strides in the past decades. Relevant factors to explain the increase in the participation rate of women are rising wages, decreasing fertility rates, and changing attitudes toward married women in the labor force. The increase in the labor force participation rate of women under age 35 is synchronized with the decline in the fertility rate. Wage increases have two offsetting effects on the employment of married women, namely an increase in the attractiveness of employment to women increasing the probability of entering the work force, and an increase in the income of the spouse reducing the probability of women entering the labor force. However, there is an agreement that there is a gap between the wages of men and women, with inequality blamed on different factors.

Advocates of pay equity believe that the gap exists, because of gender discrimination and the exclusion of women from high paying jobs. They emphasize occupational and job segregation as key elements in gender discrimination. They cite the manipulation of hiring standards in setting different titles for the same jobs, and the under-valuation of work performed by women, thereby perpetuating a prejudicial system. They point out that women overall earn less than men. Conversely, critics of pay equity believe that there are legitimate causes for the differences in salaries. They note the differences in job related characteristics, and emphasize job experience as a plausible reason for the disparity in pay. They point out that it is irrational for employers to discriminate against qualified women. In a perfect world, this would be true. However, they put the blame of job limitations on women's low expectations and their choice for motherhood. Men are not concentrated in the same occupations as women, and the concentration of women in a few occupations shows a disturbing continuity. Further, the traditional female dominated jobs are low paying for both women and men who find themselves employed in these types of occupations.

Both occupational segregation and earning differentials are persistent towards women. More than ever, discrimination is affecting more women, since they are participating in the labor force to an unprecedented degree. Some see an increase in opportunity, while others see an increase in need. There are two types of inequity, namely pure, where one is paid less for the same job, and systemic, where there are discriminatory effects to policies and practices.[48] Internal components include under-valuation, while external components include segregation into a limited number of low paying jobs. Historically, women have only had access to a limited number of occupations, in a process called 'crowding'. This has caused an oversupply of labor and has reduced wages. People employed in female dominated occupations have lower returns, so that the percentage of females within an occupation is negatively associated with earnings. Thus, there are lower earnings for women, due to a differential placement and occupational discrimination.[49]

In the fight against gender discrimination comes more discrimination through retaliatory behavior. The burden of proof for this often invisible prejudice is a hard one to meet. Therefore, the merit system is often a myth, with the victim, often the woman, not necessarily responsible for career failure. In addition, women in male dominated professions are channelled into certain types of work and are marginalized into discriminatory environments, which add to the segregationist argument. Their careers are shaped in detrimental ways, because of their gender. Further, equal employment opportunity is often a myth, because of the stereotyping of women, their work and their profession, the lack of sponsorship and role models, informal anti-women sentiment, their perceived lack of professional commitment, the unplanned nature of their career, discriminatory client expectations, and the inequality in compensation. Women are judged according to the standard set by men, even though they juggle bimodal careers. When women are dominant and in power in a particular occupation, the position in turn is systematically viewed lower. Even though women are capable, they sometimes under-perform, under-achieve and under-produce, because of the patriarchal structure which wastes female potential. Women and men are evaluated differently as to salaries, access to jobs and promotions. Therefore, women still find themselves to be an oppressed minority.

Segregation exists on two levels. There is horizontal segregation, since most men work with men. If equality existed, then there would be the same proportion of women as men in any one occupation. There is also vertical segregation, since women occupy the lower ranks of occupations. Despite equal opportunity legislation, women and men hold different jobs. The dual labor market theory postulates that direct discrimination is a minor cause, with the major element being the different labor market sectors for each sex.[50] In support of the argument of intentional channelling of female careers through the proposition of segregation, women are still found mainly in the traditional roles of teacher and administrator, and are over-represented in social work and library science.[51] There is significant occupational segregation, with half of women found in three traditional female careers, namely the clerical, sales and service sectors. Roughly only one out of five blue-collar or managerial jobs are held by women. Added to this is the fact that employers still commit gender wage discrimination, since female dominated jobs pay less than male jobs. When women are employed in male-dominated fields and are under-represented, there is found to be a stronger attachment to work and higher pay.

It has been found that there is usually instability early in life, with employment stability coming at middle age. Women, in the workforce, who have never been married work more continuously and earn more. Often, husbands are found to be hindrances to careers, and children a barrier as it is still exceptional to work immediately after having a child. Divorced women are propelled faster into the workforce due to economic conditions. Women with higher degrees are more successful than other women, with high achievers working more often, as the majority of women are found to work in the area of their degree. Therefore, the reality is that there is not equal treatment between the sexes in the workforce, in considering access, promotion and salary. Society is divided along patriarchal lines across most cultures, with gender playing a role in subordinating women to men. This hierarchy is reproduced in the diverse social structures of politics, work, education and church, thus creating gender expectations. There is a sexual division of labor, thereby leaving women at a disadvantage and in a precarious position.

Interestingly, the relationship between mothers and daughters can play an important role in the career choices of women.[52] Mothers can often have a strong influence on daughters, which far exceeds the influence that fathers may have on daughters and sons. A mother's occupational attainment has been found to have some impact in predicting a daughter's occupational inheritance and destiny. A mother is a strong gender role model, and her occupation is a significant dimension in intergenerational occupational mobility. Mothers, who worked in a field classified as professional or non-manual workers, had a positive effect on their daughter's achievement of professional work. However, mothers who were classified as semi-skilled/unskilled manual workers or housewives, had a negative effect on their daughter's chances for professional work, since daughters often significantly inherit the occupational status of their mothers.[53] This reinforces gender disparity and inequality of opportunities.

Women occupy most of the part-time and dead-end low paying jobs. They are over-represented in low wage clerical work, and under-represented in managerial and professional work. The more homogeneous the occupational group, the smaller the wage gap. Age and education alone do not account for the inequality in wages. It is possible that wage discrimination will be diminished, due to women being paid lower, meaning more will be hired, which will eventually increase their wages. However, it is also possible that wage discrimination will be increased, due to equal pay laws and the perception of women as threatening the employment of men, which will decrease their wages. There is occupational segregation by employers, where people work almost entirely with their own gender. This not only impacts access to employment, but also causes a wage gap. Overall, roughly 80 per cent of people do not work with the opposite sex.[54]

Normally, wages within the same job differ by only 1 per cent.[55] However, wages are strongly linked to the proportion of females in an occupation, as the femaleness of an occupation still correlates to lower wages. In building the argument of wage disparity, the movement from virtually 100 per cent male to 100 per cent female occupations causes roughly a 20 per cent reduction in pay for men and roughly a 3 per cent reduction for women.[56] Earning discrimination exists, along with the unequal treatment based on individual not occupational characteristics. Further, there is an added explanation for the difference in salaries, finding a salary disadvantage at the time of hiring, with the pay differential favoring men.[57] Labor market discrimination relies on group stereotyping for unequal starting salaries. There is often a temporary acceptance of lower starting salaries by women, in order to gain access, after which a larger role is played by affirmative action and legal pressures. However, the wage gap has decreased only slightly with equal employment opportunity, affirmative action, and equal education.

Equal Value and Wage Solidarity in the Labor Market

Equal pay for work of equal value was introduced in the International Labour Organisation's Equal Remuneration Convention No. 100 of 1951. Job evaluation was a management tool for wage administration, hiring, placement and supervision. However, the changes in employment for women during World War II brought about the desire to equalize wage rates for competition both in quality and in quantity. Comparative worth or equal pay for work of equal value has as its goal to raise the pay in gender segregated female dominated jobs, which have historically been undervalued. It compares the complexity and responsibility of female and male dominated jobs, and provides for pay increases to eliminate discrimination. The wage gap came about because of a cumulative history of discrimination and bias, and because of different skills, education, and individual family employment choices. Pay equity has the goal of ending wage discrimination, and comparative worth is the process through which to end it. Jobs of dissimilar nature are to be compared by knowledge, skill, effort, responsibility and work conditions for equality in value, in order to achieve pay equity.

Feminism looks to how gender is constructed and gives value to social relations, in order to end systemic inequality.[58] Systemic gender segregation along with women's historical dependence on men have served to reinforce masculinity as having mechanical and technical skills, and femininity as having patience and selfless dedication for repetitive tasks. This ideology is tantamount to a weapon that excludes women from the mainstream of society, and entrenches gender inequity. The wage difference between sectors and establishments is reinforced by the general system of job evaluation for pay equity on a per establishment basis, with little coordination across industry or country. Implementing pay equity takes negotiation, consultation and litigation.

Feminists challenge gender stratification and the discriminatory nature of the system, which undervalue performance and salaries. Opponents of pay equity state that wage hierarchies and job evaluation give value to employers. They believe that in reality, pay equity fails to bridge class divisions, and rather reinforces the separation of feminists from other groups. The public policy goal of pay equity is focused on closing that part of the gender gap, which has resulted from a systemic under-valuation of women's work. It challenges the traditional cultural assumptions of the worth of female work, and the conventional gender hierarchies. Women have come to refuse to accept less pay because of their gender.

The women's liberation movement was mainly aimed at University and professional middle class women, but working class and marginalized women were also active. Working class feminism focused on the changes experienced by women, including their participation in the labor force and their unequal position in the workplace. It covered many issues, including sexual harassment, childcare and male leader dominance. The issue of female low pay began to be a central issue for women in the 1970s, with unionism and collectivism acting as important weapons against subordination. To be an employee is to sell one's labor power within a system of management control. The system of job evaluation highly values professional skills, which ultimately reinforces status and pay within a gender hierarchy. Management control is given the highest weighting and value, serving gender discrimination. There is an assumption of the existence of fine divisions of skill and responsibility, rather than recognition of the imposed differentials between the sexes.

Pay equality has come to mean value, which masks the inequality. Equal value shows that gender bias and discrimination have prevented women from being valued on merit and achievement, denying to them their proper place. By contesting, women help to construct new structures and develop a consciousness of who has the power, who needs to become empowered and what strategies are needed to end discriminatory pay. The women's movement has had a great impact by pressing for policies and legislation to address the issue of lower pay. There have been considerable changes in the home and in the participation of women in the labor force over the last thirty years. It is important to note that women do different work from men and are occupationally segregated into lower paid jobs.

Two avenues exist in the fight for equality: 1. The equal value approach, which sees the working woman as undervalued and seeks to raise pay by using job evaluation of skill, effort, responsibility and working conditions for the same value at the same rate; and 2. The wage solidarity approach, which seeks to decrease pay differentials and raise the lowest paid by using the union strategy of power of all members.[59]

The equal value approach has become the chosen strategy for feminists, who view the oppression of women as endemic to the system.[60] Those who favor it believe that it will revalue women's work and eliminate inequality in women's substantially lower pay. It compares job content in gender neutral systems, instead of the present job evaluation scheme, which legitimizes class differentials. Those who oppose it believe that it is not possible to compare and differentiate between jobs based on job content. Value in the market place means value to the employer, who justifies existing hierarchies and women's subordination. On the other hand, even though the wage solidarity approach has been less popular than the dominant strategy for raising pay, the equal value approach, job evaluation has been a means for justifying women's lower pay. It involves 1. The description and analysis of job content, skill, effort, responsibility and working conditions; 2. The evaluation of relative value to the job; and 3. The wage setting of internal and external comparisons in the labor market.[61] Equal value advocates have criticized the present system of job evaluation, because different plans are used for men and women, perpetuating gender bias. Adjustments are needed for an objective job evaluation in the determination of just wages, regardless of gender. However, evaluation systems reflect and rationalize the unequal class structure, since heavy weight is assigned to skill and responsibility rather than effort and working conditions. The standards of occupational worth in job evaluation plans have been inegalitarian and meritocratic within a class hierarchy. Gender bias and discrimination have prevented women from being valued on merit and achievement. The demand is for women to be given their proper place in the hierarchy, in order to rectify past distortions. However, equal value does not question the unequal structuring of the system, with women generally at the bottom. The determination of equal value should not be left to job evaluation consultants and experts, who constructed gender biased plans. Gender, race and class inequalities need to be exposed.

Importantly, the integration of both the equal value approach and the wage solidarity approach is essential in the fight against gender bias and discrimination, with women still occupying the most subordinate and controlled positions. Equal value is needed, because women are paid less and their work is undervalued. Wage solidarity is also needed, because women are drawn into the subordinate positions due to their limited bargaining power, low pay and little opportunity for promotion.

The structure of the class system degraded and deskilled jobs, by separating management from execution, thus causing subordination. Skilled tasks are those which have control, and unskilled tasks are those that lack self-control and follow the rules. Women have been routinized by monotonous tasks within subordinate dead-end jobs, while men have had opportunities within superior administrative positions along the corporate ladder. Therefore, men do different work from women. Men's jobs usually involve responsibility, skill and control over women, the subordinates. Women are more likely to be workers not bosses, directed by men or machines. Of the workers who exercise control over others, roughly only 27 per cent are women. Women have less power and are vertically separated. The organization of work and the management control of the labor process have led to a white male dominated hierarchy.

The career mobility of men has been possible due to the support of women in the subordinate positions at the office, as well as their physical and emotional support at home. However, the justification for lower pay has been strengthened by segregation, which has made for the assumption that female work should be slotted in a lower position. As well, different job titles for men and women has led to the perception of different work. While men direct and do, women coordinate and assist, at the bottom of the ladder in less powerful positions. An important factor in the inability for women to improve their position is that women did not form a permanent part of the paid labour force until recently. However, women's growing independence from men has not brought about substantially higher wages, thereby forcing a continued dependence on men.

To decrease the division among members of the workforce, the unequal pay of women has to be treated as main business. Therefore, there is a need for the integration of the wage solidarity approach with the equal value approach. Few jobs have been created in the better paid occupations, which have traditionally been in the primary sector, which is unionised and male dominated. Women have been primarily in the low paid jobs, which are often only part-time and non-unionized. While women have been striving for equal value, employers have been reducing labor costs in order to raise profits, by moving capital and jobs to low wage countries. The cheaper labor of women has contributed to the restructuring of work for lower costs. Therefore, the wage solidarity approach must also cover those outside the organized labor movement, in order to raise minimum wages and to unionize the unorganized to stop exploitation.

Occupational segregation comes from gender and class forces both in the family and in society. A new strategy of wage and work solidarity would improve the situation, through a sharing with the marginal groups like women and minorities in the integration of equality and equal pay. One problem has been the definition by unions of fair wages. The definition has been tied to conventions and practices, which have legitimized and perpetuated an inegalitarian income hierarchy between men and women. Although unionization generally results in better wages, women are not necessarily in a fairer position than men. It has been found that white men have the highest income, followed by non-white men, white women and non-white women, in that order.[62] Therefore, union practices help to reproduce wage inequality. However, unions have undergone a major change in the last fifteen years, with women gaining more power. Women now represent roughly 40 per cent of unionized workers compared to 16.6 per cent in 1965.

There have been three ways of looking at wages: 1. Wages for skill, whereby equal pay for equal work is sought, emphasizing skills and job content; 2. Wages for living, whereby a living wage below subsistence levels has been often tolerated by women, because of their subordinated status in the family unit as secondary wage earners dependent on men for living costs; and 3. Wages for the family head, whereby males are positioned as the head of the house, and women are placed simply as mothers and wives, not co-workers.[63] Therefore, women's issues need to be integrated into the policy-making of unions to have a valid effect. The marginalization of union policy with attempts to raise women's pay have only served to create gender conflict and competition. This in turn weakens unions, and also the move for solidarity. Mainstream union practices have worked against the fight for pay equity, with some negating the effects of reevaluating women's work.

Women's demand for the redefinition of skills seeks to include recognizing the skills of caring, supporting and nurturing. Large wage differentials and hierarchies still exist. Pay equity has not challenged the concept of hierarchy, occupational segregation, or the quality of jobs. The standard norm is still male wages and skill, which are applied to women. Thus, women will not often score highly by these male standards, with their lower rank in the hierarchy further legitimized. When changes do occur in the gender order, it threatens management and those who want to maintain the status quo. Attempts to break occupational segregation brings resistance from men and also women. Economic and political conditions are making it harder for wage equality. There is increased competition for scarce resources and jobs. The structure of production, employment and technology has changed dramatically over the years.

Global competition and trade harmonization with the advent of free trade have made for increased production but with fewer workers, due to new technology and methods. The drop in blue-collar manufacturing and industrial jobs, and the expansion of marginal employment have led to greater polarization between core and periphery workers. The full-time permanent pensionable core is mostly made up of white males, while the periphery consists of women, youth and minorities. Women are the working poor. It is increasingly more difficult to achieve equal pay gains, due to increased gender and racial conflict. Women still take most of the responsibility in the home, which affects their capacity in the workplace and in unions. The family wage concept serves to prevent women from being fully integrated into the system, and to reassert that the home is the woman's proper place.

Women's inequality must be at the centre of the debate. Policies favoring solidarity between men and women, as well as minorities, must be sought to heal the divisions. Wage solidarity seeks to push up the wages of the lowest paid to an acceptable living standard, flattening the hierarchy and eliminating gender bias in pay differentials. Businesses desire to accumulate capital, through increased production and reduced labor costs. This is accomplished by separating the execution from the conception of tasks. Solidarity demands the requalification of work, adjusting for the knowledge and experience of all workers while increasing the range of tasks and responsibilities. Women, however, remain outside the demand for the reevaluation of work.

Therefore, solidarity must include the home front, not just the job sphere. Since part-time and casual workers are mainly women, the equitable distribution of paid work would remove a barrier to men's participation in domestic work. Restrictions on overtime would benefit women and the unemployed. It would free women to take more responsibility in the paid labor force, and it would free men to take more responsibility at home. Solidarity recognizes gender and race differences, and the fact that these groups have been excluded from the mainstream policies. As a demand for quality jobs and quality pay for all working men and women, solidarity has the potential to combine with various other initiatives, such as reevaluation of women's work in raising the wages of the lowest paid and affirmative action in ending occupational segregation.[64]

With fierce global competition and economic restructuring, there are fewer jobs in the industrial and manufacturing sectors. In contrast, there are more non-standard part-time part-year service work in small organizations, with a shift to contracting out, in a more flexible labor force. Unions need to equalize the relationship between labor and management, with the key demand being a decent living wage and the right to work. Personal empowerment, political awareness and collective solidarity are needed. Unions ultimately need women as members. Unions have to increase their representation in the private sector where most of the women are found. With the increased participation of women in the workforce, unions must incorporate the feminist perspective to survive and flourish.

Important women's issues such as sexual harassment, childcare, maternity, affirmative action and pay equity must be addressed. Women need to increase their representation in elected positions, and priority must be given to women's issues in collective bargaining towards alliances to link legislation with the community. The challenge of inequity is also the challenge of economic restructuring. Unions, however, provide for gender segmentation of the market, support the traditional ideology of women's work and male breadwinners, resist broader bargaining, and enforce a patriarchal bureaucratic hierarchy.[65] Labor strategies have changed, with more part-time, intensive and seasonal work. There is a need for prorated benefits, job security for part-time part-year workers, affirmative action to integrate women into the highly paid jobs, and equally shared responsibility in the home. Unions must 1. Make gender visible, addressing gender specific needs and seeking a feminization of labor, the work force, unions and the concept of militancy; 2. Challenge male standards and the belief that women are atypical; 3. Build alliances and coalitions, linking the labor movement with outside forces, for a class specific understanding of women's realities; and 4. Fight workplace discrimination in order for women to have a fuller place inside the union movement.[66]

Career strategies in the past have promoted career changes as a solution to the problem, to the neglect of low paid unskilled jobs. There is a disproportionate responsibility given to women in the home, which is exploited by employers. There needs to be recruitment in male occupations in order to break horizontal gender segregation, and promotion to climbing the corporate ladder within these occupations in order to break vertical gender segregation. However, institutional and cultural means impede women. Procedural justice theory calls for adequate explanations of decision-making policies, and interpersonal treatment for interactional justice. It is important to maintain consistency in pay allocation procedures and in basing pay decisions on accurate performance information. Employees expect adequate accounts of decisions, the suppression of personal bias, consistent decision-making criteria, timely feedback and consideration of other views, since interpersonal ethical treatment affects people's perception of fairness.

There is a common pattern in comparative worth whereby legislation and collective bargaining are formulated to establish a policy, jobs are evaluated for wage disparity, and a plan for equity adjustment is formulated and instituted through politics and bargaining.[67] Women suffer, because of gender segregation, low wages, intermittent employment, and subordination both at work and at home. However, many men benefit by gender segregation, higher wages, lifelong employment, and little contact with women both at work and at home through dominance. What is needed is an unbiased gender neutral job evaluation system. Better wages for women, especially for those in low paying jobs, would help to ease poverty, draw women into better jobs and into unions, and improve labor issues.

Equal pay for equal work means that people performing the same job or like jobs must be paid the same wage, regardless of their gender. Pay equality concerns equal pay for equal work, for the same jobs and qualifications. Further, equal pay for work of equal value adds to this by requiring that all jobs within an organization be compared on the basis of their value to the employer, not limiting comparisons to similar work. Legislation requires four factors be taken into account for measuring the value of a job: skill, effort, responsibility required in the performance, and the conditions under which it is performed. Therefore, pay equity concerns equal pay for work of equal value for jobs with similar characteristics. However, a gender-neutral system measuring the four factors needs to be applied for an effective result. Employers must review their compensation systems to determine whether sex based discriminatory pay practices exist, with corrective action taken to eliminate and ensure it does not recur. The benefits to employers are: a successful defence against a complaint of pay inequity; an accurate up-to-date job description system for the appraisal of performance, an incentive plan and the establishment of criteria for hiring employees; the development of a formalized salary administration system; and the attraction, retention and motivation of a competent work force.[68]

Women will be the main beneficiaries of the fight for pay equity. However, men employed in female dominated occupations will also benefit in the implementation of an equitable method of determining wages that is not based on historical pay practices or discriminatory bargaining patterns. Affirmative action provides positive measures to remedy the effects of past discrimination. Remedial measures can be court ordered, required by law or voluntarily adopted. The proportion of protected groups in various job categories should be monitored for equity. Any positive efforts by businesses or educational institutions can advance the employment status of target groups. Equality of opportunity is affected when there is under-representation in significant positions due to the explicit use of gender characteristics for discrimination.

In order to have a responsible and effective society, there needs to be an improvement in the financial position of women and men through the elimination of segregation. There must also be changes in the perception of members of certain groups as second-class citizens, to eliminate social and economic barriers. The goal of affirmative action is to replace the illusion with the reality of equality of opportunity. Its success will be an effective plan to reduce and eventually eliminate the disparity between the sexes, without substantially reducing material or emotional benefits, or alienating a significant portion of the workforce in the pursuit of justice. In the end, in some cases, one must overcome the stigma of feeling personally responsible for one's disadvantages.

Conclusion

The yearning for freedom and justice is instinctively present in all human beings. For women, justice can mean equal pay for equal work, or equal treatment under the law. Feminist practice at the end of the last century and the beginning of this century remains political.[69] It is the practice of accountability in a relational and a collective mode, which aims at unveiling relations and reducing power differentials. There have been two major changes recently, namely the globalization of the late 20th century and a shift to post modernity. The marginalization and suppression of women's interests and the female identity have occurred. Patriarchy has obscured individual differences of class, color and gender, significant for women as for men.

In the 19th century, women fought for the right to education and to suitable employment. In the 1960s and 1970s came the women's liberation movement because of a dissatisfaction with women's rights. There was an ambivalence to the term equality, with women wanting to be accepted like men, while at the same time wanting to be accepted as women. Today, there have been important changes for women, with increased access to education, less frequency to childbearing, and less complexity for housework. Women are more available and willing to work. Therefore, wage inequity and limited access to employment continue to persist. Horizontal and vertical segregation are still real problems, which women must encounter in the workplace everyday. This is unacceptable.

Although, there has been a feminization of the labor force both as to numbers and as to length of employment, lower pay is still a reality for women, with fewer occupations open to them. Inequity starts in the home. Pay equity seeks to positively mobilize women, in order to break the isolating barriers of the home, to delegitimize the ideological and material incentives of a family wage dependent on men, to chip away at the economic dependence of women on men and on the state, and to alleviate feminine poverty. A revised employment standards policy is needed for a living minimum wage, in order to protect from exploitative and discriminatory treatment. Pay equity has ignored flexible and temporary workers, as well as those who work at home. Therefore, statutory domestic responsibility leave needs to be adopted, in order to undermine impediments to pay equity, and to provide some flexibility in the balancing of work with domestic responsibility. Women, who have made it into the executive and management positions, have a duty as primary forces to see that the rest are not forgotten.

Notes

1 Rothblatt, Martine, *The Apartheid of Sex*, 1995, p.57.
2 Flax, Jane, 'Beyond Equality: Gender, Justice and Difference', in Gisela Bock and Susan James, *Beyond Equality and Difference, Citizens, Feminist Politics and Female Subjectivity*, Routledge, 1992, p.193.
3 *Ibid.*, at p.205.
4 Mackinnon, Catharine, *Feminism Unmodified*, 1987.
5 Hughes, Patricia, 'Fighting the Good Fight', in Angela Miles and Geraldine Finn, *Feminism*, 1989l, p.405.
6 Tietjens Meyers, Diana, *Feminists Rethink the Self*, 1997, p.1.
7 Evans, Judith, *Feminist Theory Today*, 1995, p.44.
8 Coppock, Vicki, *The Illusions of Post Feminism*, 1995, p.10.
9 Charles, Nickie, *Practising Feminism*, 1996, p.142.
10 *Supra* note 7, at p.4.
11 Lorde, Audre, *Sister Outsider*, 1984, p.102.
12 Firestone, Shulamith, *The Dialectic of Sex*, 1971, p.274.
13 *Supra* note 8, at p.32.
14 *Supra* note 7, at p.18.
15 *Ibid.*, at p.21.
16 *Ibid.*, at p.125.
17 *Supra* note 8, at p.4.

[18] *Supra* note 7, at p.23.
[19] Hollows, Joanne, *Feminism, Femininity and Popular Culture*, 2000, p.190.
[20] Doucet, Andrea, 'Can Boys Grow into Mothers?, Maternal Thinking and Fathers' Reflections', in Andrea O'Reilly, *Mothers and Sons: Feminism, Masculinity and the Struggle to Raise Our Sons*, 2001, p.173.
[21] Olivier, Christiane, *Jocasta's Children, The Imprint of the Mother*, 1989, p.xi.
[22] Habermas, Jurgen, *Between Facts and Norms*, 1998, p.xxxii.
[23] *Supra* note 4, at p.216.
[24] *Ibid.*, at p.229.
[25] *Ibid.*, at p.234.
[26] *Ibid.*, at p.219.
[27] Meehan, Johanna, *Feminists Read Habermas*, 1995, p.1.
[28] Lahey, Kathleen, 'Celebration and Struggle', in Angela Miles and Geraldine Finn, *Feminism*, 1989, p.102.
[29] Equal Employment Opportunity Commission v. Sears Roebuck & Company, 839 F.2d 301 (1988).
[30] *Ibid.*
[31] *Ibid.*
[32] *Supra* note 1, at p.12.
[33] *Supra* note 22, at p.425.
[34] *Supra* note 28, at p.107.
[35] *Ibid.*, at p.115.
[36] Van Lenning, Alkeline, *Feminist Utopias in a Postmodern Era*, 1997, p.5.
[37] Acker, Joan, *Doing Comparative Worth*, 1989, p.17.
[38] Piori, Michael, *Dualism and Discontinuity in Industrial Societies*, 1980, p.7.
[39] *Ibid.*, at p.8.
[40] Courchane, Marsha and Redish, Angela, 'Women in the Labour Force, 1911-1986', in Robert Allen, Rosenbluth, Gideon, *False Promises*, 1992, p.153.
[41] *Supra* note 37, at p.5.
[42] Kaufman, Bruce E., *How Labor Markets Work*, 1988, p.128.
[43] Schwartz, Barry, *Queuing and Waiting*, 1975.
[44] Reskin, Barbara and Roos, Patricia, *Job Queues, Gender Queues*, 1990, p.31.
[45] *Supra* note 42, at p.7.
[46] *Supra* note 43.
[47] *Ibid.*, at p.309.
[48] Argawal, Naresh, 'Pay Equity in Canada', *Labour Law Journal*, Vol.41, 1990, p.518.
[49] Gerhart, Barry and El Cheich, Nabil, 'Earnings and Percentage Female', *Industrial Relations*, Vol.30, N.1, 1991, p.62.
[50] Wickham, James, *Industrializing Work and Unemployment*, 1986, p.87.
[51] Yohalem, Alice, *The Careers of Professional Women*, 1979, p.63.
[52] Hayes, Bernadette, 'Female Intergenerational Occupational Mobility Within Northern Ireland and the Republic of Ireland', *British Journal of Sociology*, Vol.38, May 1987, p.66.
[53] *Ibid.*, at p.74.
[54] Goshen, Erica, 'Structure of Female/Male Wage Differentials', *Journal of Human Resources*, Vol.26, Summer 1991, p.457, at p.465.
[55] *Ibid.*, at p.457.
[56] *Supra* note 48, at p.73.
[57] Gerhart Barry, 'Gender Differences in Current and Starting Salaries', *Industrial and Labor Relations Review*, Vol.43, N.4, 1990, p.418.
[58] Fudge, Judy, *Just Wages, Feminine Perspective of Pay Equity*, 1991, p.5.

59 Warskett, Rosemary, 'Wage Solidarity and Equal Value: Or Gender and Class in the Structuring of Work Place Hierarchies', *Studies in Political Economy* 1990, p.32, at p.57.

60 Warskett, Rosemary, 'Political Power, Technical Disputes, and Unequal Pay: A Federal Case', in Judy Fudge, *Just Wages, Feminine Perspective of Pay Equity*, 1991, p.172.

61 *Ibid.*, at p.66.

62 Warskett, Rosemary, 'Can a Disappearing Pie Be Shared Equally?: Unions, Women, and Wage Fairness, in Linda Briskin, *Women Challenging Unions: Feminism, Democracy and Militancy*, 1993, p.250.

63 *Ibid.*, at p.252.

64 *Ibid.*, at p.262.

65 Briskin, Linda, *Women Challenging Unions, Feminism, Democracy and Militance*, 1993, p.7.

66 *Ibid.*, at 16.

67 *Supra* note 36, at p.9.

68 Labour Canada, *Equal Pay for Work of Equal Value*, 1986, p.4-2.

69 Braidotti, Rosi, 'Becoming Women, Rethinking the Positivity of Difference', in Elizabeth Bronfen, *Feminist Consequences, Theory for the New Century*, 2001, p.381.

References

Acker, Joan (1989), *Doing Comparative Worth.*

Ali, Suki (2000), *Global Feminist Politics*, Routledge, London.

Argawal, Naresh, 'Pay Equity in Canada', *Labour Law Journal*, Vol.41, 1990, p.518.

Baumeister, Andrea (2000), *Liberalism and the Politics of Difference*, Edinburgh University Press, Edinburgh.

Bhavnani, Kum-Kum (2001), *Feminism and Race*, Oxford University Press, Oxford.

Braidotti, Rosi, 'Becoming Women, Rethinking the Positivity of Difference', in Elizabeth Bronfen (2001), *Feminist Consequences, Theory for the New Century*, Columbia University Press, New York.

Briskin, Linda (1993), *Women Challenging Unions, Feminism, Democracy and Militance*, University of Toronto Press, Toronto.

Catterall, Miriam (2000), *Marketing and Feminism*, Routledge, London.

Charles, Nickie (1996), *Practising Feminism*, Routledge, New York.

Coppock, Vicki (1995), *The Illusions of Post Feminism*, Taylor & Francis, London.

Courchane, Marsha and Redish, Angela, 'Women in the Labour Force, 1911-1986', in Robert Allen (1992), Rosenbluth, Gideon, *False Promises*, New Star Books, Vancouver.

Delamont, Sara (2001), *Changing Women, Unchanged Men*, Open University Press, Buckingham.

Doucet, Andrea, 'Can Boys Grow into Mothers?, Maternal Thinking and Fathers' Reflections', in Andrea O'Reilly (2001), *Mothers and Sons: Feminism, Masculinity and the Struggle to Raise Our Sons*, Routledge, London.

Equal Employment Opportunity Commission v. Sears Roebuck & Company, 839 F.2d 301 (1988).

Evans, Judith (1995), *Feminist Theory Today*, Sage Publications, Thousand Oaks.

Evans, Mary (1997), *Introducing Contemporary Feminist Thought*, Polity Press, Cambridge.

Fawcett, Barbara (2000), *Practice and Research in Social Work, Postmodern Feminist Perspective*, Routledge, London.

Firestone, Shulamith (1971), *The Dialectic of Sex*, Jonathan Cape, London.
Flax, Jane, 'Beyond Equality: Gender, Justice and Difference', in Gisela Bock and Susan James (1992), *Beyond Equality and Difference, Citizens, Feminist Politics and Female Subjectivity*, Routledge, London.
Fox-Genovese, Elizabeth (1996), *Feminism Is Not the Story of My Life*, Doubleday, New York.
Freedman, Jane (2001), *Feminism*, Open University Press, Buckingham.
Fried, Morton (1967), *The Evolution of Political Society*, Random House, New York.
Friedan, Betty (1963), *The Feminine Mystique*, Penguin, Harmondsworth.
Friedan, Betty (1983), *The Second Stage*, Sphere Books, London.
Fudge, Judy (1991), *Just Wages, Feminine Perspective of Pay Equity*, University of Toronto Press, Toronto.
Gerhart Barry, 'Gender Differences in Current and Starting Salaries', *Industrial and Labor Relations Review*, Vol.43, N.4, 1990, p.418.
Gerhart, Barry and El Cheich, Nabil, 'Earnings and Percentage Female', *Industrial Relations*, Vol.30, N.1, 1991, p.62.
Goshen, Erica, 'Structure of Female/Male Wage Differentials', *Journal of Human Resources*, Vol.26, Summer 1991, p.457.
Grande Jensen, Pamela (1996), *Finding a New Feminism*, Rowman & Littlefield Publishers, Lanham.
Greer, Germaine (2000), *The Whole Woman*, Anchor, London.
Habermas, Jurgen (1998), *Between Facts and Norms*, MIT Press, Massachussetts.
Hayes, Bernadette, 'Female Intergenerational Occupational Mobility Within Northern Ireland and the Republic of Ireland', *British Journal of Sociology*, Vol.38, May 1987, p.66.
Hollows, Joanne (2000), Feminism, *Femininity and Popular Culture*, Manchester University Press, Manchester.
Hughes, Patricia, 'Fighting the Good Fight', in Angela Miles and Geraldine Finn (1989), *Feminism*, Black Rose Books, Montreal.
Irigaray, Luce (2000), *Democracy Begins Between Two*, Athlone Press, London.
Jung, Anees (1997), *Breaking the Silence*, Penguin Books, New York.
Kaufman, Bruce E. (1988), *How Labor Markets Work*, Lexington Books, Lexington.
Kokott, Juliane, 'European Communities, Equal Pay for Men and Women, DeFacto Discrimination', *American Journal of International Law*, Vol.86, N.2, 1991, p.348.
Labour Canada (1986), *Equal Pay for Work of Equal Value*, Ottawa.
Lahey, Kathleen, 'Celebration and Struggle', in Angela Miles and Geraldine Finn (1989), *Feminism*, Black Rose Books, Montreal.
Lasch, Christopher (1977), *Haven in a Heartless World, The Family Besieged*, Basic Books, New York.
Lasch, Christopher (1979), *The Culture of Narcissism*, W.W.Norton & Co., New York.
Lee, Yong, 'Shaping Judicial Response to Gender Discrimination in Employment Compensation', *Public Administration Review*, Sept. 1989, p.420.
Lorde, Audre (1984), *Sister Outsider*, The Crossing Press, Freedom.
Mackinnon, Catharine (1987), *Feminism Unmodified*, Harvard University Press, Cambridge.
Mackinnon, Catharine (1989), *Toward a Feminist Theory of the State*, Harvard University Press, Cambridge.
Mackinnon, Catharine (1993), *Only Words*, Harvard University Press, Cambridge.
McCarty, Claire, 'The International Aspects of Procedural Justice', *Labor Law Journal*, Vol.41, 1990, p.580.
McRobbie, Angela (2000), *Feminism and Youth Culture*, Macmillan, Basingstoke.

Meehan, Johanna (1995), *Feminists Read Habermas*, Routledge, New York.
Nussbaum, Martha (2000), *Women and Human Development*, Cambridge University Press, Cambridge.
Olivier, Christiane (1989), *Jocasta's Children, The Imprint of the Mother*, Routledge, London.
O'Reilly, Andrea (2001), *Mothers and Sons: Feminism, Masculinity and the Struggle to Raise Our Sons*, Routledge, London.
Orenstein, Peggy (2000), *Women on Work, Love, Children and Life*, Piatkus, London.
Pease, Bob (2000), *Recreating Men, Postmodern Masculinity Politics*, Sage, London.
Piori, Michael (1980), *Dualism and Discontinuity in Industrial Societies*, Cambridge University Press, Cambridge.
Rado, Lisa (1997), *Modernism, Gender and Culture*, Garland Publishing, New York.
Reskin, Barbara and Roos, Patricia (1990), *Job Queues, Gender Queues*, Temple University Press, Philadelphia.
Rothblatt, Martine (1995), *The Apartheid of Sex*, Crown Publishers, New York.
Sargeant, Georgia, 'Pay Equity: Lagging in Court, Gaining at the Bargaining Table', *Trial*, Vol.26, N.2, 1990, p.98.
Schwartz, Barry (1975), *Queuing and Waiting*, University of Chicago Press, Chicago.
Scott, Hilda (1984), *Working Your Way to the Bottom*, Pandora Press, London.
Scott, Joan (1988), *Gender and the Politics of History*, Columbia University Press, New York.
Scott, Joan (1996), *Feminism and History*, Oxford University Press, Oxford.
Sterba, James (2001), *Controversies in Feminism*, Rowman & Littlefield, Oxford.
Thompson, Denise (2001), *Radical Feminism Today*, Sage, London.
Tietjens Meyers, Diana (1993), *Kindred Matters, Rethinking the Philosophy of the Family*, Cornell University Press, Ithaca.
Tietjens Meyers, Diana (1997), *Feminists Rethink the Self*, Westview Press, Boulder.
Van Lenning, Alkeline (1997), *Feminist Utopias in a Postmodern Era*, Tilburg University Press, Tilburg.
Walter, Natasha (2000), *On the Move, Feminism for a New Generation*, Virago, London.
Warskett, Rosemary, 'Wage Solidarity and Equal Value: Or Gender and Class in the Structuring of Work Place Hierarchies', *Studies in Political Economy* 1990, p. 32.
Warskett, Rosemary, 'Political Power, Technical Disputes, and Unequal Pay: A Federal Case', in Judy Fudge (1991), *Just Wages Feminine Perspective of Pay Equity*, University of Toronto Press, Toronto.
Warskett, Rosemary, 'Can a Disappearing Pie Be Shared Equally?: Unions, Women, and Wage Fairness, in Linda Briskin (1993), *Women Challenging Unions: Feminism, Democracy and Militancy*, University of Toronto Press, Toronto.
Whelehan, Imelda (2000), *Overload, Popular Culture and the Future of Feminism*, Women's, London.
Wickham, James (1986), *Industrializing Work and Unemployment*, Ireland.
Wollstonecraft, Mary (1792), *Vindication of the Rights of Women*, Source Book Press, London.
Yohalem, Alice (1979), *The Careers of Professional Women*, Allanheld Osmun & Co., Montclair.

Chapter 3

Gender Injustice and the United Nations

Introduction

This chapter will examine Gender Injustice and the United Nations. It will look at the important United Nations' legislation impacting women's rights in the fight against gender discrimination and in the pursuit of gender equality, namely the Universal Declaration of Human Rights; the Charter of the United Nations; the Statute of the International Court of Justice; the Equal Remuneration Convention (ILO No. 100); the Discrimination (Employment and Occupation) Convention; the International Covenant on Civil and Political Rights; the International Covenant on Economic, Social and Cultural Rights; the Optional Protocol to the International Covenant on Civil and Political Rights; the Convention on the Elimination of All Forms of Discrimination against Women (CEDAW); the Optional Protocol to the Convention on the Elimination of All Forms of Discrimination against Women; the International Convention on the Elimination of All Forms of Racial Discrimination; and the Beijing Declaration.

The Universal Declaration of Human Rights

The Universal Declaration of Human Rights was adopted by the United Nations, on December 10, 1948. The Preamble of the Universal Declaration of Human Rights states:

> Whereas recognition of the inherent dignity and of the equal and inalienable rights of all members of the human family is the foundation of freedom, justice and peace in the world,
>
> Whereas disregard and contempt for human rights have resulted in barbarous acts which have outraged the conscience of mankind, and the advent of a world in which human beings shall enjoy freedom of speech and belief and freedom from fear and want has been proclaimed as the highest aspiration of the common people,
>
> Whereas it is essential, if man is not to be compelled to have recourse, as a last resort, to rebellion against tyranny and oppression, that human rights should be protected by the rule of law,
>
> Whereas it is essential to promote the development of friendly relations between nations,

Whereas the peoples of the United Nations have in the Charter reaffirmed their faith in fundamental human rights, in the dignity and worth of the human person and in the equal rights of men and women and have determined to promote social progress and better standards of life in larger freedom,

Whereas Member States have pledged themselves to achieve, in co-operation with the United Nations, the promotion of universal respect for and observance of human rights and fundamental freedoms,

Whereas a common understanding of these rights and freedoms is of the greatest importance for the full realization of this pledge.

The General Assembly of the United Nations proclaims:

THIS UNIVERSAL DECLARATION OF HUMAN RIGHTS as a common standard of achievement for all peoples and all nations, to the end that every individual and every organ of society, keeping this Declaration constantly in mind, shall strive by teaching and education to promote respect for these rights and freedoms and by progressive measures, national and international, to secure their universal and effective recognition and observance, both among the peoples of Member States themselves and among the peoples of territories under their jurisdiction.[1]

Article 1 guarantees that all human beings are born free and equal in dignity and rights. They are endowed with reason and conscience and should act towards one another in a spirit of brotherhood.[2] In the fight against gender discrimination, Article 2 is a helpful tool, since it holds that everyone is entitled to all the rights and freedoms set forth in this Declaration, without distinction of any kind, such as race, color, sex, language, religion, political or other opinion, national or social origin, property, birth or other status.[3]

Importantly, equality before the law without discrimination is guaranteed in Article 7:

7. All are equal before the law and are entitled without any discrimination to equal protection of the law. All are entitled to equal protection against any discrimination in violation of this Declaration and against any incitement to such discrimination.[4]

In the effort to redress discriminatory action, Article 8 establishes that everyone has the right to an effective remedy by the competent national tribunals for acts violating the fundamental rights granted him by the constitution or by law.[5]

Employment rights, including equal pay for equal work, are protected under Article 23:

23. (1) Everyone has the right to work, to free choice of employment, to just and favourable conditions of work and to protection against unemployment.

(2) Everyone, without any discrimination, has the right to equal pay for equal work.

(3) Everyone who works has the right to just and favourable remuneration ensuring for himself and his family an existence worthy of human dignity, and supplemented, if necessary, by other means of social protection.
(4) Everyone has the right to form and to join trade unions for the protection of his interests.[6]

The right to education as a means of enhancement is established in Article 26, which holds that everyone has the right to education. Education shall be free, at least in the elementary and fundamental stages. Elementary education shall be compulsory. Technical and professional education shall be made generally available and higher education shall be equally accessible to all on the basis of merit. Further, education shall be directed to the full development of the human personality and to the strengthening of respect for human rights and fundamental freedoms. It shall promote understanding, tolerance and friendship among all nations, racial or religious groups, and shall further the activities of the United Nations for the maintenance of peace.[7]

The Universal Declaration of Human Rights of 1948 was codified into two Covenants, which the General Assembly adopted on December 16, 1966, and they are the International Covenant on Civil and Political Rights and the International Covenant on Economic, Social and Cultural Rights. Described as the 'International Bill of Human Rights', the Covenants along with the Optional Protocols are landmarks in the efforts of the international community to promote human rights.

The Charter of the United Nations

The Preamble of the Charter of the United Nations states:

WE THE PEOPLES OF THE UNITED NATIONS DETERMINED

to save succeeding generations from the scourge of war, which twice in our lifetime has brought untold sorrow to mankind, and
to reaffirm faith in fundamental human rights, in the dignity and worth of the human person, in the equal rights of men and women and of nations large and small, and
to establish conditions under which justice and respect for the obligations arising from treaties and other sources of international law can be maintained, and
to promote social progress and better standards of life in larger freedom,

AND FOR THESE ENDS

to practice tolerance and live together in peace with one another as good neighbours, and
to unite our strength to maintain international peace and security, and
to ensure, by the acceptance of principles and the institution of methods, that armed force shall not be used, save in the common interest, and

> to employ international machinery for the promotion of the economic and social advancement of all peoples,
>
> HAVE RESOLVED TO COMBINE OUR EFFORTS TO ACCOMPLISH THESE AIMS
>
> Accordingly, our respective Governments, through representatives assembled in the city of San Francisco, who have exhibited their full powers found to be in good and due form, have agreed to the present Charter of the United Nations and do hereby establish an international organization to be known as the United Nations.[8]

The purposes of the United Nations as outlined in Article 1 are to maintain international peace and security, and to that end to take effective collective measures for the prevention and removal of threats to the peace, and for the suppression of acts of aggression or other breaches of the peace, and to bring about by peaceful means, and in conformity with the principles of justice and international law, adjustment or settlement of international disputes or situations which might lead to a breach of the peace; to develop friendly relations among nations based on respect for the principle of equal rights and self-determination of peoples, and to take other appropriate measures to strengthen universal peace; to achieve international cooperation in solving international problems of an economic, social, cultural, or humanitarian character, and in promoting and encouraging respect for human rights and for fundamental freedoms for all without distinction as to race, sex, language, or religion; and to be a center for harmonizing the actions of nations in the attainment of these common ends.[9]

In terms of International Economic and Social Co-operation, Article 55 guarantees equal rights in employment without regard to gender:

> 55. With a view to the creation of conditions of stability and well-being which are necessary for peaceful and friendly relations among nations based on respect for the principle of equal rights and self-determination of peoples, the United Nations shall promote:
> a. higher standards of living, full employment, and conditions of economic and social progress and development;
> b. solutions of international economic, social, health, and related problems; and international cultural and educational cooperation; and
> c. universal respect for, and observance of, human rights and fundamental freedoms for all without distinction as to race, sex, language, or religion.[10]

The International Court of Justice (ICJ) is established under Article 92 as the principal judicial organ of the United Nations, functioning in accordance with the Statute of the Permanent Court of International Justice.[11] Article 94 binds Member States in their compliance with the decisions of the ICJ in that each Member of the United Nations undertakes to comply with the decision of the International Court of Justice in any case to which it is a party; and if any party to a case fails to perform the obligations incumbent upon it under a judgment rendered by the Court, the other party may have recourse to the Security Council, which may, if it deems necessary, make recommendations or decide upon measures to be taken to give effect to the judgment.[12]

Further, Article 95 holds that nothing in the present Charter shall prevent Members of the United Nations from entrusting the solution of their differences to other tribunals by virtue of agreements already in existence or which may be concluded in the future.[13] By virtue of Article 96, the General Assembly, the Security Council, and other organs of the United Nations and specialized agencies may request the International Court of Justice to give an advisory opinion on any legal question.[14]

The Statute of the International Court of Justice

Article 1 of the Statute of the International Court of Justice holds that the International Court of Justice (ICJ) established by the Charter of the United Nations as the principal judicial organ of the United Nations shall be constituted and shall function in accordance with the provisions of the present Statute.[15] By virtue of Article 34, only States may be parties in cases before the Court which, subject to and in conformity with its Rules, may request of public international organizations information relevant to cases before it, and shall receive such information presented by such organizations on their own initiative.[16]

Jurisdiction of the Court is established under Article 36 as comprising all cases which the parties refer to it and all matters specially provided for in the Charter of the United Nations or in treaties and conventions in force. Further, the States Parties to the present Statute may at any time declare that they recognize as compulsory ipso facto and without special agreement, in relation to any other State accepting the same obligation, the jurisdiction of the Court in all legal disputes concerning the interpretation of a treaty; any question of international law; the existence of any fact which, if established, would constitute a breach of an international obligation; and the nature or extent of the reparation to be made for the breach of an international obligation.[17]

As to the application of choice of law, Article 38 maintains that the Court, whose function is to decide in accordance with international law such disputes as are submitted to it, shall apply international conventions, whether general or particular, establishing rules expressly recognized by the contesting States; international custom, as evidence of a general practice accepted as law; the general principles of law recognized by civilized nations; and judicial decisions and the teachings of the most highly qualified publicists of the various nations, as subsidiary means for the determination of rules of law.[18]

The Equal Remuneration Convention (ILO No. 100)

According to the Equal Remuneration Convention (ILO No. 100) of 1951, the term 'remuneration' is defined in Article 1 as the ordinary, basic or minimum wage or salary and any additional emoluments whatsoever payable directly or indirectly, whether in cash or in kind, by the employer to the worker and arising out of the worker's employment.[19] Further, the term 'equal remuneration for men and women workers for work of equal value' is defined as rates of remuneration established without discrimination based on sex.[20]

Article 2 promotes equal remuneration for men and women:

> 2(1) Each Member shall, by means appropriate to the methods in operation for determining rates of remuneration, promote and, in so far as is consistent with such methods, ensure the application to all workers of the principle of equal remuneration for men and women workers for work of equal value.
> (2) This principle may be applied by means of:
> (a) National laws or regulations;
> (b) Legally established or recognised machinery for wage determination;
> (c) Collective agreements between employers and workers; or
> (d) A combination of these various means.[21]

In the promotion of an objective appraisal of jobs on the basis of the work to be performed, Article 3 takes into account that differential rates between workers, which correspond, without regard to sex, to differences, as determined by such objective appraisal, in the work to be performed, shall not be considered as being contrary to the principle of equal remuneration for men and women workers for work of equal value.[22]

The Discrimination (Employment and Occupation) Convention

According to the Discrimination (Employment and Occupation) Convention of 1958, considering that the Declaration of Philadelphia affirms that all human beings, irrespective of race, creed or sex, have the right to pursue both their material well-being and their spiritual development in conditions of freedom and dignity, of economic security and equal opportunity, and considering further that discrimination constitutes a violation of rights enunciated by the Universal Declaration of Human Rights, the term 'discrimination', including gender discrimination, is defined in Article 1(1) as any distinction, exclusion or preference made on the basis of race, color, sex, religion, political opinion, national extraction or social origin, which has the effect of nullifying or impairing equality of opportunity or treatment in employment or occupation; and such other distinction, exclusion or preference which has the effect of nullifying or impairing equality of opportunity or treatment in employment or occupation as may be determined by the Member concerned after consultation with representative employer's and worker's organizations, where such exist, and with other appropriate bodies.[23]

An exception is contained in Article 1(2) under the term 'inherent requirements' in employment, defined as any distinction, exclusion or preference in respect of a particular job based on the inherent requirements thereof shall not be deemed to be discrimination.[24]

Equal opportunity and equal treatment in employment are guaranteed under Article 2, which states that each Member for which this Convention is in force undertakes to declare and pursue a national policy designed to promote, by methods appropriate to national conditions and practice, equality of opportunity and treatment in respect of employment and occupation, with a view to eliminating any discrimination in respect thereof.[25]

Article 3 holds that each Member for which this Convention is in force undertakes, by methods appropriate to national conditions and practice to seek the cooperation of employers' and workers' organizations and other appropriate bodies in promoting the acceptance and observance of this policy; to enact such legislation and to promote such educational programs as may be calculated to secure the acceptance and observance of the policy; to repeal any statutory provisions and modify any administrative instructions or practices which are inconsistent with the policy; to pursue the policy in respect of employment under the direct control of a national authority; to ensure observance of the policy in the activities of vocational guidance, vocational training and placement services under the direction of a national authority; and to indicate in its annual reports on the application of the Convention the action taken in pursuance of the policy and the results secured by such action.[26]

Affirmative action to correct gender discrimination is recognized under Article 5:

> 5(1). Special measures of protection or assistance provided for in other Conventions or Recommendations adopted by the International Labour Conference shall not be deemed to be discrimination.
> (2). Any Member may, after consultation with representative employers' and workers' organisations, where such exist, determine that other special measures designed to meet the particular requirements of persons who, for reasons such as sex, age, disablement, family responsibilities or social or cultural status, are generally recognised to require special protection or assistance, shall not be deemed to be discrimination.[27]

The International Covenant on Civil and Political Rights (ICCPR)

The International Covenant on Civil and Political Rights was adopted and opened for signature, ratification and accession by the United Nations General Assembly in resolution 2200A (XXI) of December 16, 1966, and entered into force on March 23, 1976.[28] The Covenant is divided into six parts: Part I reaffirms the right of self-determination; Part II formulates general obligations by States Parties, notably to implement the Covenant through legislative and other measures, to provide effective remedies to victims and to ensure gender equality, and it restricts the possibility of derogation; Part III outlines the general civil and political rights, including the right to life, the prohibition of torture, the right to liberty and security of person, the right to freedom of movement, the right to a fair hearing, the right to privacy, the right to freedom of religion, freedom of expression, freedom of peaceful assembly, the right to family life, the rights of children to special protection, the right to participate in the conduct of public affairs, the overarching right to equal treatment, and the special rights of persons belonging to ethnic, religious and linguistic minorities; Part IV regulates the election of members of the Human Rights Committee, the State reporting procedure and the interstate complaints mechanism; Part V stipulates that nothing in the Covenant shall be interpreted as impairing the inherent right of all peoples to fully enjoy and to utilize their natural resources; and Part VI provides that the Covenant shall extend to all parts of federal States and sets out the amendment procedure. The Covenant is not subject to denunciation.

The Human Rights Committee monitors implementation by States Parties in a variety of ways, and initial and periodic reports are examined by the plenary, which formulates concluding observations with concrete recommendations. In order to assist States Parties in preparing reports, the Committee has formulated 28 general comments, which constitute a commentary on the provisions of the Covenant, and in advance of the examination of a report, the Committee forwards a list of issues to the State Party concerned. The list is prepared by the members and takes into consideration information received from other United Nations organs and specialized agencies as well as from Non-Governmental Organizations (NGOs).

In the Preamble of the Covenant on Civil and Political Rights, the States Parties to the present Covenant undertake the agreement:

> Considering that, in accordance with the principles proclaimed in the Charter of the United Nations, recognition of the inherent dignity and of the equal and inalienable rights of all members of the human family is the foundation of freedom, justice and peace in the world,
>
> Recognizing that these rights derive from the inherent dignity of the human person,
>
> Recognizing that, in accordance with the Universal Declaration of Human Rights, the ideal of free human beings enjoying civil and political freedom and freedom from fear and want can only be achieved if conditions are created whereby everyone may enjoy his civil and political rights, as well as his economic, social and cultural rights,
>
> Considering the obligation of States under the Charter of the United Nations to promote universal respect for, and observance of, human rights and freedoms,
>
> Realizing that the individual, having duties to other individuals and to the community to which he belongs, is under a responsibility to strive for the promotion and observance of the rights recognized in the present Covenant.[29]

The obligations of Member States are established in Article 2 without regard to gender, in that:

> Each State Party to the present Covenant undertakes to respect and to ensure to all individuals within its territory and subject to its jurisdiction the rights recognized

in the present Covenant, without distinction of any kind, such as race, colour, sex, language, religion, political or other opinion, national or social origin, property, birth or other status.[30]

Further, where not already provided for by existing legislative or other measures, each State Party to the present Covenant undertakes to take the necessary steps in accordance with its constitutional processes and with the provisions of the present Covenant, to adopt such legislative or other measures as may be necessary to give effect to the rights recognized in the present Covenant; and each State Party to the present Covenant undertakes to ensure that any person whose rights or freedoms as herein recognized are violated shall have an effective remedy, notwithstanding that the violation has been committed by persons acting in an official capacity; to ensure that any person claiming such a remedy shall have his rights thereto determined by competent judicial, administrative or legislative authorities, or by any other competent authority provided for by the legal system of the State, and to develop the possibilities of judicial remedy; and to ensure that the competent authorities shall enforce such remedies when granted.

Article 3 guarantees the equal rights of men and women:

3.The States Parties to the present Covenant undertake to ensure the equal right of men and women to the enjoyment of all civil and political rights set forth in the present Covenant.[31]

Further, equality before the law is guaranteed under Article 26:

26. All persons are equal before the law and are entitled without any discrimination to the equal protection of the law. In this respect, the law shall prohibit any discrimination and guarantee to all persons equal and effective protection against discrimination on any ground such as race, colour, sex, language, religion, political or other opinion, national or social origin, property, birth or other status.[32]

Importantly, Article 23 recognizes that the family is the natural and fundamental group unit of society and is entitled to protection by both society and the State.[33]

Article 28 establishes the Human Rights Committee, consisting of eighteen members and shall carry out the functions provided.[34] Additionally, the submission of reports in compliance with the Covenant is required in Article 40 and Article 45. Under Article 40, the States Parties to the present Covenant undertake to submit reports on the measures they have adopted which give effect to the rights recognized herein and on the progress made in the enjoyment of those rights within one year of the entry into force of the present Covenant for the States Parties concerned; and thereafter whenever the Committee so requests. Reports shall indicate the factors and difficulties, if any, affecting the implementation of the present Covenant. The Committee shall study the reports submitted by the States Parties to the present Covenant, and shall transmit its reports, and such general comments as it may consider appropriate, to the States Parties.[35] Under Article 45, the Committee shall submit to the General Assembly of the United Nations, through the Economic and Social council, an annual report on its activities.[36]

Other procedures of recourse are permitted under Article 44, which states that the provisions for the implementation of the present Covenant shall apply without prejudice to the procedures prescribed in the field of human rights by or under the constituent instruments and the conventions of the United Nations and of the specialized agencies and shall not prevent the States Parties to the present Covenant from having recourse to other procedures for settling a dispute in accordance with general or special international agreements in force between them.[37]

The Optional Protocol to the International Covenant on Civil and Political Rights

The Optional Protocol to the International Covenant on Civil and Political Rights (ICCPR) allows individuals, whose countries are party to the ICCPR and the protocol, who claim their rights under the ICCPR have been violated, and who have exhausted all domestic remedies, to submit written communications to the UN Human Rights Committee. States Parties to the ICCPR undertake to ensure that women and men enjoy all the civil and political rights in the Covenant on a basis of equality. In addition, article 26 of the ICCPR provides that all people are equal before the law, are entitled to equal protection of the law without discrimination, and that the law shall guarantee equal and effective protection against discrimination. It prohibits discrimination in law or in fact in any field regulated by public authorities and its scope is not limited to civil and political rights, so that it can be used to challenge discriminatory laws whether or not they relate to civil and political rights.[38]

The International Covenant on Economic, Social and Cultural Rights (ICESCR)

The International Covenant on Economic, Social and Cultural Rights was adopted and opened for signature, ratification and accession by General Assembly resolution 2200A (XXI) of December 16, 1966, and entered into force January 3, 1976.[39] Economic, social and cultural rights are designed to ensure the protection of people as full persons, based on a perspective in which people can enjoy rights, freedoms and social justice. In a world where, according to the United Nations Development Programme (UNDP), 'a fifth of the developing world's population goes hungry every night, a quarter lacks access to even a basic necessity like safe drinking water, and a third lives in a state of abject poverty at such a margin of human existence that words simply fail to describe it',[40] the importance of renewed attention and commitment to the full realization of economic, social and cultural rights is self-evident with such marginalization. Despite significant progress since the establishment of the United Nations in addressing problems of human deprivation, well over 1 billion people live in circumstances of extreme poverty, homelessness, hunger and malnutrition, unemployment, illiteracy and chronic ill-health. More than 1.5 billion people lack access to clean drinking water and sanitation, and some 500 million children do not have access to even primary education, with more than 1 billion adults not able to read and write.

Of all the basic human rights standards, the International Covenant on Economic, Social and Cultural Rights provides one of the most important international legal frameworks for protecting basic human rights. The Covenant contains significant international legal provisions establishing economic, social and cultural rights, including rights relating to work in just and favorable conditions, social protection, an adequate standard of living, the highest attainable standards of physical and mental health, education, and enjoyment of the benefits of cultural freedom and scientific progress. It also provides for the right of self-determination; equal rights for men and women; the right to work; the right to just and favorable conditions of work; the right to form and join trade unions; the right to social security and social insurance; protection and assistance to the family; the right to adequate standard of living; the right to the highest attainable standard of physical and mental health; the right to education; the right to take part in cultural life; and the right to enjoy the benefits of scientific progress.

Compliance by States Parties with their obligations under the Covenant and the level of implementation of the rights and duties in question is monitored by the Committee on Economic, Social and Cultural Rights, which submits annual reports on its activities to the Economic and Social Council. The Committee works on the basis of many sources of information, including reports submitted by States Parties and information from United Nations specialized agencies, including the International Labour Organisation, the United Nations Educational, Scientific and Cultural Organization, the World Health Organization, the Food and Agriculture Organization of the United Nations, the World Bank, and the International Monetary Fund. In addition, information is submitted from the United Nations Development Programme, the Office of the United Nations High Commissioner for Refugees, and the United Nations Centre for Human Settlements (Habitat). It also makes use of information from other United Nations treaty bodies, from national non-governmental and community-based organizations working in States which have ratified the Covenant, and from international human rights and other Non-Governmental Organizations (NGOs).

In the Preamble of the International Covenant on Economic, Social and Cultural Rights, the States Parties to the present Covenant undertake the agreement:

> Considering that, in accordance with the principles proclaimed in the Charter of the United Nations, recognition of the inherent dignity and of the equal and inalienable rights of all the members of the human family is the foundation of freedom, justice and peace in world,
>
> Recognizing that these rights derive from the inherent dignity of the human person,

> Recognizing that, in accordance with the Universal Declaration of Human Rights, the ideal of free human beings enjoying freedom from fear and want can only be achieved if conditions are created whereby everyone may enjoy his economic, social and cultural rights, as well as his civil and political rights and freedom,
>
> Realizing that the individual, having duties to other individuals and to the community to which he belongs, is under a responsibility to strive for the promotion and observance of the rights recognized in the present Covenant.[41]

Member States' obligations are outlined in Article 2, which holds that each State Party to the present Covenant undertakes to take steps, individually and through international assistance and cooperation, especially economic and technical, to the maximum of its available resources, with a view to achieving progressively the full realization of the rights recognized in the present Covenant by all appropriate means, including particularly the adoption of legislative measures. Further, the States Parties to present Covenant undertake to guarantee that the rights enunciated in the present Covenant will be exercised without discrimination of any kind as to race, color, sex, language, religion, political or other opinion, national or social origin, property, birth or other status.[42]

Article 3 establishes the equal right of men and women:

> 3. The States Parties to the present Covenant undertake to ensure the equal right of men and women to the enjoyment of all economic, social and cultural rights set forth in the present Covenant.[43]

Employment rights under Article 6 establishes that the States Parties to the present Covenant recognize the right to work, which includes the right of everyone to the opportunity to gain his living by work which he freely chooses or accepts, and will take appropriate steps to safeguard this right. Further, the steps to be taken by a State Party to the present Covenant to achieve the full realization of this right shall include technical and vocational guidance and training programmes, policies and techniques to achieve steady economic, social and cultural development, and full and productive employment under conditions safeguarding fundamental political and economic freedoms to the individual.

Article 7 is an important guarantee for equal rights in terms of equal pay and access to employment:

> 7. The States to the present Covenant recognize the right of everyone to the enjoyment of just and favourable conditions of work which ensure, in particular:
> (1) Remuneration which provides all workers, as a minimum, with:
>
> > 1. Fair wages and equal remuneration for work of equal value without distinction of any kind, in particular women being guaranteed conditions of work not inferior to those enjoyed by men, with equal pay for equal work;
> > 2. A decent living for themselves and their families in accordance with the provisions of the present Covenant;
>
> (2) Safe and healthy working conditions;

(3) Equal opportunity for everyone to be promoted in his employment to an appropriate higher level, subject to no considerations other than those of seniority and competence;
(4) Rest, leisure and reasonable limitation of working hours and periodic holidays with pay, as well as remuneration for public holidays.[44]

The family and working mothers are afforded special protection under Article 10 as the States Parties to the present Covenant recognize that the widest possible protection and assistance should be accorded to the family, which is the natural and fundamental group unit of society, particularly for its establishment and while it is responsible for the care and education of dependent children. Further, special protection should be accorded to mothers during a reasonable period before and after childbirth, and during such period, working mothers should be accorded paid leave or leave with adequate social security benefits.[45]

Article 13 guarantees the right to education for the enhancement of the person in that the States Parties to the present Covenant recognize the right of everyone to education. They agree that education shall be directed to the full development of the human personality and the sense of its dignity, and shall strengthen the respect for human rights and fundamental freedoms. They further agree that education shall enable all persons to participate effectively in a free society, promote understanding, tolerance and friendship among all nations and all racial, ethnic or religious groups, and further the activities of the United Nations for the maintenance of peace.[46]

The Convention on the Elimination of All Forms of Discrimination against Women (CEDAW)

The Convention on the Elimination of All Forms of Discrimination against Women (CEDAW) was adopted on December 18, 1979.[47] It is the most comprehensive treaty specifically on the human rights of women, establishing legally binding obligations to end discrimination. Described as the 'International Bill of Rights for Women', the Convention provides for equality between women and men in the enjoyment of civil, political, economic, social and cultural rights. Discrimination against women is to be eliminated through legal, policy and programmatic measures, and through temporary special measures to accelerate women's equality, which are defined as non-discriminatory. States Parties are required to end all forms of discrimination against women and to ensure their equality with men in political and public life with regard to nationality, education, employment, health, and economic and social benefits. Obligations are also imposed to eliminate discrimination against women in marriage and family life, and to ensure that women and men are treated equally before the law. States are required to take account of the particular problems of women in rural areas, and their special roles in the economic survival of the family.

The Convention obliges States Parties to modify the social and cultural patterns of conduct of men and women, in order to eliminate prejudices and customs and all other practices, which are based on the idea of the inferiority or superiority of either of the sexes or on stereotyped roles for men and women. The Convention establishes a monitoring body, the Committee on the Elimination of Discrimination against Women, which comprises 23 independent experts. The Committee is mandated to consider reports from States Parties, and to make suggestions and general recommendations based on these reports. The Committee directs its suggestions to the United Nations system and its general recommendations to States Parties.

Consisting of a preamble and 30 articles, CEDAW defines what constitutes discrimination against women and sets up an agenda for national action to end such discrimination. Countries that have ratified or acceded to the Convention are legally bound to put its provisions into practice, and are also committed to submit national reports, at least every four years, on measures they have taken to comply with their treaty obligations. As of March 2003, the Convention, which entered into force on September 3, 1981, had 171 signatory States Parties to the Convention, which represents almost 90 per cent of the members of the United Nations.

In the Preamble of the Convention on the Elimination of All Forms of Discrimination against Women, the State Parties undertake the agreement:

> Noting that the Charter of the United Nations reaffirms faith in fundamental human rights, in the dignity and worth of the human person and in the equal rights of men and women,
>
> Noting that the Universal Declaration of Human Rights affirms the principle of the inadmissibility of discrimination and proclaims that all human beings are born free and equal in dignity and rights and that everyone is entitled to all the rights and freedoms set forth therein, without distinction of any kind, including distinction based on sex,
>
> Noting that the States Parties to the International Covenants on Human Rights have the obligation to ensure the equal rights of men and women to enjoy all economic, social, cultural, civil and political rights,
>
> Considering the international conventions concluded under the auspices of the United Nations and the specialized agencies promoting equality of rights of men and women,
>
> Noting also the resolutions, declarations and recommendations adopted by the United Nations and the specialized agencies promoting equality of rights of men and women,
>
> Concerned, however, that despite these various instruments extensive discrimination against women continues to exist,
>
> Recalling that discrimination against women violates the principles of equality of rights and respect for human dignity, is an obstacle to the participation of women, on equal terms with men, in the political, social, economic and cultural life of their

countries, hampers the growth of the prosperity of society and the family and makes more difficult the full development of the potentialities of women in the service of their countries and of humanity,

Concerned that in situations of poverty women have the least access to food, health, education, training and opportunities for employment and other needs,

Convinced that the establishment of the new international economic order based on equity and justice will contribute significantly towards the promotion of equality between men and women,

Emphasizing that the eradication of apartheid, all forms of racism, racial discrimination, colonialism, neo-colonialism, aggression, foreign occupation and domination and interference in the internal affairs of States is essential to the full enjoyment of the rights of men and women,

Affirming that the strengthening of international peace and security, the relaxation of international tension, mutual co-operation among all States irrespective of their social and economic systems, general and complete disarmament, in particular nuclear disarmament under strict and effective international control, the affirmation of the principles of justice, equality and mutual benefit in relations among countries and the realization of the right of peoples under alien and colonial domination and foreign occupation to self-determination and independence, as well as respect for national sovereignty and territorial integrity, will promote social progress and development and as a consequence will contribute to the attainment of full equality between men and women,

Convinced that the full and complete development of a country, the welfare of the world and the cause of peace require the maximum participation of women on equal terms with men in all fields,

Bearing in mind the great contribution of women to the welfare of the family and to the development of society, so far not fully recognized, the social significance of maternity and the role of both parents in the family and in the upbringing of children, and aware that the role of women in procreation should not be a basis for discrimination but that the upbringing of children requires a sharing of responsibility between men and women and society as a whole,

Aware that a change in the traditional role of men as well as the role of women in society and in the family is needed to achieve full equality between men and women,

Determined to implement the principles set forth in the Declaration on the Elimination of Discrimination against Women and, for that purpose, to adopt the measures required for the elimination of such discrimination in all its forms and manifestations.[48]

Discrimination against women is defined in Article 1 as to mean any distinction, exclusion or restriction made on the basis of sex which has the effect or purpose of impairing or nullifying the recognition, enjoyment or exercise by women, irrespective of their marital status, on a basis of equality of men and women, of human rights and fundamental freedoms in the political, economic, social, cultural, civil or any other field.[49]

Importantly, States stand firm against discrimination and commit to implement a policy to eliminate discrimination against women in Article 2:

> 2. States Parties condemn discrimination against women in all its forms, agree to pursue by all appropriate means and without delay a policy of eliminating discrimination against women and, to this end, undertake:
> (a) To embody the principle of the equality of men and women in their national constitutions or other appropriate legislation if not yet incorporated therein and to ensure, through law and other appropriate means, the practical realization of this principle;
> (b) To adopt appropriate legislative and other measures, including sanctions where appropriate, prohibiting all discrimination against women;
> (c) To establish legal protection of the rights of women on an equal basis with men and to ensure through competent national tribunals and other public institutions the effective protection of women against any act of discrimination;
> (d) To refrain from engaging in any act or practice of discrimination against women and to ensure that public authorities and institutions shall act in conformity with this obligation;
> (e) To take all appropriate measures to eliminate discrimination against women by any person, organization or enterprise;
> (f) To take all appropriate measures, including legislation, to modify or abolish existing laws, regulations, customs and practices which constitute discrimination against women;
> (g) To repeal all national penal provisions which constitute discrimination against women.[50]

Further, in Article 3, to ensure the full participation of women in various spheres, States Parties shall take in all fields, in particular in the political, social, economic and cultural fields, all appropriate measures, including legislation, to ensure the full development and advancement of women, for the purpose of guaranteeing them the exercise and enjoyment of human rights and fundamental freedoms on a basis of equality with men.[51]

Article 4 contains an affirmative action strategy in that adoption by States Parties of temporary special measures aimed at accelerating de facto equality between men and women shall not be considered discrimination as defined in the present Convention, but shall in no way entail as a consequence the maintenance of unequal or separate standards; these measures shall be discontinued when the objectives of equality of opportunity and treatment have been achieved. Further, adoption by States Parties of special measures, including those measures contained in the present Convention, aimed at protecting maternity shall not be considered discriminatory.[52]

In order to eliminate prejudices and customary practices, Article 5 establishes that States Parties shall take all appropriate measures to modify the social and cultural patterns of conduct of men and women, with a view to achieving the elimination of prejudices and customary and all other practices which are based on the idea of the inferiority or the superiority of either of the sexes or on stereotyped roles for men and women; and to ensure that family education includes a proper understanding of maternity as a social function and the recognition of the common responsibility of men and women in the upbringing and development of their children, it being understood that the interest of the children is the primordial consideration in all cases.[53] Further, in order to counter the exploitation of women, Article 6 holds that States Parties shall take all appropriate measures, including legislation, to suppress all forms of traffic in women and exploitation of prostitution of women.[54]

The public life stream is protected under Article 7 in that States Parties shall take all appropriate measures to eliminate discrimination against women in the political and public life of the country and, in particular, shall ensure to women, on equal terms with men, the right to vote in all elections and public referenda and to be eligible for election to all publicly elected bodies; to participate in the formulation of government policy and the implementation thereof, and to hold public office and perform all public functions at all levels of government; and to participate in Non-Governmental Organizations (NGOs) and associations concerned with the public and political life of the country.[55] Further, according to Article 8, States Parties shall take all appropriate measures to ensure to women, on equal terms with men and without any discrimination, the opportunity to represent their Governments at the international level and to participate in the work of international organizations.[56]

The importance of education for the advancement and the enhancement of women is emphasized in Article 10, which holds that States Parties shall take all appropriate measures to eliminate discrimination against women in order to ensure to them equal rights with men in the field of education and in particular to ensure, on a basis of equality of men and women the same conditions for career and vocational guidance, for access to studies and for the achievement of diplomas in educational establishments of all categories in rural as well as in urban areas, and this equality shall be ensured in pre-school, general, technical, professional and higher technical education, as well as in all types of vocational training; the elimination of any stereotyped concept of the roles of men and women at all levels and in all forms of education by encouraging coeducation and other types of education which will help to achieve this aim and, in particular, by the revision of textbooks and school programs and the adaptation of teaching methods; the same opportunities to benefit from scholarships and other study grants; the same opportunities for access to programs of continuing education, including adult and functional literacy programs, particulary those aimed at reducing, at the earliest possible time, any gap in education existing between men and women; the reduction of female student drop-out rates, and the organization of programs for girls and women who have left school prematurely; and the same opportunities to participate actively in sports and physical education.[57]

Crucially, Article 11 (1) guarantees employment rights for women in terms of access to employment and equal pay:

> 11(1). States Parties shall take all appropriate measures to eliminate discrimination against women in the field of employment in order to ensure, on a basis of equality of men and women, the same rights, in particular:
> (a) The right to work as an inalienable right of all human beings;
> (b) The right to the same employment opportunities, including the application of the same criteria for selection in matters of employment;
> (c) The right to free choice of profession and employment, the right to promotion, job security and all benefits and conditions of service and the right to receive vocational training and retraining, including apprenticeships, advanced vocational training and recurrent training;
> (d) The right to equal remuneration, including benefits, and to equal treatment in respect of work of equal value, as well as equality of treatment in the evaluation of the quality of work;
> (e) The right to social security, particularly in cases of retirement, unemployment, sickness, invalidity and old age and other incapacity to work, as well as the right to paid leave;
> (f) The right to protection of health and to safety in working conditions, including the safeguarding of the function of reproduction.[58]

Women are protected further in the employment area by Article 11(2) as to issues of marriage and maternity, which states that in order to prevent discrimination against women on the grounds of marriage or maternity and to ensure their effective right to work, States Parties shall take appropriate measures to prohibit, subject to the imposition of sanctions, dismissal on the grounds of pregnancy or of maternity leave and discrimination in dismissals on the basis of marital status; to introduce maternity leave with pay or with comparable social benefits without loss of former employment, seniority or social allowances; and to encourage the provision of the necessary supporting social services to enable parents to combine family obligations with work responsibilities and participation in public life, in particular through promoting the establishment and development of a network of childcare facilities.[59]

Further, economic and social life is emphasized in Article 13, which holds that States Parties shall take all appropriate measures to eliminate discrimination against women in other areas of economic and social life in order to ensure, on a basis of equality of men and women, the same rights, in particular the right to family benefits; the right to bank loans, mortgages and other forms of financial credit; and the right to participate in recreational activities, sports and all aspects of cultural life.[60]

Women in rural areas are given added protection in light of their situation in Article 14, which recognizes that States Parties shall take into account the particular problems faced by rural women and the significant roles they play in the economic survival of their families, including their work in the non-monetized sectors of the economy. Further, States Parties shall take all appropriate measures to eliminate discrimination against women in rural areas in order to ensure, on a basis of equality of men and women, that they participate in and benefit from rural development and, in particular, shall ensure to such women the right to participate in the elaboration and implementation of development planning at all levels; to have access to adequate health care facilities, including information, counselling and services in family planning; to benefit directly from social security programmes; to obtain all types of training and education, formal and non-formal, including that relating to functional literacy, as well as the benefit of all community and extension services, in order to increase their technical proficiency; to organize self-help groups and cooperatives in order to obtain equal access to economic opportunities through employment or self employment; to participate in all community activities; to have access to agricultural credit and loans, marketing facilities, appropriate technology, and equal treatment in land and agrarian reform as well as in land resettlement schemes; and to enjoy adequate living conditions, particularly in relation to housing, sanitation, electricity and water supply, transport and communications.[61]

The important concept of equality before the law is guaranteed in Article 15:

> 15(1). States Parties shall accord to women equality with men before the law.
> (2). States Parties shall accord to women, in civil matters, a legal capacity identical to that of men and the same opportunities to exercise that capacity. In particular, they shall give women equal rights to conclude contracts and to administer property and shall treat them equally in all stages of procedure in courts and tribunals.
> (3). States Parties agree that all contracts and all other private instruments of any kind with a legal effect which is directed at restricting the legal capacity of women shall be deemed null and void.[62]

In view of the issue of marital responsibility, Article 16 enunciates the concept of equality of women and men in marriage, in that States Parties shall take all appropriate measures to eliminate discrimination against women in all matters relating to marriage and family relations and in particular shall ensure, on a basis of equality of men and women, the same rights and responsibilities during marriage and at its dissolution.[63]

Under Article 17, for the purpose of considering the progress made in the implementation of the Convention, a Committee on the Elimination of Discrimination against Women is established to ensure equality of men and women.[64] In the on-going monitoring process, Article 18 holds that States Parties undertake to submit to the Secretary-General of the United Nations, for consideration by the Committee, a report on the legislative, judicial, administrative or other measures which they have adopted to give effect to the provisions of the present Convention and on the progress made in this respect within one year after the entry into force for the State concerned; and thereafter at least every four years and further whenever the Committee so requests. Further, reports may indicate factors and difficulties affecting the degree of fulfillment of obligations under the present Convention.[65] Likewise, under Article 21, the Committee shall, through the Economic and Social Council, report annually to the General Assembly of the United Nations on its activities and may make suggestions and general recommendations based on the examination of reports and information received from the States Parties, and such suggestions and general recommendations shall be included in the report of the Committee together with comments, if any, from States Parties. Further, the Secretary-General of the United Nations shall transmit the reports of the Committee to the Commission on the Status of Women for its information.[66]

As for greater measures as well as the necessary measures taken by State Parties to combat discrimination, Article 23 states that nothing in the present Convention shall affect any provisions that are more conducive to the achievement of equality between men and women which may be contained in the legislation of a State Party; or in any other international convention, treaty or agreement in force for that State. Further, States Parties undertake to adopt all necessary measures at the national level aimed at achieving the full realization of the rights recognized in the present Convention.[67]

The Optional Protocol to the Convention on the Elimination of All Forms of Discrimination against Women

The Optional Protocol to the Convention on the Elimination of All Forms of Discrimination Against Women (CEDAW) was adopted by the United Nations Commission on the Status of Women on March 2, 1999.[68] It has yet to be adopted by the United Nations General Assembly, but if adopted, it will allow individuals and groups to bring petitions before the CEDAW Committee. Human rights issues of racism and ethnocentrism continue to mar progress towards women's empowerment where minorities continue to be over-represented among the poor and face systemic barriers that prevent them from accessing the opportunities created for the achievement of gender equality.

The objective of the Optional Protocol is to allow individuals or groups of individuals who have exhausted national remedies to petition the Committee directly about alleged violations of the Convention by their Governments. The Optional Protocol also permits the Committee to conduct inquiries into grave or systematic violations of the Convention in countries that are parties to the Convention and to the Optional Protocol.

By the Optional Protocol, States Parties undertake to make the Convention and the Protocol widely known and to facilitate access to information about the views and recommendations of the Committee. They are also required to take all appropriate measures to ensure that individuals under their jurisdiction are not subjected to ill-treatment or intimidation when they take advantage of the Protocol's procedure or provide information associated with these procedures. States which ratify or accede to the Optional Protocol may not enter reservations to its terms, may opt-out of the inquiry procedure.

Essentially, an optional protocol is an additional enforcement mechanism for the original convention. The motivation behind the development of an Optional Protocol for CEDAW was to bring CEDAW itself on an equal footing with other international human rights instruments, enhancing its enforcement mechanisms. Although CEDAW represents a strong and valuable statement of women's human rights, it is essentially a weak and often ignored instrument among the States party to it, since signatories to CEDAW have made more reservations to its provisions than any other UN convention.

As the principal document enunciating women's rights, CEDAW is an important instrument for half of the world's population. The significance of CEDAW, however, is not matched by its lack of implementation strength, since human rights are only as effective as their ability to be implemented. The CEDAW Committee has limited powers to promote the implementation of the Convention, since it is unable to pronounce a State Party in violation of CEDAW, or to order a remedy for violation.

However, the Optional Protocol has provided an opportunity to strengthen the weak enforcement ability of CEDAW. The Optional Protocol gives individual women and groups of women the ability to make a direct complaint to the CEDAW Committee, which only considers complaints related to incidents within the domestic jurisdiction of State Parties to the Optional Protocol and only when the complainant has demonstrated that available domestic remedies have been exhausted. This latter requirement will be lifted if it can be shown that the application of domestic remedies is unreasonably prolonged or unlikely to bring effective relief. Complaints made must concern an alleged breach of the rights enshrined in CEDAW, which encompass issues of political participation, health, education, employment, marriage, family relations and equality before the law. The Optional Protocol does not create new rights, but merely creates a new enforcement mechanism for these rights.

The Optional Protocol has been approved by the United Nations General Assembly, and it is open for signature. It provides a 'backup' for domestic enforcement mechanisms to ensure that they are adequate and effective. In States with a federalist system, regional and federal governments may have separate and independent legislative power, with the actions of one level of government perhaps being contrary to CEDAW, and the Optional Protocol would help to ensure that all levels of government find domestic methods to set uniform standards in accordance with CEDAW. It is important for States with good domestic protection for women to become a party to the Optional Protocol to demonstrate leadership for other States with less effective mechanisms.

The Optional Protocol to CEDAW has an inquiry procedure, which allows individuals, groups of individuals and NGOs to have standing to submit communications. As well, the Optional Protocol incorporates a settlement procedure, which would allow the Committee to facilitate settlements of disputes in some circumstances. The Committee's views on communications would amount to jurisprudence, that is case law used for guidance in interpreting laws, providing clarification and guidance for States and for individuals about States' obligations under CEDAW. In order to stimulate changes in discriminatory laws and practices, the Committee would be able to request the State Party concerned to take specific measures to remedy violations of CEDAW, such as the amendment of legislation, the ending of discriminatory practices, and the implementation of affirmative action measures. In order to enhance existing mechanisms for the implementation of human rights within the UN system, the Optional Protocol to CEDAW is effectively the first gender specific international complaints procedure. As well as putting CEDAW on a par with human rights treaties which have a complaints process, it enhances existing mechanisms by specifically incorporating practices and procedures that have been developed under other international complaints procedures, such as the International Covenant on Civil and Political Rights (ICCPR) and its Protocol; the Convention on the Elimination of All Forms of Racial Discrimination; and the Convention Against Torture and Other Cruel, Inhuman or Degrading Treatment or Punishment.

In the Preamble of the Optional Protocol to the Convention on the Elimination of All Forms of Discrimination against Women, the State Parties undertake the agreement:

> Noting that the Charter of the United Nations reaffirms faith in fundamental human rights, in the dignity and worth of the human person and in the equal rights of men and women,
>
> Also noting that the Universal Declaration of Human Rights proclaims that all human beings are born free and equal in dignity and rights and that everyone is entitled to all the rights and freedoms set forth therein, without distinction of any kind, including distinction based on sex,
>
> Recalling that the International Covenants on Human Rights and other international human rights instruments prohibit discrimination on the basis of sex,
>
> Also recalling the Convention on the Elimination of All Forms of Discrimination against Women ('the Convention'), in which the States Parties thereto condemn discrimination against women in all its forms and agree to pursue by all appropriate means and without delay a policy of eliminating discrimination against women,
>
> Reaffirming their determination to ensure the full and equal enjoyment by women of all human rights and fundamental freedoms and to take effective action to prevent violations of these rights and freedoms.[69]

Article 1 establishes that States who become Parties to the optional protocol recognize the competence of the Committee to receive and consider communications under the protocol.[70] According to Article 2, communications may be submitted by or on behalf of individuals or groups of individuals, under the jurisdiction of a State Party, claiming to be victims of a violation of any of the rights set forth in the Convention by that State Party. Where a communication is submitted on behalf of individuals or groups of individuals, this shall be with their consent unless the author can justify acting on their behalf without such consent.[71] However, under Article 4, the Committee shall not consider a communication unless it has ascertained that all available domestic remedies have been exhausted unless the application of such remedies is unreasonably prolonged or unlikely to bring effective relief.[72]

Article 4 stipulates admissibility criteria of communications in that before a complaint is considered, the Committee must determine that all available domestic remedies have been exhausted and the complaint is not, nor has been examined by the Committee or has been or is being examined under another procedure of international investigation or settlement. In addition, a complaint will only be admissible provided the complaint is compatible with the provisions of the Convention, is not an abuse of the right to submit a communication, the claimants' allegations can be substantiated, and the facts presented occurred after the State Party ratified the Protocol.[73] Further, Article 5 holds that, after receipt of a communication and prior to its final decision, the Committee has the option of contacting the State Party with an urgent request that the State Party take steps to protect the alleged victim or victims from irreparable harm.[74]

Article 7 outlines the process of complaint consideration in that the Committee will examine and consider all information provided by a complaint in closed meetings, and the Committee's views and recommendations will be transmitted to the parties concerned. The State Party has six months to consider the views of the Committee and provide a written response, including remedial steps taken, and the Committee may request additional information from the State Party, including in subsequent reports.[75] Further, Article 8 establishes an inquiry procedure that allows the Committee to initiate a confidential investigation by one or more of its members where it has received reliable information of grave or systematic violations by a State Party of rights established in the Convention, and any findings, comments or recommendations will be transmitted to the State Party concerned, to which it may respond within six months.[76] As well, Article 9 holds that the State Party may be invited to provide the Committee with details of any remedial efforts taken following an inquiry.[77]

Article 10 provides an opt-out clause, since ratification of the Optional Protocol, a State Party has the option of refusing to recognize the competence of the Committee to initiate and conduct an inquiry as established under articles 8 and 9; however, this declaration may be withdrawn at a later time.[78] Further, under Article 11, a State Party shall take all appropriate steps to ensure that individuals under its jurisdiction are not subjected to ill treatment or intimidation as a consequence of communicating with the Committee pursuant to the present Protocol.[79] Finally, Article 13 establishes a requirement that States Parties widely publicize the Convention and its Protocol, and provide access to the views and recommendations of the Committee.[80]

There are currently two ways CEDAW is enforced: The Reporting Procedure, in that States Parties have to submit a national report to the Committee within one year of accession or ratification of CEDAW and thereafter every four years or when the Committee requests, and in the reports, States must indicate the measures they have adopted to give effect to the provisions of CEDAW, and the Committee discusses these reports with Government representatives and explores areas for further action by the specific country; and The Interstate Procedure, in that under article 29 of CEDAW, two or more State Parties can refer disputes about the interpretation and implementation of CEDAW to arbitration, and if the dispute is not settled, it can be referred to the International Court of Justice.

The International Convention on the Elimination of All Forms of Racial Discrimination (ICEAFRD)

Impacting on minority women, the International Convention on the Elimination of All Forms of Racial Discrimination was adopted on March 7, 1966.[81] The Convention defines and condemns racial discrimination, and commits States to change national laws and policies, which create or perpetuate racial discrimination. It was the first human rights instrument to establish an international monitoring system and was also revolutionary in its provision of national measures toward the advancement of specific racial or ethnic groups.

One of the main objectives of the Convention is to promote racial equality, and as such, the Convention not only aims to achieve de jure racial equality but also de facto equality, which allows the various ethnic, racial and national groups to enjoy the same social development. Furthermore, the Convention recognizes that certain racial or ethnic groups may need special protection or may need to be assisted by special measures in order to achieve adequate development, and the Convention provides that such special measures shall not be considered racial discrimination as long as they are not continued after the objectives for which they were taken have been achieved.

The Convention defines the concept of racial discrimination, covering indirect discrimination or unjustifiable disparate impact. The Convention shall not apply to distinctions, exclusions, restrictions or preferences made by a State Party between citizens and non-citizens. Other important provisions include imperative stipulations obliging States Parties to adopt legislation to criminalize and punish the dissemination of ideas based on racial superiority or hatred, incitement to racial discrimination, and acts of violence against any race or group of persons of another color or ethnic origin.

The Convention contains a non-exhaustive list of rights and freedoms in the enjoyment of which racial discrimination shall be prohibited and eliminated, which includes certain rights not expressly contained in the Universal Declaration of Human Rights, such as the right to inherit and the right of access to any place or service intended for use by the general public, and includes rights in regard to which racial discrimination is prohibited, such as the right to work, the right to join trade unions and the right to housing.

In order to monitor and review actions taken by States to fulfill their obligations, the Convention established the Committee on the Elimination of Racial Discrimination (CERD), which was the first body created by the United Nations to monitor the implementation by States of a human rights treaty. Its mandate is to review the legal, judicial, administrative and other steps taken by individual States to fulfill their obligations to combat racial discrimination. The Convention establishes three procedures to facilitate CERD's review: periodic reports submitted to the Committee by all States Parties to the Convention; State-to-State complaints; and a complaint lodged against the alleged offending State by an individual or a group of persons who claim to be victims of racial discrimination.

The Beijing Declaration and the Platform for Action

The Beijing Declaration, the Fourth World Conference on Women, states:

1. We, the Governments participating in the Fourth World Conference on Women,

2. Gathered here in Beijing in September 1995, the year of the fiftieth anniversary of the founding of the United Nations,

3. Determined to advance the goals of equality, development and peace for all women everywhere in the interest of all humanity,

4. Acknowledging the voices of all women everywhere and taking note of the diversity of women and their roles and circumstances, honouring the women who paved the way and inspired by the hope present in the world's youth,

5. Recognize that the status of women has advanced in some important respects in the past decade but that progress has been uneven, inequalities between women and men have persisted and major obstacles remain, with serious consequences for the well-being of all people,

6. Also recognize that this situation is exacerbated by the increasing poverty that is affecting the lives of the majority of the world's people, in particular women and children, with origins in both the national and international domains,

7. Dedicate ourselves unreservedly to addressing these constraints and obstacles and thus enhancing further the advancement and empowerment of women all over the world, and agree that this requires urgent action in the spirit of determination, hope, cooperation and solidarity, now and to carry us forward into the next century.

The States reaffirm a commitment to:

8. The equal rights and inherent human dignity of women and men and other purposes and principles enshrined in the Charter of the United Nations, to the Universal Declaration of Human Rights and other international human rights instruments, in particular the Convention on the Elimination of All Forms of Discrimination against Women and the Convention on the Rights of the Child, as well as the Declaration on the Elimination of Violence against Women and the Declaration on the Right to Development;

9. Ensure the full implementation of the human rights of women and of the girl child as an inalienable, integral and indivisible part of all human rights and fundamental freedoms;

10. Build on consensus and progress made at previous United Nations conferences and summits on women in Nairobi in 1985, on children in New York in 1990, on environment and development in Rio de Janeiro in 1992, on human rights in Vienna in 1993, on population and development in Cairo in 1994 and on social

development in Copenhagen in 1995 with the objective of achieving equality, development and peace;

11. Achieve the full and effective implementation of the Nairobi Forward-looking Strategies for the Advancement of Women;

12. The empowerment and advancement of women, including the right to freedom of thought, conscience, religion and belief, thus contributing to the moral, ethical, spiritual and intellectual needs of women and men, individually or in community with others and thereby guaranteeing them the possibility of realizing their full potential in society and shaping their lives in accordance with their own aspirations.

The States are convinced that:

13. Women's empowerment and their full participation on the basis of equality in all spheres of society, including participation in the decision-making process and access to power, are fundamental for the achievement of equality, development and peace;

14. Women's rights are human rights;

15. Equal rights, opportunities and access to resources, equal sharing of responsibilities for the family by men and women, and a harmonious partnership between them are critical to their well-being and that of their families as well as to the consolidation of democracy;

16. Eradication of poverty based on sustained economic growth, social development, environmental protection and social justice requires the involvement of women in economic and social development, equal opportunities and the full and equal participation of women and men as agents and beneficiaries of people-centred sustainable development;

17. The explicit recognition and reaffirmation of the right of all women to control all aspects of their health, in particular their own fertility, is basic to their empowerment;

18. Local, national, regional and global peace is attainable and is inextricably linked with the advancement of women, who are a fundamental force for leadership, conflict resolution and the promotion of lasting peace at all levels;

19. It is essential to design, implement and monitor, with the full participation of women, effective, efficient and mutually reinforcing gender-sensitive policies and programmes, including development policies and programmes, at all levels that will foster the empowerment and advancement of women;

20. The participation and contribution of all actors of civil society, particularly women's groups and networks and other non-governmental organizations and community-based organizations, with full respect for their autonomy, in

cooperation with Governments, are important to the effective implementation and follow-up of the Platform for Action;

21. The implementation of the Platform for Action requires commitment from Governments and the international community. By making national and international commitments for action, including those made at the Conference, Governments and the international community recognize the need to take priority action for the empowerment and advancement of women.

The States are determined to:

22. Intensify efforts and actions to achieve the goals of the Nairobi Forward-looking Strategies for the Advancement of Women by the end of this century;

23. Ensure the full enjoyment by women and the girl child of all human rights and fundamental freedoms and take effective action against violations of these rights and freedoms;

24. Take all necessary measures to eliminate all forms of discrimination against women and the girl child and remove all obstacles to gender equality and the advancement and empowerment of women;

25. Encourage men to participate fully in all actions towards equality;

26. Promote women's economic independence, including employment, and eradicate the persistent and increasing burden of poverty on women by addressing the structural causes of poverty through changes in economic structures, ensuring equal access for all women, including those in rural areas, as vital development agents, to productive resources, opportunities and public services;

27. Promote people-centred sustainable development, including sustained economic growth, through the provision of basic education, life-long education, literacy and training, and primary health care for girls and women;

28. Take positive steps to ensure peace for the advancement of women and, recognizing the leading role that women have played in the peace movement, work actively towards general and complete disarmament under strict and effective international control, and support negotiations on the conclusion, without delay, of a universal and multilaterally and effectively verifiable comprehensive nuclear-test-ban treaty which contributes to nuclear disarmament and the prevention of the proliferation of nuclear weapons in all its aspects;

29. Prevent and eliminate all forms of violence against women and girls;

30. Ensure equal access to and equal treatment of women and men in education and health care and enhance women's sexual and reproductive health as well as education;

31. Promote and protect all human rights of women and girls;

32. Intensify efforts to ensure equal enjoyment of all human rights and fundamental freedoms for all women and girls who face multiple barriers to their empowerment and advancement because of such factors as their race, age, language, ethnicity, culture, religion, or disability, or because they are indigenous people;

33. Ensure respect for international law, including humanitarian law, in order to protect women and girls in particular;

34. Develop the fullest potential of girls and women of all ages, ensure their full and equal participation in building a better world for all and enhance their role in the development process.

The States are determined to:

35. Ensure women's equal access to economic resources, including land, credit, science and technology, vocational training, information, communication and markets, as a means to further the advancement and empowerment of women and girls, including through the enhancement of their capacities to enjoy the benefits of equal access to these resources, inter alia, by means of international cooperation;

36. Ensure the success of the Platform for Action, which will require a strong commitment on the part of Governments, international organizations and institutions at all levels. We are deeply convinced that economic development, social development and environmental protection are interdependent and mutually reinforcing components of sustainable development, which is the framework for our efforts to achieve a higher quality of life for all people. Equitable social development that recognizes empowering the poor, particularly women living in poverty, to utilize environmental resources sustainably is a necessary foundation for sustainable development. We also recognize that broad-based and sustained economic growth in the context of sustainable development is necessary to sustain social development and social justice. The success of the Platform for Action will also require adequate mobilization of resources at the national and international levels as well as new and additional resources to the developing countries from all available funding mechanisms, including multilateral, bilateral and private sources for the advancement of women; financial resources to strengthen the capacity of national, subregional, regional and international institutions; a commitment to equal rights, equal responsibilities and equal opportunities and to the equal participation of women and men in all national, regional and international bodies and policy-making processes; and the establishment or strengthening of mechanisms at all levels for accountability to the world's women;

37. Ensure also the success of the Platform for Action in countries with economies in transition, which will require continued international cooperation and assistance;

38. We hereby adopt and commit ourselves as Governments to implement the following Platform for Action, ensuring that a gender perspective is reflected in all our policies and programmes. We urge the United Nations system, regional and

international financial institutions, other relevant regional and international institutions and all women and men, as well as non-governmental organizations, with full respect for their autonomy, and all sectors of civil society, in cooperation with Governments, to fully commit themselves and contribute to the implementation of this Platform for Action.[82]

According to the Fourth World Conference on Women's Platform for Action, Governments, the international community and civil society, including Non-Governmental Organizations (NGOs) and the private sector, are called upon to take strategic action in the following critical areas of concern: The ever persistent and increasing burden of poverty on women; Inequalities and inadequacies in and unequal access to education and training; Inequalities and inadequacies in and unequal access to health care and related services; Violence against women; The effects of armed or other kinds of conflict on women, including those living under foreign occupation; Inequality in economic structures and policies, in all forms of productive activities and in access to resources; Inequality between men and women in the sharing of power and decision-making at all levels; Insufficient mechanisms at all levels to promote the advancement of women; Lack of respect for and inadequate promotion and protection of the human rights of women; Stereotyping of women and inequality in women's access to and participation in all communication systems, especially in the media; Gender inequalities in the management of natural resources and in the safeguarding of the environment; and Persistent discrimination against and violation of the rights of the girl child.[83]

In terms of women and the economy, the following are the strategic objectives and the actions to be taken by the various stakeholders:

Strategic Objective 1: Promote women's economic rights and independence, including access to employment, appropriate working conditions and control over economic resources.

Actions to be taken by Governments include:

(a) Enact and enforce legislation to guarantee the rights of women and men to equal pay for equal work or work of equal value;
(b) Adopt and implement laws against discrimination based on sex in the labor market, especially considering older women workers, hiring and promotion, the extension of employment benefits and social security, and working conditions;
(c) Eliminate discriminatory practices by employers and take appropriate measures in consideration of women's reproductive role and functions, such as the denial of employment and dismissal due to pregnancy or breast-feeding, or requiring proof of contraceptive use, and take effective measures to ensure that pregnant women, women on maternity leave or women re-entering the labor market after childbearing are not discriminated against;
(d) Devise mechanisms and take positive action to enable women to gain access to full and equal participation in the formulation of policies and definition of structures through such bodies as ministries of

finance and trade, national economic commissions, economic research institutes and other key agencies, as well as through their participation in appropriate international bodies;

(e) Undertake legislation and administrative reforms to give women equal rights with men to economic resources, including access to ownership and control over land and other forms of property, credit, inheritance, natural resources and appropriate new technology;

(f) Conduct reviews of national income and inheritance tax, and social security systems to eliminate any existing bias against women;

(g) Seek to develop a more comprehensive knowledge of work and employment through efforts to measure and better understand the type, extent and distribution of unremunerated work, particularly work in caring for dependants and unremunerated work done for family farms or businesses, and encourage the sharing and dissemination of information on studies and experience in this field, including the development of methods for assessing its value in quantitative terms, for possible reflection in accounts that may be produced separately from, but consistent with, core national accounts;

(h) Review and amend laws governing the operation of financial institutions to ensure that they provide services to women and men on an equal basis;

(i) Facilitate, at appropriate levels, more open and transparent budget processes;

(j) Revise and implement national policies that support the traditional savings, credit and lending mechanisms for women;

(k) Seek to ensure that national policies related to international and regional trade agreements do not have an adverse impact on women's new and traditional economic activities;

(l) Ensure that all corporations, including transnational corporations, comply with national laws and codes, social security regulations, applicable international agreements, instruments and conventions, including those related to the environment, and other relevant laws;

(m) Adjust employment policies to facilitate the restructuring of work patterns in order to promote the sharing of family responsibilities;

(n) Establish mechanisms and other forums to enable women entrepreneurs and women workers to contribute to the formulation of policies and programs being developed by economic ministries and financial institutions;

(o) Enact and enforce equal opportunity laws, take positive action and ensure compliance by the public and private sectors through various means;

(p) Use gender-impact analyses in the development of macro and micro-economic and social policies in order to monitor such impact and restructure policies in cases where harmful impact occurs;

(q) Promote gender-sensitive policies and measures to empower women as equal partners with men in technical, managerial and entrepreneurial fields;

(r) Reform laws or enact national policies that support the establishment of labor laws to ensure the protection of all women workers, including safe work practices, the right to organize and access to justice.[84]

Strategic Objective 2: Facilitate women's equal access to resources, employment, markets and trade.

Actions to be taken by Governments include:

(a) Promote and support women's self-employment and the development of small enterprises, and strengthen women's access to credit and capital on appropriate terms equal to those of men through the scaling-up of institutions dedicated to promoting women's entrepreneurship, including, as appropriate, non-traditional and mutual credit schemes, as well as innovative linkages with financial institutions;

(b) Strengthen the incentive role of the State as employer to develop a policy of equal opportunities for women and men;

(c) Enhance, at the national and local levels, rural women's income-generating potential by facilitating their equal access to and control over productive resources, land, credit, capital, property rights, development programs and cooperative structures;

(d) Promote and strengthen micro-enterprises, new small businesses, cooperative enterprises, expanded markets and other employment opportunities and, where appropriate, facilitate the transition from the informal to the formal sector, especially in rural areas;

(e) Create and modify programs and policies that recognize and strengthen women's vital role in food security and provide paid and unpaid women producers, especially those involved in food production, such as farming, fishing and aquaculture, as well as urban enterprises, with equal access to appropriate technologies, transportation, extension services, marketing and credit facilities at the local and community levels;

(f) Establish appropriate mechanisms and encourage intersectoral institutions that enable women's cooperatives to optimize access to necessary services;

(g) Increase the proportion of women extension workers and other government personnel who provide technical assistance or administer economic programs;

(h) Review, reformulate and implement policies, including business, commercial and contract law, as well as government regulations, to ensure that they do not discriminate against micro, small and medium-scale enterprises owned by women in rural and urban areas;

(i) Analyze, advise on, coordinate and implement policies that integrate the needs and interests of employed, self-employed and entrepreneurial women into sectoral and interministerial policies, programs and budgets;
(j) Ensure equal access for women to effective job training, retraining, counselling and placement services that are not limited to traditional employment areas;
(k) Remove policy and regulatory obstacles faced by women in social and development programs that discourage private and individual initiative;
(l) Safeguard and promote respect for basic workers' rights, including the prohibition of forced labor and child labor, freedom of association and the right to organize and bargain collectively, equal remuneration for men and women for work of equal value and non-discrimination in employment, fully implementing the conventions of the International Labour Organisation in the case of States Parties to those conventions and, taking into account the principles embodied in the case of those countries that are not parties to those conventions in order to achieve truly sustained economic growth and sustainable development.[85]

Actions to be taken by Governments, central banks and national development banks, and private banking institutions include:

(a) Increase the participation of women, including women entrepreneurs, in advisory boards and other forums to enable women entrepreneurs from all sectors and their organizations to contribute to the formulation and review of policies and programs being developed by economic ministries and banking institutions;
(b) Mobilize the banking sector to increase lending and refinancing through incentives and the development of intermediaries that serve the needs of women entrepreneurs and producers in both rural and urban areas, and include women in their leadership, planning and decision-making;
(c) Structure services to reach rural and urban women involved in micro, small and medium-scale enterprises, with special attention to young women, low-income women, those belonging to ethnic and racial minorities, and indigenous women who lack access to capital and assets; and expand women's access to financial markets by identifying and encouraging financial supervisory and regulatory reforms that support financial institutions' direct and indirect efforts to better meet the credit and other financial needs of the micro, small and medium-scale enterprises of women;
(d) Ensure that women's priorities are included in public investment programs for economic infrastructure, such as water and sanitation, electrification and energy conservation, transport and road construction; promote greater involvement of women beneficiaries at

the project planning and implementation stages to ensure access to jobs and contracts.[86]

Actions to be taken by Governments and Non-Governmental Organizations (NGOs) include:

(a) Pay special attention to women's needs when disseminating market, trade and resource information and provide appropriate training in these fields;
(b) Encourage community economic development strategies that build on partnerships among Governments, and encourage members of civil society to create jobs and address the social circumstances of individuals, families and communities.[87]

Actions to be taken by multilateral funders and regional development banks, as well as bilateral and private funding agencies, at the international, regional and sub-regional levels include:

(a) Review, where necessary reformulate, and implement policies, programs and projects, to ensure that a higher proportion of resources reach women in rural and remote areas;
(b) Develop flexible funding arrangements to finance intermediary institutions that target women's economic activities, and promote self-sufficiency and increased capacity in and profitability of women's economic enterprises;
(c) Develop strategies to consolidate and strengthen their assistance to the micro, small and medium-scale enterprise sector, in order to enhance the opportunities for women to participate fully and equally and work together to coordinate and enhance the effectiveness of this sector, drawing upon expertise and financial resources from within their own organizations as well as from bilateral agencies, Governments and non-governmental organizations.[88]

Actions to be taken by international, multilateral and bilateral development cooperation organizations include: Support, through the provision of capital and resources, financial institutions that serve low-income, small and micro-scale women entrepreneurs and producers in both the formal and informal sectors.[89]

Actions to be taken by international organizations include: Provide adequate support for programs and projects designed to promote sustainable and productive entrepreneurial activities among women, in particular the disadvantaged.[90]

Strategic Objective 3: Provide business services, training and access to markets, information and technology, particularly to low-income women.

Actions to be taken by Governments in cooperation with Non-Governmental Organizations (NGOs) and the private sector:

(a) Provide public infrastructure to ensure equal market access for women and men entrepreneurs;
(b) Develop programs that provide training and retraining, particularly in new technologies, and affordable services to women in business

management, product development, financing, production and quality control, marketing and the legal aspects of business;

(c) Provide outreach programs to inform low-income and poor women, particularly in rural and remote areas, of opportunities for market and technology access, and provide assistance in taking advantage of such opportunities;

(d) Create non-discriminatory support services, including investment funds for women's businesses, and target women, particularly low-income women, in trade promotion programs;

(e) Disseminate information about successful women entrepreneurs in both traditional and non-traditional economic activities and the skills necessary to achieve success, and facilitate networking and the exchange of information;

(f) Take measures to ensure equal access of women to ongoing training in the workplace, including unemployed women, single parents, women re-entering the labor market after an extended temporary exit from employment owing to family responsibilities and other causes, and women displaced by new forms of production or by retrenchment, and increase incentives to enterprises to expand the number of vocational and training centers that provide training for women in non-traditional areas;

(g) Provide affordable support services, such as high-quality, flexible and affordable childcare services, that take into account the needs of working men and women.[91]

Actions to be taken by local, national, regional and international business organizations and non-governmental organizations concerned with women's issues include: Advocate, at all levels, for the promotion and support of women's businesses and enterprises, including those in the informal sector, and the equal access of women to productive resources.[92]

Strategic Objective 4: Strengthen women's economic capacity and commercial networks.

Actions to be taken by Governments:

(a) Adopt policies that support business organizations, Non-Governmental Organizations (NGOs), cooperatives, revolving loan funds, credit unions, grass-roots organizations, women's self-help groups and other groups in order to provide services to women entrepreneurs in rural and urban areas;

(b) Integrate a gender perspective into all economic restructuring and structural adjustment policies and design programs for women who are affected by economic restructuring, including structural adjustment programs, and for women who work in the informal sector;

(c) Adopt policies that create an enabling environment for women's self-help groups, workers' organizations and cooperatives through nonconventional forms of support and by recognizing the right to freedom of association and the right to organize;

(d) Support programs that enhance the self-reliance of special groups of women, such as young women, women with disabilities, elderly women and women belonging to racial and ethnic minorities;

(e) Promote gender equality through the promotion of women's studies and through the use of the results of studies and gender research in all fields, including the economic, scientific and technological fields;

(f) Support the economic activities of indigenous women, taking into account their traditional knowledge, so as to improve their situation and development;

(g) Adopt policies to extend or maintain the protection of labor laws and social security provisions for those who do paid work in the home;

(h) Recognize and encourage the contribution of research by women scientists and technologists;

(i) Ensure that policies and regulations do not discriminate against micro, small and medium-scale enterprises run by women.[93]

Actions to be taken by financial intermediaries, national training institutes, credit unions, Non-Governmental Organizations (NGOs), women's associations, professional organizations and the private sector include:

(a) Provide, at the national, regional and international levels, training in a variety of business-related and financial management and technical skills to enable women, especially young women, to participate in economic policy-making at those levels;

(b) Provide business services, including marketing and trade information, product design and innovation, technology transfer and quality, to women's business enterprises, including those in export sectors of the economy;

(c) Promote technical and commercial links and establish joint ventures among women entrepreneurs at the national, regional and international levels to support community-based initiatives;

(d) Strengthen the participation of women, including marginalized women, in production and marketing cooperatives by providing marketing and financial support, especially in rural and remote areas;

(e) Promote and strengthen women's micro-enterprises, new small businesses, cooperative enterprises, expanded markets and other employment opportunities and, where appropriate, facilitate the transition from the informal to the formal sector, in rural and urban areas;

(f) Invest capital and develop investment portfolios to finance women's business enterprises;

(g) Give adequate attention to providing technical assistance, advisory services, training and retraining for women connected with the entry to the market economy;

(h) Support credit networks and innovative ventures, including traditional savings schemes;

(i) Provide networking arrangements for entrepreneurial women, including opportunities for the mentoring of inexperienced women by the more experienced;

(j) Encourage community organizations and public authorities to establish loan pools for women entrepreneurs, drawing on successful small-scale cooperative models.[94]

Actions to be taken by the private sector, including transnational and national corporations include:

(a) Adopt policies and establish mechanisms to grant contracts on a non-discriminatory basis;

(b) Recruit women for leadership, decision-making and management and provide training programs, all on an equal basis with men;

(c) Observe national labor, environment, consumer, health and safety laws, particularly those that affect women.[95]

Strategic Objective 5: Eliminate occupational segregation and all forms of employment discrimination.

Actions to be taken by Governments, employers, employees, trade unions and women's organizations include:

(a) Implement and enforce laws and regulations and encourage voluntary codes of conduct that ensure that international labor standards, such as International Labour Organization Convention No. 100 on equal pay and workers' rights, apply equally to female and male workers;

(b) Enact and enforce laws and introduce implementing measures, including means of redress and access to justice in cases of noncompliance, to prohibit direct and indirect discrimination on grounds of gender, including by reference to marital or family status, in relation to access to employment, conditions of employment, including training, promotion, health and safety, as well as termination of employment and social security of workers, including legal protection against sexual and racial harassment;

(c) Enact and enforce laws and develop workplace policies against gender discrimination in the labor market, especially considering older women workers, in hiring and promotion, and in the extension of employment benefits and social security, as well as regarding discriminatory working conditions and sexual harassment; mechanisms should be developed for the regular review and monitoring of such laws;

(d) Eliminate discriminatory practices by employers on the basis of women's reproductive roles and functions, including refusal of employment and dismissal of women due to pregnancy and breast-feeding responsibilities;

(e) Develop and promote employment programs and services for women entering and re-entering the labor market, especially poor urban, rural and young women, the self-employed and those negatively affected by structural adjustment;

(f) Implement and monitor positive public and private-sector employment, equity and positive action programs to address systemic discrimination against women in the labor force, in particular women with disabilities and women belonging to other disadvantaged groups, with respect to hiring, retention and promotion, and vocational training of women in all sectors;
(g) Eliminate occupational segregation, especially by promoting the equal participation of women in highly skilled jobs and senior management positions, and through other measures, such as counselling and placement, that stimulate their on-the-job career development and upward mobility in the labor market, and by stimulating the diversification of occupational choices by both women and men; encourage women to take up non-traditional jobs, especially in science and technology, and encourage men to seek employment in the social sector;
(h) Recognize collective bargaining as a right and as an important mechanism for eliminating wage inequality for women and to improve working conditions;
(i) Promote the election of women trade union officials and ensure that trade union officials elected to represent women are given job protection and physical security in connection with the discharge of their functions;
(j) Ensure access to and develop special programs to enable women with disabilities to obtain and retain employment, and ensure access to education and training at all proper levels, in accordance with the Standard Rules on the Equalization of Opportunities for Persons with Disabilities; adjust working conditions, to the extent possible, in order to suit the needs of women with disabilities, who should be assured legal protection against unfounded job loss on account of their disabilities;
(k) increase efforts to close the gap between women's and men's pay, take steps to implement the principle of equal remuneration for equal work of equal value by strengthening legislation, including compliance with international labor laws and standards, and encourage job evaluation schemes with gender-neutral criteria;
(l) Establish and strengthen mechanisms to adjudicate matters relating to wage discrimination;
(m) Set specific target dates for eliminating all forms of child labor that are contrary to accepted international standards and ensure the full enforcement of relevant existing laws and, where appropriate, enact the legislation necessary to implement the Convention on the Rights of the Child and International Labour Organization standards, ensuring the protection of working children, in particular, street children, through the provision of appropriate health, education and other social services;

(n) Ensure that strategies to eliminate child labor also address the excessive demands made on some girls for unpaid work in their household and other households, where applicable;
(o) Review, analyze and, where appropriate, reformulate the wage structures in female-dominated professions, such as teaching, nursing and childcare, with a view to raising their low status and earnings;
(p) Facilitate the productive employment of documented migrant women, including women who have been determined refugees according to the 1951 Convention relating to the Status of Refugees, through greater recognition of foreign education and credentials, and by adopting an integrated approach to labor market training that incorporates language training.[96]

Strategic Objective 6: Promote harmonization of work and family responsibilities for women and men.

Actions to be taken by Governments include:
(a) Adopt policies to ensure the appropriate protection of labor laws and social security benefits for part-time, temporary, seasonal and home-based workers; promote career development based on work conditions that harmonize work and family responsibilities;
(b) Ensure that full and part-time work can be freely chosen by women and men on an equal basis, and consider appropriate protection for atypical workers in terms of access to employment, working conditions and social security;
(c) Ensure, through legislation, incentives and encouragement, opportunities for women and men to take job-protected parental leave and to have parental benefits; promote the equal sharing of responsibilities for the family by men and women, including through appropriate legislation, incentives and encouragement, and also promote the facilitation of breast-feeding for working mothers;
(d) Develop policies in education to change attitudes that reinforce the division of labor based on gender in order to promote the concept of shared family responsibility for work in the home, particularly in relation to children and elder care;
(e) Improve the development of, and access to, technologies that facilitate occupational as well as domestic work, encourage self-support, generate income, transform gender-prescribed roles within the productive process and enable women to move out of low-paying jobs;
(f) Examine a range of policies and programs, including social security legislation and taxation systems, in accordance with national priorities and policies, to determine how to promote gender equality and flexibility in the way people divide their time between and derive benefits from education and training, paid employment, family responsibilities, volunteer activity, and other socially useful forms of work, rest and leisure.[97]

Actions to be taken by Governments, the private sector and Non-Governmental Organizations (NGOs), trade unions and the United Nations include:

(a) Adopt appropriate measures involving relevant governmental bodies and employers' and employees' associations so that women and men are able to take temporary leave from employment, have transferable employment and retirement benefits and make arrangements to modify work hours without sacrificing their prospects for development and advancement at work and in their careers;

(b) Design and provide educational programs through innovative media campaigns, and school and community education programs to raise awareness on gender equality and non-stereotyped gender roles of women and men within the family; provide support services and facilities, such as on-site child care at workplaces and flexible working arrangements;

(c) Enact and enforce laws against sexual and other forms of harassment in all workplaces.[98]

Important issues for women's economic security and rights are: Engendering macroeconomic frameworks and building capacities of countries to manage globalization and economic transition from the perspective of poor women; Promoting enabling institutional, legal and regulatory environments for women's equal ownership and access to economic resources and assets, such as finance, land and property; Strengthening women's economic capacity and rights as entrepreneurs, producers and home-based workers; and Mainstreaming gender to economic policies and to the distribution, use and generation of public resources by means of gender responsive budget analysis.[99]

In terms of Institutional Mechanisms for the Advancement of Women, the following are the strategic objective and the actions to be taken by the various stakeholders:

Strategic Objective: Integrate gender perspectives in legislation, public policies, programs and projects.

Actions to be taken by Governments include:

(a) Seek to ensure that before policy decisions are taken, an analysis of their impact on women and men, respectively, is carried out;

(b) Regularly review national policies, programs and projects, as well as their implementation, evaluating the impact of employment and income policies in order to guarantee that women are direct beneficiaries of development and that their full contribution to development, both remunerated and unremunerated, is considered in economic policy and planning;

(c) Promote national strategies and aims on equality between women and men in order to eliminate obstacles to the exercise of women's rights and eradicate all forms of discrimination against women;

(d) Work with members of legislative bodies, as appropriate, to promote a gender perspective in all legislation and policies;

(e) Give all ministries the mandate to review policies and programs from a gender perspective and in the light of the Platform for Action. Locate the responsibility for the implementation of that mandate at the highest possible level. Establish and strengthen an inter-ministerial coordination structure to carry out this mandate and monitor progress and to network with relevant machineries.[100]

Actions to be taken by national machinery:

(a) Facilitate the formulation and implementation of government policies on equality between women and men, develop appropriate strategies and methodologies, and promote coordination and cooperation within the central government in order to ensure mainstreaming of a gender perspective in all policy-making processes;

(b) Promote and establish cooperative relationships with relevant branches of government, centers for women's studies and research, academic and educational institutions, the private sector, the media, Non-Governmental Organizations (NGOs), especially women's organizations, and all other actors of civil society;

(c)&(d) Undertake activities focusing on legal reform with regard, to the family, conditions of employment, social security, income tax, equal opportunity in education, positive measures to promote the advancement of women, and the perception of attitudes and a culture favorable to equality, as well as promote a gender perspective in legal policy and programing reforms;

(e) Promote the increased participation of women as both active agents and beneficiaries of the development process, which would result in an improvement of quality of life for all;

(f) Establish direct links with national, regional and international bodies dealing with the advancement of women;

(g) Provide training and advisory assistance to government agencies in order to integrate a gender perspective in their policies and programs.[101]

In terms of Human Rights of Women, the following are the strategic objective and the actions to be taken by the various stakeholders:

Strategic Objective: Ensure equality and non-discrimination under the law and in practice.

Actions to be taken by Governments:

(a) Give priority to promoting and protecting the full and equal enjoyment by women and men of all human rights and fundamental freedoms without distinction of any kind as to race, color, sex, language, religion, political or other opinions, national or social origins, property, birth or other status;

(b) Provide constitutional guarantees and enact appropriate legislation to prohibit discrimination on the basis of sex for all women and girls of all ages and assure women of all ages equal rights and their full enjoyment;

(c) Embody the principle of the equality of men and women in their legislation and ensure, through law and other appropriate means, the practical realization of this principle;

(d) Review national laws, including customary laws and legal practices in the areas of family, civil, penal, labor and commercial law in order to ensure the implementation of the principles and procedures of all relevant international human rights instruments by means of national legislation, and revoke any remaining laws that discriminate on the basis of sex and remove gender bias in the administration of justice;

(e) Strengthen and encourage the development of programs to protect the human rights of women in the national institutions on human rights that carry out programs, such as human rights commissions or ombudspersons, according them appropriate status, resources and access to the Government to assist individuals, in particular women, and ensure that these institutions pay adequate attention to problems involving the violation of the human rights of women;

(f) Take action to ensure that the human rights of women are fully respected and protected;

(g) Take urgent action to combat and eliminate violence against women, which is a human rights violation, resulting from harmful traditional or customary practices, cultural prejudices and extremism;

(g) Prohibit female genital mutilation wherever it exists and give vigorous support to efforts among non-governmental and community organizations and religious institutions to eliminate such practices;

(i) Provide gender-sensitive human rights education and training to public officials, including police and military personnel, corrections officers, health and medical personnel, and social workers, including people who deal with migration and refugee issues, and teachers at all levels of the educational system, and make available such education and training also to the judiciary and members of parliament in order to enable them to better exercise their public responsibilities;

(j) Promote the equal right of women to be members of trade unions and other professional and social organizations;

(k) Establish effective mechanisms for investigating violations of the human rights of women perpetrated by any public official and take the necessary punitive legal measures in accordance with national laws;

(l) Review and amend criminal laws and procedures, as necessary, to eliminate any discrimination against women in order to ensure that criminal law and procedures guarantee women effective protection against, and prosecution of, crimes directed at or disproportionately affecting women, regardless of the relationship between the perpetrator and the victim, and ensure that women defendants, victims and witnesses are not revictimized or discriminated against in the investigation and prosecution of crimes;

(m) Ensure that women have the same right as men to be judges, advocates or other officers of the court, as well as police officers and prison and detention officers, among other things;

(n) Strengthen existing or establish readily available and free or affordable alternative administrative mechanisms and legal aid programs to assist disadvantaged women seeking redress for violations of their rights;

(o) Ensure that all women and Non-Governmental Organizations (NGOs) and their members in the field of protection and promotion of all human rights, civil, cultural, economic, political and social rights, including the right to development, enjoy fully all human rights and freedoms in accordance with the Universal Declaration of Human Rights and all other human rights instruments and the protection of national laws;

(p) Strengthen and encourage the implementation of the recommendations contained in the Standard Rules on the Equalization of Opportunities for Persons with Disabilities, paying special attention to ensure non-discrimination and equal enjoyment of all human rights and fundamental freedoms by women and girls with disabilities, including their access to information and services in the field of violence against women, as well as their active participation in and economic contribution to all aspects of society;

(q) Encourage the development of gender-sensitive human rights programs.[102]

All human rights, civil, cultural, economic, political and social, including the right to development, are universal, indivisible, interdependent and interrelated. Governments and others must not only refrain from violating the human rights of all women, but must work actively to promote and protect these rights. Recognition of the importance of the human rights of women is reflected in the fact that three quarters of the States Members of the United Nations have become parties to the Convention on the Elimination of All Forms of Discrimination against Women. In order to protect the human rights of women, it is necessary to avoid, as far as possible, resorting to reservations and to ensure that no reservation is incompatible with the object and purpose of the Convention or is otherwise incompatible with international treaty law. Further, women's full enjoyment of equal rights is undermined by the discrepancies between some national legislation and international law and international instruments on human rights. Overly complex administrative procedures, lack of awareness within the judicial process and inadequate monitoring of the violation of the human rights of all women, coupled with the underrepresentation of women in justice systems, insufficient information on existing rights and persistent attitudes and practices perpetuate women's de facto inequality, which is also perpetuated by the lack of enforcement of family, civil, penal, labor and commercial laws or codes, or administrative rules and regulations intended to ensure women's full enjoyment of human rights and fundamental freedoms.[103]

The World Conference to Review and Appraise the Achievements of the United Nations Decade for Women: Equality, Development and Peace, held at Nairobi in 1985, with the adoption of the Nairobi Forward-looking Strategies for the Advancement of Women, recognized that the human rights of women and the girl child are an inalienable, integral and indivisible part of universal human rights. The full and equal participation of women in political, civil, economic, social and cultural life at the national, regional and international levels, and the eradication of all forms of discrimination on the grounds of gender are priority objectives of the international community. The World Conference on Human Rights reaffirmed the solemn commitment of all States to fulfill their obligations to promote universal respect for, and observance and protection of, all human rights and fundamental freedoms for all in accordance with the Charter of the United Nations, as well as other instruments related to human rights and international law.[104]

The Platform for Action is an agenda for women's empowerment. It aims at accelerating the implementation of the Nairobi Forward-looking Strategies for the Advancement of Women and at removing all the obstacles to women's active participation in all spheres of public and private life through a full and equal share in economic, social, cultural and political decision-making. The principle of shared power and responsibility should be established between women and men at home, in the workplace, and in the wider national and international communities. Equality between men and women is a matter of human rights and a condition for social justice, and is also a necessary and fundamental prerequisite for equality, development and peace. A transformed partnership based on equality between men and women is a condition for people-centered sustainable development, and a long-term commitment is essential, so that women and men can work together for themselves, for their children and for society to meet the challenges of the twenty-first century.

Committed to furthering the fundamental principle set forth in the Vienna Declaration and Program of Action, adopted by the World Conference on Human Rights, that the human rights of women are an inalienable, integral and indivisible part of universal human rights, the Beijing Platform seeks to promote and protect the full enjoyment of human rights and fundamental freedoms of all women throughout their life cycle. The Platform for Action emphasizes that women share common concerns that can be addressed only by working together and in partnership with men towards the common goal of gender equality around the world. It respects and values the full diversity of women's situations and conditions, and recognizes that some women face particular barriers to their empowerment.

The Platform for Action upholds the Convention on the Elimination of All Forms of Discrimination against Women and builds upon the Nairobi Forward-looking Strategies for the Advancement of Women, as well as relevant resolutions adopted by the Economic and Social Council and the General Assembly. Its formulation is aimed at establishing a basic group of priority actions. It recognizes the importance of such agreements as the World Summit for Children, the United

Nations Conference on Environment and Development, the World Conference on Human Rights, the International Conference on Population and Development, and the World Summit for Social Development, which set out specific approaches and commitments to fostering sustainable development and international cooperation, and to strengthening the role of the United Nations to that end. Similarly, the Global Conference on the Sustainable Development of Small Island Developing States, the International Conference on Nutrition, the International Conference on Primary Health Care and the World Conference on Education for All have addressed the various facets of development and human rights, paying significant attention to the role of women and girls. In addition, the International Year for the World's Indigenous People, the International Year of the Family, the United Nations Year for Tolerance, the Geneva Declaration for Rural Women, and the Declaration on the Elimination of Violence against Women have also emphasized the issues of women's empowerment and equality.

The Fourth World Conference on Women was to be a conference of commitments made in the legal area, where governments agreed to revise existing, or introduce new laws and regulations to advance the status of women and eliminate de jure discrimination.[105] In the important area of women and the economy, countries stressed the necessity of improving the situation of women in the labor market, bridging the pay gap between men and women, enhancing women's access to capital and productive resources. Further, in the critical area of human rights of women, countries committed themselves to promote and protect these rights, and to ensure equality under the law and in practice. Several countries decided to sign or ratify international conventions for the advancement of women, including CEDAW and some relevant ILO conventions.

The general objective of the Platform for Action, which is in full conformity with the purposes and principles of the Charter of the United Nations and international law, is the complete realization of human rights and fundamental freedoms of all women, essential for the empowerment of women. While the significance of national and regional particularities and various historical, cultural and religious backgrounds must be borne in mind, it is the duty of States, regardless of their political, economic and cultural systems, to promote and protect human rights and fundamental freedoms of all people. The implementation of this Platform, including through national laws, strategies, policies, programs and development priorities, is the sovereign responsibility of each State, in conformity with human rights and fundamental freedoms. The significance of and full respect for various religious, philosophical and ethical values, and cultural and racial backgrounds of individuals and communities should contribute to the full enjoyment by women of their human rights, in order to achieve equality, development and peace.

The Platform for Action requires immediate and concerted action by all to create a peaceful, just and humane world based on human rights and fundamental freedoms, including the principle of equality for all people of all ages and from all walks of life, and to this end, recognizes that broad-based and sustained economic growth in the context of sustainable development is necessary to sustain social development and social justice. Its success will require a strong commitment on the part of Governments, international organizations and institutions at all levels. It will also require adequate mobilization of resources from multilateral, bilateral and private sources for the advancement of women for strengthening the capacity of national, sub-regional, regional and international institutions; a commitment to equal rights, equal responsibilities and equal opportunities for the equal participation of women and men in all national, regional and international bodies in the policy-making processes; and the establishing or strengthening of mechanisms at all levels for accountability to the world's women.

In looking at the economic stream, recent international economic developments have had a disproportionate impact on women and children. Economic recession in many 'developed' and 'developing' countries, as well as ongoing restructuring in countries with economies in transition, have had a disproportionately negative impact on women's employment. Women often have no choice but to take employment that lacks long-term job security or involves dangerous working conditions, or to be unemployed. Many women enter the labor market in under-remunerated and undervalued jobs, seeking to improve their household income. This has increased the total burden of work for women.

Macro and micro-economic policies and programs, including structural adjustment, have not always been designed to take account of their impact on women, especially those living in poverty, in both urban and remote rural areas. Importantly, women are key contributors to the economy and to combating poverty through both remunerated and unremunerated work at home, in the community and in the workplace. Growing numbers of women have achieved economic independence through gainful employment. One fourth of all households world wide are headed by women, and many other households are dependent on female income even where men are present. Unfortunately, female-maintained households are very often among the poorest, because of wage discrimination, occupational segregation patterns in the labor market and other gender-based barriers.

As globalization continues to influence economic opportunities worldwide, its effects remain uneven, creating both risks and opportunities for different groups. For many women, globalization has intensified existing inequalities and insecurities, often translating into the loss of livelihoods, labor rights, and social benefits.[106] Member States of the United Nations have endorsed the Millennium Development Goals of halving extreme poverty by 2015 and of achieving gender equality. Social movements are fueling increased global networking, civil society activism, and consumer awareness. Women's organizations and networks are taking on issues of social justice and equal rights to influence economic policies and decisions at the micro, meso and macro levels. Women's economic security and rights means more than helping women find employment. It means improving the power relationships in a woman's home, in her community and in the marketplace, so that she can take advantage of growing international markets. Ultimately, it means helping women lift themselves and their families out of poverty for a better future.

Even with economic growth, conditions can arise which can aggravate social inequality and marginalization. Hence, it is indispensable to search for new alternatives that ensure that all members of society benefit from economic growth based on a holistic approach to all aspects of development: equality between women and men, social justice, conservation and protection of the environment, sustainability, solidarity, participation, peace and respect for human rights. Of the more than 1 billion people living in abject poverty, women are an overwhelming majority. The rapid process of adjustment due to downsizing in sectors has also led to increased unemployment and underemployment, having a particular impact on women. Structural adjustment programs have not been successfully designed to minimize their negative effects on vulnerable and disadvantaged groups, such as women, or to assure positive effects on those groups by preventing their marginalization in society.

The Final Act of the Uruguay Round of multilateral trade negotiations underscored the increasing interdependence of national economies, as well as the importance of trade liberalization and access to open dynamic markets. The feminization of poverty, unemployment, the increasing fragility of the environment, continued violence against women, and the widespread exclusion of half of humanity from institutions of power and governance underscore the need to continue the search for development, peace and security, and for ways of assuring people-centered sustainable development. The participation and leadership of the half of humanity that is female is essential. Therefore, only a new era of international cooperation among peoples based on a spirit of partnership within an equitable international social and economic environment, along with a radical transformation of the relationship between men and women to one of full and equal partnership will enable the world to meet the challenges of the twenty-first century.

Interestingly, the growing strength of the non-governmental sector, particularly women's organizations and feminist groups, has become a driving force for change. Non-Governmental Organizations (NGOs) have played an important advocacy role in advancing legislation or mechanisms to ensure the promotion of women, and have become catalysts for new approaches to development. Women, through NGOs, have participated in and strongly influenced community, national, regional and global forums, and international debates.

However, equality between men and women has still not been achieved. In leadership roles, women represent a mere 10 per cent of all elected legislators worldwide, and in most national and international administrative structures, both public and private, including the United Nations, they remain underrepresented. In examining the policy stream, a world-wide movement towards democratization has opened up the political process in many nations, but the popular participation of women in key decision-making arenas as full and equal partners with men, has not yet been achieved.

Further, in examining the family, women play a critical role, as the family is the basic unit of society. Today, in different cultural, political and social systems, various forms of the family exist. Women make a great contribution to the welfare of the family and hence to the development of society, which is still not recognized for its full importance. The social significance of the role of parents and society as a whole in the upbringing of children should be acknowledged. Further, recognition should also be given to the important role often played by women in caring for other members of their family. Major demographic trends have had profound repercussions on the dependency ratio within families. Care of children, the sick and the elderly is a responsibility that falls disproportionately on women, owing to the lack of equality and the unbalanced distribution of remunerated and unremunerated work between women and men.

In addition, in the past 20 years, the world has seen an explosion in the field of global communications, which have been used to spread stereotyped and demeaning images of women for narrow commercial and consumerist purposes. Until women participate equally in the decision-making areas of the mass media, they will continue to be misrepresented, and the awareness of the reality of women's lives will continue to be lacking. The media have a great potential to promote the advancement and the equality of women, by portraying both women and men in a non-stereotypical, diverse and balanced manner, and by respecting the dignity and worth of the human person.

The Platform of Action's strategic objectives and the actions to be taken by all parties cut across the boundaries of equality, development and peace, the goals of the Nairobi Forward-looking Strategies for the Advancement of Women, and reflect their interdependence. It is intended to improve the situation of all women who often face similar barriers, while special attention is to be given to groups that are the most disadvantaged. The Platform for Action recognizes that women face barriers to full equality and advancement, because of such factors as race, ethnicity, culture, indigenousness, age, language, religion, or disability. Many women encounter specific obstacles related to their family status, particularly as single parents, and to their socio-economic status, including their living conditions in rural, isolated or impoverished areas. Additional barriers also exist for refugee women and other displaced and immigrant women, as well as migrant women workers. Many are also particularly affected by environmental disasters, serious and infectious diseases, and various forms of violence against women.

Actions to be taken at the national and international levels by governments, the United Nations system, international and regional organizations, including international financial institutions, the private sector, Non-Governmental Organizations (NGOs) and other actors of civil society, include the creation and maintenance of a non-discriminatory, as well as a gender sensitive legal environment through review of legislation with a view to striving to remove discriminatory provisions. Problems continue to persist in addressing the challenges of poverty eradication, gender inequalities, empowerment, and advancement of women and employment.[107]

It is hoped that the outcomes of the Fourth World Conference on Women will accelerate the process that formally began in 1975, the International Year of the Woman. It was a turning-point in that it put women's issues on the agenda. The United Nations Decade for Women, 1976-1985, was a worldwide effort to examine the status and rights of women, and to bring women into decision-making at all levels. During that decade, the General Assembly adopted the Convention on the Elimination of All Forms of Discrimination against Women, which set an international standard for what was meant by equality between women and men. As well, it saw the formulation of the Nairobi Forward-looking Strategies for the Advancement of Women. In the interim, many governments have enacted legislation to promote equality between women and men and have established national machineries to ensure the mainstreaming of gender perspectives in all spheres of society. International agencies have focused greater attention on women's status and roles.

Since 1975, knowledge of the relationship between the sexes has increased, and is contributing to further actions aimed at promoting equality between men and women. The boundaries of the gender division of labor between productive and reproductive roles are gradually being crossed, as women have started to enter formerly male-dominated areas of work, and men have started to accept greater responsibility for domestic tasks and childcare. However, changes in women's roles have been greater and much more rapid than changes in men's roles. In many countries, the differences between women's and men's achievements and activities are still not recognized as the consequences of false socially constructed gender roles, rather than immutable biological differences.

Unfortunately, most of the goals set out in the Nairobi Forward-looking Strategies for the Advancement of Women have not yet been achieved. Barriers to women's empowerment remain, despite the efforts of women and men everywhere. Vast political, economic and ecological crises, systematic or de facto discrimination, violations of and failure to protect human rights and fundamental freedoms, and ingrained prejudicial attitudes towards women are impediments to equality.

Throughout the entire life cycle, women's daily existence and long-term aspirations are restricted by discriminatory attitudes, unjust social and economic structures, and a lack of resources in most countries that prevent their full and equal participation. Discrimination against women begins at the earliest stages of life. The girl child of today is the woman of tomorrow. Women should be equal partners with men, in every aspect of life and development. Special measures must be taken to ensure that young women have the life skills necessary for active and effective participation in all facets of society. It will be critical for the international community to demonstrate a new commitment for the future to inspire a new generation of women and men to work together for a more just society. The advancement of women and the achievement of equality between men and women are a matter of human rights and a condition for social justice, and should not be seen in isolation as women's issues.

Conclusion

On the international level, attempts have been made to provide legislatively for equality and pay equity. Since 1919, the International Labour Organisation's objective has been the principle that men and women should receive equal remuneration for work of equal value. The universal concord is a 'fair day's pay for a fair day's work'. Internationally, the fundamental concept of human rights is one which human beings have striven both to suppress and promote.

Historically, women have had no input in the Constitution and the laws of the land.[108] From the feminist perspective, it is important that the needs and interests of women be valued as highly as those of men, and viewed in the social context in which women are often devalued. Despite their numbers, women are still severely under-represented in government and the judiciary. Constitutional rules have been interpreted and implemented without much participation of women. Women's issues are still at the margins of the national agenda. In recycling discrimination, 'the stream always tries to return to its habitual course'.[109]

Notes

1 Universal Declaration of Human Rights, Preamble.
2 *Ibid.*, at Article 1.
3 *Ibid.*, at Article 3.
4 *Ibid.*, at Article 7.
5 *Ibid.*, at Article 8.
6 *Ibid.*, at Article 23.
7 *Ibid.*, at Article 26.
8 Charter of the United Nations, Preamble.
9 *Ibid.*, at Article 1.
10 *Ibid.*, at Article 55.
11 *Ibid.*, at Article 92.
12 *Ibid.*, at Article 94.
13 *Ibid.*, at Article 95.
14 *Ibid.*, at Article 96.
15 Statute of the International Court of Justice, Article 1.
16 *Ibid.*, at Article 34.
17 *Ibid.*, at Article 36.
18 *Ibid.*, at Article 38.
19 Equal Remuneration Convention (ILO No. 100), Article 1.
20 *Ibid.*
21 *Ibid.*, at Article 2.
22 *Ibid.*, at Article 3.
23 *Ibid.*, at Article 1(1).
24 *Ibid.*, at Article 1(2).
25 *Ibid.*, at Article 2.
26 *Ibid.*, at Article 3.
27 *Ibid.*, at Article 5.
28 International Covenant on Civil and Political Rights.
29 International Covenant on Civil and Political Rights, Preamble.
30 *Ibid.*, at Article 2.
31 *Ibid.*, at Article 3.
32 *Ibid.*, at Article 26.
33 *Ibid.*, at Article 23.
34 *Ibid.*, at Article 28.
35 *Ibid.*, at Article 40.
36 *Ibid.*, at Article 45.
37 *Ibid.*, at Article 44.
38 Optional Protocol to the International Covenant on Civil and Political Rights.
39 International Covenant on Economic, Social and Cultural Rights.
40 United Nations Development Program, *Human Development Report*, Oxford University Press, 1994, p.2.

41 *Supra* note 39, at Preamble.
42 *Ibid.*, at Article 2.
43 *Ibid.*, at Article 3.
44 *Ibid.*, at Article 7.
45 *Ibid.*, at Article 10.
46 *Ibid.*, at Article 13.
47 Convention on the Elimination of All Forms of Discrimination against Women.
48 *Ibid.*, at Preamble.
49 *Ibid.*, at Article 1.
50 *Ibid.*, at Article 2.
51 *Ibid.*, at Article 3.
52 *Ibid.*, at Article 4.
53 *Ibid.*, at Article 5.
54 *Ibid.*, at Article 6.
55 *Ibid.*, at Article 7.
56 *Ibid.*, at Article 8.
57 *Ibid.*, at Article 10.
58 *Ibid.*, at Article 11(1).
59 *Ibid.*, at Article 11(2).
60 *Ibid.*, at Article 13.
61 *Ibid.*, at Article 14.
62 *Ibid.*, at Article 15.
63 *Ibid.*, at Article 16.
64 *Ibid.*, at Article 17.
65 *Ibid.*, at Article 18.
66 *Ibid.*, at Article 21.
67 *Ibid.*, at Article 23.
68 Optional Protocol to the Convention on the Elimination of All Forms of Discrimination against Women.
69 *Ibid.*, at Preamble.
70 *Ibid.*, at Article 1.
71 *Ibid.*, at Article 2.
72 *Ibid.*, at Article 4.
73 *Ibid.*, at Article 4.
74 *Ibid.*, at Article 5.
75 *Ibid.*, at Article 7.
76 *Ibid.*, at Article 8.
77 *Ibid.*, at Article 9.
78 *Ibid.*, at Article 10.
79 *Ibid.*, at Article 11.
80 *Ibid.*, at Article 13.
81 International Convention on the Elimination of All Forms of Racial Discrimination.
82 Beijing Declaration.
83 United Nations, *Beijing Declaration and Platform for Action, Fourth World Conference on Women.*
84 *Ibid.*, at Strategic Objective F1.
85 *Ibid.*, at Strategic Objective F2.
86 *Ibid.*, at Strategic Objective F2.
87 *Ibid.*, at Strategic Objective F2.
88 *Ibid.*, at Strategic Objective F2.
89 *Ibid.*, at Strategic Objective F2.

[90] *Ibid.*, at Strategic Objective F2.
[91] *Ibid.*, at Strategic Objective F3.
[92] *Ibid.*, at Strategic Objective F3.
[93] *Ibid.*, at Strategic Objective F4.
[94] *Ibid.*, at Strategic Objective F4.
[95] *Ibid.*, at Strategic Objective F4.
[96] *Ibid.*, at Strategic Objective F5.
[97] *Ibid.*, at Strategic Objective F6.
[98] *Ibid.*, at Strategic Objective F6.
[99] *Ibid.*
[100] *Ibid.*, at Strategic Objective H2.
[101] *Ibid.*, at Strategic Objective H2.
[102] *Ibid.*, at Strategic Objective I1.
[103] *Ibid.*, at Strategic Objective I.
[104] *Supra* note 83.
[105] United Nations Women Watch, *Commitments of Governments to Implement the Beijing Platform for Action.*
[106] United Nations Women Watch, *Progress of the World's Women*, 2000.
[107] United Nations Women Watch, *Beijing+5 Process and Beyond.*
[108] Canadian Advisory Council on the Status of Women, *Feminist Guide to the Canadian Constitution*, Ottawa, 1992.
[109] *Ibid.*, at p.57.

References

Beijing Declaration.

Canadian Advisory Council on the Status of Women (1992), *Feminist Guide to the Canadian Constitution*, Ottawa.

Charter of the United Nations.

Convention on the Elimination of all Forms of Discrimination Against Women.

Discrimination (Employment and Occupation) Convention.

Equal Remuneration Convention (ILO No. 100).

International Convention on the Elimination of All Forms of Racial Discrimination.

International Covenant on Civil and Political Rights.

International Covenant on Economic, Social and Cultural Rights.

Optional Protocol to the Convention on the Elimination of All Forms of Discrimination against Women.

Optional Protocol to the International Covenant on Civil and Political Rights.

Statute of the International Court of Justice.

United Nations Development Program (1994), *Human Development Report*, Oxford University Press.

United Nations Women Watch, *Beijing+5 Process and Beyond.*

United Nations Women Watch, *Commitments of Governments to Implement the Beijing Platform for Action.*

United Nations, *Beijing Declaration and Platform for Action, Fourth World Conference on Women.*

United Nations Women Watch (2000), *Progress of the World's Women.*

Universal Declaration of Human Rights.

Chapter 4

Gender Injustice in Australia and New Zealand

Introduction

This chapter will examine Gender Injustice in Australia and New Zealand. It will initially look at the role of women in society, and will then examine important legislation impacting women, namely in Australia, the Sex Discrimination Act, and in New Zealand, the Bill of Rights Act and the Human Rights Act.

Australia

The Role of Women in Australia

In the one hundred years since the Commonwealth Franchise Act granted most Australian women the right to vote and stand in Commonwealth elections, female dynamics have changed greatly.[1] In 1902, there were 1,831,787 women living in Australia, making up 47.6 per cent of the population, and by 2001, there were 9,731,241 women, comprising 50.2 per cent of the population.

The representation of women in the workplace has more than doubled in the last century. In 1911, the labor force participation rate of women aged 15 and over was 25 per cent, compared to 55 per cent in 2002. Over the century, women's labor force participation rates have increased in every age group up to 64 years of age. Women have also continued to make significant contributions to the Australian workforce. Between 1996 and 2002, employment increased by 971,800, and over 52 per cent of these new jobs were filled by women. In 2002, there were 4,108,700 women in employment, an increase of 505,800 or 14.0 per cent since 1996 alone. In 2002, the labor force participation rate of women of workforce age, that is 15-64, was 66.2 per cent. Further, women's unemployment rate was 5.8 per cent in 2002, 1.8 per cent lower than in 1996, and in 2000, it reached 5.6 per cent, the lowest level in over 20 years.

Additionally, in 1997, 462,300 women were small business operators, accounting for 35 per cent of Australia's 1.3 million small business operators. In the private sector, the proportion of women occupying board positions has doubled over the past five years. In 1999, over 13 per cent of non-executive directors were women, an increase from 4 per cent in 1995, and the number of women in private sector managerial positions has risen from 17.2 per cent in 1990 to 24.7 per cent in 2001.

The gap between men and women's earnings has fallen over time. In 2002, the ratio of female-to-male full time average weekly ordinary time earnings stood at 84.6 per cent, compared with 83.2 per cent in 1996. The gap has also narrowed when comparing average hourly pay rates, which takes account of the large proportion of women who work on a part-time basis. The ratio of female to male average hourly time earnings stood at 92.6 per cent in 2002, compared with 87.1 per cent in 1996.

Pay equity is about providing equal remuneration for work of equal value. For employers, that means: Paying men and women equally for work that is of equal skill and responsibility, and is performed under comparable conditions; and Ensuring that all workers have the same access to benefits, superannuation, allowances and other discretionary payments. According to the Australian Bureau of Statistics (ABS), women currently earn on average roughly 84 per cent of what men earn, and thus a significant pay gap between men and women still exists. Women in full-time employment earn just 84.3 per cent of male earnings, and women in all types of employment, that is full-time, part-time and overtime employment, earn just 66.3 per cent of male earnings. The gap between men's and women's earnings is caused by many contributing factors, most notably equal pay factors and equal opportunity factors. Equal pay factors include: Undervaluation of women's work and skills; Undervaluation of women's occupations; and Unequal remuneration structures. Equal opportunity factors include: Occupational segregation; Unequal workforce participation; and Unequal distribution of carer responsibility.

Each year sees new records in access to education and training for women. In 2001, women made up 57 per cent of the higher education students commencing an undergraduate qualification, and 50.5 per cent of postgraduate commencements. In addition, 18 per cent of the total female student population is undertaking postgraduate work, almost matching the 20 per cent of the total male population. Women have made inroads into some nontraditional areas of study, including engineering and architecture, and women continue to be well represented across a range of undergraduate studies, including law and medicine. Now more than ever, not only do women have increased access to education but they are also forming an increasing majority of the teaching profession.

Educational opportunities and outcomes have continued to grow strongly for women since the mid-1990s. More young women than men undertake the senior years of secondary schooling, 77.9 per cent for girls, compared to 65.9 per cent for boys. Women make up more than half of all higher education students in Australia since 1987, and the proportion of female students has increased steadily. The proportion of women entering higher education increased from 56.5 per cent in 1995 to 56.9 per cent in 1998. In vocational educational and training (VET), women have almost reached parity with men, rising from 47.2 per cent in 1995 to 48.5 per cent in 1998. Dramatic improvements have occurred in the area of employment based training, with the proportion of women entering apprenticeships and traineeships, increasing from approximately 25 per cent in 1995 to more than 40 per cent in 1998. Women have also made significant inroads into several traditional male areas of study, such as science, engineering and medicine, and more women today are studying mathematics and technology-based subjects than ever before.[2]

It is important to create a workplace environment that helps parents meet the challenges they face in juggling their work and family commitments for increased family-friendly employment conditions. In 2001, 73 per cent of women covered by certified agreements had access to family/carer's leave provisions, and 38 per cent had access to paid maternity leave provisions.

Additionally, life expectancy has increased dramatically in the one hundred years since the Commonwealth Franchise Act, granting most Australian women the right to vote and stand in Commonwealth elections. Women are living much longer and the population is ageing. In the 1901 Census, 3.7 per cent of women were aged over 65 years, and 0.1 per cent were aged over 85 years, whereas in 2001, 13.8 per cent of women were aged over 65 years, and 1.8 per cent were aged over 85 years. Due to the ageing population, the traditional concerns of financial security and health have an increased prominence on the nation's agenda as key issues for women.

Further, Australia has taken practical steps to improve women's access to justice and protection under the law in the pursuit of gender equality, and it is committed to providing more accessible, low cost alternative dispute resolution options. Australia has a regime of legislation and institutional mechanisms to protect women against discrimination, and is committed to promoting, supporting and protecting the human rights of women. It supports women's human rights in relevant international fora, including the United Nations General Assembly, the Commission on Human Rights and the Commission on the Status of Women.

Legislation

In looking at important dates for women in Australian history, in 1885, the Victorian Married Women's Property Act allowed Victorian married women to own and dispose of property in their own right. In 1908, the minimum wage for women's work was set in the First Federal Arbitration Award for Women, and until 1950, this was usually 54 per cent of the male rate. In 1949 and 1950, the Basic Wage Inquiry was held in which, for the first time, women's organizations, namely the National Council of Women and the Australian Federation of Business and Professional Clubs, made submissions for equal pay, and although the female basic wage was established, equal pay was not achieved. In 1969, the equal pay determination, by the then Commonwealth Conciliation and Arbitration Commission, introduced the principle of 'equal pay for work of equal value'. Further, in 1972, the Australian Conciliation and Arbitration Commission adopted the principle of 'equal pay for work of equal value'. However, it was estimated that only 18 per cent of adult female employees obtained equal pay under this ruling, because in most cases females and males worked under different awards. The Commission continued to find that the male wage took account of family considerations and would not apply to females.

Further, the Federal Childcare Act 1972 was enacted which provided the first direct Federal Government participation in childcare. In 1973, Paid Maternity

Leave was granted for the Commonwealth Public Service. In 1975, the Federal Family Law Act, subsequently amended in 1983, introduced a no-fault divorce system, and irretrievable breakdown of marriage became the only ground for divorce, and legislative recognition of the economic value of women's traditional work in the home was given in the division of assets on divorce.

The Sex Discrimination Act 1975, the first sex discrimination act in Australia, was passed by the South Australian Parliament and came into operation on August 12, 1976. The legislation was complaints-based, defining indirect discrimination. In 1977, the Maternity Leave Test Case decision of the then Australian Conciliation and Arbitration Commission granted a 12 month maternity leave entitlement to all permanent workers, guaranteeing continuity of employment following leave for the birth of a child. In 1981, the Federal Human Rights Commission Act came into force, based on the United Nations International Covenant on Civil and Political Rights.

In 1983, the National Wage Case was held, in which the Australian Conciliation and Arbitration Commission (ACAC) acknowledged women's work as undervalued and underpaid, but it was stressed that the economy could not afford to pay commensurate women's wages. As well, the same year, Australia ratified the United Nations Convention on the Elimination of All Forms of Discrimination Against Women (CEDAW), and in 1984, the Federal Sex Discrimination Act was passed, based on the United Nations Convention on the Elimination of All Forms of Discrimination Against Women. As well, the First Federal Government Women's Budget Statement was tabled, and the Public Service Reform Act introduced Equal Employment Opportunity Programmes into the Australian Public Service. Further, both the Affirmative Action (Equal Employment Opportunity for Women) Act, and the Commonwealth Human Rights and Equal Opportunity Commission Act were passed.

In 1988, Australia launched the first National Agenda for Women, based on the United Nation's Nairobi Forward Looking Strategies for the Advancement of Women, and equality became a national objective of all programs. In 1989, Australia ratified the International Labour Organisation Convention No 156, Workers with Family Responsibilities. Further, in 1993, the Commonwealth Sex Discrimination Act 1984 was strengthened, with such amendments as dismissal on the grounds of family responsibilities a ground for complaint, and a redefinition of sexual harassment not requiring a showing of disadvantage or detriment. Additionally, in 1995, the Sex Discrimination Act had further amendments to include discrimination on the ground of potential pregnancies. The Workplace Relations Act 1996 was enacted, a central objective of which is to assist employees to balance their work and family responsibilities effectively through the development of mutually beneficial work practices with employers. The Equal Opportunity for Women in the Workplace Act was introduced into Parliament on September 22, 1999, replacing the Affirmative Action Act 1986.[3]

Importantly, the Human Rights and Equal Opportunity Commission (HREOC) inquires into complaints under federal anti-discrimination law and educates the community about obligations under domestic legislation. HREOC is charged with increasing the understanding, acceptance and observance of human rights in Australia, and has a mandate to carry out related research and education activities. HREOC liaises internationally with governments and agencies in respect of international treaties and ensures that Australia meets its obligations under international instruments.

The Sex Discrimination Act The Sex Discrimination Act 1984 prohibits discrimination on the grounds of gender, marital status, pregnancy, and potential pregnancy and family responsibilities, and is administered by the Sex Discrimination Commissioner under the auspices of the Human Rights & Equal Opportunity Commission. Section 3 outlines the objects of the Act:

> 3 (a) to give effect to certain provisions of the Convention on the Elimination of All Forms of Discrimination Against Women; and
> (b) to eliminate, so far as is possible, discrimination against persons on the ground of sex, marital status, pregnancy or potential pregnancy in the areas of work, accommodation, education, the provision of goods, facilities and services, the disposal of land, the activities of clubs and the administration of Commonwealth laws and programs; and
> (ba) to eliminate, so far as possible, discrimination involving dismissal of employees on the ground of family responsibilities; and
> (c) to eliminate, so far as is possible, discrimination involving sexual harassment in the workplace, in educational institutions and in other areas of public activity; and
> (d) to promote recognition and acceptance within the community of the principle of the equality of men and women.[4]

Importantly, Section 5 deals directly with the definition of gender discrimination:

> 5(1) For the purposes of this Act, a person (in this subsection referred to as the discriminator) discriminates against another person (in this subsection referred to as the aggrieved person) on the ground of the sex of the aggrieved person if, by reason of:
> (a) the sex of the aggrieved person;
> (b) a characteristic that appertains generally to persons of the sex of the aggrieved person; or
> (c) a characteristic that is generally imputed to persons of the sex of the aggrieved person; the discriminator treats the aggrieved person less favourably than, in circumstances that are the same or are not materially different, the discriminator treats or would treat a person of the opposite sex.
> (2) For the purposes of this Act, a person (the discriminator) discriminates against another person (the aggrieved person) on the ground of the sex of the aggrieved person if the discriminator imposes, or proposes to impose, a condition, requirement or practice that has, or is likely to have, the effect of disadvantaging persons of the same sex as the aggrieved person.[5]

Indirect discrimination and the reasonableness test are dealt with under Section 7B, which holds that a person does not discriminate against another person by imposing, or proposing to impose, a condition, requirement or practice that has, or is likely to have, the disadvantaging effect mentioned in subsection 5(2) if the condition, requirement or practice is reasonable in the circumstances. The matters to be taken into account in deciding whether a condition, requirement or practice is reasonable in the circumstances include the nature and extent of the disadvantage resulting from the imposition, or proposed imposition, of the condition, requirement or practice; and the feasibility of overcoming or mitigating the disadvantage; and whether the disadvantage is proportionate to the result sought by the person who imposes, or proposes to impose, the condition, requirement or practice.[6] Further, Section 7C states that the burden of proving that an act does not constitute discrimination because of section 7B lies on the person who did the act.[7]

In terms of affirmative action, Section 7D stipulates that a person may take special measures for the purpose of achieving substantive equality between men and women; or people of different marital status; or women who are pregnant and people who are not pregnant; or women who are potentially pregnant and people who are not potentially pregnant.[8]

Importantly, in terms of equality in access to employment, Section 14 establishes that it is unlawful for an employer to discriminate against a person on the ground of the person's sex, marital status, pregnancy or potential pregnancy in the arrangements made for the purpose of determining who should be offered employment; in determining who should be offered employment; or in the terms or conditions on which employment is offered; in the terms or conditions of employment that the employer affords the employee; by denying the employee access, or limiting the employee's access, to opportunities for promotion, transfer or training, or to any other benefits associated with employment; by dismissing the employee; or by subjecting the employee to any other detriment. Further, it is unlawful for an employer to discriminate against an employee on the ground of the employee's family responsibilities by dismissing the employee.[9]

However, in terms of genuine occupational qualification, Section 30 holds that it is not unlawful for a person to discriminate against another person, on the ground of the other person's sex, in connection with a position as an employee, commission agent or contract worker, being a position in relation to which it is a genuine occupational qualification to be a person of the opposite sex to the sex of the other person. It is considered a genuine occupational qualification, in relation to a particular position, to be a person of a particular sex if, among other things, the duties of the position can be performed only by a person having particular physical attributes other than attributes of strength or stamina that are not possessed by persons of the opposite sex to the relevant sex; and the position is declared to be a position in relation to which it is a genuine occupational qualification to be a person of a particular sex.[10]

The Act provides an important role for the Human Rights and Equal Opportunity Commission in addressing the issue of gender discrimination. Its functions are defined under Section 48, namely to promote an understanding and acceptance of, and compliance with, this Act; to undertake research and educational programs, and other programs, on behalf of the Commonwealth for the purpose of promoting the objects of this Act; to examine enactments, and proposed enactments, for the purpose of ascertaining whether they are or would be inconsistent with or contrary to the objects of this Act, and to report to the Minister the results of any such examination. Further, on issues of discrimination on the ground of gender, marital status, pregnancy or potential pregnancy or discrimination involving sexual harassment, the Human Rights and Equal Opportunity Commission is to report to the Minister as to the laws that should be made by the Parliament, or action that should be taken by the Commonwealth; to prepare, and to publish in such manner as the Commission considers appropriate, guidelines for the avoidance of discrimination; and where the Commission considers it appropriate to do so, with the leave of the court and subject to any conditions imposed by the court, to intervene in proceedings.[11]

As well as the Sex Discrimination Act, the following legislative provisions may be relevant to cases of gender discrimination or equal pay:

The Racial Discrimination Act 1975 Further, the Racial Discrimination Act 1975 prohibits discrimination on the grounds of race, color, descent and national or ethnic origin. Indigenous women and women from diverse cultural backgrounds who experience this form of discrimination can lodge a complaint with the HREOC Race Commissioner.[12] Further, a close interest that specifically relates to both the International Decade of the World's Indigenous Peoples and to the development on the Rights of Indigenous Peoples is required.

The Disability Discrimination Act 1992 The Disability Discrimination Act 1992 prohibits discrimination on the ground of disability. Disability is broadly defined to include the loss, partial loss or impairment of physical or mental functions, and the presence in the body of organisms causing or capable of causing disease or illness.[13] Women with disabilities who have experienced discrimination can lodge a complaint with the HREOC Disability Commissioner. The human rights of people with disabilities are of particular concern to women, the effects of which can compound gender disadvantage.

The Affirmative Action (Equal Employment Opportunity for Women) Act 1986 The Affirmative Action (Equal Employment Opportunity for Women) Act 1986 ensures equal opportunity for women in Australian workplaces.[14] Changes to the Act will improve its operation through the appointment of an advisory board to the Equal Opportunity for Women in the Workplace Agency to strengthen links with business; the increase in education and the facilitation of outcomes for women in the workplace; and the streamlining of reporting procedures to identify key issues to be addressed by particular workplaces.

The Workplace Relations Act 1996 The Workplace Relations Act 1996 has provisions to safeguard women and other groups of workers, including youth and those from culturally and linguistically diverse backgrounds.[15] The Act provides for equal remuneration for work of equal value without discrimination on the grounds of gender. The Act provides a legislative entitlement to 12 months' parental leave for most employees after 12 months of continuous service, up until the child's first birthday. It also requires a periodic report to the Parliament on outcomes for women.

The Beijing Platform for Action Australia's Beijing Plus Five Action Plan 2001-2005, an implementation strategy, takes forward the outcomes of the UN Special Session of the General Assembly, in close consultation with women and other key stakeholders, such as governments, communities, the media, businesses and women's groups. The Australia Action Plan aims to bolster the efforts of all government agencies, the private sector, the community and individuals to achieve equality for women, through, namely advancing outcomes for women in areas where there is discrimination and inequality; improving outcomes for women with special needs including women with disabilities, Indigenous women, women in rural and remote regions, women from a non-English speaking background and older women; encouraging increased efforts by State/Territory and Commonwealth agencies to develop gender-inclusive policies, programs and services; encouraging and facilitating the increased involvement of the private sector, community groups and men in taking responsibility for addressing discrimination and inequality; and raising community awareness of Beijing Plus Five and government efforts to advance equality for women.[16]

Australia has made efforts to implement the Beijing Platform for Action.[17] In terms of women and poverty, the critical area of concern is the persistent and increasing burden of poverty on women, with corrective action to review, adopt and maintain macroeconomic policies and development strategies that address the needs and efforts of address in poverty; revise laws and administrative practices to ensure women's equal rights and access to economic resources; provide women with access to savings and credit mechanisms and institutions; and develop gender-based methodologies and conduct research to address the feminization of poverty. Economic security is essential to providing women with the ability to make life choices. Historically, however, women have had less access to economic opportunities and resources than men, and fewer opportunities to live their full potential through access to education and paid employment.

Most women's life patterns continue to be different to those of men. Many women have primary responsibility for caring for children, the elderly and the sick. This means that significantly more women than men have disrupted work patterns and have taken on part-time and casual jobs. Women's capacity to achieve financial security depends on access to education and training, jobs, superannuation, affordable childcare, equal pay, a fair division of family responsibility, and adequate income security.

In terms of education and training of women, the critical area of concern is inequalities and inadequacies in and unequal access to education and training, with corrective action to ensure equal access to education; eradicate illiteracy among women; improve women's access to vocational training, science and technology, and continuing education; develop non-discriminatory education and training; allocate sufficient resources for and monitor the implementation of educational reforms; and promote life-long education and training for girls and women. Access to education and training is vital for women. Education remains the key to improving economic status in a changing economy and equipping individuals to achieve their goals and widen their life choices. A well functioning economy needs a workforce that fully utilizes all its human capital, and promotes skills development and education without discrimination on the grounds of gender.

In terms of violence against women, the critical area of concern is the violence itself, with corrective action to take integrated measures to prevent and eliminate violence against women. Violence and the threat of violence against women and girls is a fundamental violation of human rights. It is also a form of discrimination that prevents women from achieving full social and economic equality.

In terms of women and the economy, the critical area of concern is the inequality in economic structures and policies, in all forms of productive activities and in access to resources, with corrective action to promote women's economic rights and independence, including access to employment, appropriate working conditions and control over economic resources; facilitate women's equal access to resources, employment, markets and trade; provide business services, training and access to markets, information and technology, particularly to low-income women; strengthen women's economic capacity and commercial networks; eliminate occupational segregation and all forms of employment discrimination; and promote harmonization of work and family responsibilities for women and men.

Policies to improve opportunities and choices for women are essential whether participating in the paid workforce or full-time parents or carers. Reforms to workplace relations are providing greater flexibility for women and men to combine work and family responsibilities, while maintaining a safety net of fair minimum wages and conditions of employment, as well as opening up a far wider range of employment options for women. Further, there are more opportunities for women to participate in part-time jobs, job-sharing and home-based work, and more women are entering non-traditional areas of the labor force.

In terms of women in power and decision-making the critical area of concern is the inequality between men and women in the sharing of power and decision-making at all levels, with correction action to take measures to ensure women's equal access to and full participation in power structures and decision-making; and increase women's capacity to participate in decision-making and leadership. Women have a right and a responsibility to participate in the decision-making processes that shape the nation. Unless women are full and active participants in all spheres of public and private life, across a wide range of decision-making positions, the future will not reflect the talents, experience and aspirations of all citizens.

Greater diversity should be encouraged among those occupying senior decision-making positions, and opportunities should be expanded to participate in high-level positions, in order to create or strengthen national machineries and other governmental bodies; integrate gender perspectives in legislation, public policies, programs and projects; and generate and disseminate gender-disaggregated data and information for planning and evaluation. The participation of women on equal terms with men in political, social, economic and cultural life is essential to the progress of women and the well-being of society in general.

In terms of women and the media, the critical area of concern is the stereotyping of women and inequality in women's access to and participation in all communication systems, especially in the media, with corrective action to promote a balanced and non-stereotyped portrayal of women in the media.

In terms of human rights of women, the critical area of concern is the lack of respect for and adequate promotion and protection of the human rights of women, with corrective action to promote and protect the human rights of women, through the full implementation of all human rights instruments, especially the Convention on the Elimination of All Forms of Discrimination against Women; ensure equality and non-discrimination under the law and in practice; and achieve legal literacy. Women are particularly concerned about the level of access to and participation in processes relating to Australia's obligations under international instruments on the rights of women, including reporting and monitoring obligations. Human rights of women are an inalienable, integral and indivisible aspect of human rights, in the legislative protections and the existence of agencies to enable citizens to exercise their rights and responsibilities.[18]

New Zealand

The Role of Women in New Zealand

The population of New Zealand is estimated to be roughly 3,670,000 people.[19] While half the resident population is under the age of 33 years, one-quarter of the population is aged 50 years or over, reflecting the fact that New Zealand's population is ageing, with women accounting for 53.3 per cent of the population aged over 50 years and 56.9 per cent of the population aged 65 years and over.

Over the years, there has been an increase in the percentage of working age women joining the labor force and an increase in the numbers of women in self-employment. According to the latest statistics, the percentage of working age women that is 15 years and over joining the labor force continues to increase, since women comprise 51.2 per cent of the working age population and 44.7 per cent of the labor force. While 52 per cent of working age women are in the labor force, 62 per cent of employed women are working full-time and 38 per cent are working part-time.

Ethnicity plays a factor in gender discrimination. In New Zealand, although participation rates for Maori and Pacific women have risen over the past six years, Maori, Pacific and women from 'other' ethnic groups are currently less likely to participate in the labor force than European/Pakeha women. The decrease in participation by women from 'other' ethnic groups is likely to be influenced by the high level of immigration. While Maori and Pacific women, and women from 'other' ethnic groups face higher rates of unemployment than European/Pakeha women, there has been a significant improvement in the unemployment rates for Maori and Pacific women in the last six years.

Turning to the issue of work and age, there is a significant variation in the labor force participation for women of different age groups. The highest rate of participation occurs when women are between 40 and 54 years of age. The smallest difference between men's and women's participation occurs from 15 to 24 years and from 65 years and over. Unemployment rates are highest for those 15 to 24 years, both women and men.

A major difference between men and women is in hours of work. Although an increasing proportion of men and women are working part-time, women are more than twice as likely to work part-time than men, as 38 per cent of women employed were in part-time work compared to 12 per cent of men employed. Women comprise 73 per cent of all part-time workers. Many women work part-time to allow them to combine paid work and family responsibilities. However, many part-timers are working fewer hours than they would like, since 35 per cent of men and 27 per cent of women working part-time would prefer more hours. Of all part-time workers wanting more hours, 67 per cent are women, since women working part-time also work shorter hours than their male counterparts.

In terms of occupation, women continue to work in different occupations from men and are concentrated in a narrower range of occupations. Over 90 per cent of early childhood workers are women, and approximately 80 per cent of primary teachers are women. However, there has been an increase over the years in the proportion of women working as legislators, administrators and managers, from 8.1 per cent in 1991 to 9.3 per cent in 1997; and working as technicians from 11.1 per cent in 1991 to 13.2 per cent in 1997. Occupation is also a major factor influencing earning capacity. A higher proportion of women work in lower paid clerical, sales and service occupations. However, within every occupation, male full-time employees receive higher incomes than female full-time employees. In percentage terms, the largest income gap is among service and sales workers, and the smallest income gap is among clerical workers.

In looking at women in self-employment and small business, women's self-employment grew by 31.5 per cent between 1991 and 1996, with the largest increases in community, social and personal services, in finance, insurance, real estate and business industries, and in manufacturing. As well, almost twice as many women as men of working age are not in the labor force, with the reason being the doing of unpaid work at home, caring for children and dependent older relatives. In looking at women in self-employment, 40 per cent of new businesses are started up by women, and this is predicted to increase to 50 per cent within the next few years, since the numbers of women going into self-employment are increasing at a rate of 20 per working day. Further, women setting up their own businesses are increasing at a faster rate than men, with women considered to be 49 per cent more successful than men in such ventures. Of women with their own business, 55 per cent were under 40 when they set up in business.

In examining earnings, the average ordinary time weekly earnings for females was $537.65 in 1997, that is 76.8 per cent of males' average ordinary time weekly pay of $700.02. Women's average hourly earnings were 81.2 per cent of men's. Part of the difference in men's and women's average weekly earnings is attributable to differences in the hours spent in paid employment, since male employees tend to work longer hours and receive more paid overtime than women.

The gap between female and male average ordinary time hourly earnings in the public sector is wider than that in the private sector, since the average ordinary time hourly earnings for female employees in the public sector is at 76.2 per cent, and in the private sector at 80.2 per cent of that for males. Other significant factors affecting earnings are the level of seniority, the level of skills, experience and job-related training, and the duration and continuity of employment.

In looking at the distribution of family/household income, it was found that the more a woman contributes to household income, the more she is likely to have some say in household financial decisions. Men exert various forms of direct and indirect control over money that inhibits women spending on themselves for things unrelated to the role of housewife and mother, such as health care, dentistry, and further education or retraining to enhance employment prospects. Women in all ethnic groups prioritize their children's needs over their own.

In terms of the economic consequences of marriage breakdown, women's income and standard of living drop significantly after divorce and often never fully recover. This is largely due to the fact that women still retain primary care of children after marriage breakdown, and may, as a result, have a weakened attachment to the labor market. This is known as the 'equality is not equity' phenomenon, which is a barrier to equality of outcomes following marriage breakdown. In looking at family responsibilities, there have been changes over the years to family composition, which affect women. There is a significant increase in the number of sole parent families, that is 28.3 per cent of all families with children in New Zealand, the majority headed by women. As a result, there is a recognition of reconstituted or 'blended' families resulting from remarriage after death or divorce.

Overall, as a result of social attitudes to and distinctions made on the basis of gender, women experience particularly daunting barriers when seeking access to legal services, and consequently to courts and tribunals. The evidence suggests that women usually become involved in legal proceedings when the circumstances are such that, effectively, they have no choice but to become involved. This is the case in family matters and in criminal matters. Women find it especially problematic to obtain information about legal rights and processes; experience difficulties finding an appropriate legal advisor as most lawyers are men, and have limited opportunities during their education and training to become informed about the effects of gender; and find the cost of legal services too high, deterring women from proceeding to protect and enforce their legal rights. For a great many women, 'access to justice' means ready access to quality legal services and procedures, measured to a significant extent by the responsiveness of legal services to clients' social and economic situation and cultural background.

Legislation

New Zealand has ratified international covenants, which obligate governments to ensure women's and men's equal rights to enjoy all economic, social, cultural, civil and political rights. Although international agreements do not automatically become part of New Zealand domestic law upon ratification but must be enacted into law by Parliament, jurisprudence has developed in New Zealand that recognizes the value of international agreements as tools for interpreting the legislative provisions which implement them into domestic law. In addressing the barriers to equality in employment and equal employment opportunities (EEO) in the public sector, New Zealand endorsed the document EEO Policy to 2010, which seeks improvements in four areas of the public sector, namely leadership, organizational culture and strategic human resource management, employment of EEO groups, and monitoring and evaluation. Chief executives of government agencies are responsible and accountable for delivery of agreed EEO goals in their organizations.

The Bill of Rights Act 1990 According to the Preamble of the New Zealand Bill of Rights Act, as amended by the Human Rights Act, the Bill of Rights aims to affirm, protect, and promote human rights and fundamental freedoms in New Zealand; and to affirm New Zealand's commitment to the International Covenant on Civil and Political Rights.[20]

Freedom from Discrimination is guaranteed under Section 19:

> 19(1) Everyone has the right to freedom from discrimination on the grounds of discrimination in the Human Rights Act 1993.
> (2) Measures taken in good faith for the purpose of assisting or advancing persons or groups of persons disadvantaged because of discrimination that is unlawful by virtue of Part II of the Human Rights Act 1993 do not constitute discrimination.[21]

Remedies are contained in Section 27:

> 27(1) Every person has the right to the observance of the principles of natural justice by any tribunal or other public authority which has the power to make a determination in respect of that person's right, obligations, or interests protected or recognised by law.
> (2) Every person whose rights, obligations, or interests protected or recognised by law have been affected by a determination of any tribunal or other public authority has the right to apply, in accordance with law, for judicial review of that determination.
> (3) Every person has the right to bring civil proceedings against, and to defend civil proceedings brought by, the Crown, and to have those proceedings heard, according to law, in the same way as civil proceedings between individuals.[22]

The Bill of Rights Act 1990 aims to affirm, protect and promote human rights and fundamental freedoms in New Zealand; and to affirm New Zealand's commitment to the International Covenant on Civil and Political Rights. It applies to acts done by the legislative, executive and judicial branches of the Government, or by any person or body in the performance of any public function, power or duty conferred or imposed on that person or body by or pursuant to law. It also affirms the right of everyone to freedom from discrimination on all the grounds set out in the Human Rights Act 1993.

The Human Rights Act 1993 Gender is a prohibited ground of discrimination under Section 21(1)(a) of the New Zealand Human Rights Act.[23] Further, as regards discrimination in employment, Section 22(1) states:

> 22(1) Where an applicant for employment or an employee is qualified for work of any description, it shall be unlawful for an employer, or any person acting or purporting to act on behalf of an employer:
>
> (a) to refuse or omit to employ the applicant on work of that description which is available; or
>
> (b) to offer or afford the applicant or the employee less favourable terms of employment, conditions of work, superannuation or other fringe benefits, and opportunities for training, promotion, and transfer than are made available to applicants or employees of the same or substantially similar capabilities employed in the same or substantially similar circumstances on work of that description; or
>
> (c) to terminate the employment of the employee, or subject the employee to any detriment, in circumstances in which the employment of other employees employed on work of that description would not be terminated, or in which other employees employed on work of that description would not be subjected to such detriment; or
>
> (d) to retire the employee, or to require or cause the employee to retire or resign (applies to all (a), (b), (c) and (d), by reason of any of the prohibited grounds of discrimination.[24]

Indirect discrimination is defined in Section 65:

> 65. Where any conduct, practice, requirement, or condition that is not apparently in contravention of any provision of this Part of this Act has the effect of treating a person or group of persons differently on one of the prohibited grounds of discrimination in a situation where such treatment would be unlawful under any provision of this Part of this Act other than this section, that conduct, practice, condition, or requirement shall be unlawful under that provision unless the person whose conduct or practice is in issue, or who imposes the condition or requirement, establishes good reason for it.[25]

The Act contains exceptions in terms of a genuine occupational qualification as to crews of ships and aircraft (Section 24),[26] work involving national security (Section 25),[27] work performed outside New Zealand (Section 26),[28] authenticity and privacy (Section 27),[29] purposes of religion (Section 28),[30] disability (Section 29),[31] age (Section 30),[32] employment of a political nature (Section 31),[33] family status (Section 32),[34] Armed Forces (Section 33),[35] and Regular Forces and Police (Section 34).[36] Further, Section 35 outlines the general qualification on exceptions:

> 35. No employer shall be entitled...to accord to any person in respect of any position different treatment based on a prohibited ground of discrimination even though some of the duties of that position would fall within any of those exceptions if, with some adjustment of the activities of the employer (not being an adjustment involving unreasonable disruption of the activities of the employer), some other employee could carry out those particular duties.[37]

Section 66 guards against victimization in that it shall be unlawful for any person to treat or to threaten to treat any other person less favorably than he would treat other persons in the same or substantially similar circumstances, on the ground that that person, or any relative or associate of that person, intends to make use of his rights under this Act; or has made use of his rights, or promoted the rights of some other person, under this Act; or has given information or evidence in relation to any complaint, investigation, or proceeding under this Act; or has declined to do an act that would contravene this Act; or has otherwise done anything under or by reference to this Act.[38]

Measures to ensure equality are established under Section 73:

> 73 (1) Anything done or omitted which would otherwise constitute a breach of any of the provisions of this Part of this Act shall not constitute such a breach if:
>
> (a) it is done or omitted in good faith for the purpose of assisting or advancing persons or groups of persons, being in each case persons against whom discrimination is unlawful by virtue of this Part of this Act; and
>
> (b) those persons or groups need or may reasonably be supposed to need assistance or advancement in order to achieve an equal place with other members of the community.[39]

Further, Section 5(1) outlines the functions and powers of the Human Rights Commission, some of which are to encourage, by education and publicity, respect for and observance of human rights; to encourage and coordinate programs and activities in the field of human rights; to make public statements in relation to any matter affecting human rights, including statements promoting an understanding of, and compliance with, this Act; to prepare and publish, as the Commission considers appropriate, guidelines for the avoidance of acts or practices that may be inconsistent with, or contrary to, the provisions of this Act; to receive and invite representations from members of the public on any matter affecting human rights; to consult and cooperate with other persons and bodies concerned with the protection of human rights; to inquire generally into any matter, including any enactment or law, or any practice, or any procedure, whether governmental or nongovernmental, if it appears to the Commission that human rights are, or may be, infringed thereby; and to report to the Prime Minister from time to time on any matter affecting human rights, including the desirability of legislative, administrative, or other action to give better protection to human rights and to ensure better compliance with standards laid down in international instruments on human rights, the desirability of New Zealand becoming bound by any international instrument on human rights, and the implications of any proposed legislation or proposed policy of the Government that the Commission considers may affect human rights.[40]

Interestingly, the combined gender discrimination complaints and sexual harassment complaints account for roughly 45 per cent of all complaints received by the Human Rights Commission, and the vast majority of gender discrimination and sexual harassment complainants are women. Employment remains the largest area of complaints at 62 per cent.

The Human Rights Act prohibits discrimination in a number of areas, which include employment matters; access to public places, vehicles and facilities; provision of goods and services; provision of land, housing and other accommodation; and access to educational establishments. In compliance, governmental domestic policy and practice will be required to be non-discriminatory under the terms of the Human Rights Act, unless that policy or practice is authorized by legislation or regulation; Chief executives of government departments will be responsible for making sure that their department is complying with the Human Rights Act; Existing legislation is to be considered with human rights principles, and any justification for inconsistency will be assessed on an ongoing basis as it comes up for amendment; and all proposed new legislation will be required to be vetted for compliance with the New Zealand Bill of Rights Act, containing the same anti-discrimination grounds as the Human Rights Act.

As well as the Bill of Rights Act and the Human Rights Act, the following legislative provisions may be relevant to cases of gender discrimination or equal pay:

The Health and Disability Commissioner Act 1994 and Code of Health & Disability Services Consumers' Rights Under the auspices of the Health and Disability Commissioner, a Code of Health and Disability Services Consumers' Rights came into force on July 1, 1996.[41] It aims to promote the rights of consumers to receive services of an appropriate standard, and to facilitate the fair, simple, and speedy resolution of complaints related to these rights. In particular, Right 2 of the Code states that every consumer has the right to be free from discrimination, coercion, harassment, and sexual, financial or other exploitation.[42] Discrimination is defined in the Code as discrimination that is unlawful under Part II of the Human Rights Act 1993.[43] Exploitation includes any abuse of a position of trust, breach of a fiduciary duty, or exercise of undue influence.[44] The Health and Disability Commissioner may investigate alleged breaches by providers, as they relate to the quality and delivery of health and disability services, and in instances of possible discrimination by the provider, may be referred by the Commissioner to the Human Rights Commission.

The Domestic Violence Act 1995 The Domestic Violence Act 1995 came into force on July 1, 1996. The definition of violence in the Act closely resembles the definition of violence used in the Declaration on the Elimination of Violence Against Women. The key legislative changes contained in the Act include changes to the meaning of violence to take into account psychological abuse; free legal aid for protection orders; and special information, education and support programs for women and children.[45]

The Employment Contracts Act 1991 The Employment Contracts Act 1991 provides women with the right to take gender discrimination cases including cases of sexual harassment to the Employment Court as a personal grievance. The complainant must choose either the Employment Contracts Act or the Human Rights Act as the forum for a complaint, and cases cannot be transferred from one jurisdiction to another.[46]

The Parental Leave and Employment Act 1997 The Parental Leave and Employment Protection Act 1987 provides for job protection, and access to maternity, paternity and extended parental leave. However, access to leave was likely to be limited for those in casual or seasonal work, because of legislative eligibility criteria.[47] Between a quarter and a third of organizations provided parental leave beyond that required by legislation, with by far the highest proportion were in the education sector at 65 per cent. Just over a third of public sector organizations and state-owned enterprises provided parental leave, as did a quarter of the private sector companies.

The Beijing Platform for Action As a result of the Beijing Platform for Action and the Fourth World Conference on Women of 1995, New Zealand identified six cross-cutting themes where further action would be taken to improve the status of women: mainstreaming a gender perspective into the development of all policies and programs; women's unremunerated work; the gender pay gap; the need for more and better data collection on all aspects of women's lives; the Platform's recommendations relevant to Indigenous Maori women; and the enhancement of women's role in decision-making. Significant progress has been achieved in implementing the Beijing Platform for Action in several areas: the introduction of the Domestic Violence Act 1995; the implementation of a national breast cancer screening program; the implementation of the Code of Health and Disability Services Consumers' Rights; and the protection of children from sexual exploitation by New Zealand nationals in other countries.

In terms of mainstreaming gender analysis in response to the Beijing Platform for Action, the Government directed the Ministry of Women's Affairs to work with other government departments and agencies on mainstreaming a gender perspective in the development of all policies and programs, with the focus to work on improving the quality of policy advice provided to government, by developing a means of ensuring that other agencies are accountable for implementing gender analysis in all aspects of their work.

Conclusion

Australia and New Zealand are State Parties to all the major human rights instruments, including the International Covenant on Civil and Political Rights and the Optional Protocol to the ICCPR; the International Covenant on Economic, Social and Cultural Rights; the International Convention on the Elimination of All Forms of Racial Discrimination; and importantly the Convention on the Elimination of All Forms of Discrimination against Women, including being active participants in the development of an Optional Protocol to CEDAW.

Further, the Asia Pacific Economic Cooperation (APEC), and in particular, the Women's Leaders Network (WLN) aims to ensure that the interests of businesswomen are well represented in APEC's trade liberalization and facilitation agenda across the Asia-Pacific region. Australia and New Zealand play a leading role in promoting women's increased participation in the activities of APEC, being active members of the Ad Hoc Advisory Group on Gender Integration (AGGI) established in APEC in 1999, which has responsibility for ensuring the implementation of the Framework for the Integration of Women into APEC, an action plan to increase women's participation.

However, despite strong legislative provisions both in Australia and New Zealand, there is still progress to be made to achieve equal outcomes and opportunities for men and women. Gender equality and the rights contained within legislation rely on the overall legal system, as well as cultural attitudes for implementation and enforcement. However, gaps do exist in the coverage of legislation, and in the manner by which it is enforced. Taking concrete action to advance human rights and support opportunity and choice require a concerted effort across the whole of government, in addition to the important ongoing role of specialist human rights monitoring and complaints mechanisms.

Notes

1 Commonwealth of Australia, *Women 2002*.
2 Government of Australia, *Implementation of the Beijing Platform for Action*, 2000.
3 Commonwealth Office of the Status of Women, Australia, 2002.
4 Sex Discrimination Act, Australia, Section 3.
5 *Ibid.*, at Section 5.
6 *Ibid.*, at Section 7B.
7 *Ibid.*, at Section 7C.
8 *Ibid.*, at Section 7D.
9 *Ibid.*, at Section 14.
10 *Ibid.*, at Section 30.
11 *Ibid.*, at Section 48.
12 Racial Discrimination Act, Australia.
13 Disability Discrimination Act, Australia.
14 Affirmative Action (Equal Employment Opportunity for Women) Act, Australia.
15 Workplace Relations Act, Australia.
16 Government of Australia, *Australia's Beijing Plus Five Action Plan 2001-2005*.
17 *Supra* note 2.
18 *Ibid.*
19 Ministry of Women's Affairs, New Zealand, 1998.
20 Bill of Rights Act, New Zealand, Preamble.
21 *Ibid.*, at Section 19.

[22] *Ibid.*, at Section 27.
[23] Human Rights Act, New Zealand, Section 21(1)(a).
[24] *Ibid.*, at Section 22(1).
[25] *Ibid.*, at Section 65.
[26] *Ibid.*, at Section 24.
[27] *Ibid.*, at Section 25.
[28] *Ibid.*, at Section 26.
[29] *Ibid.*, at Section 27.
[30] *Ibid.*, at Section 28.
[31] *Ibid.*, at Section 29.
[32] *Ibid.*, at Section 30.
[33] *Ibid.*, at Section 31.
[34] *Ibid.*, at Section 32.
[35] *Ibid.*, at Section 33.
[36] *Ibid.*, at Section 34.
[37] *Ibid.*, at Section 35.
[38] *Ibid.*, at Section 66.
[39] *Ibid.*, at Section 73.
[40] *Ibid.*, at Section 5(1).
[41] Health and Disability Commissioner Act and Code of Health & Disability Services Consumers' Rights, New Zealand.
[42] *Ibid.*, at Right 2.
[43] *Ibid.*
[44] *Ibid.*
[45] Domestic Violence Act, New Zealand.
[46] Employment Contracts Act, New Zealand.
[47] Parental Leave and Employment Act, New Zealand.

References

Affirmative Action (Equal Employment Opportunity for Women) Act, Australia, 1986.
Bill of Rights Act, New Zealand, 1990.
Commonwealth of Australia, *Women 2002*.
Commonwealth Office of the Status of Women, Australia, 2002.
Disability Discrimination Act, Australia, 1992.
Domestic Violence Act, New Zealand, 1995.
Employment Contracts Act, New Zealand, 1991.
Government of Australia, *Australia's Beijing Plus Five Action Plan 2001-2005*.
Government of Australia (2000), *Implementation of the Beijing Platform for Action*.
Health and Disability Commissioner Act 1994 and Code of Health & Disability Services Consumers' Rights, New Zealand.
Human Rights Act, New Zealand, 1993.
Ministry of Women's Affairs, New Zealand, 1998.
Parental Leave and Employment Act, New Zealand, 1997.
Racial Discrimination Act, Australia, 1975.
Sex Discrimination Act, Australia, 1984.
Workplace Relations Act, Australia, 1996.

Chapter 5

Gender Injustice in Africa and South Africa

Introduction

This chapter will examine gender injustice in the continent of Africa, and in South Africa. It will initially look at the situation in Africa, examining such legislation as the African Charter on Human and Peoples' Rights and the Protocol of the African Charter on Human and Peoples' Rights, and the Protocol of Rights of Women in Africa. It will then go on to look at the situation in South Africa, examining the Interim Constitution Schedule 4 and the Constitution, as well as the Employment Equity Act and the Promotion of Equality and Prevention of Unfair Discrimination Act.

Africa

The Role of Women in African Society

Women play a key, but often unrecognized, role in all the important aspects of life in Africa, as food producers, carriers of water, collectors of fuel wood, processors of food, caretakers of children and the elderly, and often times the primary earners of cash incomes.[1] The constraints faced by women influence and are influenced by activities relating to population growth, the environment and food security. Women's roles impact directly on Africa's problems of food insufficiency and environmental degradation. The pressure on women's time and the gender-specific constraints that women face, with notable limited access to the productive resources, have serious implications for the environment, agriculture and sustainable development throughout Africa. Africa's challenges and opportunities include empowering every member of the population particularly women; reducing poverty; reducing food insecurity; improving social and economic amenities in rural and urban areas; and generating and disseminating information widely.

Africa is not a single uniform entity. Within Africa there is much diversity, in terms of gender relations, culture, geography, society, family, economy, and natural resources. There is not one formula that can be applied in every case, and every community has to make its individual needs heard. As well, Africa is not static. It is a continent in flux and is rapidly undergoing fundamental changes, namely the growth of urban populations, deterioration of the environment and increasing desertification, deterioration of living standards, growing dependency on world markets, increasing numbers of young people and children, and civil strife and conflict. Development policies, plans and programs must be flexible to react and respond to these changes.

In terms of trade and its impact on women in Africa, in 2000, the United States Congress passed the African Growth and Opportunity Act (AGOA), which eliminated U.S. duties on textile imports from eligible Sub-Saharan countries.[2] Among the most visible beneficiaries of the textiles boom are women who earned low unpredictable incomes in the industry. However, to ensure long-term benefits from better access to American markets, African countries must diversify their economies, investing in the infrastructure and education that attract higher-tech companies. Further, a new round of global trade negotiations, dubbed the Doha Development Round, began in 2002, with the negotiations focused on agriculture. Africa's main goals are to substantially reduce or eliminate all tariffs on agricultural products, including quota duties; substantially reduce or eliminate tariff escalation; simplify complex tariffs by converting all tariffs to an ad valorem or fixed percentage of a product's value; substantially reduce or eliminate market-distorting export subsidies and domestic support; and recognize the special needs of the world's least developed countries.

As well, the New Partnership for Africa's Development (NEPAD) is a pledge by all of Africa's leaders to eradicate poverty and move towards sustainable growth and development. The partnership focuses on African ownership of the development process and seeks to reinvigorate the continent in all areas of human activity. Through the partnership, African leaders have agreed to promote the role of women in social and economic development; promote and protect democracy and human rights by developing standards for accountability, transparency, and participatory governance; restore and maintain macroeconomic stability; implement transparent legal and regulatory frameworks; revitalize and extend education, technical training, and health care services; and promote the development of infrastructure, agriculture, agroprocessing, and manufacturing to meet the needs of export and domestic markets and local employment.

NEPAD draws Africa's attention to the seriousness of the continent's economic challenges, the potential for addressing them and the challenge of mobilizing support. The main strategies proposed include pursuing gender equality in education, business, and public service; developing education and human resources at all levels, and in particular increasing the role of information and communication technology in education and training, inducing a 'brain gain' for Africa and eliminating gender disparities in education; and increasing domestic resource mobilization and accelerating foreign investment; creating a conducive environment for private sector activities, with an emphasis on domestic entrepreneurs.

African countries adopted the Dakar/Ngor Declaration in 1992 as the African common position to the International Conference on Population and Development (ICPD). It was recognized that population and development are inextricably linked, and that empowering women and meeting people's needs for education and health, including reproductive health, are necessary for both individual advancement and balanced development. For population and sustainable development in Africa, a key measure must be the promotion of access to equitable distribution of resources regardless of gender. Further, there needs to be a mix of macroeconomic and structural policies and programs for enhancing investment, growth, poverty reduction and social development; infrastructure improvement and institutional support services policies; and policies aimed at strengthening grassroots institutions and local participation.

The ICPD+5 Program of Action recommended a set of interdependent quantitative goals and objectives, which included universal access to primary education, with special attention to closing the gender gap in primary and secondary school education; universal access to primary health care; universal access to a full range of comprehensive reproductive health care services, including family planning; reductions in infant, child and maternal morbidity and mortality; and increased life expectancy.

Legislation

The African Charter on Human and Peoples' Rights The African Charter on Human and Peoples' Rights was adopted by the eighteenth Assembly of Heads of State and Government in June 1981 in Nairobi, Kenya. In the Preamble to the African Charter on Human and Peoples' Rights, the African States members of the Organisation of African Unity, parties to the present Convention entitled 'African Charter on Human and Peoples' Rights', undertake the agreement:

> Recalling Decision 115 (XVI) of the Assembly of Heads of State and Government at its Sixteenth Ordinary Session held in Monrovia, Liberia, from 17 to 20 July 1979 on the preparation of 'a preliminary draft on an African Charter on Human and Peoples' Rights, providing inter alia for the establishment of bodies to promote and protect human and peoples' rights';
>
> Considering the Charter of the Organisation of African Unity, which stipulates that 'freedom, equality, justice and dignity are essential objectives for the achievement of the legitimate aspirations of the African peoples';
>
> Reaffirming the pledge they solemnly made in Article 2 of the said Charter to eradicate all forms of colonialism from Africa, to coordinate and intensify their cooperation and efforts to achieve a better life for the peoples of Africa and to promote international cooperation having due regard to the Charter of the United Nations and the Universal Declaration of Human Rights;
>
> Taking into consideration the virtues of their historical tradition and the values of African civilization which should inspire and characterize their reflection on the concept of human and peoples' rights;
>
> Recognizing on the one hand, that fundamental human rights stem from the attitudes of human beings, which justifies their international protection and on the other hand that the reality and respect of peoples' rights should necessarily guarantee human rights;

> Considering that the enjoyment of rights and freedoms also implies the performance of duties on the part of everyone;
>
> Convinced that it is henceforth essential to pay particular attention to the right to development and that civil and political rights cannot be dissociated from economic, social and cultural rights in their conception as well as universality and that the satisfaction of economic, social and cultural rights is a guarantee for the enjoyment of civil and political rights;
>
> Conscious of their duty to achieve the total liberation of Africa, the peoples of which are still struggling for their dignity and genuine independence, and undertaking to eliminate colonialism, neo-colonialism, apartheid, zionism and to dismantle aggressive foreign military bases and all forms of discrimination, language, religion or political opinions;
>
> Reaffirming their adherence to the principles of human and peoples' rights and freedoms contained in the declarations, conventions and other instruments adopted by the Organisation of African Unity, the Movement of Non-Aligned Countries and the United Nations;
>
> Firmly convinced of their duty to promote and protect human and peoples' rights and freedoms and taking into account the importance traditionally attached to these rights and freedoms in Africa.[3]

Article 1 guarantees that the Member States of the Organisation of African Unity, parties to the present Charter shall recognize the rights, duties and freedoms enshrined in the Charter and shall undertake to adopt legislative or other measures to give effect to them.[4]

Rights without distinction including as to sex are guaranteed in Article 2:

> 2. Every individual shall be entitled to the enjoyment of the rights and freedoms recognised and guaranteed in the present Charter without distinction of any kind such as race, ethnic group, colour, sex, language, religion, political or any other opinion, national and social origin, fortune, birth or any status.[5]

Importantly, Article 3 establishes that every individual shall be equal before the law, and that every individual shall be entitled to equal protection of the law.[6] Further, the equality provision is contained in Article 19, which states that all peoples shall be equal; they shall enjoy the same respect and shall have the same rights, and nothing shall justify the domination of a people by another.[7]

Integrity of the person is guaranteed under Article 4 in that human beings are inviolable, and that every human being shall be entitled to respect for his life and the integrity of his person, with no one arbitrarily deprived of this right.[8] Further, Article 5 establishes that every individual shall have the right to the respect of the dignity inherent in a human being and to the recognition of his legal status.[9]

In looking at the importance of the courts in safeguarding rights, Article 7 establishes that every individual shall have the right to have his cause heard, which comprises of the right to an appeal to competent national organs against acts of violating his fundamental rights as recognized and guaranteed by conventions, laws, regulations and customs in force.[10] Further, the independence of the courts is ensured through Article 26, which states that State Parties to the present Charter shall have the duty to guarantee the independence of the Courts, and shall allow the establishment and improvement of appropriate national institutions entrusted with the promotion and protection of the rights and freedoms guaranteed by the present Charter.[11]

Article 15 is a paramount provision for employment rights and guarantees equal pay for equal work by simply stating:

> 15. Every individual shall have the right to work under equitable and satisfactory conditions, and shall receive equal pay for equal work.[12]

Further, an anti-discrimination clause is contained in Article 28:

> 28. Every individual shall have the duty to respect and consider his fellow beings without discrimination, and to maintain relations aimed at promoting, safeguarding and reinforcing mutual respect and tolerance.[13]

In terms of the important concept of education for advancement, Article 16 holds that every individual shall have the right to education.[14] Further, rights guaranteed to the family and the elimination of discrimination against women are outlined in Article 18, which recognizes that the family shall be the natural unit and basis of society, and it shall be protected by the State which shall take care of its physical health and moral. As well, the State shall ensure the elimination of every discrimination against women and also ensure the protection of the rights of women and the child as stipulated in international declarations and conventions.[15]

Article 25 outlines the duty of the State toward its citizens in terms of rights and freedoms in that State Parties to the present Charter shall have the duty to promote and ensure through teaching, education and publication, the respect of the rights and freedoms contained in the present Charter and to see to it that these freedoms and rights as well as corresponding obligations and duties are understood.[16] Further, Article 27 establishes that every individual shall have duties towards his family and society, the State and other legally recognized communities, and the international community, and the rights and freedoms of each individual shall be exercised with due regard to the rights of others, collective security, morality and common interest.[17]

Article 30 provides that an African Commission on Human and Peoples' Rights, hereinafter called 'the Commission', shall be established within the Organisation of African Unity to promote human and peoples' rights and ensure their protection in Africa.[18] Its functions are outlined in Article 45 as follows:

> 45(1) To promote human and peoples' rights and in particular:
>
> a) to collect documents, undertake studies and researches on African problems in the field of human and peoples' rights, organise seminars,

symposia and conferences, disseminate information, encourage national and local institutions concerned with human and peoples' rights and, should the case arise, give its views or make recommendations to Governments.

b) to formulate and lay down, principles and rules aimed at solving legal problems relating to human and peoples' rights and fundamental freedoms upon which African Governments may base their legislation.

c) cooperate with other African and international institutions concerned with the promotion and protection of human and peoples' rights.

(2) Ensure the protection of human and peoples' rights under conditions laid down by the present Charter.[19]

Applicable principles are outlined in Article 60 which stresses the importance of international law in that the Commission shall draw inspiration from international law on human and peoples' rights, particularly from the provisions of various African instruments on Human and Peoples' Rights, the Charter of the United Nations, the Charter of the Organisation of African Unity, the Universal Declaration of Human Rights, other instruments adopted by the United Nations and by African countries in the field of Human and Peoples' Rights, as well as from the provisions of various instruments adopted within the Specialized Agencies of the United Nations of which the Parties to the present Charter are members.[20]

Further, Article 61 holds that the Commission shall also take into consideration, as subsidiary measures to determine the principles of law, other general or special international conventions, laying down rules expressly recognized by Member States of the Organisation of African Unity, African practices consistent with international norms on Human and Peoples' Rights, customs generally accepted as law, general principles of law recognized by African States as well as legal precedents and doctrine.

The Protocol to the African Charter on Human and Peoples' Rights In the Preamble of the Protocol to the African Charter on Human and Peoples' Rights on the Establishment of an African Court on Human and Peoples' Rights, the Member States of the Organization of African Unity hereinafter referred to as the OAU, States Parties to the African Charter on Human and Peoples' Rights, undertake the agreement:

> Considering that the Charter of the Organization of African Unity recognizes that freedom, equality, justice, peace and dignity are essential objectives for the achievement of the legitimate aspirations of the African Peoples;
>
> Noting that the African Charter on Human and Peoples' Rights reaffirms adherence to the principles of Human and Peoples' Rights, freedoms and duties contained in the declarations, conventions and other instruments adopted by the Organization of African Unity, and other international organizations;
>
> Recognizing that the two-fold objective of the African Commission on Human and Peoples' Rights is to ensure on the one hand promotion and on the other protection of Human and Peoples' Rights, freedom and duties;

Recognizing further, the efforts of the African Charter on Human and Peoples' Rights in the promotion and protection of Human and Peoples' Rights since its inception in 1987;

Recalling resolution AHGéRes.230 (XXX) adopted by the Assembly of Heads of State and Government in June 1994 in Tunis, Tunisia, requesting the Secretary-General to convene a Government experts' meeting to ponder, in conjunction with the African Commission, over the means to enhance the efficiency of the African commission and to consider in particular the establishment of an African Court on Human and Peoples' Rights;

Noting the first and second Government legal experts' meeting held respectively in Cape Town, South Africa (September, 1995) and Nouakchott, Mauritania (April 1997), and the third Government Legal Experts meeting held in Addis Ababa, Ethiopia (December, 1997), which was enlarged to include Diplomats;

Firmly convinced that the attainment of the objectives of the African Charter on Human and Peoples' Rights requires the establishment of an African Court on Human and Peoples' Rights to complement and reinforce the functions of the African Commission on Human and Peoples' Rights.[21]

Article 1 states that there shall be established within the Organization of African Unity an African Court Human and Peoples' Rights hereinafter referred to as 'the Court', the organization, jurisdiction and functioning of which shall be governed by the present Protocol.[22]

The relationship between the Court and the Commission is outlined in Article 2, holding that the Court shall, bearing in mind the provisions of this Protocol, complement the protective mandate of the African Commission on Human and Peoples' Rights hereinafter referred to as 'the Commission', conferred upon it by the African Charter on Human and Peoples' Rights, hereinafter referred to as 'the Charter'.[23] Further, Article 3 states that the jurisdiction of the Court shall extend to all cases and disputes submitted to it concerning the interpretation and application of the Charter, this Protocol and any other relevant Human Rights instrument ratified by the States concerned. In the event of a dispute as to whether the Court has jurisdiction, the Court shall decide.[24]

Under Article 5, the following are entitled to submit cases to the Court: 1. The Commission; 2. The State Party, which had lodged a complaint to the Commission; 3. The State Party against which the complaint has been lodged at the Commission; 4. The State Party whose citizen is a victim of human rights violation; and 5. African Intergovernmental Organizations. When a State Party has an interest in a case, it may submit a request to the Court to be permitted to join, and the Court may entitle relevant Non-Governmental organizations (NGOs) with observer status before the Commission, and individuals to institute cases directly before it.[25]

The Protocol on Rights of Women in Africa In the Preamble to the Protocol on Rights of Women in Africa, the State Parties to the Protocol on the Rights of Women in Africa undertake the agreement:

CONSIDERING that Article 66 of the African Charter on Human and Peoples' Rights provides for special protocols or agreements, if necessary, to supplement the provisions of the African Charter, and that the OAU Assembly of Heads of State and Government meeting in its Thirty-first Ordinary Session in Addis Ababa, Ethiopia, in June 1995, endorsed by resolution AHG/Res.240 (XXXI) the recommendation of the African Commission on Human and Peoples' Rights to elaborate a Protocol on the Rights of Women in Africa;

CONSIDERING that Article 2 of the African Charter on Human and Peoples' Rights enshrines the principle of non-discrimination on the grounds of race, ethnic group, colour, sex, language, religion, political or any other opinion, national and social origin, fortune, birth or other status;

FURTHER CONSIDERING that Article 18 of the African Charter on Human and Peoples' Rights calls on all Member States to eliminate every discrimination against women and to ensure the protection of the rights of women as stipulated in international declarations and conventions;

NOTING that Articles 60 and 61 of the African Charter on Human and Peoples' Rights recognise regional and international human rights instruments and African practices consistent with international norms on human and peoples' rights as being important reference points for the application and interpretation of the African Charter;

RECALLING that women's rights have been recognised and guaranteed in all international human rights instruments, notably the Universal Declaration of Human Rights, the International Covenant on Civil and Political Rights, the International Covenant on Economic, Social and Cultural Rights, the Convention on the Elimination of All Forms of Discrimination Against Women and all other international conventions and covenants relating to the rights of women as being inalienable, interdependent and indivisible human rights;

NOTING that women's rights and women's essential role in development have been reaffirmed in the United Nations Plans of Action on the Environment and Development in 1992, on Human Rights in 1993, on Population and Development in 1994 and on Social Development in 1995;

FURTHER NOTING that the Plans of Action adopted in Dakar and in Beijing call on all Member States of the United Nations, which have made a solemn commitment to implement them, to take concrete steps to give greater attention to the human rights of women in order to eliminate all forms of discrimination and of gender-based violence against women;

BEARING IN MIND related Resolutions, Declarations, Recommendations, Decisions and other Conventions aimed at eliminating all forms of discrimination and at promoting equality between men and women;

CONCERNED that despite the ratification of the African Charter on Human and Peoples' Rights and other international human rights instruments by the majority of Member States, and their solemn commitment to eliminate all forms of discrimination and harmful practices against women, women in Africa still continue to be victims of discrimination and harmful practices;

FIRMLY CONVINCED that any practice that hinders or endangers the normal growth and affects the physical, emotional and psychological development of women and girls should be condemned and eliminated, and DETERMINED to ensure that the rights of women are protected in order to enable them to enjoy fully all their human rights.[26]

Article 1 defines 'Discrimination against women' to mean any distinction, exclusion or restriction based on sex, or any differential treatment whose objective or effects compromise or destroy the recognition, enjoyment or the exercise by women, regardless of their marital status, of human rights and fundamental freedoms in all spheres of life.[27] Further, 'Harmful Practices (HPs)' means all behavior, attitudes and practices which negatively affect the fundamental rights of women and girls, such as their right to life, health and bodily integrity.[28]

Importantly, Article 2(1) is paramount in the fight for the elimination of discrimination against women:

2(1) State Parties shall combat all forms of discrimination against women through appropriate legislative measures. In this regard they shall:

i. include in their national constitutions and other legislative instruments the principle of equality between men and women and ensure its effective application;
ii. enact and effectively implement appropriate national legislative measures to prohibit all forms of harmful practices which endanger the health and general well-being of women and girls;
iii. integrate a gender perspective in their policy decisions, legislation, development plans, activities and all other spheres of life;
iv. take positive action in those areas where discrimination against women in law and in fact continues to exist. [29]

Further, Article 2(2) holds:

2(2) State Parties shall modify the social and cultural patterns of conduct of men and women through specific actions, such as:

i. public education, with a view to achieving the elimination of harmful cultural and traditional practices and all other practices which are based on the idea of the inferiority or the superiority of either of the sexes, or on stereotyped roles for men and women;
ii. support local, national, regional and continental initiatives directed at eradicating all forms of discrimination against women. [30]

It is recognized in Article 3 that women contribute to the preservation of those African values that are based on the principles of equality, dignity, justice and democracy, and in this regard, the State Parties shall ensure that women enjoy rights and dignity inherent in all human beings, and adopt appropriate measures to prohibit any exploitation and degradation of women.[31]

Article 4 establishes that women shall be entitled to respect of their lives and the integrity of their person.[32] Additionally, Article 5 holds that State Parties shall take appropriate measures to prohibit all forms of violence against women whether physical, mental, verbal or sexual, domestic and family, whether they take place in the private sphere or in society and public life.[33]

Further, Article 6 establishes that State Parties shall condemn all harmful practices which affect the fundamental human rights of women and girls and which are contrary to recognized international standards, and undertake to take all the necessary measures to create public awareness regarding harmful practices through information, formal and informal education, communication campaigns and outreach programs targeting all stakeholders; and to rehabilitate victims of harmful practices by providing them with social support services such as health services to meet their health-care needs, emotional and psychological counselling, and skills training aimed at making them self-supporting in order to facilitate their re-integration into their families, communities and in other sectors of the society.[34]

On the issue of marriage, Article 7 guarantees that State Parties shall ensure that man and women enjoy equal rights and are regarded as equal partners in marriage. They shall enact appropriate national legislative measures to ensure that during her marriage, the women shall have the right to acquire her own property and to administer and manage it freely; and in cases of joint ownership of property the husband and wife shall have the same rights.[35]

The right to education and training for the advancement of women is outlined in Article 12 which establishes that State Parties shall take all appropriate measures to eliminate all forms of discrimination against women and girls in the sphere of education and training; and eliminate all references in textbooks and syllabuses to the stereotypes which perpetuate such discrimination. Further, State Parties shall take specific positive action to increase literacy among women; promote education and training for women and girls at all levels and in all disciplines; and promote the retention of girls in schools and other training institutions.[36]

In looking at the important concern of economic and social welfare rights, Article 13 is paramount for equal rights:

> 13. State Parties shall guarantee women equal opportunities to work. In this respect, they shall:
>
> i. promote equality in access to employment;
> ii. promote the right to equal remuneration for jobs of equal value for men and women;
> iii. ensure transparency in employment and dismissal relating to women in order to address issues of sexual harassment in the workplace;
> iv. allow women freedom to choose their occupation, and protect them from exploitation by their employers;
> v. create conditions to promote and support the occupations and economic activities dominated by women, in particular, within the informal sector;
> vi. encourage the establishment of a system of protection and social insurance for women working in the informal sector;

vii. introduce a minimum age of work and prohibit children below that age from working, and prohibit the exploitation of children, especially the girl-child;
viii. take the necessary measures to recognise the economic value of the work of women in the home;
ix. guarantee adequate pre and post-natal maternity leave;
x. ensure equality in taxation for men and women;
xi. recognise the right of salaried women to the same allowances and entitlements as those granted to salaried men for their spouses and children;
xii. recognise motherhood and the upbringing of children as a social function for which the State, the private sector and both parents must take responsibility.[37]

Further, Article 19 guarantees that women shall have the right to fully enjoy their right to sustainable development, and that State Parties shall take all appropriate measures to ensure that in the implementation of trade and economic policies and programs such as globalization, the negative effects on women are minimised.[38] Finally, special protection is afforded to elderly women and women with disabilities under Article 22, which holds that elderly women and women with disability have the right to specific measures of protection commensurate with their physical and moral needs.[39]

South Africa

The Role of Women in South African Society

In looking at the situation in South Africa, there are 19,520,886 men and 21,062,685 women.[40] In terms of the economically active population, 5,481,903 men and 3,631,944 women were employed, compared with 2,039,917 men and 2,631,730 women who were unemployed. According to staff profiles of all companies, women account for only 12 per cent of executive directors and senior management, 26 per cent of junior middle management, 29 per cent of professionals, 27 per cent of technicians and associate professionals, 54 per cent of clerical and administrative workers, 51 per cent of service and sales workers, 56 per cent of skilled agricultural and fishery workers, 5 per cent of craft and related trades, 17 per cent of operators and assemblers, and 20 per cent of laborers and related workers. Further, women represent only 22 per cent of total permanent employees and 40 per cent of temporary and casual workers. In terms of education level, there were 3,557,303 men and 4,108,495 women who were listed as having no schooling, and 657,674 men and 655,965 women who were listed at the other end of the spectrum in terms of having completed higher education, with most men at 4,372,582 men and women at 5,197,104 falling within the category of having some high school.

Legislation

Interim Constitution Schedule 4 The Constitutional Principles for the Republic of South Africa are contained in Schedule 4 of the Interim Constitution (Act 200 of 1993). Article I guarantees equality between men and women:

> I. The Constitution of South Africa shall provide for the establishment of one sovereign state, a common South African citizenship and a democratic system of government committed to achieving equality between men and women and people of all races.[41]

Article II also guarantees fundamental rights, freedoms and civil liberties by holding that everyone shall enjoy all universally accepted fundamental rights, freedoms and civil liberties, which shall be provided for and protected by entrenched and justiciable provisions in the Constitution.[42] Further, Article IV is the Supremacy clause, which states that the Constitution shall be the supreme law of the land; it shall be binding on all organs of state at all levels of government.[43]

Importantly, the prohibition against gender discrimination and the promotion of gender equality is contained within Article III:

> III. The Constitution shall prohibit racial, gender and all other forms of discrimination and shall promote racial and gender equality and national unity.[44]

The fundamental guarantee of equality of all before the law is contained in Article V:

> V. The legal system shall ensure the equality of all before the law and an equitable legal process. Equality before the law includes laws, programmes or activities that have as their object the amelioration of the conditions of the disadvantaged, including those disadvantaged on the grounds of race, colour or gender.[45]

The separation of powers for objectivity and accountability is contained in Article VI, which establishes that there shall be a separation of powers between the legislature, executive and judiciary, with appropriate checks and balances to ensure accountability, responsiveness and openness.[46] Further, the important role of the judiciary is outlined in Article VII, by holding that the judiciary shall be appropriately qualified, independent and impartial, and shall have the power and jurisdiction to safeguard and enforce the Constitution and all fundamental rights.[47]

The Constitution of South Africa The Constitution of the Republic of South Africa 1996 was first adopted by the Constitutional Assembly on May 8, 1996 (Act 108 of 1996), and was signed into law on December 10, 1996. As an integration of ideas from ordinary citizens, civil society and political parties represented in and outside of the Constitutional Assembly, the Constitution of South Africa represents the collective wisdom of the South African people and has been arrived at by general agreement. The objective in this process was to ensure that the final Constitution be legitimate, credible and accepted by all South Africans.

The Preamble of the Constitution reads:

> We, the people of South Africa,
> Recognise the injustices of our past;
> Honour those who suffered for justice and freedom in our land;
> Respect those who have worked to build and develop our country; and
> Believe that South Africa belongs to all who live in it, united in our diversity.
> We therefore, through our freely elected representatives, adopt this Constitution as the supreme law of the Republic so as to
> Heal the divisions of the past and establish a society based on democratic values, social justice and fundamental human rights;
> Lay the foundations for a democratic and open society in which government is based on the will of the people and every citizen is equally protected by law;
> Improve the quality of life of all citizens and free the potential of each person; and
> Build a united and democratic South Africa able to take its rightful place as a sovereign state in the family of nations.
> May God protect our people.
> Nkosi Sikelel' iAfrika. Morena boloka setjhaba sa heso.
> God seën Suid-Afrika. God bless South Africa.
> Mudzimu fhatutshedza Afurika. Hosi katekisa Afrika.[48]

The Founding Provisions of the Republic of South Africa are found in Article 1 of the Constitution which stresses equality and the advancement of human rights, by stating that the Republic of South Africa is one, sovereign, democratic state founded on the following values: Human dignity, the achievement of equality and the advancement of human rights and freedoms; Non-racialism and non-sexism; and the Supremacy of the constitution and the rule of law.[49]

The Supremacy Clause is found in Article 2 of the Constitution, which holds that this Constitution is the supreme law of the Republic; law or conduct inconsistent with it is invalid, and the obligations imposed by it must be fulfilled.[50] The right to equality is espoused in Article 3, which states that all citizens are equally entitled to the rights, privileges and benefits of citizenship; and equally subject to the duties and responsibilities of citizenship.[51]

Chapter 2 of the Constitution enumerates the Bill of Rights for South Africa. Article 7 states:

> 7(1) This Bill of Rights is a cornerstone of democracy in South Africa. It enshrines the rights of all people in our country and affirms the democratic values of human dignity, equality and freedom.
> (2) The state must respect, protect, promote and fulfil the rights in the Bill of Rights.
> (3) The rights in the Bill of Rights are subject to the limitations contained or referred to in section 36, or elsewhere in the Bill.[52]

Application and jurisdiction of the Bill of Rights are outlined in Article 8:

> 8(1) The Bill of Rights applies to all law, and binds the legislature, the executive, the judiciary and all organs of state.

> (2) A provision of the Bill of Rights binds a natural or a juristic person if, and to the extent that, it is applicable, taking into account the nature of the right and the nature of any duty imposed by the right.
> (3) When applying a provision of the Bill of Rights to a natural or juristic person in terms of subsection (2), a court
> a. in order to give effect to a right in the Bill, must apply, or if necessary develop, the common law to the extent that legislation does not give effect to that right; and
> b. may develop rules of the common law to limit the right, provided that the limitation is in accordance with section 36(1).
> (4) A juristic person is entitled to the rights in the Bill of Rights to the extent required by the nature of the rights and the nature of that juristic person.[53]

In terms of gender equality, Article 9 goes on to outline and guarantee the important concept of equal protection:

> 9(1) Everyone is equal before the law and has the right to equal protection and benefit of the law.
> (2) Equality includes the full and equal enjoyment of all rights and freedoms. To promote the achievement of equality, legislative and other measures designed to protect or advance persons, or categories of persons, disadvantaged by unfair discrimination may be taken.
> (3) The state may not unfairly discriminate directly or indirectly against anyone on one or more grounds, including race, gender, sex, pregnancy, marital status, ethnic or social origin, colour, sexual orientation, age, disability, religion, conscience, belief, culture, language and birth.
> (4) No person may unfairly discriminate directly or indirectly against anyone on one or more grounds in terms of subsection (3). National legislation must be enacted to prevent or prohibit unfair discrimination.
> (5) Discrimination on one or more of the grounds listed in subsection (3) is unfair unless it is established that the discrimination is fair.[54]

On human dignity, Article 10 states that everyone has inherent dignity and the right to have their dignity respected and protected.[55] Further, in the interpretation of the Bill of Rights, Article 39 states the importance of human dignity and equality:

> 39(1) When interpreting the Bill of Rights, a court, tribunal or forum
> a. must promote the values that underlie an open and democratic society based on human dignity, equality and freedom;
> b. must consider international law; and
> c. may consider foreign law.
> (2) When interpreting any legislation, and when developing the common law or customary law, every court, tribunal or forum must promote the spirit, purport and objects of the Bill of Rights.
> (3) The Bill of Rights does not deny the existence of any other rights or freedoms that are recognised or conferred by common law, customary law or legislation, to the extent that they are consistent with the Bill.[56]

In the area of employment, under the principle of freedom of trade, occupation and profession, Article 22 states that every citizen has the right to choose their trade, occupation or profession freely. The practice of a trade, occupation or profession may be regulated by law.[57] In terms of labor relations, Article 23 establishes that everyone has the right to fair labor practices. Every worker has the right to form and join a trade union; to participate in the activities and programs of a trade union; and to strike.[58]

In looking at the important right to education as a way of betterment, Article 29 states that everyone has the right to a basic education, including adult basic education; and to further education, which the state, through reasonable measures, must make progressively available and accessible.[59]

In guaranteeing the right to administrative action, Article 33 states that everyone has the right to administrative action that is lawful, reasonable and procedurally fair.[60] Further, the right to access to the courts is outlined in Article 34, which holds that everyone has the right to have any dispute that can be resolved by the application of law decided in a fair public hearing before a court or, where appropriate, another independent and impartial tribunal or forum.[61]

The Constitution also goes on to provide for a limitation of rights under Article 36(1), which provides that the rights in the Bill of Rights may be limited only in terms of law of general application to the extent that the limitation is reasonable and justifiable in an open and democratic society based on human dignity, equality and freedom, taking into account all relevant factors, including the nature of the right; the importance of the purpose of the limitation; the nature and extent of the limitation; the relation between the limitation and its purpose; and less restrictive means to achieve the purpose.[62]

In order to guarantee rights enumerated under the Constitution, Article 38 ensures the enforcement of such rights, by holding that anyone listed in this section has the right to approach a competent court, alleging that a right in the Bill of Rights has been infringed or threatened, and the court may grant appropriate relief, including a declaration of rights. The persons who may approach a court are anyone acting in their own interest; anyone acting on behalf of another person who cannot act in their own name; anyone acting as a member of, or in the interest of, a group or class of persons; anyone acting in the public interest; and an association acting in the interest of its members.[63]

The powers of the courts in constitutional matters are outlined in Article 172(1), which holds that when deciding a constitutional matter within its power, a court must declare that any law or conduct that is inconsistent with the Constitution is invalid to the extent of its inconsistency; and may make any order that is just and equitable, including an order limiting the retrospective effect of the declaration of invalidity; and an order suspending the declaration of invalidity for any period and on any conditions, to allow the competent authority to correct the defect.[64]

Under the establishment and governing principles, Article 181 lists several important institutions mandated to strengthen constitutional democracy, namely the Public Protector; the Human Rights Commission; the Commission for the Promotion and Protection of the Rights of Cultural, Religious and Linguistic Communities; the Commission for Gender Equality; the Auditor-General; and the

Electoral Commission.[65] The functions of the Human Rights Commission are listed under Article 184, which states that it must promote respect for human rights and a culture of human rights; promote the protection, development and attainment of human rights; and monitor and assess the observance of human rights in the Republic. Further, the Human Rights Commission has the powers, as regulated by national legislation, necessary to perform its functions, including the power to investigate and to report on the observance of human rights; to take steps to secure appropriate redress where human rights have been violated; and to carry out research; and to educate.[66]

The functions of the Commission for Gender Equality are listed under Article 187, which states that it must promote respect for gender equality and the protection, development and attainment of gender equality. Further, the Commission for Gender Equality has the power, as regulated by national legislation, necessary to perform its functions, including the power to monitor, investigate, research, educate, lobby, advise and report on issues concerning gender equality.[67]

The Employment Equity Act 1998 The Preamble of the South African Employment Equity Act, an Act to provide for employment equity and to provide for matters incidental thereto, states:

> Recognising
>
> that as a result of apartheid and other discriminatory laws and practices, there are disparities in employment, occupation and income within the national labour market; and that those disparities create such pronounced disadvantages for certain categories of people that they cannot be redressed simply by repealing discriminatory laws.
>
> Therefore, in order to
>
> promote the constitutional right of equality and the exercise of true democracy; eliminate unfair discrimination in employment; ensure the implementation of employment equity to redress the effects of discrimination; achieve a diverse workforce broadly representative of our people; promote economic development and efficiency in the workforce; and give effect to the obligations of the Republic as a member of the International Labour Organisation.[68]

The purpose of the Act is defined in Section 2 as to achieve equity in the workplace by promoting equal opportunity and fair treatment in employment through the elimination of unfair discrimination; and implementing affirmative action measures to redress the disadvantages in employment experienced by designated groups, in order to ensure their equitable representation in all occupational categories and levels in the workforce.[69]

According to Section 3, the Act must be interpreted in compliance with the Constitution so as to give effect to its purpose; taking into account any relevant code of good practice issued in terms of this Act or any other employment law; and in compliance with the international law obligations of the Republic, in particular those contained in the International Labour Organisation Convention (No. 111) concerning Discrimination in Respect of Employment and Occupation.[70]

The elimination and the prohibition of unfair discrimination are called for in Sections 5 and 6(1) respectively:

> 5. Every employer must take steps to promote equal opportunity in the workplace by eliminating unfair discrimination in any employment policy or practice.[71]
>
> 6(1) No person may unfairly discriminate, directly or indirectly, against an employee, in any employment policy or practice, on one or more grounds, including race, gender, sex, pregnancy, marital status, family responsibility, ethnic or social origin, colour, sexual orientation, age, disability, religion, HIV status, conscience, belief, political opinion, culture, language and birth.[72]

Section 6(2) allows for affirmative action programs and bona fide occupational qualifications:

> 6(2) It is not unfair discrimination to
> a. take affirmative action measures consistent with the purpose of this Act; or
> b. distinguish, exclude or prefer any person on the basis of an inherent requirement of a job.[73]

Further, Section 15 goes on to outline affirmative action measures which are permitted:

> 15(1) Affirmative action measures are measures designed to ensure that suitably qualified people from designated groups have equal employment opportunities and are equitably represented in all occupational categories and levels in the workforce of a designated employer.
> (2) Affirmative action measures implemented by a designated employer must include
> a. measures to identify and eliminate employment barriers, including unfair discrimination, which adversely affect people from designated groups;
> b. measures designed to further diversity in the workplace based on equal dignity and respect of all people;
> c. making reasonable accommodation for people from designated groups in order to ensure that they enjoy equal opportunities and are equitably represented in the workforce of a designated employer;
> d. subject to subsection (3), measures to
> i. ensure the equitable representation of suitably qualified people from designated groups in all occupational categories and levels in the workforce; and
> ii. retain and develop people from designated groups and to implement appropriate training measures, including measures

in terms of an Act of Parliament providing for skills development.

(3) The measures referred to in subsection (2)(d) include preferential treatment and numerical goals, but exclude quotas.[74]

According to the burden of proof outlined in Section 11, whenever unfair discrimination is alleged in terms of this Act, the employer against whom the allegation is made must establish that it is fair.[75]

To combat discrimination, Section 20 outlines the requirement of an employment equity plan:

20(1) A designated employer must prepare and implement an employment equity plan which will achieve reasonable progress towards employment equity in that employer's workforce.

(2) An employment equity plan prepared in terms of subsection (1) must state

a. the objectives to be achieved for each year of the plan;
b. the affirmative action measures to be implemented as required by section 15(2);
c. where underrepresentation of people from designated groups has been identified by the analysis, the numerical goals to achieve the equitable representation of suitably qualified people from designated groups within each occupational category and level in the workforce, the timetable within which this is to be achieved, and the strategies intended to achieve those goals;
d. the timetable for each year of the plan for the achievement of goals and objectives other than numerical goals;
e. the duration of the plan, which may not be shorter than one year or longer than five years;
f. the procedures that will be used to monitor and evaluate the implementation of the plan and whether reasonable progress is being made towards implementing employment equity;
g. the internal procedures to resolve any dispute about the interpretation or implementation of the plan;
h. the persons in the workforce, including senior managers, responsible for monitoring and implementing the plan; and
i. any other prescribed matter.[76]

The functions of the Commission for Employment Equity are enumerated in Section 30:

30(1) The Commission advises the Minister on

a. codes of good practice issued by the Minister;
b. regulations made by the Minister; and
c. policy and any other matter concerning this Act.

(2) In addition to the functions in subsection (1) the Commission may

a. make awards recognising achievements of employers in furthering the purpose of this Act;

b. research and report to the Minister on any matter relating to the application of this Act, including appropriate and well-researched norms and benchmarks for the setting of numerical goals in various sectors; and
c. perform any other prescribed function.[77]

Under Section 35, a labour inspector acting in terms of this Act has the authority to enter, question and inspect as provided.[78] Further, Section 36 holds that a labour inspector must request and obtain a written undertaking from a designated employer to comply within a specified period, if the inspector has reasonable grounds to believe that the employer has failed to consult with employees; conduct an analysis; prepare and implement an employment equity plan; submit and publish its annual report; prepare a successive employment equity plan; assign responsibility to a senior manager; inform its employees; or keep records.[79] According to Section 37, a labour inspector may issue a compliance order to a designated employer if that employer has refused to give a written undertaking; or failed to comply with a written undertaking given in terms of section 36.[80] Finally, under Section 40, a designated employer may appeal to the Labour Court against a compliance order of the Director-General within 21 days after receiving that order.[81]

In terms of a Code of Good Practice, according to the Employment Equity Act, the process of developing a plan has three sequential phases: planning, development, and implementation and monitoring. The planning phase of the process should include assignment of responsibility and accountability to one or more senior managers; a communication, awareness and training program; consultation with relevant stakeholders; an analysis of existing employment policies, procedures, and practices; an analysis of the existing workforce profile; an analysis of relevant demographic information; and the development of meaningful benchmark comparisons. The development phase should include objectives set; corrective measures formulated; time frames established; the plan drawn up; resources identified and allocated for the implementation of the plan; and the plan communicated. The implementation and monitoring phase should include implementation; monitoring and evaluating progress; reviewing the plan; and reporting on progress.

In order to identify any barriers that may be responsible for the underrepresentation or underutilization of employees from designated groups, a review of all employment policies, practices, procedures, and of the working environment should be undertaken of employment policy or practices, such as recruitment, selection, preemployment testing, and induction that could be biased, inappropriate, or unaffirming; practices related to succession and experience planning, and related promotions and transfers to establish whether designated groups are excluded or adversely impacted; utilization and job assignments to establish whether designated groups are able to meaningfully participate and contribute; current training and development methodologies and strategies; remuneration structures and practices such as equal remuneration for work of equal value; employee benefits related to retirement, risk, and medical aid to establish whether designated groups have equal access; disciplinary practices which may have a disproportionately adverse effect on designated groups that may not be justified; the number and nature of dismissals, voluntary terminations and retrenchments of employees from designated groups that may indicate internal or external equity-related factors contributing to such terminations; and corporate culture which may be characterised by exclusionary social and other practices. All practices should be assessed in terms of cross-cultural and gender fairness. The review should take into account more subtle or indirect forms of discrimination and stereo-typing which could result in certain groups of people not being employed in particular jobs, or which could preclude people from being promoted.

Affirmative action measures should be developed in terms of appointing members from designated groups for transparent and unbiased recruitment strategies; increasing the pool of available candidates; training, promoting and retaining people from designated groups; ensuring that members of designated groups are appointed in such positions that they are able to meaningfully participate in corporate decision-making processes; and transforming the corporate culture of the past in a way that affirms diversity in the workplace and harnesses the potential of all employees.

Promotion of Equality and Prevention of Unfair Discrimination Act, 2000 The preamble of the South African Promotion of Equality and Prevention of Unfair Discrimination Act, 2000 states:

> The consolidation of democracy in our country requires the eradication of social and economic inequalities, especially those that are systematic in nature, which were generated in our history by colonialism, apartheid and patriarchy, and which brought pain and suffering to the great majority of our people....
> The Constitution provides for the enactment of national legislation to prevent or prohibit unfair discrimination and to promote the achievement of equality;
> This implies the advancement, special legal and other measures, of historically disadvantaged individuals, communities and social groups who were dispossessed of their land and resources, deprived of their human dignity and who continue to endure the consequences;
> This Act endeavours to facilitate the transition to a democratic society, united in its diversity, marked by human relations that are caring and compassionate, and guided by the principles of equality, fairness, equity, social progress, justice, human dignity and freedom.[82]

Under Chapter 1, the objects of the Act are to enact legislation required by section 9 of the Constitution; to give effect to the letter and spirit of the Constitution, in particular the equal enjoyment of all rights and freedoms by every person, the promotion of equality, the values of non-racialism and non-sexism contained in section 1 of the Constitution, the prevention of unfair discrimination and protection of human dignity as contemplated in sections 9 and 10 of the Constitution, and the prohibition of advocacy of hatred based on race, ethnicity, gender or religion, that constitutes incitement to cause harm; to provide for measures to facilitate the eradication of unfair discrimination, hate speech and harassment, particularly on the grounds of race, gender and disability; and to provide for procedures for the determination of circumstances under which discrimination is unfair.[83]

Further, 'Prohibited grounds' are defined as:

> (a) race, gender, sex, pregnancy, marital status, ethnic or social origin, colour, sexual orientation, age, disability, religion, conscience, belief, culture, language and birth; or
> (b) any other ground where discrimination based on that other ground –
> (i) causes or perpetuates systematic disadvantaged:
> (ii) undermines human dignity; or
> (iii) adversely affects the equal enjoyment of a person's rights and freedoms in a serious manner that is comparable to discrimination on a ground in paragraph (a).[84]

In terms of the burden of proof in gender discrimination cases, Article 13 stipulates:

> 13(1) If the complainant makes out a prima facie case of discrimination
> (a) the respondent must prove, in the facts before the court, that the discrimination did not take place as alleged; or
> (b) the respondent must prove that the conduct is not based on one or more of the prohibited grounds.
> (2) If the discrimination did take place
> (a) on a ground in paragraph (a) of the definition of 'prohibited grounds'... then it is unfair, unless the respondent proves that the discrimination is fair;
> (b) on a ground in paragraph (b) of the definition of 'prohibited grounds', then it is unfair
> (i) if one or more of the conditions set out in paragraph (b) of the definition of 'prohibited grounds' is established; and
> (ii) unless the respondent proves that the discrimination is fair.[85]

According to Article 4, in the adjudication of any proceedings which are instituted in terms of or under this Act, the following principles should apply, namely the expeditious and informal processing of cases, which facilitate participation by the parties to the proceedings; access to justice to all persons in relevant judicial and other dispute resolution forums; the use of rules of procedure in terms of section 19 and criteria to facilitate participation; the use of corrective or restorative measures in conjunction with measures of a deterrent nature; and the development of special skills and capacity for persons applying this Act in order to ensure effective implementation and administration thereof. In the application of this Act, the following should be recognized and taken into account, namely the existence of systematic discrimination and inequalities, particularly in respect of race, gender and disability in all spheres of life as a result of past and present unfair discrimination, brought about by colonialism, the apartheid system and patriarchy; and the need to take measures at all levels to eliminate such discrimination and inequalities.[86]

It is understood that by virtue of Article 5 the Act binds the State and all persons,[87] and by virtue of Article 6 neither the State nor any person may unfairly discriminate against any person.[88] In the prohibition against discrimination on the grounds of gender, Article 8 states:

> 8. Subject to section 6, no person may unfairly discriminate against any person on the ground of gender, including
> (a) gender-based violence;
> (b) female genital mutilation;
> (c) the system of preventing women from inheriting family property:
> (d) any practice, including traditional, customary or religious practice, which impairs the dignity of women and undermines equality between women and men, including the undermining of the dignity and well-being of the girl child;
> (e) any policy or conduct that unfairly limits access of women to land rights, finance and other resources;
> (f) discrimination on the ground of pregnancy;
> (g) limiting women's access to social services or benefits, such as health, education and social security;
> (h) the denial of access to opportunities, including access to services or contractual opportunities for rendering services for consideration, or failing to take steps to reasonably accommodate the needs for such persons;
> (i) systematic inequality of access to opportunities by women as a result of the sexual division of labour.[89]

Article 14 establishes the determination of fairness or unfairness:

> 14(1) It is not unfair discrimination to take measures designed to protect or advance persons or categories of persons disadvantaged by unfair discrimination or the members of such groups or categories of persons.
> (2) In determining whether the respondent has proved that the discrimination is fair, the following must be taken into account:
> (a) the context;
> (b) the factors referred to in subsection (3);
> (c) whether the discrimination reasonably and justifiably differentiates between persons according to objectively determinable criteria, intrinsic to the activity concerned.
> (3) The factors referred to in subsection (2)(b) include the following:
> (a) whether the discrimination impairs or is likely to impair human dignity;
> (b) the impact or likely impact of the discrimination on the complainant;
> (c) the position of the complainant in society and whether he or she suffers from patterns of disadvantage or belongs to a group that suffers from patterns of disadvantage;
> (d) the nature and extent of the discrimination;
> (e) whether the discrimination is systematic in nature;
> (f) whether the discrimination has a legitimate purpose;
> (g) whether and to what extent the discrimination achieves its purpose;
> (h) whether there are less restrictive and less disadvantageous means to achieve the purpose;

(i) whether and to what extent the respondent has taken such steps as being reasonable in the circumstances to –

(i) address the disadvantage which arises from or is related to one or more of the prohibited grounds; or

(ii) accommodate diversity.[90]

According to Article 25, the State has a duty to promote equality and as such, the State must, where necessary with the assistance of the relevant constitutional institutions develop awareness of fundamental rights in order to promote a climate of understanding, mutual respect and equality; take measures to develop and implement programs in order to promote equality; and where necessary or appropriate develop action plans to address any unfair discrimination, hate speech or harassment, enact further legislation that seeks to promote equality and to establish a legislative framework in line with the objectives of this Act, develop codes of practice as contemplated in this Act in order to promote equality, and develop guidelines, including codes in respect of reasonable accommodation, provide assistance, advice and training on issues of equality, develop appropriate internal mechanisms to deal with complaints of unfair discrimination, hate speech or harassment, and conduct information campaigns to popularize this Act.[91]

Conclusion

In terms of gender issues of equality in Africa, African States should share experiences on best practices in order to complement each other so as to ensure effective gender mainstreaming; continue to ensure that gender issues are integrated in all development programs and plans; develop common indicators for monitoring gender issues at regional levels; and encourage and support the initiation and coordination of periodical conference/seminars on gender and development in relation to population issues.

Indeed, a renewal of commitment to gender equality is overdue in Africa, where there is a great disparity in the level of human rights protection available to its inhabitants. Almost all African countries have constitutions or civil codes that prohibit discrimination. But the level of protection varies from nation to nation. Entrenched attitudes and practices, as well as limited resources, limit the practical effect of these.

Notes

1 Economic Commission for Africa, *Africa's Population and Development Bulletin*, Addis Ababa, 2002.
2 Economic Commission for Africa, *Economic Report on Africa*, 2002.
3 African Charter on Human and Peoples' Rights, Preamble.
4 *Ibid.*, at Article 1.
5 *Ibid.*, at Article 2.
6 *Ibid.*, at Article 3.

[7] *Ibid.*, at Article 19.
[8] *Ibid.*, at Article 4.
[9] *Ibid.*, at Article 5.
[10] *Ibid.*, at Article 7.
[11] *Ibid.*, at Article 26.
[12] *Ibid.*, at Article 15.
[13] *Ibid.*, at Article 28.
[14] *Ibid.*, at Article 16.
[15] *Ibid.*, at Article 18.
[16] *Ibid.*, at Article 25.
[17] *Ibid.*, at Article 27.
[18] *Ibid.*, at Article 30.
[19] *Ibid.*, at Article 45.
[20] *Ibid.*, at Article 60.
[21] Protocol to the African Charter on Human and Peoples' Rights, Preamble.
[22] *Ibid.*, at Article 1.
[23] *Ibid.*, at Article 2.
[24] *Ibid.*, at Article 3.
[25] *Ibid.*, at Article 5.
[26] Protocol on the Rights of Women in Africa, Preamble.
[27] *Ibid.*, at Article 1.
[28] *Ibid.*, at Article 1.
[29] *Ibid.*, at Article 2(1).
[30] *Ibid.*, at Article 2(2).
[31] *Ibid.*, at Article 3.
[32] *Ibid.*, at Article 4.
[33] *Ibid.*, at Article 5.
[34] *Ibid.*, at Article 6.
[35] *Ibid.*, at Article 7.
[36] *Ibid.*, at Article 12.
[37] *Ibid.*, at Article 13.
[38] *Ibid.*, at Article 19.
[39] *Ibid.*, at Article 22.
[40] South African Census, 1996.
[41] Interim Constitution of South Africa, Schedule 4, Article I.
[42] *Ibid.*, at Article II.
[43] *Ibid.*, at Article IV.
[44] *Ibid.*, at Article III.
[45] *Ibid.*, at Article V.
[46] *Ibid.*, at Article VI.
[47] *Ibid.*, at Article VII.
[48] Constitution of South Africa, Preamble.
[49] *Ibid.*, at Article 1.
[50] *Ibid.*, at Article 2.
[51] *Ibid.*, at Article 3.
[52] *Ibid.*, at Article 7.
[53] *Ibid.*, at Article 8.
[54] *Ibid.*, at Article 9.
[55] *Ibid.*, at Article 10.
[56] *Ibid.*, at Article 39.
[57] *Ibid.*, at Article 22.

[58] *Ibid.*, at Article 23.
[59] *Ibid.*, at Article 29.
[60] *Ibid.*, at Article 33.
[61] *Ibid.*, at Article 34.
[62] *Ibid.*, at Article 36(1).
[63] *Ibid.*, at Article 38.
[64] *Ibid.*, at Article 172(1).
[65] *Ibid.*, at Article 181.
[66] *Ibid.*, at Article 184.
[67] *Ibid.*, at Article 187.
[68] Employment Equity Act, South Africa, Preamble.
[69] *Ibid.*, at Section 2.
[70] *Ibid.*, at Section 3.
[71] *Ibid.*, at Section 5.
[72] *Ibid.*, at Section 6(1).
[73] *Ibid.*, at Section 6.
[74] *Ibid.*, at Section 15.
[75] *Ibid.*, at Section 11.
[76] *Ibid.*, at Section 20.
[77] *Ibid.*, at Section 30.
[78] *Ibid.*, at Section 35.
[79] *Ibid.*, at Section 36.
[80] *Ibid.*, at Section 37.
[81] *Ibid.*, at Section 40.
[82] Promotion of Equality and Prevention of Unfair Discrimination Act, South Africa, Preamble.
[83] *Ibid.*, at Chapter 1.
[84] *Ibid.*
[85] *Ibid.*, at Article 13.
[86] *Ibid.*, at Article 4.
[87] *Ibid.*, at Article 5.
[88] *Ibid.*, at Article 6.
[89] *Ibid.*, at Article 8.
[90] *Ibid.*, at Article 14.
[91] *Ibid.*, at Article 25.

References

African Charter on Human and Peoples' Rights, 1981.
Constitution of South Africa, 1996.
Economic Commission for Africa (2002), *Africa's Population and Development Bulletin*, Addis Ababa.
Economic Commission for Africa (2002), *Economic Report on Africa*.
Employment Equity Act, South Africa, 1998.
Interim Constitution of South Africa, Schedule 4, 1996.
Promotion of Equality and Prevention of Unfair Discrimination Act, South Africa, 2000.
Protocol on the Rights of Women in Africa.
Protocol to the African Charter on Human and Peoples' Rights.
South African Census (1996).

Chapter 6

Gender Injustice in Canada, Mexico and the United States

Introduction

This Chapter will examine Gender Injustice in Canada, Mexico and the United States. It will initially look at the role of women in society. It will then examine legislation impacting women, namely the Constitution as well as other important legislation. Finally, in order to properly analyze the laws and the courts, cases will be reviewed not for their factual content or the judgment issued, but more importantly for the burden of proof required in gender discrimination as opposed to racial discrimination.

The British model of government, which has influenced greatly the Canadian structure, sees the legislature making the laws and the judiciary applying them.[1] Parliamentary supremacy is not founded on democratic ideals, but rather a narrow power struggle representing property. However, the American Model sees judicial activism and the judicial power as fundamentally legislative in character. Royal power is displaced and overthrown, but class power remains, with the upper class combining the popular republican form of government with the protection of property.

Canada

The Role of Women in Canadian Society

Canada has a total of 31,015,000 people, with 15,356,000 males and 15,659,000 females, according to the latest statistics.[2] Importantly, women have experienced growth in the labor force over the years. However, women are still considerably less likely to be in the workforce than men, as 5,844,800 women are employed, while 514,700 are unemployed.[3] Labor force participation rates are at 72.5 per cent for men and 57.4 per cent for women.[4] Men account for 6,613,000 of full-time jobs, compared to 4,384,000 for women, and 783,000 of part-time jobs, compared to 1,725,000 for women. The unemployment rate was 7.3 per cent for women and 7.8 per cent for men.[5] Part-time work continues to be more significant for women than for men. Women are more likely to work part-time, accounting for 69 per cent of all part-time employment. Some women work part-time because of family responsibilities, with young women more likely than older women to be in part-time positions. However, many women work part-time because they cannot find full-time employment, with 34 per cent wanting full-time work but not finding it.[6]

Women have made gains in some professional occupations. In management and professional positions, women number 2,258,000, compared to 2,190,000 men, having made tremendous gains, due in part to changes in occupational definitions. This category of management and other professional occupations includes the management and administrative sectors, and other professions such as natural sciences, social sciences, religion, teaching, medicine and art. However, women still occupy positions of less power and influence, predominating in the clerical sector, numbering 1,578,000 compared with 392,000 men. Women are also underrepresented among self-employed workers, with women accounting for roughly 10 per cent of such workers, in comparison with roughly 20 per cent for male workers. However, there has been an increase, in the last decade, in the number of women running their own businesses.

Women have less tenure in employment than men, with an average ratio of 81 months compared to 108 months at the same job. Older women have greater job tenure than younger women, but still less tenure than men. This is due in part to the tradition of many women interrupting their work in order to raise a family. However, increases in unemployment among women have been less severe than among men, so that female participants are less likely to be unemployed. Interestingly, women are more likely than men to drop out of the labor force when they lose their job. Young women are more likely to be unemployed than other women, but are less likely to be unemployed than their male counterparts. There is variation in the level of unemployment in different occupational groups. Women in the goods producing industries are more likely to be unemployed than women in the service sector, but are less likely than their male colleagues to be unemployed. There is little difference, however, between the sexes in the service sector. Unemployed women are more likely than men to be new job market entrants who have never worked, and are twice as likely as men to be re-entrants who have not worked in the past five years. Women are also more likely to have left their job for personal responsibilities, in keeping with tradition. However, women are unemployed for shorter periods, and are less likely to experience extended periods of unemployment, with older women more likely than younger women to be unemployed for longer periods.

The increased workforce participation of women is due in part to the higher levels of educational attainment. The university enrolment of women declines the higher the level of education. Women earned 72,884 bachelors and first professional degrees, compared to 53,276 for men, while women earned only 1,059 doctorates, compared to 2,588 for men. The gap will narrow in the future, since women form the majority of students attending university. Women with high levels of education are more likely than other women to be employed in the labor force and are less likely to work part-time or be unemployed. As well, female graduates have a higher income than other women. Young women are better educated than their male counterparts, with the reverse true for the older population. Women with high levels of educational attainment are less likely than other women to work part-time. However, women are more likely than their male counterparts to work part-time regardless of educational qualifications, with female university graduates over three times more likely than male graduates to have part-time employment. Women who have graduated from a post-secondary institution have lower unemployment rates than other women. However, women with a university degree have a higher unemployment rate than similarly qualified men. As well, at all levels of educational attainment, women are less likely than men to be employed.

Rapid growth has occurred in labor force participation rates for those women with children in the last decade. However, women with pre-school children are less likely than those with school-aged children to be employed. In general, women are less likely than men to be in the labor force, and women with children are more likely than other women to be employed part-time. Further, female lone parents are less likely to be employed than women in two-parent families with children. Women continue to be responsible for most of the unpaid domestic work even when employed, devoting two hours more per day than men. Domestic work activities account for most of the total unpaid work time of employed women. Employed women are nearly three times more likely than men to be absent from work, because of personal family responsibilities. Importantly, most female homemakers spend more time on unpaid household activities than the employed do at their jobs, but these women are not included in national labor market surveys.

Further, the membership of women in labor unions has increased, while that of men has declined. Women employed full-time are more likely than women employed part-time to be unionized. As well, women employed part-time are more likely than their male counterparts to be union members. However, women in general are still less likely than their male counterparts to be union members. As such, women are less likely than men to be unionized in most industries, with health and social services the only category in which females were more likely to be unionized.[7]

The past thirty years have seen the growth of dual-earner families. The number of dual-earner families has gone from 33 per cent to 60 per cent in recent years. The traditional family of a bread-winning husband and a stay at home wife has been radically changed, in less than a generation, into one where both spouses work outside the home. As well, a recent trend has been the emergence of women as primary earners and sole earners within families.[8] An interesting aspect of women working outside the home has been the growing proportion of working couples, in which the wife earns more than the husband. Over the last thirty years, the proportion of women as the primary wage earner has risen from 11 per cent to 25 per cent. As well, changes have occurred in single earner families, which has seen the proportion of families with the wife as the earning spouse grow over the years from 2 per cent to 20 per cent.

The growing number of wives who earn more than their husbands is a reflection of women's long term movement into higher paying managerial and professional occupations, with their accumulated job experience. As well, during this same period, there was slower growth in the average earnings of men. This combined for a rapid increase in the number of wives who occupied the position of primary earners. Many wives became the main breadwinners by default. Most of the full-year, full-time earners who lost their jobs were men, accounting for 84 per cent. The high-wage managerial jobs and manufacturing jobs, mostly held by men, were particularly hard hit. Therefore, the combination of recessions and women's rising earnings left many wives as primary earners in their families.

The difference in earnings between the sexes has closed in recent years mostly because of substantial increases in the earnings of women and little change in the earnings of men. Women in professional occupations have considerably higher incomes than other occupations. However, women's earnings overall continue to be significantly below those of men in all occupations. Women with a university degree have higher earnings than women with other educational qualifications. However, the earnings of women are below those of men in all educational groups. As concerns marital status, there is little difference in the participation rate or the employment levels of women. In all marital categories, women are less likely than men to be employed. Despite all the progress, women cannot match men's earning power. The average employment income of primary earner wives was $31,000, 30 per cent less than that of primary earner husbands at $43,250. Primary earner wives were more likely to be employed in managerial professional occupations, 48 per cent compared to 35 per cent for primary earner husbands. However, at the same time, these women earned one-third less than their male counterparts. Outside of the managerial professional occupations, almost 80 per cent of female primary earners worked in clerical, sales or service jobs, with an average salary ranging from $24,000 to $30,000. In contrast, 60 per cent of male primary earners worked in blue-collar occupations, with an average salary ranging from $37,000 to $40,000.

One factor for the differential is the work pattern. Women primary earners were considerably less likely to have worked full-time than their male counterparts, 86 per cent to 96 per cent respectively. Another factor is age, with the median age of female primary earners slightly younger at 38, compared with the median age of 40 for their male counterparts. Contributing to some lack of work experience, these factors helped to influence job tenure and salary level. Another phenomenon has been the steady increase in families in which the wife was the only spouse earner. This can be traced to the general ageing of the population. Sole earner wives and their husbands are generally older, with 43 per cent of such wives and 60 per cent of such husbands aged 55 and over. In contrast, in families in which the sole wage earner is the husband, 47 per cent of these men are between the ages of 25 and 44.

The generation gap suggests that the growth of female sole earner families is mainly due to the fact that husbands retire and the younger wives continue to work. The labor force participation rates of older women have steadily risen. In addition, sole earner wives are less likely to experience unemployment than their male counterparts. However, sole earner wives have an average employment income of only $18,250, while sole earner husbands made nearly twice as much at $34,750. Despite this, families in which wives were the sole earners, reported an average income of $44,250, only 12 per cent less than those of sole earner husbands. The reason for this is the fact that almost half the family income of female sole earners comes from sources other than employment, such as government transfer payments or private pensions and investments, compared to only one fifth for male sole earners.

The important contribution of primary earner wives to dual earner families has helped some to stay above the low-income level, for without them 45 per cent would have fallen below this line. So it is, as well, in male primary earner families, in which the wives' contribution is smaller, but without which 9 per cent would have fallen below the poverty line. The importance of women wage earners has grown throughout the years. Overall, wives are the primary wage earners in one quarter of dual earner families and the sole earner in one fifth of families. At the same time, however, women's salaries still lag behind men's in similar situations.[9]

Women's advancements in the labor force have contributed to another recent trend of female entrepreneurs. Self-employment or entrepreneurship has boomed in the last few decades, accounting for more than one fourth of all employment.[10] Self-employment reflects the shift to a service economy and the growth of small businesses. This has occurred as a result of corporate downsizing and restructuring, as well as contracting out and privatization. The number of entrepreneurs has risen to roughly 15 per cent of those employed. The representation of women among the self-employed has jumped to account for one in three entrepreneurs, up from one in four previously. In the last two decades, women have accounted for two thirds of all employment gains. In addition, the number of self-employed women has tripled over the years, while the number of self-employed men has doubled. Women account for 40 per cent in the rise of self-employment. Two-thirds of women entrepreneurs work full-time. While both the full-time and part-time self-employment rates have doubled among women, the rate for male entrepreneurs has fallen from 95 per cent to 90 per cent. The rate for part-time work considerably exceeds that of full-time work, by a ratio of 311 per cent to 85 per cent. In addition, women account for 22 per cent of all employers, up from 12 per cent previously. The incidence of entrepreneurship has risen with age. Due to retirement, there is a particularly high rate of entrepreneurship for both sexes, with 34 per cent of women and 55 per cent of men aged 65 and over self-employed.

Women entrepreneurs are frequently married to other entrepreneurs, reflecting changes in the way women view their role in the market place and in the family. Although men still dominate the self-employment sphere, women are playing an increasing role.[11] Overall, self-employed workers are more likely than paid workers to be married. The incidence of self-employment is only slightly higher for married than non-married women, while that of married men is almost double that of non-married men. In addition, the incidence of self-employment is considerably higher among women who did not complete high school than those who had a higher level of education, with a similar pattern for men. In looking at the different sectors and among self-employed women, 37 per cent work in the service industry, 21 per cent in sales, 17 per cent in the retail trade, 13 per cent in business, and 11 per cent in health and social services. In contrast, among self-employed men, 21 per cent work in sales, 17 per cent in the construction trade, and 13 per cent in managerial and administrative occupations. Interestingly, average annual earnings for entrepreneur women are low at $18,400, compared with $25,900 for female paid workers and contrasted with $33,400 for entrepreneur men. Several factors account for this: part-time work is more prevalent among women entrepreneurs; women entrepreneurs are concentrated in industries with lower earnings; the number of female employers is considerably lower than that of men; and the proportion of self-employed women with a university degree is lower than that of men.

Women have made considerable progress in the labor force. However, much still needs to be done to improve the lives of women, who often have to work twice as hard. Equal pay and access to employment need to become realities for women.

Legislation

The Canadian Constitution The Canadian Constitution was proclaimed into force and entrenched on April 17, 1982.[12] It is made up of three separate documents: The British North America Act and its various amendments, the Constitution Act and its amending formula, and the Canadian Charter of Rights and Freedoms. Section 32 of the Charter provides for its application to the Parliament and government of Canada, as well as to the legislature and government of each province.[13] The purpose of the Canadian Charter of Rights and Freedoms is to protect and safeguard the rights and freedoms enumerated, and to contain governmental action within reasonable limits. The supremacy of the Constitution is contained in Section 52(1) of the Constitution Act:

> 52(1) The Constitution of Canada is the supreme law of Canada and any law that is inconsistent with the provisions of the Constitution is, to the extent of the inconsistency, of no force or effect.[14]

The Charter through Section 15 guarantees equality of rights, and also deals with affirmative action programs to help reverse the discrimination process:

> 15. (1) Every individual is equal before and under the law and has the right to the equal protection and equal benefit of the law without discrimination and, in particular, without discrimination based on race, national or ethnic origin, colour, religion, sex, age or mental or physical disability.
> (2) Subsection (1) does not preclude any law, program or activity that has as its object the amelioration of conditions of disadvantaged individuals or groups including those that are disadvantaged because of race, national or ethnic origin, colour, religion, sex, age or mental or physical disability.[15]

The Charter implements gender equality through Section 28, which states:

> 28. Notwithstanding anything in this Charter, the rights and freedoms referred to in it are guaranteed equally to male and female persons.[16]

This provision contained in Section 28 cannot be overridden by legislation or act of Parliament.

However, Section 33 of the Charter is the infamous notwithstanding clause, whereby the Canadian provinces are allowed to opt out of the Constitution for successive and infinite five-year periods:

> 33. Parliament or the legislature of a province may expressly declare in an act of Parliament or of the legislature...that the act or a provision thereof shall operate notwithstanding a provision included in ...Section...15 of this Charter.[17]

The Canadian Constitution extends power to judges to review legislative action on the basis of congruence with protected values in the Charter, and treats the judicial branch of government as a partner with the legislative and executive branches, in determining the rights of citizens. However, Section 33, the overriding clause, will ensure that legislatures rather than judges have the final say on important matters of public policy, so that laws offensive to certain provisions of the Charter may be upheld.

Section 1 of the Charter is also an overriding clause:

> 1. The Canadian Charter of Rights and Freedoms set out is subject only to such reasonable limits prescribed by law as can be demonstrably justified in a free and democratic society.[18]

Thus, fundamental freedoms, as well as legal and equality rights, can be subjected to this notwithstanding clause. Remarkably, the right against gender discrimination is not absolute. The Canadian Charter of Rights and Freedoms may be used to strengthen inequalities, by weighing in on the side of power, and undermine popular movements.

Section 1 of the Charter has two functions: First, it guarantees the rights and freedoms set out in the provisions which follow it; and Second, it states explicitly the exclusive justificatory criteria, outside of Section 33 of the Charter, against which limitations on those rights and freedoms may be measured. The onus of proving that a limitation on any Charter right is reasonable and demonstrably justified in a free and democratic society rests upon the party seeking to uphold the limitation. Limits on constitutionally guaranteed rights are clearly exceptions to the general guarantee. The presumption is that Charter rights are guaranteed unless the party invoking Section 1 can bring itself within the exceptional criteria justifying their being limited. The standard of proof under Section 1 is a preponderance of probabilities. Proof beyond a reasonable doubt would be unduly onerous on the party seeking to limit the right because concepts such as 'reasonableness', 'justifiability', and 'free and democratic society' are not amenable to such a standard. Nevertheless, the preponderance of probability test must be applied rigorously.

The Supreme Court of Canada uses the purposive approach to interpret the Charter, whereby the underlying purpose of the legislative provision and the nature of the interest are identified. A two-step procedure is utilized to see whether the limit of the Charter contained in Section 1 can uphold an infringement of a right. Two questions are asked: 1. Has the right been violated?; and 2. Can the violation be justified under Section 1? The burden of proof is such that the onus of establishing a prima facie infringement of the Charter is on the person alleging it, while the onus of justifying a reasonable limit on the protected right is on the party invoking Section 1. The standard is a preponderance of probabilities. Two criteria must be satisfied in order to come within Section 1 of the Charter: 1. The objective of the limiting measure must be sufficiently important, and the concerns must be pressing and substantial to justify overriding a constitutionally protected right; and 2. The means must be reasonable and demonstrably justified according to a proportionality test, which balances the interests of society against those of individuals. There are three components to the test: 1. The measure must be carefully designed to achieve the stated objective, and must not be arbitrary, unfair or irrational; 2. The measure should impair the right as little as possible; and 3. Proportionality must exist between the effect of the limiting measure and its objectives (Regina v. Oakes, [1986] 1 S.C.R. 103).[19]

The Canadian Human Rights Act In addition to the Canadian Constitution, there is the Canadian Human Rights Act (CHRA), which came into force on March 1, 1978.[20] It has been very influential for those seeking relief through an alternate channel other than the traditional court system, namely the Canadian Human Rights Tribunal. The Canadian Human Rights Act deals with pay equity, applying the same wages where respective work is shown to be equal in value in respect to a combination of factors, influencing comparisons between dissimilar jobs. The Act was passed as a result of political lobbying by mostly highly educated women and those at the grass-roots level. It implements a complaints process through a commission, which assumes that systemic discrimination does not exist but for a few cases. It differs from a proactive approach, which places an obligation on the employer to determine if systemic gendered wage discrimination exists and to remedy it within a time frame.

The purpose of the Canadian Human Rights Act is outlined in Section 2:

> 2. The purpose of this Act is to extend the laws in Canada to give effect, within the purview of matters coming within the legislative authority of Parliament, to the principle that all individuals should have an opportunity equal with other individuals to make for themselves the lives that they are able and wish to have and to have their needs accommodated, consistent with their duties and obligations as members of society, without being hindered in or prevented from doing so by discriminatory practices based on race, national or ethnic origin, colour, religion, age, sex, sexual orientation, marital status, family status, disability or conviction for an offence for which a pardon has been granted.[21]

Under Section 11, it is discriminatory directly or indirectly to refuse to employ or, in the course of employment, to differentiate adversely against an employee in recruitment, referral, hiring, promotion, training or transfer policies:

11(1) It is a discriminatory practice for an employer to establish or maintain a difference in wages between male and female employees employed in the same establishment who are performing work of equal value;
(2) In assessing the value of work performed by employees employed in the same establishment, the criterion to be applied is the composite of the skill, effort and responsibility required in the performance of the work and the conditions under which the work is performed.[22]

Further, Section 15(1) allows for a bona fide occupational exception:

15(1) It is not a discriminatory practice if
(*a*) any refusal, exclusion, expulsion, suspension, limitation, specification or preference in relation to any employment is established by an employer to be based on a *bona fide* occupational requirement.[23]

Finally, Section 48(1) establishes the Canadian Human Rights Tribunal.[24]

The Canadian Human Rights Act looks at comparable worth, applying the same wages where respective work is shown to be equal in value through a combination of skill, effort, responsibility and working conditions. It thereby makes comparisons between dissimilar jobs, in order to reduce the historical social injustice of the under-valuation of women's work. It is a discriminatory practice to establish different wages, so that if men and women do work of equal value in the same establishment then they must be paid equally. Discriminatory practices for wage inequities include segregated employment, exclusion of females categorically from the existing evaluation system, under-valuation of female positions, fewer promotion opportunities for women, senior rules disadvantaging women, and discriminatory transfers, promotion and layoffs.[25] There are, however, some reasonable factors to permit a pay difference, such as periodic pay increases for length of service or working in remote locations. Equal value can be incorporated by a complaint driven process and a proactive requirement process on the employer to initiate plans. The government policy is that employer initiated compliance with equal pay legislation is the effective way for goodwill.

The Canadian Human Rights Commission only has jurisdiction over the federal public service and federally regulated employers in the quest for equal pay for work of equal value. One drawback to the federal law is that it is limited to comparisons within the same establishment. The Act allows anyone working within the federal jurisdiction to file a complaint with the Canadian Human Rights Commission. The Commission will then investigate by collecting job information, analyzing the job evaluation plan, and calculating the pay adjustment to eliminate the wage discrimination. If discrimination is found and there is no agreement for adjustment, a conciliator is appointed or a tribunal is established, with its decision appealable to the courts.

Discrimination includes practices or attitudes, whether by design or impact, which have the effect of limiting the individual's right to the opportunities generally available, because of attributes such as gender rather than actual characteristics. The Canadian Human Rights Tribunal has found a discriminatory practice toward women in non-traditional employment, and called for the future setting aside of jobs for women to prevent similar discrimination in the future (Action Travail des Femmes v. Canadien National, 1984 CHRT).[26]

The Canadian Human Rights Act through Section 11 prohibits discrimination by an employer between 'male and female' employees who perform work of equal value, and does not guarantee to individual employees equal pay for work of equal value irrespective of sex. In the judicial system, the Plaintiff has the burden to prove a prima facie case of discrimination. Then, the burden shifts to the Defendant who must show a reasonable explanation for the distinction. The Plaintiff must then demonstrate that it is a pretext, the true motive being discrimination. The Canadian Human Rights Tribunal found that there is not a prima facie case of discrimination when others are better-qualified (Folch v. Canadian Airlines, 1992 CHRT).[27]

The rational connection test, the potential for a rational connection between the basic fact and the presumed fact to justify a reverse onus provision, does not specifically apply to the interpretation of Section 11(d) of the Canadian Human Rights Act. A basic fact may rationally tend to prove a presumed fact, but still not prove its existence beyond a reasonable doubt, which is an important aspect of the presumption of innocence. The appropriate stage for invoking the rational connection test is therefore under Section 1 of the Charter (Regina v. Oakes, [1986] 1 S.C.R. 103).[28]

However, in terms of the onus of proof with respect to a complaint under the Act, the burden, and order, of proof in discrimination cases involving refusal of employment appears clear and constant through all Canadian jurisdictions: a complainant must first establish a prima facie case of discrimination; once that is done the burden shifts to the respondent to provide a reasonable explanation for the otherwise discriminatory behavior. Thereafter, assuming the employer has provided an explanation, the complainant has the eventual burden of showing that the explanation provided was merely 'pretext' and that the true motivation behind the employer's actions was in fact discriminatory (Basi v. Canadian National Railway (1984), 9 C.H.R.R.4. D/5029, 5037 (C.H.R.Tribunal)).[29]

In an employment complaint, the Commission usually establishes a prima facie case by proving: 1. That the Complainant was qualified for the particular employment; 2. That the complainant was not hired; and 3. That someone no better qualified but lacking the distinguishing feature which is the gravamen of the human rights complaint subsequently obtained the position. If these elements are proved, there is an evidentiary onus on the Respondent to provide an explanation of events equally consistent with the conclusion that discrimination on the basis prohibited by the Code is not the correct explanation of what occurred (Shakes v. Rex Pak Ltd. (1982), 3 C.H.R.R. D/1001, 1002).[30] Should the Respondent lead evidence of a non-discriminatory reason for refusing to employ the Complainant, the Complainant and the Commission can still establish that the reason advanced for non-employment is in fact a pretext, and that discrimination on an unlawful ground was one of the operative reasons for the Respondent's actions (Blake v. Ministry of Correctional Services and Mimico Correctional Institute (1984), 5 C.H.R.R. D/2417 (Ontario)).[31]

The ultimate onus of proof to establish the complaint on a balance of probabilities lies with the Complainant and the Commission. Discrimination can be established by direct evidence or by circumstantial evidence, which is evidence that is consistent with the fact that is sought to be proven and inconsistent with any other rational conclusion. It is not necessary to find that the Respondent intended to discriminate against the Complainant. It is sufficient to establish the complaint if it is found, on the balance of probabilities, that the Respondent in fact discriminated against the Complainant on one of the grounds alleged in her complaint (Ontario Human Rights Commission v. Simpsons-Sears Ltd., [1985] S.C.R. 536, 547).[32]

The Canadian Human Rights Commission published a document entitled 'Special Programs in Employment: Criteria for Compliance'. The purpose of a special program in employment, as intended by the Canadian Human Rights Act, is to provide the conditions which will nurture the growth of equal opportunity for among others women within the working environment. Equitable representation will be achieved by changing the composition of the internal labor force such that any underutilization or over concentration of groups within that labor force is corrected.

There are three essential steps in developing a special program: To identify as problems, areas within the organization in which the labor force is unrepresentative; To determine how the problems relate to organization policies, practices and procedures, both formal and informal; and To formulate solutions which aim to remove existing barriers and to forward equitable representation. The criteria which indicate the need for a special program are: observable absence of members of certain groups in particular job categories, or in the organization as a whole; existence of particularly high unemployment rates among certain groups; internal complaints and grievances from employees; external complaints by individuals or groups; inability of the organization to recruit or retain employees that is high turnover; and complaints filed with the CHRC alleging discriminatory practices.

The primary objective of a special program is to increase the representiveness of the organization's labor force in some specific way. In setting objectives specific to the organization, the following factors must be considered; objectives should be quantitative, namely targets or goals; objectives aim to correct underutilization or overconcentration where they occur in an organization; objectives must be specific as to target group and should also specify job category and geographical area; the objectives must be attainable within specific and reasonable timeframes. A special program is intended to be a temporary measure that should never outlive the identified problem of disadvantage, although the achievement of objectives will result in permanent organizational changes; objectives should realistically reflect the ability of the organization to respond to change; objectives must take into consideration the continuing rights of individuals, especially employees, not belonging to designated target groups; the objectives will be framed with care to be sensitive to the feelings and expectations of staff, including members of the target groups.

Canada Employment Equity Act, 1995 The purpose of the Canada Employment Equity Act as outlined in Article 2 is to achieve equality in the workplace so that no person shall be denied employment opportunities or benefits for reasons unrelated to ability and, in the fulfillment of that goal, to correct the conditions of disadvantage in employment experienced by women, aboriginal peoples, persons with disabilities and members of visible minorities by giving effect to the principle that employment equity means more than treating persons in the same way but also requires special measures and the accommodation of differences.[33]

Article 5 establishes a duty of employers:

> 5. Every employer shall implement employment equity by
> (*a*) identifying and eliminating employment barriers against persons in designated groups that result from the employer's employment systems, policies and practices that are not authorized by law; and
> (*b*) instituting such positive policies and practices and making such reasonable accommodations as will ensure that persons in designated groups achieve a degree of representation in each occupational group in the employer's workforce that reflects their representation in
> (i) the Canadian workforce, or
> (ii) those segments of the Canadian workforce that are identifiable by qualification, eligibility or geography and from which the employer may reasonably be expected to draw employees.[34]

Further, Article 6 states that the obligation to implement employment equity does not require an employer to take a particular measure to implement employment equity where the taking of that measure would cause undue hardship to the employer; to hire or promote unqualified persons; with respect to the public sector, to hire or promote persons without basing the hiring or promotion on selection according to merit in cases where the Public Service Employment Act requires that hiring or promotion be based on selection according to merit; or to create new positions in its workforce.[35]

Article 10 provides for the implementation of an employment equity plan:

> 10. (1) The employer shall prepare an employment equity plan that
> (*a*) specifies the positive policies and practices that are to be instituted by the employer in the short term for the hiring, training, promotion and retention of persons in designated groups and for the making of reasonable accommodations for those persons, to correct the underrepresentation of those persons identified by the analysis…;
> (*b*) specifies the measures to be taken by the employer in the short term for the elimination of any employment barriers identified by the review…;
> (*c*) establishes a timetable for the implementation of the matters referred to in paragraphs (*a*) and (*b*);
> (*d*) where underrepresentation has been identified by the analysis, establishes short term numerical goals for the hiring and promotion of persons in designated groups in order to increase their representation in each occupational group in the workforce in which underrepresentation has been identified and sets out measures to be taken in each year to meet those goals;

(*e*) sets out the employer's longer term goals for increasing the representation of persons in designated groups in the employer's workforce and the employer's strategy for achieving those goals; and
(*f*) provides for any other matter that may be prescribed.[36]

Under Article 29, a Tribunal may in the same manner and to the same extent as a superior court of record, summon and enforce the attendance of witnesses and compel them to give oral and written evidence on oath and to produce such documents and things as the Tribunal considers necessary for a full review; administer oaths; and receive and accept such evidence and other information, whether on oath or by affidavit or otherwise, as the Tribunal sees fit, whether or not that evidence or information would be admissible in a court of law.[37]

Mexico

Legislation

Constitución Política de los Estados Unidos Mexicanos The equality of all persons before the law is guaranteed by the Constitución Política de los Estados Unidos Mexicanos, the Political Constitution of the United Mexican States.[38] Article 1 establishes that all individuals shall enjoy the guarantees set down by the Constitution, which may not be restricted or suspended, except in those cases and conditions established therein.[39] Article 4 goes on to state that men and women are equal under the Law.[40] In terms of equality in employment, Article 123(7) establishes that equal work performed in the same post, with the same hours worked and conditions of efficiency shall also be remunerated with the same salary.[41]

Ley Federal de Trabajo The entitlement of women and men to equal opportunities is set down in Article 3 and Article 164 of the Ley Federal de Trabajo (LFT), the Federal Labor Law.[42] Article 1 states that no discrimination may be established between workers on the basis of race, gender, age, religion, political opinion or social rank.[43] Article 2 states that women shall have the same rights and obligations as men.[44] In terms of equality in employment, Article 133(1) states that it is prohibited for an employer to refuse to contract an individual, because of their age or gender.[45] Article 86 establishes that equal work performed in the same post, with the same hours worked and conditions of efficiency shall also be remunerated with the same salary.[46]

As regards maternity leave, Article 170 establishes the obligation of employers to provide female workers with six weeks leave before and six weeks after childbirth at full salaries.[47] This period may be extended as necessary, and in the event of a worker being unable to work as the result of pregnancy or child birth, she is entitled to 50 per cent of her salary for a period of up to 60 days in addition to the 12 weeks at full pay. Further, during the period of lactation, women are entitled to two extra half-hour rest periods in order to feed their infants. Importantly, as long as more than a year has not elapsed from the date of childbirth, women are entitled to return to the position they formerly occupied, and are entitled to have pre- and post-natal periods included in their seniority.

In terms of work risk indemnification financed by a premium paid by the employer, Article 166 establishes that pregnant or lactating women may not be assigned to unhealthy or dangerous work, industrial night work, in commercial or service establishments after 10 p.m. or for overtime, as a means of protecting the health of women.[48]

Although there is no unemployment insurance per se, Articles 50 and 52 of the LFT establish an obligation on the part of employers to pay compensation to unfairly dismissed workers, who also have the option to be reinstated to the same job.[49] If the worker is discharged without justification, and his employment is for a specified period, the worker is entitled to receive a severance payment equal to the wages received for half of the time of work with the same employer. For those workers with more than one year of service, severance payment is equal to six months' wages for the first year of service plus 20 days' wages for each additional year of service. For workers with labor contracts of unspecified duration, severance payment is equal to three months' wages, and they would also have the right to receive wages for the period between the day of dismissal and the day the severance compensation is paid. If a worker asks to be reinstated and the employer refuses, he has the right to receive 20 days' wages for each year of service in addition to the above.

Ley del Seguro Social Article 109 of the Ley del Seguro Social (LSS), the Social Security Law, states that in the event of a female insurance worker losing her job and having made at least eight continuous weekly contributions to the Instituto Mexicano del Seguro Social (IMSS), Mexican Institute of Social Security, she shall be entitled to receive all necessary medical, maternity, surgical, pharmaceutical and hospital assistance for eight weeks following dismissal.[50] Likewise, female workers involved in strikes are entitled to medical benefits for the duration of the strike, a requirement that applies equally to male workers.

In terms of retirement income and health benefits, the social security system administered by the IMSS covers a broad range of social insurance, including work risks, illness and maternity, disability and life, retirement and dismissal due to old age, and nursery facilities for children, as well as other social benefits. The system is financed by premiums paid by employers, employees and by contributions by the federal government. Premiums paid by the employer are equal to 8.5 per cent of insurable earnings plus 13.9 per cent of the minimum wage in the Distrito Federal for illness and maternity insurance plus a variable portion for work risks insurance. Employees' premiums are equal to 2 per cent of their insurable earnings. In the case of workers receiving the minimum wage, employers are obliged to pay the entire premium, according to Article 36.[51] The IMSS offers nursery facilities for children aged 43 days to four years of insured female workers, as provided by Article 206,[52] and the premium is entirely covered by the employer, as stated in Article 212.[53] Any female worker losing her job is entitled to make use of the nursery service for a further four weeks, according to Article 207.[54] As of July 1997, contributions for the retirement insurance scheme are administered by means of individual accounts handled by private companies known as Administradores de Fondos para el Retiro de los Trabajadores (AFORES), Worker Retirement Fund Administrators.

The United States

The Role of Women in American Society

The United States has a total of 274,087,000 people, with 133,933,000 males and 140,154,000 females, according to the latest statistics.[55] In terms of marital status of the population 15 years and older, of the 103,114,000 males and 110,660,000 females, there are 56,501,000 men and 56,501,000 women married with spouse, 1,365,000 men and 1,365,000 women married with spouse absent, 2,604,000 men and 11,061,000 women widowed, 8,572,000 men and 11,309,000 divorced, 1,818,000 men and 2,661,000 separated, and 32,253,000 men and 27,763,000 women never married. In looking at household type, of the 104,705 total households, there are 55,311 married-couple families, 18,669 male householders with no spouse, and 30,726 female householders with no spouse. While marriage was once considered a total impediment to employment, women have managed to combine both often out of necessity.

Concerning the employment status of the population 16 years and older in the civilian labor force, 74,517,000 are men, of these 3,281,000 are unemployed, and 65,937,000 are women, of these 2,835,000 are unemployed.[56] In terms of unemployment, reasons given for the unemployment of both sexes were: lost their job; left their job; re-entered the work force; or remained non-entrants. The rates for women and men were higher for re-entrants and non-entrants.[57] Additionally, men and women continue to occupy different professions. In terms of the major occupational groups, managerial and professional has 20,297,000 men and 20,196,000 women; technical, sales and administrative support 14,174,000 men and 25,367,000 women; service occupations 7,459,000 men and 11,212,000 women; precision production, craft and repair 12,975,000 men and 1,410,000 women; operators, fabricators and laborers 13,816,000 men and 4,187,000 women; and farming, forestry and fishing 2,515,000 men and 729,000 women.[58] Further, at the top of the career ladder, in the managerial and professional category, there are 10,877,000 men (15.3 per cent) and 8,888,000 women (14.1 per cent) in the decision-making executive, administrator and managerial areas. However, 9,420,000 men (13.2 per cent) and 11,309,000 women (17.9 per cent) are in the support service professional speciality area.[59] In looking more closely at the legal profession, women still account for only 29 per cent of attorneys and judges, up from 15.8 per cent a decade earlier.[60]

In terms of earnings of full-time year-round workers aged 15 years and older, most men (12,631,000 or 22.0 per cent) are found in the $35,000 to $49,999 range, while most women (9,410,000 or 23.3 per cent) are less well-off in the

$25,000 to $34,999 range. The highest level $75,000 and over held 13 per cent of the male figures and only 3.7 per cent of the female figures.[61] Women still earn roughly 75 per cent of what men earn, with the wage gap persisting.[62] Of the total money income of families by type, most of the married couples (33.6 per cent) are in the $75,000 and more range, while male householders (19.3 per cent) are lower in the $50,000 to $74,999 range, and female householders (15.2 per cent) even lower in the $25,000 to $34,999 range.[63]

In terms of educational attainment of the population 25 years and older, of the 83,611,000 total male population and 91,620,000 total female population, 13,215,000 males and 14,638,000 females have less than a high school diploma, and 70,395,000 males and 76,982,000 females are high school graduates or more. In other terms, 60,359,000 males and 70,025 females have less than a University bachelor's degree, and 23,251,000 males and 21,595,000 females have a University bachelor's degree or more. On opposite scales, there are 5,918,000 men and 6,261,000 women who have less than 9th grade education, and 8,342,000 men and 6,664,000 women who hold an advanced University degree.[64] Education has had an important impact on the lives of both sexes, but especially women. Female labor force participation rates are at 47.2 per cent for those with less than high school, 68.9 per cent for high school graduates, 77.3 per cent for those with some University and 82.5 per cent for University graduates, while male labor force participation rates are at 72 per cent for those with less than high school, 86.9 per cent for high school graduates, 90.1 per cent for those with some University and 93.8 per cent for University graduates.[65]

Interestingly, in terms of the poverty status of the population in examining overall achievement, 13,813,000 men (10.3 per cent) and 18,445,000 (13.2 per cent) women are below the poverty line. In looking at the poverty status of families by family type, 4.8 per cent (2,673,000) married couple families are below the poverty line, compared to 11.7 per cent (472,000) of male householders, and 27.8 per cent (3,531,000) of female householders.[66]

In the United States, the return on education for women is particularly high for those with a third-level qualification. Looking at earnings data for full-time women classified by educational attainment, women without a high school diploma earned only 40 per cent as much as women with a college degree, and women with just some college education or an associate degree made just 67 per cent of the earnings of their counterparts with a 4-year degree. However, regardless of education level, female full-time workers earned less than men, with the gap being relatively similar for all of the education groups. In looking at temporary contract and part-time workers, and in particular weekly hours worked by men and women full-time in the United States, men were more than twice as likely as women to work 49 or more hours in a week, and women were three times as likely as men to work 35 to 39 hours per week. The possible reasons for the difference in work hours could be attributed to women being more likely to be engaged in family caretaking responsibilities, or to men being more likely to work in occupations and industries where overtime or extended hours are required or frequently available. In looking at discrimination, while the unadjusted gender pay gap in the United States is around 73 per cent, the gap narrowed to 81 per cent after adjusting for human capital differences and to 88 per cent when adjusting for other variables such as occupation and industry. So while the gap in pay was reduced significantly after accounting for other variables, a substantial proportion remained due to discrimination.[67]

Women continue to make significant strides in the labor force. However, women still lag behind men overall, making it more difficult for women to advance in their career and in life. The United States Department of Labor will work with employers to develop more equitable pay and promotion policies, and will help employees to balance the twin responsibilities of family and work. Further, the Agency for International Development will work to establish important initiatives to increase women's participation in political processes and to promote the enforcement of women's legal rights.

Legislation

The Declaration of Independence The concepts of equality and good government were equally important principles to the Founding Fathers of the United States. The Declaration of Independence, the bedrock of the United States' jurisprudence system, was enshrined on July 4, 1776. It fundamentally states:

> We hold these truths to be self-evident, that all men are created equal; that they are endowed by their Creator with certain unalienable rights; that among these are life, liberty and the pursuit of happiness. That, to secure these rights, governments are instituted among men, deriving their just powers from the consent of the governed; that whenever any form of government becomes destructive of these ends, it is the right of the people to alter or to abolish it, and to institute a new government, laying its foundation on such principles, and organize its powers in such form, as to them shall seem most likely to effect their safety and happiness.[68]

The Federalist Papers Influential thinkers, such as Jefferson, Madison and Jay, believed in a national government and a Bill of Rights, which they outlined in the Federalist Papers. Government was seen as essential to the security of liberty, with every citizen ceding some rights for the protection thereof. The diversities in the faculties of men are where property rights originate. The objective of government is to secure the public good and private rights against the danger of factions. The most common source of faction is the unequal distribution of property. The purpose of the Union is the common defence of the members, so that the means are proportionate to the ends. Government must act before the public, and must be derived from the body of society. The Constitution is founded on the assent and ratification of the people, and every man who loves liberty must cherish the attachment to the Union and preserve it. Among the three branches of government, the Judicial branch is considered the least dangerous to the political rights of the Constitution. The Executive branch dispenses the honors and holds the sword, the Legislative branch controls the purse and prescribes the rules to regulate duties and rights, and the Judiciary has no influence over the sword or the purse, needing the aid of the Executive for the efficacy of judgments. Oppression can proceed from the Courts, but liberty will not be endangered if the branches are separate. The Constitution is the fundamental law of the land. 'We, the people of the United States, to secure the blessings of liberty to ourselves and our prosperity, do ordain and establish this Constitution for the United States of America'. This is a recognition of popular rights. The judgments of many unite into one, with the voluntary consent of a whole people.[69]

The Federalist Papers give us an important insight into the making of the Constitution, showing us early on the concept of equality of man and the formation of one government out of many people. The importance of the Judiciary must not be overlooked, as it is a major contributor of policy through its judgments, often itself influencing the sword, the Executive, and the purse, the Legislative. American constitutionalism is the product of the revolutionary movement in political thought of Hobbes, the parent of the modern American political process.[70] The chief purpose of political institutions is the management of social conflict. According to Hobbes, the only source of public authority is the private need of independently situated political actors, with a prior right to act based on self-defined standards of conscience and interest. If used wisely, the Constitution can serve to remedy past injustices of gender discrimination.

The United States Constitution The American Founding Fathers designed the United States Constitution to be a set of broad guidelines established by free and intelligent men for the government of free and intelligent people for successive generations. It has survived for over two hundred years due to the common sense of the American people, the prudence of their representatives, and the calculated wisdom of its judicial interpreters, the Supreme Court of the United States.[71] Chief Justice Marshall said of the Constitution, 'it was intended to endure for ages to come and consequentially to be adapted to the various crises of human affairs' (McCullough v. Maryland, 4 Wheaton 415 (1819)).[72] It was a common opinion that each branch of government in matters pertaining to itself be the final judge of its own powers. However, it was the function of the judiciary, and especially the Supreme Court, to construe in the last resort the meaning of the Constitution, with its opinion final and binding. Justice Hughes stated, 'We are under a Constitution but the Constitution is what the judges say it is'. The seminal case of Marbury v. Madison, 1 Cranch 137 (1803), brought forth the important principles that 1. The Constitution is the supreme law of the land; 2. The powers granted to various branches of government are limited; and 3. The sole and essential function of the Court is to determine which law should prevail in conflict of laws.[73]

In a dynamic society, the creativity of judges is important for the development of law and the adaptability of the Constitution to the needs of modern society, according to the Realist Theory. Courts are the best means for recognizing social change, in order to focus social attitudes on unachieved goals and assist in their attainment through a decision-making process of judgments and thus policy-making, according to the Free Legal Decision Sociological Jurisprudence Theory.[74] History has a record of the past and provides the Court with a reservoir of social wisdom and political insight. It points out the evils against which the great constitutional clauses were designed as remedies.

The adjudicative process depends on a delicate symbiotic relationship, whereby the Court must know us better than we know ourselves, acting as a voice of the spirit to remind us of our better selves.[75] It provides a stimulus and quickens moral education. However, the roots of the Supreme Court's decisions must be already in the nation. The aspirations voiced by the Court must be those the community is willing not only to avow but in the end to live by. For the power of the great constitutional decisions rests upon the accuracy of the Court's perceptions of this kind of common will and upon its ability ultimately to command a consensus. The rule of law, the capacity to command free assent, is the substitute for power.[76] Law is the fabric of a free society, organized with a minimum of force and a maximum of reason, in an ideal sense of right and justice. A neutral government, with its various branches, serves only as a participant in the inhumanities of its citizens.

The United States Constitution, through Article 6(2) known as the Supremacy Clause, is the supreme law of the land:

> 6(2) This Constitution, and the Laws of the United States which shall be made in Pursuance thereof; and all Treaties made, or which shall be made, under the Authority of the United States, shall be the supreme Law of the Land; and the Judges in every State shall be bound thereby, any Thing in the Constitution or Laws of any State to the Contrary notwithstanding.[77]

The 39th Article of the Magna Carta of 1215 is a foundation for the 5th and 14th Amendments of the American Constitution regarding due process and the rights of life, liberty and property. The Magna Carta states:

> No free man shall be taken or imprisoned or dispossessed, or outlawed or banished, or in any way destroyed, nor will we go upon him nor send upon him, except by the legal judgement of his peers or by the law of the land.[78]

The 5th and 14th Amendments to the Constitution provide due process of law and equal protection to citizens from federal and state actions, respectively. They state:

> 5. No person shall... be deprived of life, liberty or protection without due process of law.[79]
> 14(1) Nor shall any state deprive any person of life, liberty, or property, without due process of law; nor deny to any person within its jurisdiction the equal protection of the laws.[80]

The due process clause of the 5th Amendment includes an equal protection component, which prohibits government from invidious discrimination. These provisions are of paramount importance to the courts in fighting discrimination. In discrimination cases, the United States Supreme Court examines the legislative purpose of the governmental action alleged to be contrary to the constitutional amendments. Rather than the strict scrutiny level of review applied where the classification is suspect, affecting fundamental rights, or the minimum rationality level of scrutiny applied to see the rational basis for the means to the ends, a middle level of heightened scrutiny is applied to quasi-suspect cases, such as gender. The cause of action is examined to see whether a plaintiff is a member of a class, which as a matter of law can invoke the power of the court. Sex discrimination, with its exaggerated stereotyping of women as unsuited to the working world, is an ideology rampant throughout the male dominated working world and legislature calling for constitutional suspicion of blocked access.[81]

The equal protection clause and the due process clause of the Amendments confer a constitutional right to be free from gender discrimination, which does not serve an important government objective or is not substantially related to the achievement of the objective (Davis v. Passman, 442 U.S. 228 (1979)).[82] In the past, the Supreme Court has found that it was a mistake to resolve 5th Amendment cases through the Civil Rights Act, since a law, which has a disproportionate impact, is not necessarily unconstitutional, and therefore, the statutory standards of the Civil Rights Act are more prohibiting to judicial review.

Although, the American Constitution is the paramount tool for redressing wrongs, the judicial system in the United States has seen the use of two acts, the Equal Pay Act and the Civil Rights Act as alternatives to the Constitution, with the latter having been the most successful in guarding against discrimination.

The Equal Pay Act The Equal Pay Act of 1963 established that it was unlawful for an employer to pay unequal wages for equal work based on gender.[83] An exception was made where there was a system of 1. Seniority; 2. Merit; 3. Earnings based on quantity or quality of production; or 4. Something other than gender. Section 16 of the Equal Pay Act states:

> 16. No employer having employees...shall discriminate, within any establishment...between employees on the basis of sex by paying wages to employees in such establishment at a rate less than the rate at which he pays wages to employees of the opposite sex in such establishment for equal work on jobs the performance of which requires equal skill, effort and responsibility, and which are performed under similar working conditions except where such payment is made pursuant to 1. a seniority system, 2. a merit system, 3. a system which measures earnings by quantity or quality of product or 4. a differential based on any other factor other than sex.[84]

The Equal Pay Act only includes jobs that are very much alike or closely related, considered virtually or substantially identical (Brennan v. City Stores, 479 F.2d. 235 (1973)).[85] Jobs though not identical can be considered equal for Equal Pay Act standards, if there is only an insubstantial difference in skill, effort and responsibility (Murphy v. Miller Brewer Co., 307 F.Supp. 829 (1969)).[86] For the Equal Pay Act, there is sex discrimination when there is a different wage rate for equal work, that is work which requires equal skill, effort and responsibility under similar working conditions (Corning Glass v. Brennan, 417 U.S. 188 (1974)).[87] Equal protection is violated only by intentional discrimination, and a different impact standing alone is not enough. There is the need for a failure to act, or a desire to benefit men at the expense of women. Further, there is no legal duty to undo the effects of previous discrimination (American Nurses' Association v. State of Illinois, 783 F.2d. 716 (1986)).[88]

Therefore, the Plaintiff has the burden of establishing that equal pay for equal work was not received. Then, the Defendant must show the different wages were based on seniority, merit, a quantitative or qualitative system, or reasons other than sex (Spaulding v. University of Washington, 740 F.2d. 686 (1984)).[89] The court, however, is concerned with the actual job performance and content, not job description, titles or classifications, and the scrutiny is done on a case by case basis. If skill is irrelevant to job requirements, it is not considered. Therefore, a non-job related pretext can act as a shield for invidious discrimination.

The Civil Rights Act The Civil Rights Act of 1964 was implemented to safeguard important civil liberties. It serves to strengthen legislation, thereby helping the courts rule against discrimination. Section 703(a) of Title VII, the Civil Rights Act, states:

> 703(a) It shall be an unlawful employment practice for an employer, (1) to fail or refuse to hire or to discharge any individual, or otherwise to discriminate against any individual with respect to his compensation, terms, conditions, or privilege of employment, because of such individual's race, color, religion, sex, or national origin, or (2) to limit, segregate, or classify his employees or applicants for employment in any way which would deprive or tend to deprive any individual of employment opportunities or otherwise adversely affect his status as an employee, because of such individual's race, color, religion, sex, or national origin.[90]

Further, the Civil Rights Act incorporates the Equal Pay Act with the Bennett Act Amendment, which states:

> 703(h) Notwithstanding any other provision of this title, it shall be a lawful employment practice for an employer to apply different standards of compensation, or different terms, conditions, or privileges of employment pursuant to a bona fide seniority or merit system, or a system which measures earnings by quantity or quality of production or to employees who work different locations, provided that such are not the result of an intention to discriminate because of race, color, religion, sex, or national origin. It shall not be an unlawful employment practice under this title for any employer to differentiate upon the basis of sex in determining the amount of wages or compensation paid to employees of such employer if such differentiation is authorized by the provisions of Section 6(d) of the Fair Standards Act.[91]

Section 706(g) provides for adjudicative relief:

> 706(g) If the court finds that the respondent has intentionally engaged in or is intentionally engaging in an unlawful employment practice charged in the complaint, the court may enjoin the respondent from engaging in such unlawful employment practice, and order such affirmative action as may be appropriate, which may include, but is not limited to, reinstatement or hiring of employees, with or without back pay..., or any other equitable relief as the court deems

> appropriate....No order of the court shall require the admission or reinstatement of an individual as a member of a union, or the hiring, reinstatement, or promotion of an individual as an employee, or the payment to him of any back pay, if such individual was refused admission, suspended, or expelled, or was refused employment or advancement or was suspended or discharged for any reason other than discrimination on account of race, color, religion, sex, or national origin or in violation of section 704(a).[92]

Finally, Section 704(a) holds that it shall be an unlawful employment practice for an employer to discriminate against any of his employees or applicants for employment because he has made a charge, testified, assisted, or participated in any manner in an investigation, proceeding, or hearing under this title.[93]

The Civil Rights Act goes further than the Equal Pay Act by not requiring equal work. It is flexible enough to include all forms of pay discrimination, namely unequal pay for equal work, unequal pay for comparable worth, adverse impact involving a neutral but unequal impact, and disparate treatment involving an intent for a less favorable treatment. More cases today are brought under the Civil Rights Act, because it expands the availability of relief. Title VII prohibits sex discrimination allowing for compensation, thus recognizing equal pay as a legal right (American Federation of State, County and Municipal Employees v. Washington, 770 F.2d. 1401 (1985)).[94] The Civil Rights Act eliminates artificial, arbitrary and unnecessary barriers to employment in the form of invidious discrimination, unless there is a demonstrably reasonable measure of job performance (Griggs v. Duke Power, 401 U.S. 424, 429 (1971)).[95] According to Section 703(a) of the Civil Rights Act, persons of like qualifications must be given employment opportunities regardless of their gender (Phillips v. Martin Marietta, 400 U.S. 542 (1971)).[96] There cannot be different hiring practices for each sex. However, there can arguably be a basis for a distinction based on gender, since conflicting family obligations can be considered in the employment of a woman with school age children, if it is demonstrably more relevant to job performance.

For cases brought under the Civil Rights Act, the Plaintiff has the burden to show he belongs to a minority, has applied for a job and was qualified for the job that the employer tried, though qualified was rejected, and the employer continued to seek applicants with plaintiff's qualifications (McDonnell Douglas v. Green, 411 U.S. 792, 802 (1973)).[97] Then, in rebutting a prima facie case, the Defendant must articulate a legitimate non-discriminatory reason for the employee's rejection (McDonnell Douglas v. Green, 411 U.S. 792, 803 (1973), Board of Trustees of Can State College v. Sweeney, 439 U.S. 24 (1978)).[98] The Bennett Amendment does not restrict Title VII's prohibition of sex-based wage discrimination to claims for equal pay for 'equal work'. Rather, claims for sex-based wage discrimination can also be brought under Title VII even though no member of the opposite sex holds an equal but higher paying job, provided that the challenged wage rate is not exempted under the Equal Pay Act's affirmative defenses as to wage differentials attributable to seniority, merit, quantity or quality of production, or any other factor other than sex (County of Washington v. Gunther, 452 U.S. 161, 162 (1981)).[99]

The Civil Rights Act is often used to fight sex discrimination in compensation, with a differentiation made between disparate treatment and impact. Disparate treatment is concerned with direct or circumstantial discriminatory motives, which lack a well-defined criteria (Spaulding v. University of Washington, 740 F.2d. 686 (1984)).[100] It involves intent or motive as an essential element of liability concerning the effects of a chosen policy, with awareness alone of adverse consequences on a group not enough (American Federation of State, County and Municipal Employees v. Washington, 770 F.2d. 1401 (1985)).[101] In a disparate treatment approach, the Plaintiff in a prima facie case is required to show by a preponderance of the evidence the overt motive. In turn, the Defendant must prove that it was non-discriminatory either by the four exceptions, by necessity or by a bona fide occupational qualification. On the other hand, disparate impact is more than an inference of discriminatory impact of outwardly neutral employment practices and adversity (Spaulding v. University of Washington (740 F.2d. 686 (1984)).[102] It does not need a profession of intent by the employer to discriminate, only a clearly delineated employment practice (American Federation of State, County and Municipal Employees v. Washington, 770 F.2d. 1401 (1985)).[103] In a disparate impact approach, the Plaintiff need only show the disproportionate impact, thus the burden would then shift to the Defendant to show that it was non-discriminatory.

Under an affirmative action plan, the Supreme Court has found that the consideration of gender as to a female employee, as a factor in her promotion over an equally qualified employee of the male sex, does not violate the Civil Rights Act, if a moderate, gradual approach to eliminating the imbalance in the work force is taken, one which establishes realistic guidance for employment decisions, and which visits minimal intrusion on the legitimate expectations of other employees (Johnson v. Transportation Agency, 480 U.S. 616, 637 (1987)).[104] Therefore, in order to expand job opportunities, the sex of a qualified applicant can be considered, when promoting into a position within a traditionally underrepresented job sphere. However, it must be shown that there is an inconspicuous imbalance in these traditionally segregated job categories, and that there is no unnecessary trampling of the rights of male employees.

Women and the Burden of Proof in the United States

The concept of the burden of proof is an important element in court cases, especially those impacting gender. The court must choose among three levels of scrutiny in evaluating a case: rational basis, the lowest level, where the Plaintiff must show that there is no rational basis for the State restriction, which is a hard burden to meet; heightened scrutiny, the intermediary level, where the Defendant government must show that the restriction has a substantial relationship to an important government interest, which is used in gender cases; and strict scrutiny, the highest level, where the Defendant government must show a compelling interest for the restriction, a hard burden to meet which is used in such suspect cases as race.

Women have been discriminated against for centuries, often being put on a pedestal or being treated as inferior citizens. Because of the unresponsive rendering of rights through the rational basis test, the burden of proof, the lowest level, the heightened scrutiny test was developed to better protect women. However, today more than ever, there is a greater push to better recognize gender discrimination and to elevate it to the strict scrutiny test, the highest level of review. Just over a century ago, the Court distinguished between the sexes. In a demand by a woman to practice as an attorney, the Court, in Bradwell v. State, 16 Wall. 130 (1873), enunciated the roles of women in society, in distinguishing between womanhood and personhood.

> That God designed the sexes to occupy different spheres of action, and that it belonged to men to make, apply, and execute the laws, was regarded as an almost axiomatic truth....In view of these facts, we are certainly warranted in saying that when the legislature gave to this court the power of granting licenses to practice law, it was with not the slightest expectation that this privilege would be extended to women.[105]

In denying her claim, Mr. Justice Bradley stated:

> The civil law, as well as nature herself, has always recognized a wide difference in the respective spheres and destinies of man and woman. Man is, or should be, woman's protector and defender. The natural and proper timidity and delicacy which belongs to the female sex evidently unfits it for many of the occupations of civil life....The harmony, not to say the identity, of interests and views which belong, or should belong, to the family institution is repugnant to the idea of a woman adopting a distinct and independent career from that of her husband.[106]

The Court went on to state:

> The paramount destiny and mission of woman are to fulfil the noble and benign offices of wife and mother. This is the law of the Creator. And the rules of civil society must be adapted to the general constitution of things, and cannot be based upon exceptional cases.[107]

Hence, certain virtues were seen as prerogatives within the domain of a particular gender, and this way of thinking persisted for a long time with the help of the courts. The Court continued to hold that the 'Fourteenth Amendment did not tear history up by the roots; the fact that women may have achieved the virtues that men have long claimed as their prerogatives and now indulge in vices that men have long practiced, does not preclude the States from drawing a sharp line between the sexes, since the Constitution does not require legislatures to reflect sociological insight, or shifting social standards' Goesaert v. Cleary, 335 U.S. 464, 466 (1948).[108]

In using the rationality test, the least protective, the Court continued to see certain virtues as the prerogatives of the domain of men, even though it was recognized by the legal system that there had been many changes in the social position of women. In a case involving the denial of a woman's opportunity to serve the judicial system as a juror, the Court found that 'despite the enlightened emancipation of women from the restrictions and protections of bygone years, and their entry into many parts of community life formerly considered to be reserved to men, woman is still regarded as the center of home and family life' (Hoyt v. Florida, 368 U.S. 57, 62 (1961)).[109]

The lowest standard of scrutiny, the rationality test, finds that the State has a legitimate interest in regulating an activity within its jurisdiction. Under the rationality test, a Statute should be reviewed keeping in mind that: 1. The equal-protection clause of the 14th Amendment does not take from the state the power to classify in the adoption of police laws, but admits of the exercise of a wide scope of discretion in that regard, and avoids what is done only when it is without any reasonable basis, and therefore is purely arbitrary; 2. A classification having some reasonable basis does not offend against that clause merely because it is not made with mathematical nicety, or because in practice it results in some inequality; 3. When the classification in such a law is called in question, if any state of facts reasonably can be conceived that would sustain it, the existence of that state of facts at the time the law was enacted must be assumed; and 4. One who assails the classification in such a law must carry the burden of showing that it does not rest upon any reasonable basis, but is essentially arbitrary (Lindsley v. Natural Carbonic Gas Co., 220 U.S. 61, 78 (1911)).[110]

Thus, the Court pronounced that the governmental classification will not offend the Constitution's equal protection clause 'simply because it is not made with material nicety' (Dandridge v. William, 397 U.S. 471, 485 (1970)).[111] 'To be able to find fault with a law is not to demonstrate its invalidity. It may seem unjust and oppressive, yet be free from judicial interference....The problems of government are practical ones and may justify, if they do not require, rough accommodations, illogical, it may be, and unscientific.... What is best is not always discernible; the wisdom of any choice may be disputed or condemned. Mere errors of government are not subject to our judicial review. It is only its palpably arbitrary exercises which can be declared void under the 14th Amendment' (Metropolis Theatre Co. v. City of Chicago, 228 U.S. 61, 69 (1913)).[112] 'A statutory discrimination will not be set aside if any state of facts reasonably may be conceived to justify it', but it will fail if the unequal distinction 'rests on grounds wholly irrelevant to the achievement of the State's objective' (McGowan v. Maryland, 366 U.S. 420, 425 (1961)).[113] As such, this lowest standard was not adequate to meet the needs of women, and hence, gender discrimination persisted.

A different outlook of women was taken in the 1970s. Gender discrimination was not as readily upheld by the Court, unless it met the higher intermediate level, the heightened scrutiny test, which required the justification for limiting a right be substantially related to an important government objective. The first case in which the heightened scrutiny test was used was Reed v. Reed, 404 U.S. 71 (1971), in which a restriction based on gender was struck down.[114] Where a statutory scheme 'provides that different treatment be accorded . . . on the basis of . . . sex; it thus establishes a classification subject to scrutiny under the Equal Protection Clause. In applying that clause, this Court has consistently recognized that the Fourteenth Amendment does not deny to States the power to treat different classes of persons in different ways. The Equal Protection Clause of that amendment does, however, deny to States the power to legislate that different treatment be accorded to persons placed by a statute into different classes on the basis of criteria wholly unrelated to the objective of that statute' (Reed v. Reed, 404 U.S. 71, 76 (1971)).[115] A classification 'must be reasonable, not arbitrary, and must rest upon some ground of difference having a fair and substantial relation to the object of the legislation, so that all persons similarly circumstanced shall be treated alike' (F.S. Royster Guano Co. v. Com of Virginia, 253 U.S. 412, 415 (1920)).[116]

A mandatory preference solely on the basis of gender through an arbitrary legislative choice was forbidden. The Court stated that the classification must be reasonable not arbitrary, and must rest upon a ground which is fair and substantially related to the objective of the legislation. Even though the Court purported to apply 'any rational basis', the lowest standard, the language used in the judgment in Reed resulted in a more stringent standard for gender cases. It was an important case, which hinted at a special type of scrutiny, higher than the mere rational basis test. Further decisions drained the previous reasoning of Bradwell, Goesart and Hoyt. In contravention of Hoyt, the court in Taylor v. Louisiana, 419 U.S. 522 (1975), found that administrative convenience was not justified in excluding women from juries, dismissing the antiquated notion that society cannot spare any women from the home.[117] 'The thought is that the factors which tend to influence the action of women are the same as those which influence the action of men, personality, background, economic status, and not sex....The truth is that the two sexes are not fungible; a community made up exclusively of one is different from a community composed of both; the subtle interplay of influence one on the other is among the imponderables....Yet a flavor, a distinct quality is lost if either sex is excluded' (Ballard v. United States, 329 U.S. 187, 194 (1946)).[118]

Further, contrary to the principles enunciated in Bradwell, regarding the notion of age of majority of both sexes 'in the context of child support, the classification effectuated by the challenged statute denies the equal protection of the laws, as guaranteed by the Fourteenth Amendment. Notwithstanding the 'old notions' cited by the state court that it is the man's primary responsibility to provide a home, that it is salutary for him to have education and training before he assumes that responsibility, and that females tend to mature and marry earlier than males, there is nothing rational in the statutory distinction between males and females,...thus imposing criteria wholly unrelated to the objective of that statute' (Stanton v. Stanton, 421 U.S. 7, 17 (1975)).[119]

The seminal far reaching case of Craig v. Boren, 429 U.S. 190 (1976), was the first Supreme Court decision to officially recognize the heightened scrutiny test for gender.[120] It noted that Reed emphasized that statutory classifications which distinguish between males and females are subject to scrutiny under the Equal Protection Clause. Therefore, to withstand constitutional challenge, 'classifications by gender must serve important governmental objectives and must be substantially related to achievement of those objectives' Craig v. Boren, 429 U.S. 190, 197 (1976).[121] Craig further noted that Reed 'provided the underpinning for decisions that have invalidated statutes employing gender as an inaccurate proxy for other, more germane bases of classification. Hence, 'archaic and overbroad' generalizations could not justify use of a gender line in determining eligibility for certain governmental entitlements. Similarly, increasingly outdated misconceptions concerning the role of females in the home rather than in the 'marketplace and world of ideas' were rejected as loose-fitting characterizations incapable of supporting state statutory schemes that were premised upon their accuracy. In light of the weak congruence between gender and the characteristic or trait that gender purported to represent, it was necessary that the legislatures choose either to realign their substantive laws in a gender-neutral fashion, or to adopt procedures for identifying those instances where the sex-centered generalization actually comported with fact' (Craig v. Boren, 429 U.S. 190, 199 (1976)).[122]

It is important to understand that the intermediate level of scrutiny, used for gender discrimination cases, is a lower burden than the one used for fundamental rights or suspect classifications, which requires an overwhelming and compelling state interest to contravene a right. This higher burden, the strict scrutiny test, is used for racial and national origin classifications only. In Craig, the distinction on the basis of sex was found not to be invidious, in this case being against males who were not considered to be a discreet and insular minority, therefore an inoffensive legislative purpose. The minority opinion still rejected the notion of a higher standard beyond the rational basis test, holding that a more active review was reserved for discriminated members of discrete insular minorities, and women were not included in this. While invalidating a discriminatory statute, the Court, in a unanimous decision, further stressed that the party wishing to uphold a classification on the basis of gender must show 'an exceedingly persuasive justification' for it (Kirchberg v. Feenstra, 450 U.S. 455 (1981)).[123]

In the fight against gender discrimination, the court has sometimes moved beyond the concept of equality for women. The Supreme Court has recognized the concept of 'benign' discrimination, when one is being treated differently as a means for compensation for past and present injustices. The problem occurs when one is compensated and the other is denied compensation, and they were not parties to the original injustice. One of the first modern cases to deal with benign discrimination found that widows should be treated more favorably than widowers, since women have been negatively impacted by discrimination, with the Court finding that a state law is not arbitrary although it 'discriminate[s] in favor of a certain class . . . if the discrimination is founded upon a reasonable distinction, or difference in state policy', one of cushioning the financial impact of spousal loss upon the sex for which that loss imposes a disproportionately heavy burden (Kahn v. Shevin, 416 U.S. 351, 355 (1974)).[124] The Court made a distinction between gender and race, but allowed benign discrimination. To remedy past discrimination, the Court permitted the favoring of women by rejecting gender equality, finding that men had more of an opportunity in the past, in such matters as promotion in the military service and emphasizing the prior treatment in society toward the sexes (Schlesinger v. Ballard, 419 U.S. 498 (1975)).[125]

In the case of Orr v. Orr, 440 U.S. 268 (1979),[126] Justice Brennan had cautioned against classifications on the basis of sex, in that 'legislative classifications which distribute benefits and burdens on the basis of gender carry the inherent risk of reinforcing stereotypes about the proper place of women and their need for special protection. Thus, even statutes purportedly designed to compensate for and ameliorate the effects of past discrimination must be carefully tailored. Where...the State's compensatory and ameliorative purposes are as well served by a gender-neutral classification as one that gender classifies and therefore carries with it the baggage of sexual stereotypes, the State cannot be permitted to classify on the basis of sex. And this is doubly so where the choice made by the State appears to redound, if only indirectly, to the benefit of those without need for special solicitude' (Orr v. Orr, 440 U.S. 268, 283 (1979)).[127]

In the 1980s, more cases were decided which impaired the move toward equal citizens without distinction as to gender. Gender stereotyping was again evident when the Court upheld a Congressional exemption of women in the draft, dismissing the potential contribution of women (Rotsker v. Goldberg, 453 U.S. 57 (1981)).[128] Further, the Court upheld a discriminatory statutory rape law which was applied against males only, and did not preclude women as the 'fair sex' from engaging in the same conduct (Michael M v. Superior Court, 450 U.S. 464 (1981)).[129] This trend brought forth the idea, some would feel, that men do not need the protection of the courts and legislatures as much as women.

Importantly, equal rights advocates and women's groups have rallied to argue for the adoption of the highest standard of review, that of strict scrutiny to gender discrimination cases. It requires a precisely tailored objective to a compelling government interest, with no less drastic means available. It is used where there has been 'a history of purposeful unequal treatment...and a position of political powerlessness' (San Antonio Independent School Division v. Rodriguez, 411 U.S. 1, 16 (1973)).[130]

The closest that the United States Supreme Court has come to the strict scrutiny test for gender differentiations was in the important case of Frontiero v. Richardson, 411 U.S. 677 (1973). Judges Brennan, Douglas, White and Marshall decided that gender 'frequently bears no relation to ability to perform or contribute to society', so that statutory distinctions based on gender have invidious effects.[131] Under 'traditional' equal protection analysis, a legislative classification must be sustained unless it is 'patently arbitrary' and bears no rational relationship to a legitimate governmental interest. Therefore, the departure from 'traditional' rational-basis analysis with respect to sex-based classifications is clearly justified.

> There can be no doubt that our Nation has had a long and unfortunate history of sex discrimination. Traditionally, such discrimination was rationalized by an attitude of 'romantic paternalism' which, in practical effect, put women, not on a pedestal, but in a cage....As a result of notions such as these, our statute books gradually became laden with gross, stereotyped distinctions between the sexes and, indeed, throughout much of the 19th century the position of women in our

> society was, in many respects, comparable to that of blacks under the pre-Civil War slave codes. Neither slaves nor women could hold office, serve on juries, or bring suit in their own names, and married women traditionally were denied the legal capacity to hold or convey property or to serve as legal guardians of their own children. And although blacks were guaranteed the right to vote in 1870, women were denied even that right which is itself 'preservative of other basic civil and political rights' until adoption of the Nineteenth Amendment half a century later. It is true, of course, that the position of women in America has improved markedly in recent decades.[132]

Judges Brennan, Douglas, White and Marshall found that gender should be a suspect classification like race and national origin.

> Nevertheless, it can hardly be doubted that, in part because of the high visibility of the sex characteristic, women still face pervasive, although at times more subtle, discrimination in our educational institutions, in the job market and, perhaps most conspicuously, in the political arena. Moreover, since sex, like race and national origin, is an immutable characteristic determined solely by the accident of birth, the imposition of special disabilities upon the members of a particular sex because of their sex would seem to violate 'the basic concept of our system that legal burdens should bear some relationship to individual responsibility...[133].

Justice Brennan postulated the suspect nature of gender comparing it to race. Gender is to be considered as immutable, like race is, since one cannot change one's gender, and gender like race has historically been suspect to invidious discrimination, relegating an entire class to an inferior legal status without regard to actual individual capabilities. Members of both groups carry an obvious badge by sight, causing de jure discrimination not simply de facto discrimination.

> And what differentiates sex from such nonsuspect statuses as intelligence or physical disability, and aligns it with the recognized suspect criteria, is that the sex characteristic frequently bears no relation to ability to perform or contribute to society. As a result, statutory distinctions between the sexes often have the effect of invidiously relegating the entire class of females to inferior legal status without regard to the actual capabilities of its individual members....Congress itself has concluded that classifications based upon sex are inherently invidious, and this conclusion of a coequal branch of Government is not without significance to the question presently under consideration.[134]

Any statutory scheme which draws a sharp line between the sexes, solely for the purpose of achieving administrative convenience, necessarily commands 'dissimilar treatment for men and women who are...similarly situated', and therefore involves the 'very kind of arbitrary legislative choice forbidden by the Constitution'. Therefore, 'With these considerations in mind, we can only conclude that classifications based upon sex, like classifications based upon race, alienage, or national origin, are inherently suspect, and must therefore be subjected to strict judicial scrutiny.'[135]

Conclusion

In the fight for equal rights without regard to gender, it is true that women have achieved some gains, the biggest being the United States Supreme Court developing a higher standard of review of heightened scrutiny, which has stopped some discrimination. However, I would argue that gender, like race, should be considered suspect and thus be subject to the highest level of review, that of strict scrutiny. Laws and court judgments must stamp out gender discrimination. It is now time to give to women, who have long suffered through gender discrimination, full equality rights and the best possible protection of the law for true equality between the sexes. The importance of sensitivity to gender issues should be emphasized. Non-discriminatory equitable pay is a basic human right guaranteed to every employee by natural and positive law that must be respected and enforced in full.

Notes

1 Mandel, Michael, *The Charter of Rights and the Legalization of Politics in Canada*, Wall & Thompson, Toronto, 1989, p.4.

2 United Nations, *The World's Women 2000: Trends and Statistics*, 2000.

3 Statistics Canada, *Women in the Labour Force*, 1994, p.8.

4 Minister of Industry, *Canada Yearbook*, 1997.

5 *Supra* note 2.

6 *Supra* note 3, p.14.

7 *Ibid.*

8 Crompton, Susan and Geran, Leslie, *Women as Main Wage-Earners*, Perspectives, 1995.

9 *Ibid.*, at p.29.

10 Cohen, Gary L., *Women Entrepreneurs*, Perspectives, 1996.

11 *Ibid.*

12 Canadian Constitution.

13 Canadian Charter of Rights and Freedoms, Section 32.

14 Constitution Act, Section 52(1)

15 Canadian Charter of Rights and Freedoms, Section 15.

16 *Ibid.*, at Section 28.

17 *Ibid.*, at Section 33.

18 *Ibid.*, at Section 1.

19 Regina v. Oakes, [1986] 1 S.C.R. 103.

20 Canadian Human Rights Act.

21 *Ibid.*, at Section 2.

22 *Ibid.*, at Section 11.

23 *Ibid.*, at Section 15(1).

24 *Ibid.*, at Section 48(1).

25 Labour Canada, *Equal Pay for Work of Equal Value*, Ottawa, 1986, p.21.

26 Action Travail des Femmes v. Canadien National, 1984 CHRT.

27 Folch v. Canadian Airlines, 1992 CHRT.

28 *Supra* note 19.

29 Basi v. Canadian National Railway (1984), 9 C.H.R.R.4. D/5029, 5037 (C.H.R.Tribunal).
30 Shakes v. Rex Pak Ltd. (1982), 3 C.H.R.R. D/1001, 1002.
31 Blake v. Ministry of Correctional Services and Mimico Correctional Institute (1984), 5 C.H.R.R. D/2417 (Ontario).
32 Ontario Human Rights Commission v. Simpsons-Sears Ltd., [1985] S.C.R. 536, 547.
33 Canada Employment Equity Act, 1995, Article 2.
34 *Ibid.*, at Article 5.
35 *Ibid.*, at Article 6.
36 *Ibid.*, at Article 10.
37 *Ibid.*, at Article 29.
38 Constitución Política de los Estados Unidos Mexicanos.
39 *Ibid.*, at Article 1.
40 *Ibid.*, at Article 4.
41 *Ibid.*, at Article 123(7).
42 Ley Federal de Trabajo, Articles 3 and 164.
43 *Ibid.*, at Article 1.
44 *Ibid.*, at Article 2.
45 *Ibid.*, at Article 133(1).
46 *Ibid.*, at Article 86.
47 *Ibid.*, at Article 170.
48 *Ibid.*, at Article 166.
49 *Ibid.*, at Articles 50 and 52.
50 Ley del Seguro Social, Article 109.
51 *Ibid.*, at Article 36.
52 *Ibid.*, at Article 206.
53 *Ibid.*, at Article 212.
54 *Ibid.*, at Article 207.
55 United States Census Bureau, *Women in the United States*, 2000.
56 *Ibid.*
57 United States Census Bureau, *Statistical Abstract*, 1997.
58 *Supra* note 55.
59 *Ibid.*
60 *Supra* note 57.
61 *Supra* note 55.
62 *Supra* note 57.
63 *Supra* note 55.
64 *Ibid.*
65 *Supra* note 57.
66 *Supra* note 55.
67 Department of Justice, Equality & Law Reform, *Developing Sectoral Strategies to Address Gender Pay Gaps*, 2003.
68 Declaration of Independence.
69 Federalist Papers.
70 Coleman, Frank, *Hobbes and America*, University of Toronto, Toronto, 1977, p.3.
71 North, Arthur, *The Supreme Court, Judicial Process and Judicial Politics*, Appleton Century Crofts, New York, 1964, p.2.
72 McCullough v. Maryland, 4 Wheaton 415 (1819).
73 Marbury v. Madison, 1 Cranch 137 (1803).
74 *Supra* note 71, at p.8.

75 Cox, Archibald, *The Role of the Supreme Court in American Government*, Oxford University Press, New York, 1976, p.117.
76 Cox, Archibald, *Civil Rights, The Constitution and the Court*, Harvard University Press, Cambridge, 1967, p.21.
77 United States Constitution, Art. 6(2).
78 Magna Carta.
79 United States Constitution, 5th Amendment.
80 *Ibid.*, at 14th Amendment.
81 Ely, J., *Democracy and Distrust*, Harvard University Press, Cambridge, 1980, p.166.
82 Davis v. Passman, 442 U.S. 228 (1979).
83 Equal Pay Act.
84 *Ibid.*, at Section 16.
85 Brennan v. City Stores, 479 F.2d. 235 (1973).
86 Murphy v. Miller Brewer Co., 307 F.Supp. 829 (1969).
87 Corning Glass Works v. Brennan, 417 U.S. 188 (1974).
88 American Nurses' Association v. State of Illinois, 783 F.2d. 716 (1986).
89 Spaulding v. University of Washington, 740 F.2d. 686 (1984).
90 Civil Rights Act, Section 703(a).
91 *Ibid.*, at Section 703(h).
92 *Ibid.*, at Section 706(g).
93 *Ibid.*, at Section 704(a).
94 American Federation of State, County and Municipal Employees v. Washington, 770 F.2d. 1401 (1985).
95 Griggs v. Duke Power Co., 401 U.S. 424, 429 (1971).
96 Phillips v. Martin Marietta Corp., 400 U.S. 542 (1971).
97 McDonnell Douglas Corp. v. Green, 411 U.S. 792, 802 (1973).
98 McDonnell Douglas Corp. v. Green, 411 U.S. 792, 803 (1973), Board of Trustees v. Sweeney, 439 U.S. 24 (1978).
99 County of Washington v. Gunther, 452 U.S. 161, 162 (1981).
100 Spaulding v. University of Washington, 740 F.2d. 686 (1984).
101 American Federation of State, County and Municipal Employees v. Washington, 770 F.2d. 1401 (1985).
102 Spaulding v. University of Washington, 740 F.2d. 686 (1984).
103 American Federation of State, County and Municipal Employees v. Washington, 770 F.2d. 1401 (1985).
104 Johnson v. Transportation Agency, 480 U.S. 616 (1987).
105 Bradwell v. State, 16 Wall. 130 (1873).
106 Bradwell v. State, 16 Wall. 130 (1873).
107 Bradwell v. State, 16 Wall. 130 (1873).
108 Goesaert v. Cleary, 335 U.S. 464, 466 (1948).
109 Hoyt v. Florida, 368 U.S. 57, 62 (1961).
110 Lindsley v. Natural Carbonic Gas Co., 220 U.S. 61, 78 (1911).
111 Dandridge v. William, 397 U.S. 471, 485 (1970).
112 Metropolis Theatre Co. v. City of Chicago, 228 U.S. 61, 69 (1913).
113 McGowan v. Maryland, 366 U.S. 420, 425 (1961).
114 Reed v. Reed, 404 U.S. 71 (1971).
115 Reed v. Reed, 404 U.S. 71, 76 (1971).
116 F.S. Royster Guano Co. v. Com of Virginia, 253 U.S. 412, 415 (1920).
117 Taylor v. Louisiana, 419 U.S. 522 (1975).
118 Ballard v. United States, 329 U.S. 187, 194 (1946).
119 Stanton v. Stanton, 421 U.S. 7, 17 (1975).

120 Craig v. Boren, 429 U.S. 190 (1976).
121 Craig v. Boren, 429 U.S. 190, 197 (1976).
122 Craig v. Boren, 429 U.S. 190, 199 (1976).
123 Kirchberg v. Feenstra, 450 U.S. 455 (1981).
124 Kahn v. Shevin, 416 U.S. 351, 355 (1974).
125 Schlesinger v. Ballard, 419 U.S. 498 (1975).
126 Orr v. Orr, 440 U.S. 268 (1979).
127 Orr v. Orr, 440 U.S. 268, 283 (1979).
128 Rotsker v. Goldberg, 453 U.S. 57 (1981).
129 Michael M v. Sonoma County Superior Court, 450 U.S. 464 (1981).
130 San Antonio Independent School Division v. Rodriguez, 411 U.S. 1, 16 (1973).
131 Frontiero v. Richardson, 411 U.S. 677 (1973).
132 Frontiero v. Richardson, 411 U.S. 677, 686 (1973).
133 Frontiero v. Richardson, 411 U.S. 677, 687 (1973).
134 Frontiero v. Richardson, 411 U.S. 677, 688 (1973).
135 Frontiero v. Richardson, 411 U.S. 677 (1973).

References

Action Travail des Femmes v. Canadien National, 1984 CHRT.

American Federation of State, County and Municipal Employees v. Washington,770 F.2d. 1401 (1985).

American Nurses Association v. State of Illinois,783 F.2d. 716 (1985).

Andry, Jacqueline Hunt, 'The Supreme Court Tightens the Reins on Heightened Scrutiny', *Loyola Law Review*, Vol. 35, 1989, p.267.

Ballard v. United States, 329 U.S. 187 (1946).

Basi v. Canadian National Railway (1984), 9 C.H.R.R.4. D/5029 (C.H.R.Tribunal).

Blake v. Ministry of Correctional Services and Mimico Correctional Institute (1984), 5 C.H.R.R. D/2417 (Ontario).

Board of Trustees v. Sweeney, 439 U.S. 24 (1978).

Bradwell v. State, 16 Wall. 130 (1873).

Brennan v. City Stores, 479 F.2d. 235 (1973).

British North America Act, 1867.

Canada Employment Equity Act, 1995.

Canadian Bill of Rights, 1960.

Canadian Human Rights Act, 1978.

Canadian Charter of Rights and Freedoms, 1982.

Canadian Advisory Council on the Status of Women (1992), *Feminist Guide to the Canadian Constitution*, Ottawa.

Canadian Constitution, 1982.

Cohen, Gary L., *Women Entrepreneurs*, Perspectives, 1996.

Coleman, Frank (1977), *Hobbes and America*, University of Toronto, Toronto.

Constitución Política de los Estados Unidos Mexicanos.

Corning Glass Works v. Brennan, 417 U.S. 188 (1974).

County of Washington v. Gunther, 452 U.S. 161 (1981).

Cox, Archibald (1967), *Civil Rights, The Constitution and the Court*, Harvard University Press, Cambridge.

Cox, Archibald (1976), *The Role of the Supreme Court in American Government*, New York: Oxford University Press, New York.

Craig v. Boren, 429 U.S. 190 (1976).
Crompton, Susan and Geran, Leslie (1995), *Women as Main Wage-Earners*, Perspectives.
Dandridge v. William, 397 U.S. 471 (1970).
Davis v. Passman, 442 U.S. 228 (1979).
Department of Justice, Equality & Law Reform (2003), *Developing Sectoral Strategies to Address Gender Pay Gaps*.
Ely, J. (1980), *Democracy and Distrust*, Harvard University Press, Cambridge.
Federalist Papers, 1787-1788.
Folch v. Canadian Airlines, 1992 CHRT.
Frontiero v. Richardson, 411 U.S. 677 (1973).
F.S. Royster Guano Co. v. Com of Virginia, 253 U.S. 412 (1920).
Goesaert v. Cleary, 335 U.S. 464 (1948).
Griggs v. Duke Power Co., 401 U.S. 424 (1971).
Hoyt v. Florida, 368 U.S. 57 (1961).
Johnson v. Transportation Agency, 480 U.S. 616 (1987).
Kahn v. Shevin, 416 U.S. 351 (1974).
Kanowitz, Leo, 'Benign Sex Discrimination: Its Troubles and Their Cure', *Hastings Law Journal*, Vol. 31, 1980, p.1379.
Kirchberg v. Feenstra, 450 U.S. 455 (1981).
Klarman, Michael, 'Interpretive History of Equal Protection', *Michigan Law Review*, Vol. 90, 1991, p.213.
Kouba v. Allstate, 691 F.2d. 873 (1982).
Labour Canada (1986), *Equal Pay for Work of Equal Value*, Ottawa.
Ley del Seguro Social, Mexico.
Ley Federal de Trabajo, Mexico.
Lindsley v. Natural Carbonic Gas Co., 220 U.S. 61 (1911).
Loewy, Arnold, 'Returned to the Pedestal the Supreme Court and Gender Classification Cases: 1980 Term', *North Carolina Law Review*, Vol. 60, 1981, p.87.
Magna Carta, 1215.
Maltz, Earl, 'Legislative Inputs and Gender-Based Discrimination in the Burger Court', *Michigan Law Review*, Vol. 90, 1992, p.1023.
Mandel, Michael (1989), *The Charter of Rights and the Legalization of Politics in Canada*, Wall & Thompson, Toronto.
Marbury v. Madison, 1 Cranch 137 (1803).
McCullough v. Maryland, 4 Wheaton 415 (1819).
McDonnell Douglas Corp. v. Green, 411 U.S. 792 (1973).
McGowan v. Maryland, 366 U.S. 420 (1961).
Michael M v. Sonoma County Superior Court, 450 U.S. 464 (1981).
Metropolis Theatre Co. v. City of Chicago, 228 U.S. 61 (1913).
Mexican Investment Board (1994), *Mexico Your Partner for Growth, Regulatory Reform and Competition Policy, Setting the Incentives for an Efficient Economy*, Mexico.
Minister of Industry (1997), Canada Yearbook.
Murphy v. Miller Brewer Co., 307 F.Supp. 829 (1969).
North, Arthur (1964), *The Supreme Court, Judicial Process and Judicial Politics*, Appleton Century Crofts, New York.
Ontario Human Rights Commission v. Simpsons-Sears Ltd., [1985] S.C.R. 536.
Orr v. Orr, 440 U.S. 268 (1979).
Phillips v. Martin Marietta Corp., 400 U.S. 542 (1971).
Reed v. Reed, 404 U.S. 71 (1971).
Regina v. Oakes, [1986] 1 S.C.R. 103.
Rotsker v. Goldberg, 453 U.S. 57 (1981).

San Antonio Independent School Division v. Rodriguez, 411 U.S. 1 (1973).
Schlesinger v. Ballard, 419 U.S. 498 (1975).
Shakes v. Rex Pak Ltd. (1982), 3 C.H.R.R. D/1001.
Shultz v. Wheaton Glass, 421 F.2d. 259 (1970).
Spaulding v. University of Washington, 740 F.2d. 686 (1984).
Stanton v. Stanton, 421 U.S. 7 (1975).
Statistics Canada (1996), *Canada at a Glance.*
Statistics Canada (1994), *Women in the Labour Force.*
Taylor v. Louisiana, 419 U.S. 522 (1975).
United Nations (2000), *The World's Women 2000: Trends and Statistics.*
United States Census Bureau (1997), *Statistical Abstract.*
United States Census Bureau (2000), *Women in the United States.*
United States Civil Rights Act, 1964.
United States Constitution, 1776.
United States Declaration of Independence, 1776.
United States Equal Pay Act, 1963.
Washington v. Davis, 426 U.S. 229 (1976).

Chapter 7

Gender Injustice and the North American Free Trade Agreement

Introduction

This Chapter will examine Gender Injustice and the North American Free Trade Agreement (NAFTA), which was the largest economic and legal undertaking ever attempted, having an important impact on women and the labor force. It will look at the North American Free Trade Agreement from its inception, examining first its benefits and then its drawbacks, in general and in regard to women. It will also look at the North American Agreement on Labor Cooperation (NAALC) and the Free Trade Area of the Americas (FTAA).

Toward the North American Free Trade Agreement (NAFTA)

'Free trade' is an economic association, first brought about in North America in 1854. Prior to this, however, there were several developments in the relationship between the United States and British North America, what was to become Canada. The War of 1812 brought an end to the fear of American annexation of Canada, with rather a new view of commercial and economic rivalry between the two countries. The Canadian national sentiment favored trade with the United States through transportation via the railways and the waterways. With the industrial movement in the 1850s came the Grand Trunk, with an investment of $100 million in transportation and communication.[1] The construction of canals and railways were a move toward the avoidance of continental integration with the United States. The United States, with these developments, was not seen as the enemy but a concurrent competitor, with Canada furnishing natural resources. It was more economical for the United States to pass exports by Montreal through the St. Lawrence seaway in order to lower transportation costs. To assist them, the English, who controlled Canada at the time, would exempt the Americans from duties, treating them like Canadians. Among the market terminals of North America, Mississippi, the Hudson, New Orleans, New York and Montreal, the latter two were rivals, with New York prevailing. North American seaboard centers participated actively in the prosperity brought about by commercialism.

The first major trade pact between the United States and Canada was the Elgin-Marcy Reciprocity Treaty of 1854. Reciprocity was an attempt to create, in North America, a single market area covering several distinct political jurisdictions, where specified types of products were freely exchanged for a partial and limited economic union between British North America and the United States.[2] This was thought to be the only feasible alternative to annexation. However, the American Civil War influenced the economic development of British North America, with new markets in the United States opened for Canadian exports. At the end of the war, the removal of restraints on the expansion of American settlement west of the Mississippi jeopardized the security of the Canadian west and hastened Confederation.[3] However, the waterways were a uniting force. The businessmen from Upper Canada, what was to become the Canadian Province of Ontario, were the first to seize the idea of reciprocity. Nevertheless, immediate economic and political union with the United States would have sacrificed valued institutions, national identity and loyalty to Britain for Canada.

In the United States, the South with its plantations wanted low tariffs to lower prices of imported goods and to reduce the costs of production for exports of raw materials. On the other hand, the North, with its small farms and factories, was protectionist. There was little enthusiasm for reciprocity in the United States. It was seen as simply a concession for the inclusion of fisheries, the immediate and urgent objective. Thus, the Treaty was abrogated by the United States on March 17, 1866. British support for the Confederacy during the Civil War and new Canadian tariffs served to antagonize the United States.[4] Other factors played a role, namely the disastrous effects on timber and grain growing regions of the United States, the resentment by farming and lumber interests of Canadian competition, the jealousy by shipping and forwarding interests in Buffalo and Philadelphia of the St Lawrence Route and of the Grand Trunk with the Victoria Bridge completion in Montreal in 1860 furthering competition, and the manufacturing interests blaming Canadian tariffs for the decline of certain exports. All were a rallying cry for its end.

Canada's policy in economic relations was to favour east-west relations. However, the natural tendencies were the opposite, north-south. Shortly after the death of the Reciprocity Treaty until the advent of the 1911 'free trade' election in Canada, free trade with the United States had been the central issue in Canadian politics. Canadian Prime Minister Laurier was the first continentalist Prime Minister to appreciate that Canada shares North America with the United States, which shapes the national destiny. With the 1911 Free Trade Agreement, Canada built up its own manufacturing protection tariff. In 1911, there was the sentiment in Canada of 'no truck or trade with the Yankees'.[5] However, with the exception of Great Britain, Canada was the chief trading partner of the United States. In 1910 alone, Canada bought \$242 million and sold \$97 million to the United States.[6] American President Taft negotiated for full-scale reciprocity for better trade relations between the United States and Canada. Common interests called for special arrangements. Canadians and Americans were reminded that there were 3000 miles of joint border between the two countries.

The 1911 free trade agreement was similar to the 1854 pact, but was not a treaty, and thus did not require the two-thirds approval of the American Senate. Most American tariffs on manufacturing goods were reduced, while most Canadian manufacturing tariffs remained. It was passed by Congress and signed by American President Taft. However, Canadian Prime Minister Borden, who defeated Prime Minister Laurier in 1911, opposed the trade legislation and did not put the reciprocity agreement to a vote, with the United States rescinding its vote eight years later. Other agreements were entered into over the years, and Canada wished for trade on a liberalized basis, the first Article of the General Agreement on Tariffs and Trade (GATT), as well as same treatment. GATT provided for an impressive reduction of tariffs, with some having impeded economic efficiency, production, competition and growth. GATT, through Article 24, permitted the United States and Canada to enter into free trade, with an agreement to remove customs duties and other restrictions on substantially all bilateral trade.[7] Over the last years of GATT and the World Trade Organization (WTO), Canadian exports have multiplied ten times, the national wealth has more than tripled and the number of jobs has doubled.[8] On the other hand, unemployment has also risen over this period, which raises important questions about the benefits of free trade.

Wartime demands required greater cooperation on a continental basis, with Canada and Mexico being prime sources of raw materials for American factories. In 1947, American President Truman and Canadian Prime Minister King had private negotiations on free trade once again, in an era of the Marshall Plan, and of American economic assistance to Western Europe and Japan. King approved the agreement in October 1947, but it was later vetoed in May 1948, because he feared the Canadian public would label it continentalist and anti-British.[9] Overall, by examining the years leading to the advent of the Free Trade Agreement of the 1980s, we can observe a number of characteristics of the trade relationship between the two countries: 1. Canada has been the initiator in free trade on almost all the occasions; 2. The United States has been largely indifferent except for President Taft in 1911; 3. In the two most important negotiations of the 20th century, 1911 and 1947, Canada had second thoughts and put an end to the agreement; 4. The United States is a formidable obstacle to closer economic ties between the two nations; 5. The 1911 and 1947 deals provided for more American concessions; 6. Statements made by the United States were cannon fodder for groups in Canada which were opposed to annexation; 7. Canadian opponents that find economic costs to free trade outweigh economic benefits, and they react on an emotional, loyal, national, love of country level, branding those in favor as stooges of American financial interests; 8. While there is more emphasis today on business, commercial and economic issues, Canada on the other hand has cultural, regional economic development, social welfare and sovereignty concerns; and 9. When times are tough, Canada wants improved access to United States' markets while the United States turns inward toward protectionism.[10]

There is a regional aspect to the overall economic evolution of the North American continent. Canada's industrial development has been North American, with its development based on its natural resources, and its expansion characterized by large-scale monopolistic industries. Over time, Canada's dealings with Britain and the United States changed. Canada once had an autonomous relationship with Britain, producing an unAmerican sentiment. Great Britain was once the major investor in Canada. However, over the years, the United States has replaced it. Canada went from dependence on the British to dependence on the Americans, with its foreign controlled economy. In addition, the nature of foreign investment had changed, since the British invested indirectly through obligations and finance, while Americans invested directly, usually as proprietors funding production. Tariffs and natural resources attracted American enterprises, and Canada benefited from their capital, technological advancement and mass production. The United States invested $168 billion in 1900 and $881 billion in 1914. The Canadian policy was to increase tariffs and oblige American companies wishing to do business to build factories in Canada. The United States penetrated the Canadian economy by installing branch plants for American made products. By 1932, the United States had dominated the industrial sector, accounting for 82 per cent of car production, 68 per cent of electricity, one third of pulp and paper, and was solidly ahead in petroleum, pharmaceuticals, rubber, machinery and non metallic minerals. Of the American enterprises in Canada, 36 per cent of them were established in the period between 1920 to 1929. Today, Canada sends more than three-quarters of all its exports to the United States, accounting for 25 per cent of its annual gross national product.[11]

American policies are destined to affect the policies of Canada and North America as a whole. Canada is carried into the whirlpool of common points of view, to the advantage of the United States, and its own point of view is easily overwhelmed. It is important to understand the way the biases of information would be used to control what individuals do and think. Approaches should be adopted by which cultural traits of civilization might persist, with the least possible depreciation of the national sensibility and dependence of Canadians upon Americans. Canada's trade pattern from the outset was based on the importing of manufactured goods in return for the exporting of staples. This staple approach views staple exports to more advanced industrialized economies as the engine of growth of the Canadian economy.[12] The commercial rather than industrial bias of the Canadian capitalist class, along with dependent branch plant industrialization flowed from the unequal alliance with American foreign ownership and capital.

This policy process resulted in the overwhelming trade dependence of Canada on the United States over the years. Canada was within the tight embrace of the American empire, and occupied whatever room was left open by American capital. It became the exemplary client State. Today, the United States makes up 70 per cent of Canada's total exports. At the same time, Canada takes in over 20 per cent of United States' exports, and has a direct investment of roughly $20 billion.[13] It is not a zero sum gain with one benefiting at the expense of the other. Canada's prosperity depends on trade with other countries, with one third of its jobs and one quarter of its wealth tied to international trade.[14] From the outset, Canada was torn between republicanism and conservatism, trying to forge a national identity. Canada has wished to be more independent in its foreign policy. At the same time, it has had to guard against the departure of Canadian firms going south in search of cheaper labor and less regulation.

Free trade continentalism, according to its advocates, involves 1. Tariff liberalization; 2. A high volume of trade with the United States; 3. Meagre diversification; 4. Some protectionism by the United States; 5. Restructuration of the Canadian economy for a more competitive industrial society; and 6. Transborder transregionalism between provinces and states. Continentalism is a process of microregional (subcontinental) integration, which is transnational (multinational corporations, unions, economic elites) and transgovernmental (direct contacts between two central bureaucracies, relations between provinces and states), with closer Canada-United States transactional ties (diplomatic, administrative, commercial, cultural) and structural interpenetration (economic).[15] Canada and the United States are similar as societies with transnational and transgovernmental relationships, attitudes and values, strong social factors and a deep rooted structural economic interpenetration, in a widespread integration pattern. Canada is strategically situated, with its border close to American development centers.

The free trade zone has eliminated trade barriers as to goods. However, the movement of capital in production has caused negative integration generating disturbances and distortions in the economy. This occurs especially if there is asymmetry within the society, causing imbalances, both regionally and between partners in interactions. The freeing of circulation of goods creates initial imbalances and economic distortions. Before World War II, Canada's prosperity depended on resource industries, which required a high cost in order to protect the manufacturing sector serving the home market. However, in the 1980s, the prosperity of resource based industries was seriously hurt by international development in the areas of new sources of supply and man-made substitutes for natural materials.[16] Export and service-related products depended on hard pressed resource-based industries. This created uncertainties in business and job dislocations.[17] However, free trade advocates argued that it was important to secure continued access to the United States' market and to work against protectionism, for benefits to producers in sales and to consumers in prices.[18]

Greater specialization in North America brings greater international competition, encouraging more rapid diffusion of new technology, new management and organizational production. Textile and clothing industries were vulnerable in trade liberalization. The clothing industry would be hard pressed in lowering prices, except for high volume segments that are successful when moving into particular niches for export. Canada has specialized and expanded its primary and manufacturing sectors, which the proponents of free trade argue has afforded a net benefit through access to the vital American market that is less restrictive and more secure today. The tertiary service industries are more sharply differentiated among countries by the varied regulatory environments. In the goods producing industry, tariffs or quotas have been the main barrier. The service industry has subtle impediments, with discrimination being a barrier because of immigration labor laws. National treatment calls for no regulatory distinction between foreign and domestic firms, which is good if there are similar industries for reciprocity and market access.[19] These laws restrict one country's firms transferring staff to the other country. Trade in services encompasses a large number of areas, having different characteristics of trade and efforts for international rule-making.

Considering these factors, sectoral trade discussions in 1983 later gave way to a comprehensive free trade approach in 1985. American President Reagan and Canadian Prime Minister Mulroney launched an initiative for a bilateral trade agreement, with its goal to remove all or most remaining barriers to cross border trade in goods and services, and to create an enlarged body of agreed rules to govern trade, which produced the 1989 Canada-United States Free Trade Agreement (FTA). President Reagan called this Free Trade Agreement, signed on January 2, 1988, the most important bilateral trade negotiation ever undertaken by the United States. It was horizontal not sectoral for market access, and called for mutual restraint on unilateral commercial policies. It was believed that there would be a direct link between productivity and jobs, with higher productivity and additional spending power leading to higher incomes and more jobs.[20] Free trade is thought to afford a longer cycle of production, investment and specialization. This Free Trade Agreement was the biggest trade agreement ever reached between two countries, in excess of $200 billion in trade of goods and services.[21]

Canada exports more per citizen than any counterpart in any other industrial power. Thirty per cent of its national income is generated by exports, and more than three million jobs depend on these exports. The United States absorbs 80 per cent of Canada's exports, in a southward flow.[22] The Canada-United States Free Trade Agreement involved a trading relationship, which was the world's largest at the time, before the North American Free Trade Agreement. The United States has an economy ten times bigger than Canada's, affording the latter greater access to opportunities. The relationship encourages lower cost production in factories, and more specialized and efficient industries, thereby strengthening the capacity to compete in the global market. The goal is to generate growth and production, in order to increase the standard of living for challenging and rewarding careers.

The benefits of free trade, according to its advocates, are: 1. Increased specialization; 2. Rationalization, eliminating some production and expanding in others while introducing new production techniques; 3. Longer production runs in larger specialized plants; and 4. Easier transfer of technology. The costs of free trade are 1. Transition; and 2. Harmonization requirements.[23] Rationalization entails: 1. A reduction in the number of manufacturing plants; 2. An increase in production runs; 3. An increase in trade between the United States and Canada; and 4. A reduction in production costs.[24] Those in favor of the North American Free Trade Agreement argue that free trade improves efficiency and competition, stimulates production and economic growth, and opens new opportunities, supplementing and broadening GATT.[25] The United States, thereby, consolidates access to the biggest export market.

The North American Free Trade Agreement (NAFTA)

In June 1991, Canada, the United States and Mexico began negotiations in earnest for the North American Free Trade Agreement (NAFTA). The free trade agenda shifted from a sectoral approach to a comprehensive accord between the United States, Canada and Mexico, because of a difficulty in matching sectors and in accommodating regional concerns. The 1989 Canada-United States Free Trade Agreement laid the foundation for the North American Free Trade Agreement, which secured Canada's economic relationship with the United States.

The Preamble of the North American Free Trade Agreement states that the Government of Canada, the Government of the United Mexican States and the Government of the United States of America, have agreed to NAFTA, resolved to:

> STRENGTHEN the special bonds of friendship and cooperation among their nations;
> CONTRIBUTE to the harmonious development and expansion of world trade and provide a catalyst to broader international cooperation;
> CREATE an expanded and secure market for the goods and services produced in their territories;
> REDUCE distortions to trade;
> ESTABLISH clear and mutually advantageous rules governing their trade;
> ENSURE a predictable commercial framework for business planning and investment;
> BUILD on their respective rights and obligations under the General Agreement on Tariffs and Trade and other multilateral and bilateral instruments of cooperation;
> ENHANCE the competitiveness of their firms in global markets;
> FOSTER creativity and innovation, and promote trade in goods and services that are the subject of intellectual property rights;
> CREATE new employment opportunities and improve working conditions and living standards in their respective territories;
> UNDERTAKE each of the preceding in a manner consistent with environmental protection and conservation;
> PRESERVE their flexibility to safeguard the public welfare;
> PROMOTE sustainable development;
> STRENGTHEN the development and enforcement of environmental laws and regulations; and
> PROTECT, enhance and enforce basic workers' rights.[26]

Prior to NAFTA coming into effect on January 1, 1994, trade between the United States and Canada had never been larger and was growing faster than the rest of the economy. As well, the flow of trade and investment among the United States, Canada and Mexico was $500 billion per year. Mexico has a rapidly growing market of over 85 million people, which historically was hard to penetrate because of strict Mexican barriers to trade. Before NAFTA, Mexico was restrictive on foreign investment. However, with NAFTA, Mexican tariffs are phased out over time. Mexico's border is aligned with the United States and its coastline faces Europe and Asia. It has a key global strategic advantage with its unique geographic position, and is considered the gateway to Latin America, being ranked 12th in area among the world's nations.[27] Regulations give legal security to market transactions, protect consumers and the environment, and safeguard intellectual property rights. Free trade promotes competition and provides adequate incentives for private decision-making in a free market. However, the regulatory environment must ensure the rules of the game are clear and uniformly applied, subject to monitoring.

The North American Free Trade Agreement was the biggest trade agreement ever reached. It covers 360 million consumers and is far-reaching, removing all tariffs and liberalizing non-tariff barriers to trade. NAFTA regulates trade in services, liberalizes investment, promotes specialization, and implements a mechanism for a binding resolution to disputes, which is unprecedented in free trade. The objectives of the North American Free Trade Agreement are the removal of tariff and non-tariff barriers for goods and services, the neutralization of government policies, practices and procedures, and a consistency with the GATT agreement to cover all trade.[28] The long-term goals of free trade are the improvement of real income wages and production, an increase in the number of jobs, a reduction of protectionism, a decrease in competitive pressures from developing and newly industrialized countries, and the mitigation of pressures due to global imbalances.[29]

The United States had several objectives of its own, namely the elimination of tariffs, the reduction of non-tariff barriers, the development of rules governing trade in services, trucking and insurance, the improvement of protection to intellectual property, greater discipline over subsidies, and an open and secure environment for foreign investment. Canada, for its part, had several goals, as well, namely the improved access to the United States and Mexico for goods and services, the strengthening of the initial Canada-United States Free Trade Agreement, and the guarantee of its position as a prime location for investors to serve all the North American Continent. Canada hopes that NAFTA will supply it with a sharper edge for international competitiveness, by widening trade horizons and providing a bigger stage on which to demonstrate and prove its economic expertise and leadership.

NAFTA provided that tariffs would be removed within 10 years in the traditional sectors, accounting for half of the trade, and removed either immediately, in five or exceptionally in twenty years for the remainder. It moves toward a harmonized system of tariff nomenclature. It has quantitative restrictions, which build on GATT, and has a sectoral perspective as to agriculture, foods, automotives and energy. There are new elements to the agreement, which include the restriction of investment, the freedom in the future to regulate in conformity with the basic principles of non-discrimination, and the principles of national treatment, right of establishment and right of commercial presence. NAFTA sets out strict rules of origin, requiring that products originate in North America to qualify for preferential duties. For those not meeting this, larger quotas for preferential access to the American market have been included, with these new levels helping textile and apparel manufacturers expand their exports of products to the lucrative American market. Canadian and Mexican tariffs on apparel were eliminated within 10 years, and tariffs on textiles within eight years. Mexico has concentrated on less expensive lower quality items, while Canada is moving toward higher value textiles and quality designer fashions. So too, the financial industry was first included in the Canadian-United States Free Trade Agreement. It believed that freer market access for financial services would help trade flow more easily. The United States agreed to national treatment, market access and most favored nation status being applied to financial services, fully subjecting the sector to dispute settlement.

The NAFTA Secretariat, comprised of the Canadian, American and Mexican Sections, is an organization, established by the Free Trade Commission, pursuant to Article 2002, Chapter 20 of the North American Free Trade Agreement. It is responsible for the administration of the dispute settlement provisions of the Agreement, and its mandate includes the provision of assistance to the Commission, and support for various non-dispute related committees and working groups. Each national Section maintains a court-like registry relating to panel, committee and tribunal proceedings. A similar administrative body, the Binational Secretariat, existed under the Canada-United States Free Trade Agreement (FTA). The Parties have established permanent, national Section offices, which are 'mirror-images' of one another, and are located in Ottawa, Washington and Mexico City.

The principle dispute settlement mechanisms of NAFTA are found in Chapters 11, 14, 19 and 20 of the Agreement. NAFTA establishes a mechanism for the settlement of disputes that assures both equal treatment among Parties in accordance with the principle of international reciprocity and due process before an impartial tribunal. Alternatively, the investor may choose the remedies available in the host country's domestic courts. An important feature of the arbitral provisions is the enforceability in domestic courts of final awards by arbitration tribunals.

An important role of the Commission is to consider matters relating to the Agreement which are under dispute. NAFTA provides for a trade commission in charge of political management, which includes a dispute settlement mechanism in the form of a panel. When general disputes concerning NAFTA are not resolved through consultation within a specified period of time, the matter may be referred at the request of either Party to a non-binding panel under Article 2008. Various third Party provisions are necessarily included in Chapter 20, as a third Party that considers it has a substantial interest in a disputed matter is entitled to join consultations or a proceeding as a complaining Party on written notice. If a third Party does not join as a complainant, upon written notice, it is entitled to attend hearings, make written and oral submissions and receive written submissions of the disputing Parties. Chapter 20 also provides for an advisory committee to be established to provide recommendations to the Commission on the use of arbitration and other procedures for the resolution of international private commercial disputes.

If nothing results from the notification of a consultation action, then a panel review ensues with recommendations that are binding if both sides agree. The dispute settlement is also binding when one side believes that a surge of imports is damaging to it, thereby receiving compensation while the other side is snapped back to a most favored nation tariff. This procedure was in effect for the first ten years of the agreement, providing steps for negotiation, legislation specificity and panel review. The settlement mechanism calls for compulsory consultation on changes of law, and an evaluation procedure by a panel, with the right to retaliate or withdraw if the panel so favors. NAFTA also provides, for the first time, a system of settling private investment disputes. Disputes between an investor from a NAFTA country and another NAFTA government can be settled at the investor's option by binding international arbitration, with all investors treated equally. The NAFTA dispute settlement provisions call for the rapid and fair settlement of disputes, including the use of impartial panels. There are three basic steps to the process, namely consultation among the three countries for a satisfactory settlement. If the first round fails, the NAFTA trade commission, which is comprised of cabinet level representatives, will examine the case for interpretation of trade rules; and if this fails, in order to promote an impartial decision, the issue will be reviewed by a specially selected panel. This panel is composed of five members chosen from a trilaterally agreed roster, with two panellists from the complaining party selected by the defending party, two from the defending party nominated by the complainant and the panel's chair allowed to be a representative from the third NAFTA country or another neutral country chosen by mutual agreement or drawn by lot.

NAFTA has the first international code of binding rules and principles for services. The elimination of tariffs is important for a reduction of protectionism and a climate of open investment. Further, there is a provision for access for temporary personnel in the service and manufacturing sectors, and business recognition of professional and sales services in the spirit of freedom of movement. This latter aspect, however, has not yet been extended to blue collar workers. NAFTA obliges one country's service providers to treat the other country's no less favorably than their own for domestic and cross border sales, distribution, and the right of establishment of facilities, providing for mutually acceptable professional licensing standards. However, this equal employment provision in the Member States must go further to protect against any form of discrimination, including gender.

Cross border trade in services was first included in the Canada-United States Free Trade Agreement, and NAFTA has extended these provisions with procedures to encourage the recognition of licenses and certificates through mutually acceptable professional standards and criteria, such as education, experience and professional development. It opens up temporary entry across the border for over 60 professions. Canada's service industry is the fastest growing sector of the economy, accounting for the employment of roughly ten million Canadians, two thirds of the workforce. The service sector has provided 90 per cent of all new jobs in Canada in the last several years. More Canadians now work in software than in the auto industry. Canada's export of services around the world totals an average of $24 billion per year, with business and professional services accounting for 20 per cent of these exports.

While the Canada-United States Free Trade Agreement established the first comprehensive set of principles governing services trade, NAFTA broadens these protections and extends them to Mexico. Virtually all services are covered by NAFTA, with key sectors being: Accounting, Architecture, Land Transport, Publishing, Consulting, Commercial Education, Environmental Services, Enhanced Telecommunications, Advertising, Broadcasting, Construction, Tourism, Engineering, Health Care, Management, and Legal Services. Each country has also excluded certain sensitive sectors from coverage, such that Mexico will not liberalize services of public notaries, which are specifically reserved to Mexicans by the Mexican Constitution, and Canada has retained its cultural exclusion, which affects the entertainment and publishing industries. NAFTA does not remove or weaken licensing and certification requirements, but consistent with the NAFTA principle of non-discrimination, licensing of professionals, such as lawyers, doctors, and accountants, should be based on objective criteria aimed at ensuring competence, not on nationality. NAFTA does not permit American, Mexican or Canadian professionals to practice in the other Member countries, unless they have undergone the same licensing and certification procedures as a National professional.

Specifically, under the agreement, in terms of service providers, Article 1201 applies to measures adopted or maintained by a Party relating to cross-border trade in services by service providers of another Party, including measures respecting the production, distribution, marketing, sale and delivery of a service; the purchase or use of, or payment for, a service; the access to and use of distribution and transportation systems in connection with the provision of a service; the presence in its territory of a service provider of another Party; and the provision of a bond or other form of financial security as a condition for the provision of a service.[30]

In terms of national treatment and most-favored nation treatment, Articles 1202 and 1203 respectively provide that each Party shall accord to service providers of another Party treatment no less favorable than that it accords, in like circumstances, to service providers of any other Party or of a non-Party.[31] Further, Article 1208 maintains that each Party shall set out in its Schedule to Annex VI its commitments to liberalize quantitative restrictions, licensing requirements, performance requirements or other non-discriminatory measures.[32]

Importantly, Article 1210 provides for Licensing and Certification requirements:

> 1210.1. With a view to ensuring that any measure adopted or maintained by a Party relating to the licensing or certification of nationals of another Party does not constitute an unnecessary barrier to trade, each Party shall endeavor to ensure that any such measure:
> (a) is based on objective and transparent criteria, such as competence and the ability to provide a service;
> (b) is not more burdensome than necessary to ensure the quality of a service; and
> (c) does not constitute a disguised restriction on the cross-border provision of a service.
> 2. Where a Party recognizes, unilaterally or by agreement, education, experience, licenses or certifications obtained in the territory of another Party or of a non-Party:
> (a) nothing in Article 1203 shall be construed to require the Party to accord such recognition to education, experience, licenses or certifications obtained in the territory of another Party; and
> (b) the Party shall afford another Party an adequate opportunity to demonstrate that education, experience, licenses or certifications obtained in that other Party's territory should also be recognized or to conclude an agreement or arrangement of comparable effect.
> 3. Each Party shall...eliminate any citizenship or permanent residency requirement...that it maintains for the licensing or certification of professional service providers of another Party....[33]

Professional services are defined in Article 1213 to mean services, the provision of which requires specialized post-secondary education, or equivalent training or experience, and for which the right to practice is granted or restricted by a Party, but does not include services provided by trades-persons or vessel and aircraft crew members.[34]

Annex 1210.5.A.2 regarding Professional Services holds that the Parties shall encourage the relevant bodies in their respective territories to develop mutually acceptable standards and criteria for licensing and certification of professional service providers, providing recommendations on mutual recognition to the Commission with regard to the following matters:

> Annex 1210.5.A.3.
> (a) education accreditation of schools or academic programs;
> (b) examinations qualifying examinations for licensing, including alternative methods of assessment such as oral examinations and interviews;
> (c) experience length and nature of experience required for licensing;
> (d) conduct and ethics standards of professional conduct and the nature of disciplinary action for non-conformity with those standards;
> (e) professional development and re-certification continuing education and ongoing requirements to maintain professional certification;
> (f) scope of practice extent of, or limitations on, permissible activities;
> (g) local knowledge requirements for knowledge of such matters as local laws, regulations, language, geography or climate; and
> (h) consumer protection alternatives to residency requirements, including bonding, professional liability insurance and client restitution funds, to provide for the protection of consumers.[35]

Further, Annex 1210.5.B.1 provides that each Party shall, in implementing its obligations and commitments regarding foreign legal consultants as set out in its relevant Schedules and subject to any reservations therein, ensure that a national of another Party is permitted to practice or advise on the law of any country in which that national is authorized to practice as a lawyer.[36]

In terms of Business visitors, Annex 1603.A.1 stipulates:

> Annex 1603.A.1. Each Party shall grant temporary entry to a business person seeking to engage in a business activity..., without requiring that person to obtain an employment authorization, provided that the business person otherwise complies with existing immigration measures applicable to temporary entry, on presentation of:
> (a) proof of citizenship of a Party;
> (b) documentation demonstrating that the business person will be so engaged and describing the purpose of entry; and
> (c) evidence demonstrating that the proposed business activity is international in scope and that the business person is not seeking to enter the local labor market.[37]

Further, in terms of traders and investors, Annex 1603.B.1 provides:

Annex 1603.B.1. Each Party shall grant temporary entry and provide confirming documentation to a business person seeking to:
(a) carry on substantial trade in goods or services principally between the territory of the Party of which the business person is a citizen and the territory of the Party into which entry is sought, or
(b) establish, develop, administer or provide advice or key technical services to the operation of an investment to which the business person or the business person's enterprise has committed, or is in the process of committing, a substantial amount of capital, in a capacity that is supervisory, executive or involves essential skills, provided that the business person otherwise complies with existing immigration measures applicable to temporary entry.[38]

In terms of Intra-Company Transferees, Annex 1603.C.1 holds:

1603.C.1. Each Party shall grant temporary entry and provide confirming documentation to a business person employed by an enterprise who seeks to render services to that enterprise or a subsidiary or affiliate thereof, in a capacity that is managerial, executive or involves specialized knowledge, provided that the business person otherwise complies with existing immigration measures applicable to temporary entry. A Party may require the business person to have been employed continuously by the enterprise for one year within the three-year period immediately preceding the date of the application for admission.[39]

Finally, in terms of Professionals, Annex 1603.D.1 provides:

1603.D.1. Each Party shall grant temporary entry and provide confirming documentation to a business person seeking to engage in a business activity at a professional level in a profession..., if the business person otherwise complies with existing immigration measures applicable to temporary entry, on presentation of:
(a) proof of citizenship of a Party; and
(b) documentation demonstrating that the business person will be so engaged and describing the purpose of entry.[40]

In terms of Dispute Settlements, Article 1606.1 provides:

1606.1. A Party may not initiate proceedings...regarding a refusal to grant temporary entry under this Chapter...unless:
(a) the matter involves a pattern of practice; and
(b) the business person has exhausted available administrative remedies regarding the particular matter, provided that such remedies shall be deemed to be exhausted if a final determination in the matter has not been issued by the competent authority within one year of the institution of an administrative proceeding, and the failure to issue a determination is not attributable to delay caused by the business person.[41]

The North American Agreement on Labor Cooperation (NAALC)

The North American Agreement on Labor Cooperation (NAALC), a side agreement to NAFTA, promotes the enforcement of national labor laws and transparency in their administration. Through the North American Agreement on Labor Cooperation (NAALC) the NAFTA partners seek to improve working conditions and living standards, and commit themselves to promoting principles that protect, enhance and enforce basic workers' rights. To accomplish these goals, the NAALC creates mechanisms for cooperative activities and intergovernmental consultations, as well as for independent evaluations and dispute settlement related to the enforcement of labor laws. Public submissions made under the NAALC have led to public hearings, ministerial consultations, and action plans to address concerns raised. In addition, NAFTA partners have established cooperative programs and technical exchanges on industrial relations, health and safety, child labor, gender equity and migrant worker issues.

The Preamble to the North American Agreement on Labor Cooperation (NAALC) states that the Government of the United States of America, the Government of Canada and the Government of the United Mexican States undertake the agreement:

> RECALLING their resolve in the North American Free Trade Agreement (NAFTA) to:
> create an expanded and secure market for the goods and services produced in their territories,
> enhance the competitiveness of their firms in global markets,
> create new employment opportunities and improve working conditions and living standards in their respective territories, and
> protect, enhance and enforce basic workers' rights;
>
> AFFIRMING their continuing respect for each Party's constitution and law;
>
> DESIRING to build on their respective international commitments and to strengthen their cooperation on labor matters;
>
> RECOGNIZING that their mutual prosperity depends on the promotion of competition based on innovation and rising levels of productivity and quality;
>
> SEEKING to complement the economic opportunities created by the NAFTA with the human resource development, labor-management cooperation and continuous learning that characterize high-productivity economies;
>
> ACKNOWLEDGING that protecting basic workers' rights will encourage firms to adopt high-productivity competitive strategies;
>
> RESOLVED to promote, in accordance with their respective laws, high-skill, high-productivity economic development in North America by:
> investing in continuous human resource development, including for entry into the workforce and during periods of unemployment;

promoting employment security and career opportunities for all workers through referral and other employment services;
strengthening labor-management cooperation to promote greater dialogue between worker organizations and employers and to foster creativity and productivity in the workplace;
promoting higher living standards as productivity increases;
encouraging consultation and dialogue between labor, business and government both in each country and in North America;
fostering investment with due regard for the importance of labor laws and principles;
encouraging employers and employees in each country to comply with labor laws and to work together in maintaining a progressive, fair, safe and healthy working environment;

BUILDING on existing institutions and mechanisms in Canada, Mexico and the United States to achieve the preceding economic and social goals; and

CONVINCED of the benefits to be gained from further cooperation between them on labor matters.[42]

The objectives of the agreement are outlined in Article 1:

1(a) improve working conditions and living standards in each Party's territory;
(b) promote, to the maximum extent possible, the labor principles set out in Annex 1;
(c) encourage cooperation to promote innovation and rising levels of productivity and quality;
(d) encourage publication and exchange of information, data development and coordination, and joint studies to enhance mutually beneficial understanding of the laws and institutions governing labor in each Party's territory;
(e) pursue cooperative labor-related activities on the basis of mutual benefit;
(f) promote compliance with, and effective enforcement by each Party of, its labor law; and
(g) foster transparency in the administration of labor law.[43]

The Preamble to NAALC reaffirms relevant provisions of the NAFTA preamble and adds further shared goals related to labor matters. Importantly, each Party is committed, in accordance with its domestic laws, to promote the equal pay for men and women, and the elimination of employment discrimination. Further, each is committed to the following labor principles: the freedom of association, the right to bargain collectively, the right to strike, prohibition of forced labor, restrictions on labor by children and young people, minimum employment standards, prevention of occupational accidents and diseases, compensation in cases of work accidents or occupational diseases, and protection of migrant workers. The Agreement sets forth the following general objectives: improving working conditions and living standards, promoting compliance with and effective enforcement of labor laws, promoting the Agreement's principles through cooperation and coordination, and promoting publication and exchange of information to enhance mutual understanding of Parties' laws, institutions and legal systems.

The general obligation of each Party is to ensure the effective enforcement of its own labor law. Specific obligations refer to publication of labor laws and related regulations and procedures, and to promotion of awareness of and compliance with them. Parties will also ensure availability of public information related to its labor law, and enforcement and compliance procedures. Other obligations include government enforcement actions for promoting compliance and effective enforcement of its labor law, covering such matters as: appointing and training of inspectors, monitoring compliance and examining suspected violations; carrying out inspections, mandatory reporting and record keeping; encouraging worker-management committees; providing mediation, conciliation, or arbitration services; and initiating in a timely manner enforcement actions seeking appropriate remedies. Each Party is committed to ensuring access by persons with a legally recognized interest to administrative, judicial, and related tribunals, including recourse to procedures by which labor rights can be enforced in a binding fashion. The Agreement also provides that such tribunals and proceedings before them would be fair and comply with due process.

The intention of the Parties in the Agreement on Labor Cooperation is to pursue a set of general objectives, which aim at complementing NAFTA by promoting the improvement of working conditions and living standards in all three countries. The Commission for Labor Cooperation is trilateral and consists of a Ministerial Council and a Secretariat. The Council oversees the implementation of the agreement, promotes cooperative activities and directs the work of the Secretariat. The agreement reflects the shared recognition of the United States, Mexico, and Canada that their mutual prosperity depends on the promotion of fair and open competition based on innovation and rising levels of productivity and quality with due regard for the importance of labor laws and principles. The Agreement increases cooperation and promotes greater understanding among the Parties in a broad range of labor areas; establishes the obligation of each Party to ensure the enforcement of its domestic labor laws; provides mechanisms to permit problem-solving consultations; enables the Parties to initiate evaluations of patterns of practice by independent committees of experts; and allows for dispute settlement procedures.

A trinational Labor Commission is created to facilitate the achievement of the objectives of the Agreement and to deal with labor issues in a cooperative, and consultative manner that duly respects the three nations' sovereignty. The Labor Commission consists of a Ministerial Council, an International Coordinating Secretariat, and three National Administrative Offices (NAOs). The Ministerial Council consists of the labor Ministers from the three signatory countries, who supervise the implementation of the Agreement, including the work of the International Coordinating Secretariat (ICS). An ICS, under the direction of the Ministerial Council, carries out the day-to-day work of the Commission, and is responsible for assisting the Council in its work, for gathering and periodically publishing information on labor matters in Canada, the United States, and Mexico for planning and coordinating cooperative activities, and for supporting any working groups or evaluation committees established by the Ministerial Council. The NAOs, established by each Party, serve as a point of contact for and facilitate the provision of information to other Parties on domestic law and practice; receive public communications; conduct preliminary reviews; and promote the exchange of information relevant to the Agreement.

As to resolution of disputes, if the Council cannot resolve a dispute involving a Party's alleged persistent pattern of failure to effectively enforce labor laws with respect to health and safety, child labor and minimum wage, relating to a situation involving mutually recognized labor laws and the production of goods or services traded between the Parties, any Party may request an arbitral panel. A panel will be established on a two-thirds vote of the council, and panelists will normally be chosen from a previously agreed roster of experts, including experts on labor matters. With the approval of the disputing Parties, a panel may seek information and technical advice from any person or body that it deems appropriate, and the report of the panel will be made publicly available five days after it is transmitted to the Parties.

If a panel makes a finding that a Party has engaged in a persistent pattern of failure to effectively enforce its labor laws, the Parties may, within 60 days, agree on a mutually satisfactory action plan to remedy the non-enforcement. If there is no agreed action plan, then between 60 and 120 days after the final panel report, the panel may be reconvened to evaluate an action plan proposed by the Party complained against or to set out an action plan in its stead. The panel would also make a determination on the imposition of monetary enforcement assessments on the alleged offending Party. The panel may be reconvened at any time to determine if an action plan is being fully implemented, and if not, the panel is to impose a monetary enforcement assessment on the alleged offending Party. In the event that a Party complained against fails to pay a monetary enforcement assessment or continues in its failure to enforce its labor law and minimum wage, the Party is liable to ongoing enforcement actions. In the case of Canada, the Commission, on the request of a complaining Party, collects the monetary enforcement assessment and enforces an action plan in summary proceedings before a Canadian court of competent jurisdiction. In the case of Mexico and the United States, the complaining Party or Parties may suspend NAFTA benefits based on the amount of the assessment.

Specifically, in terms of Obligations of the Parties and the Levels of Protection, Article 2 holds that affirming full respect for each Party's constitution, and recognizing the right of each Party to establish its own domestic labor standards, and to adopt or modify accordingly its labor laws and regulations, each Party shall ensure that its labor laws and regulations provide for high labor standards, consistent with high quality and productivity workplaces, and shall continue to strive to improve those standards in that light.[44]

Government Enforcement Action is established under Article 3, which states that each Party shall promote compliance with and effectively enforce of its labor law through appropriate government action, such as:

3(a) appointing and training inspectors;

(b) monitoring compliance and investigating suspected violations, including through on-site inspections;
(c) seeking assurances of voluntary compliance;
(d) requiring record keeping and reporting;
(e) encouraging the establishment of worker-management committees to address labor regulation of the workplace;
(f) providing or encouraging mediation, conciliation and arbitration services; or
(g) initiating, in a timely manner, proceedings to seek appropriate sanctions or remedies for violations of its labor law.[45]

The agreement safeguards private action in Article 4, which holds that each Party shall ensure that persons with a legally recognized interest under its law in a particular matter have appropriate access to administrative, quasi-judicial, judicial or labor tribunals for the enforcement of the Party's labor law. Further, each Party's law shall ensure that such persons may have recourse to, as appropriate, procedures by which rights arising under its labor law, including in respect of occupational safety and health, employment standards, industrial relations and migrant workers, and collective agreements, can be enforced.[46]

Under procedural guarantees, Article 5 establishes that each Party shall ensure that its administrative, quasi-judicial, judicial and labor tribunal proceedings for the enforcement of its labor law are fair, equitable and transparent and, to this end, each Party shall provide that such proceedings comply with due process of law; any hearings in such proceedings are open to the public, except where the administration of justice otherwise requires; the parties to such proceedings are entitled to support or defend their respective positions and to present information or evidence; and such proceedings are not unnecessarily complicated and do not entail unreasonable charges or time limits or unwarranted delays. Further, each Party shall provide that final decisions on the merits of the case in such proceedings are in writing and preferably state the reasons on which the decisions are based; made available without undue delay to the parties to the proceedings and, consistent with its law, to the public; and based on information or evidence in respect of which the parties were offered the opportunity to be heard. Each Party shall provide, as appropriate, that parties to such proceedings have the right, in accordance with its law, to seek review and, where warranted, correction of final decisions issued in such proceedings. Additionally, each Party shall ensure that tribunals that conduct or review such proceedings are impartial and independent and do not have any substantial interest in the outcome of the matter. Each Party shall provide that the parties to administrative, quasi-judicial, judicial or labor tribunal proceedings may seek remedies to ensure the enforcement of their labor rights. Such remedies may include, as appropriate, orders, compliance agreements, fines, penalties, imprisonment, injunctions or emergency workplace closures. Each Party may, as appropriate, adopt or maintain labor defense offices to represent or advise workers or their organizations. Nothing in this Article shall be construed to require a Party to establish, or to prevent a Party from establishing, a judicial system for the enforcement of its labor law distinct from its system for the enforcement of laws in general. Finally, for greater certainty, decisions by each Party's administrative, quasi-judicial, judicial or labor tribunals, or pending decisions, as well as related proceedings shall not be subject to revision or reopened under the provisions of this Agreement.[47]

In terms of cooperative activities, Article 11 underlines the importance of labor practices for equality:

> 11(1) The Council shall promote cooperative activities between the Parties, as appropriate, regarding:
> (j) employment standards and their implementation;
> (l) legislation relating to the formation and operation of unions, collective bargaining and the resolution of labor disputes, and its implementation;
> (m) the equality of women and men in the workplace.[48]

Article 49 defines labor law as laws and regulations, or provisions thereof, that are directly related to, among other things, the elimination of employment discrimination on the basis of grounds such as race, religion, age, sex, or other grounds as determined by each Party's domestic laws; and equal pay for men and women.[49]

Annex 1 outlines guiding principles that the Parties are committed to promote, subject to each Party's domestic law but not establishing common minimum standards for their domestic law, and indicates broad areas of concern where the Parties have developed, each in its own way, laws, regulations, procedures and practices that protect the rights and interests of their respective workforces. These include the elimination of employment discrimination on such grounds as race, religion, age, sex or other grounds, subject to certain reasonable exceptions, such as, where applicable, bona fide occupational requirements or qualifications and established practices or rules governing retirement ages, and special measures of protection or assistance for particular groups designed to take into account the effects of discrimination; and equal wages for women and men by applying the principle of equal pay for equal work in the same establishment.[50]

NAFTA Benefits and Concerns

The North American Free Trade Agreement, the advocates argue, provides several benefits: 1. Improved access to the North American market of 360 million consumers, as to manufactured goods, and business and professional services; 2. Opportunities to export more products and services to Mexico, which needs capital goods, services and investment; 3. New export and investment opportunities for companies in different markets; 4. A more equitable trading relationship through the elimination of almost all Mexican tariffs and imports, with Mexico being the largest trading partner in Latin America; 5. Strengthened and precise North American rules of origin to determine which goods qualify for duty free treatment in North America; 6. Opportunities to bid on large government procurement contracts, with equal access to the bid process in some sectors; 7. Improved methods to settle trade disputes among Canada, Mexico and the United States; 8. Protection of key domestic interests, including culture, education, water, health and social services, such as childcare, the environment and aboriginal people; 9. Increased market opportunities in Latin America; and 10. Enhancement of the area as a foreign investment destination through secure access to the North American market for foreign investors, with key selling points of strong transportation and telecommunication infrastructures, abundant energy resources, a highly educated and skilled workforce, comprehensive social and health services, and a stable political and economic environment.[51]

NAFTA eliminates the majority of current tariffs and import licenses on all manufactured goods, provides greater access for service industries, permits more mobility for professional and business workers, and allows easier entry into the North American market of over 300 million consumers. By recognizing that we share a hemisphere, it sets an important precedent for north-south continental trade, and looks toward the future by allowing for participation by other countries, if they meet the membership criteria set by the three founding nations. Latin American countries have expressed an interest in becoming signatory members of the Free Trade Agreement. As well, the Canadian Province of Quebec has already given thought to joining as a separate member in the event it becomes a separate nation. Quebec wishes to maintain the current division of legislative powers, respect fully its unique social policy, language and culture, maintain a leeway to modernize and develop its economy, provide for transitional periods for businesses in less competitive sectors, adopt a dispute settlement mechanism, maintain its special status for agriculture and fisheries, and protect its right to decide on the Agreement in light of its interests.

By lowering trade barriers, the agreement has expanded trade in all three countries. This, some argue, has led to increased employment, more choices for consumers at competitive prices, and rising prosperity. From 1993, the year preceding the start of NAFTA implementation, to 2001, trade among the NAFTA nations climbed 109 per cent, from US$297 billion to US$622 billion. Each day the NAFTA parties conduct nearly US$1.7 billion in trilateral trade. Because of NAFTA, North America is one of the most competitive, prosperous and economically integrated regions in the world. From 1993 to 2001, in looking at the Canadian situation, Canada's merchandise exports to its NAFTA partners climbed 95 per cent, from US$117 billion to US$229 billion. By contrast, such exports to the rest of the world in the period increased only 5 per cent. In looking at the Mexican situation, Mexico exported US$139 billion to its NAFTA partners, an increase of 225 per cent. By comparison, exports to the rest of the world increased 93 per cent, and growth in Mexican exports accounted for more than half of the increase in Mexico's real gross domestic product. In looking at the American situation, United States merchandise exports to NAFTA partners nearly doubled from US$142 billion to US$265 billion. This was significantly higher than the 44 per cent growth in exports to the rest of the world.[52]

An increasingly integrated North American market has stimulated capital flows, promoted the spread of technology, and contributed to increasing productivity and higher wages. Between 1994 and 2000, Foreign Direct Investment (FDI) inflows in the NAFTA countries reached US$1.3 trillion, or about 28 per cent of the world total, spurring economic development and growth throughout

North America. Between 1994 and 2000, the United States received large flows of foreign capital, approximately US$110.2 billion per year, and Mexico's annual average capital inflow reached US$11.7 billion, three times the annual received in the seven years prior to the Agreement.

The dynamic performance of exports and investment in North America has boosted economic activity and production in the region, and some argue has contributed to the creation of more and better paying jobs in all three countries. In Canada, the hourly wage rate in export-supported jobs is 35 per cent higher than in the non-export sector. In Mexico, the export sector is the country's leading job creation engine, accounting for more than half of Mexican manufacturing jobs gained between 1994 and 2000, with these jobs paying nearly 40 per cent more than those in the rest of the manufacturing sector. In the United States, employment supported by merchandise exports to NAFTA countries grew to an estimated 2.9 million jobs, with these jobs paying between 13 and 18 per cent more than the average American national wage.

Aside from a handful of tariffs, all NAFTA commitments have been fully implemented, including trade rules on services, investment, procurement, and standards. The NAFTA partners are committed to completing the full implementation of the Agreement according to the established schedule. Eight years of expanded trade, increased employment and investment, and enhanced opportunity for the citizens of all three countries have demonstrated that NAFTA works, and will continue to work.

The North American Free Trade Agreement, according to its critics who paint a more realistic picture, is not free, since Canada has paid a high price to gain greater access to the American and Mexican markets. Canadian consumers have seen prices rise along with the advent of the Goods and Services Tax, and thousands of jobs have been lost, with unemployment hovering around the 9 per cent level.[53] The structural adjustment costs such as a rise in unemployment tend to be underestimated by free trade advocates. Further, the agreement is also not about trade, and is more about the creation of a new continental model of development for the regulation of capitalism.[54] It serves more as a corporate bill of rights entrenching deregulation and market orientation in an international treaty, while at the same time eroding national economic, social and political institutions. Neo-conservatives in Canada and the Unites States wanted a deregulated continental model of development to increase capital mobility in order to restore profitability. Corporate managers have worked in a continent-wide drive to bring down wages and welfare state spending, by playing communities off against one another. The goal is to harmonize and integrate Canadian standards and institutions with the United States. Canada's economy, political system and labor practices have been significantly altered as a result of closer ties with the United States' economy. Canada has been forced to acquiesce to the continental model of development by continental market forces and American geopolitical pressures. Free trade is designed to restructure society to suit corporate needs, causing a threat to communities, by capital enhanced geographic mobility, which is not universally beneficial.

Many have benefitted, but in the eyes of the critics, many more have been hurt. Sovereignty has been compromised, and the three most important industries for Canada, wood exports, agriculture and automobile manufacturing, have been hurt. 'The burden of Free Trade driven restructuring was shared unequally on a national, regional, class and gender basis'.[55] The critics argue that the new capital labor accord relies on domination instead of negotiation. Canadian workers are suffering from a 'whiplash process', being forced concessions on wage benefits and work rules. Mergers, temporary and part-time workers, and cheap labor increase competitiveness. Failure to acquiesce has resulted in relocation out of Canada. Free trade generated jobs have not materialized as promised by the advocates. The Continental Model has led to polarization and segmentation of the Canadian labor force. The discourse of universality has ended, so that there is more social inequality across Canada. The Welfare State is viewed as an impediment to profit in the eyes of business, which has chipped away at it, giving way to a 'policy of stealth'.

With deregulation, budget cuts and privatization, importance is given to corporate profit at the expense of social equality. 'Continental free trade has helped to create a neo-conservative utopia where issues such as social justice and regional equality have become relics' of a bygone era.[56] Opponents of free trade are said to suffer from 'emporiophobia', a fear of free trade. Yet, the effects of free trade are something to fear, since hemispheric free trade is now a possibility. It was argued that there would be a 'sucking sound' of jobs going south of the border, ultimately to Mexico.[57] However, no tripartite treaty will disturb the overwhelming dominance that accrues to the United States, because of its geographic position, between Canada and Mexico. A borderland is a region jointly shared by two nations that houses people with common social characteristics in spite of the political boundaries between them, and thus the United States has a strong influence on the other two countries bordering it.

The outflow of investment and the haemorrhaging of profits and service payments out of Canada is intrinsically intertwined with the North American Free Trade Agreement.[58] According to the critics, the human and economic debris will be with us for as long as we can see into the future. The single most important impact of NAFTA is the decline in the standard of living of Canadians, which has coincided with the agreements. We need to reform democracy and political institutions so citizens and not just corporate business benefit from change. There is presently more foreign ownership and control, with fewer jobs and poorer jobs. More imports of goods and services should be sourced in Canada, but there is a failure to develop new competitive products while at the same time having less diversification of exports.

Northrop Frye pointed out long ago, 'Why go to the trouble of annexing a country that is so easy to exploit without taking any responsibility for it'.[59] Economic penetration has proven simpler than military force. The North American Free Trade agreement, according to its critics, is a neo-conservative Americanization of Canada.[60] The pre-agreement years saw trade on a multilateral level, without abandoning national control of the foreign market. The agreement is seen as a straightjacket, because it is difficult to introduce new measures to strengthen or expand national control of firms and industries. It can be argued that it is a dangerous and indefensible gamble for Canada to commit to a binding dispute settlement mechanism with a trading partner, the United States, which has such a disproportionate power.

The North American Free Trade Agreement has set up a trading bloc designed to fit Canada and Mexico into the American model of development, keeping Europe and Japan out. There is no willingness to share political powers like in the European Community, but simply the use of American power. However, Mexico is an attractive site for low wage production of standardized industrial goods, and with this comes Canadian and American job losses with production shifts to Mexico and a downward pressure on wages. Workers have been displaced from industries and are vulnerable to competition from low wage countries, with the loss especially to low income jobs. The North American Free Trade Agreement does nothing for basic labor. Obviously, the job crisis existed before free trade and was not confined to Canada. However, there is a conflict between the profitability of individual corporations and the pressures of global capabilities against human needs for high employment levels, decent pay, healthy working conditions and job security. What has occurred is a decrease in full-time employment and an increase in part-time and temporary employment, as well as an increase in unemployment and in welfare levels. This has been 'the longest and deepest unemployment crisis since the Great Depression', with inappropriate monetary policy playing a major role.[61]

There is a gap in the free trade effect between the top corporate executive and the average shop floor worker. Free trade encourages self-reinforcing cycles of destructive competition, exerting great pressure on the Continent. It has eliminated jobs, depressed incomes and standards, and aggregated demands. The effects of investment diversion and export harassment far outweigh the positive effects of tariff reductions. There is a one-sided advantage for a corporate elite that is globally competitive, increasing profits, surviving and growing unfettered by government controls, and securing the highest rate of return for the interests of financial capital. Decent jobs and decent living standards have become unimportant. Employment needs of society must be paramount, and therefore, corporate interests must yield to broader public interests. However, the North American Free Trade Agreement is tilted in the wrong direction. Multilateral trading arrangements with the European Community and Japan would be alternatives to the North American Free Trade Agreement and its shortfalls.

Canada's social programs are a contrast to those of the United States. Americanization is balkanizing Canada. Regional equality is promised, but individuals, families, communities and regions are being abandoned. Canada was founded on the national principle of building strong communities and regions to serve the needs of their residents, not to deplete these areas in order to supply land and factories for economic interests. With lay-offs and closures, there is a bitter legacy of unemployment, poverty and inequality, with society becoming distinctly harsher. Those who are able to thrive are doing very well, but the societal gap is growing so that there is a chasm between rich and poor, young and old, men and women, with a disappearing middle class. There is a severe strain on the societal fabric, with a sacrificing of the needs of many for the demands of few.

Among those who were opposed to the Free Trade agreement, Canadian Mitchell Sharp, who has been a mentor to the current Prime Minister Jean Chrétien, stated it best:

> From the very beginnings of our country, we have sought to preserve a separate identity, to live in harmony with our next door neighbour but as an independent country. By entering into this...preferential agreement, we would be deciding no longer to resist the continental pull. On the contrary, we would be accelerating the process of the Americanisation of Canada.[62]

Many believe that free trade challenges the fundamentals of Canada's nationhood, with its powers limited by interdependence and domination from foreign multinationals. The benefits of free trade do not fall equally. Free trade serves to undermine full employment.[63] The first essential ingredient for free trade should be a commitment to full employment. Sufficient independence for blueprint choices and for flexible alternatives for long-term planning is needed, looking away from integration.

The advocates argue that there will be an increase in the wages of the skilled in manufacturing, and that this will spill over into the other sectors. However, it will not occur where unemployment is high, since high-paying and secure jobs require an overall low unemployment rate.[64] By operating under the deceptive banner of 'free' trade, multinational corporations are working hard to expand their control over the international economy, and to dismantle vital health, safety and environmental protections, which in recent decades have been won by citizens' movements across the globe. According to Consumer advocate Ralph Nader, this serves to devalue jobs, depress wage levels, make workplaces less safe, destroy family farms, and undermine consumer protections.[65]

Because of the North American Free Trade Agreement, large global companies have capitalized on poverty in the Third World, by lowering safety and wages in employment. As such, workers, consumers and communities will continue to lose, while short-term profits soar and big business wins, in a threat to move South. The centralization of commercial power is unsound. There is a need for community oriented production in smaller scale operations, along with more flexibility and adaptability to local needs for sustainable production methods and democratic controls. Thus, the allocation of power to lower levels of government bodies tends to increase citizen power. There is a race 'to the bottom' pitting State against State, for the lowest wage levels, lowest environmental policies and lowest consumer safety standards.[66]

In terms of women, there is a gender gap on the issue of free trade, according to the Canadian National Action Committee on the Status of Women. More women than men are against the free trade deal, because it affects every issue women in this country are concerned about, including day care, health care, the environment, consumer protection and prices. The North American Free Trade Agreement has forced Canada to harmonize its social and economic policies to conform to the United States. Free trade calls for privatization and deregulation, but policy intervention is needed to reduce unemployment and raise wage rates.

Women and the types of jobs they occupy are especially vulnerable to free trade. Over 60 per cent of women work in the sectors of manufacturing, textiles, clothing, food processing, electrical, and leather products. There has been a shift away from service type jobs in which women are heavily concentrated, with pressure to decrease wages and provide fewer benefits. There has been major job loss by sourcing services outside Canada.[67] It is important to negotiate over the right of establishment and the right to national treatment. Manufacturing is vulnerable to trade liberalization, which will lead to an increase in female unemployment, confinement of female work to certain occupations, and adverse working conditions.

The United States has an advantage over Canada, because of cheap material, capital intensiveness and technological advancement. Due to its size and climate, Canada is again at a disadvantage in the food industry, with its imports being greater in female concentrated jobs. The United States is again favored in the electrical field, where there is a rationalization of production for specializations, leaving women at a disadvantage. There is a 'going South' policy. Firms want to locate elsewhere, while still having access to the Canadian market. At the same time, by phasing out import restrictions, the domestic sector is not protected. From 1911-21, there was a move away by women from the manufacturing sector, from 26 per cent to 18 per cent, to the clerical sector, from 9 per cent to 19 per cent. As well, from 1941-51, there was an increase of working married women in the labor force.[68] With restructuring in the 1970s, it was found that women were hit harder, with the older married low-skill worker more affected. Women found it more difficult to find work than men at a rate of 38 per cent to 62 per cent, suffered longer unemployment, and moved out of the labor force at a rate of 15 per cent to 9 per cent.[69] There was a shifting of jobs, by which men were afforded a wider variety of employment while women were forced to move most often into clerical work and gender segregation.

American legislation for realignment, it is argued, will curtail equal rights legislation, since equal pay is too costly for the industry. Free trade will erode the domestic service economy, which is predominated by women, and no women's sector will experience real growth under free trade.[70] Of the three major categories of sectors, the primary (agriculture and resource extracting), the secondary (construction and manufacturing) and the tertiary (service), the latter sector contains the largest number of women, and therefore has the most to lose in the loss of jobs and the replacement of domestic with imports. The service sector accounts for two-thirds of the national income and 70 per cent of jobs in Canada. As such, there have been important changes in women's labor over the years.

Foreign service industry activity is limited by non-tariff barriers, through control over investment, ownership and trade levels. The United States, however, believes that government intervention as a matter of security and sovereignty is an unfair practice. The United States accounts for roughly 80 per cent of Canada's trade. The expansion of the clerical and public service areas is necessary for women's participation. However, the Canadian market is vulnerable, because of the large percentage of American-owned businesses, which causes an indirect pressure to conform to United States policy.

The United States has easier access to Canada than Canada to the United States. The American trade remedy legislation imposes pressure upon Canada to harmonize, which impacts social services, job loss, wages, working conditions and types of employment. Women become the losers in the reorganization of production for export. It is found that trade-led growth is not always an adequate economic policy. Free trade is a means not an end.

Conclusion

The NAFTA partners are cooperating to advance trade liberalization not only within North America, but also in the negotiations for the Free Trade Area of the Americas (FTAA). Recognizing their shared interests, the NAFTA partners have worked together to advance trade liberalization. In 2001, Canada hosted the Summit of the Americas, a gathering of the 34 democratically elected Heads of State of the Western Hemisphere. As one of the key elements of the Summit Agenda, NAFTA partners are working together to ensure that the Free Trade Area of the Americas (FTAA) negotiations continue to progress toward the goal of conclusion of an agreement by 2005. The FTAA would eliminate trade and investment barriers on virtually all goods and services traded by member countries, reducing prices for consumers and creating new markets for producers throughout the hemisphere.

President John F. Kennedy's statement concerning the relationship between Canada and the United States is still applicable today and can even be further extended to North America: 'Geography has made us neighbors, history has made us friends, the economy has made us partners and necessity has made us allies'.[71] In this spirit, we need to work together to bring about full equality in employment for men and women in the Americas.

Notes

1 Hamelin, Jean, *Histoire du Québec*, Edisem, St. Hyacinthe, 1976, p.371.

2 Easterbrook, W.T. and Aitken, Hugh, *Canadian Economic History*, Macmillan, Toronto, 1976, p.362.

3 *Ibid.*, at p.361.

4 Fry, Earl, 'Trends in Canada-U.S. Free Trade Discussions', in A.R. Riggs and Tom Welk, *Canadian-American Free Trade: Historical, Political and Economic Dimensions*, The Institute for Research in Public Policy, Montreal, 1987, p.28.

5 d'Aquino, Thomas, 'Truck and Trade with the Yankees, The Case for a Canada-U.S. Comprehensive Trade Agreement', in A.R. Riggs and Tom Velk, *Canadian-American Free Trade: Historical, Political and Economic Dimensions*, The Institute for Research on Public Policy, Montreal, 1987, p.74.

6 Velk, Tom and Riggs, A.R., 'The Ongoing Debate Over Free Trade', in A.R. Riggs and Tom Velk, *Canadian-American Free Trade: (The Sequel) Historical, Political and*

Economic Dimensions, The Institute for Research on Public Policy, Montreal, 1988, p.93.

7 General Agreement on Tariffs and Trade, Article 24.

8 Laun, Louis, 'U.S.-Canada Free Trade Negotiations: Historical Opportunities', in A.R. Riggs and Tom Velk, *Canadian-American Free Trade: Historical, Political and Economic Dimensions*, The Institute for Research in Public Policy, Montreal, 1987, p.205.

9 *Supra* note 4, at p.9.

10 *Ibid.*, at p.34.

11 *Ibid.*, at p. 27.

12 Watkins, Mel, 'The Political Economy of Growth', in Wallace Clement and Glen Williams, *The New Canadian Political Economy*, McGill-Queen's University Press, Kingston, 1989, p.17.

13 *Supra* note 8, at p.205.

14 Government of Canada, *The North American Free Trade Agreement At A Glance*, Ottawa, p.1.

15 Soldatos, P., 'Canada's Foreign Policy in Search of a Fourth Option: Continuity and Change in Orientation Towards the U.S.', in A.R. Riggs and Tom Velk, *Canadian-American Free Trade: (The Sequel) Historical, Political and Economic Dimensions*, The Institute for Research on Public Policy, Montreal, 1988, p.41.

16 Lipsey, Richard, 'Canada's Trade Options', in A.R. Riggs and Tom Velk, *Canadian-American Free Trade: Historical, Political and Economic Dimensions*, The Institute for Research on Public Policy, Montreal, 1987, p.59.

17 Brecher, Irving, 'The Free Trade Initiative, On Course or Off', in A.R. Riggs and Tom Velk, *Canadian-American Free Trade: Historical, Political and Economic Dimensions*, The Institute for Research in Public Policy, Montreal, 1987, p.67.

18 Neufeld, E.P, 'Financial and Economic Dimensions of Free Trade', in A.R. Riggs and Tom Velk, *Canadian-American Free Trade: Historical, Political and Economic Dimensions*, The Institute for Research on Public Policy, Montreal, 1987, p.152.

19 *Ibid.*, at p.155.

20 Layton, Robert, 'Why Canada Needs Free Trade', in A.R. Riggs and Tom Velk, *Canadian-American Free Trade: Historical, Political and Economic Dimensions*, The Institute for Research in Public Policy, Montreal, 1987, p.200.

21 *Supra* note 6, at p. 3.

22 *Supra* note 5, at p.74.

23 Raynauld, Andre, 'Looking Outward Again', in A.R. Riggs and Tom Velk, *Canadian-American Free Trade: Historical, Political and Economic Dimensions*, The Institute for Research on Public Policy, Montreal, 1987, p.86.

24 Wigle, Randall, 'The Received Wisdom of the Canada-U.S. Free Trade', Qualifications, in A.R. Riggs and Tom Velk, *Canadian-American Free Trade: Historical, Political and Economic Dimensions*, The Institute for Research in Public Policy, Montreal, 1987, p.92.

25 Stone, Frank, 'Removing Barriers to Canada', in A.R. Riggs and Tom Velk, *Canadian-American Free Trade: Historical, Political and Economic Dimensions*, The Institute for Research in Public Policy, Montreal, 1987, p.183.

26 North American Free Trade Agreement, Preamble.

27 Mexican Investment Board, *Mexico Your Partner for Growth, Regulatory Reform and Competition Policy, Setting the Incentives for an Efficient Economy*, Mexico, 1994, p.1.

28 *Supra* note 8, at p.208.

29 Harris, Richard, 'Some Observations on the Canada-U.S. Free Trade Deal', in A.R. Riggs and Tom Velk, *Canadian-American Free Trade: (The Sequel) Historical,*

Political and Economic Dimensions, The Institute for Research on Public Policy, Montreal 1988, p.52.

30 *Supra* note 26, at Article 1201.

31 *Ibid.*, at Article 1202, 1203.

32 *Ibid.*, at Article 1208.

33 *Ibid.*, at Article 1210.

34 *Ibid.*, at Article 1213.

35 *Ibid.*, at Annexes 1210.5.A.2, and 1210.5.A.3.

36 *Ibid.*, at Annex 1210.5.B.1.

37 *Ibid,*. at Annex 1603 A.1.

38 *Ibid.*, at Annex 1603.B.1.

39 *Ibid.*, at Annex 1603.C.1.

40 *Ibid.*, at Annex 1603.D.1.

41 *Ibid.*, at Article 1606.1.

42 North American Agreement on Labor Cooperation (NAALC), Preamble.

43 *Ibid.*, at Article 1.

44 *Ibid.*, at Article 2.

45 *Ibid.*, at Article 3.

46 *Ibid.*, at Article 4.

47 *Ibid.*, at Article 5.

48 *Ibid.*, at Article 11.

49 *Ibid.*, at Article 49.

50 *Ibid.*, at Annex 1.

51 *Supra* note 14, p.3.

52 Government of Canada, *NAFTA at Eight*, 2002.

53 Merrett, Christopher, *Free Trade, Neither Free Nor About Trade*, Black Rose Books, New York, 1996, p.270.

54 *Ibid.*, at p.95.

55 *Ibid.*, at p.271.

56 *Ibid.*, at p.279.

57 McPhail, Brenda, *NAFTA Now, University Press of America*, Lanham, 1985, p.44.

58 Hurtig, Mel, *The Betrayal of Canada*, Stoddart Publishing, Toronto, 1991, p.303.

59 *Ibid.*, at p.89.

60 *Supra* note 12, at p.3.

61 Campbell, Bruce, *Free Trade, Destroyer of Jobs*, Canadian Centre for Policy Alternatives, Ottawa. 1993, p.2.

62 Axworthy, Lloyd, 'Free Trade, The Costs for Canada', in A.R. Riggs and Tom Velk, *Canadian-American Free Trade: (The Sequel) Historical, Political and Economic Dimensions*, The Institute for Research on Public Policy, Montreal, 1988, p.38.

63 *Ibid.*, at p.39.

64 Harris, Richard, 'Some Observations on the Canada-U.S. Free Trade Deal', in A.R. Riggs and Tom Velk, *Canadian-American Free Trade: (The Sequel) Historical, Political and Economic Dimensions*, The Institute for Research on Public Policy, Montreal, 1988, p.53.

65 Nader, Ralph, *The Case Against Free Trade*, Earth Island Press, San Francisco, 1993, p.1.

66 *Ibid.*, at p.6.

67 Griffin Cohen, Marjorie, *Free Trade and the Future of Women's Work, Manufacturing and Service Industries*, Garamond Press, Toronto, 1987, p.16.

68 *Ibid.*, at p.60.

69 *Ibid.*, at p.37.

70 *Ibid.*, at p.49.
71 Kennedy, President John F.

References

Armstrong, Donald (1987), 'Canada-U.S. Free Trade and Canadian Culture', in A.R. Riggs and Tom Velk, *Canadian-American Free Trade: Historical, Political and Economic Dimensions*, The Institute for Research in Public Policy, Montreal.

Axworthy, Lloyd (1988), 'Free Trade, The Costs for Canada', in A.R. Riggs and Tom Velk, *Canadian-American Free Trade: (The Sequel) Historical, Political and Economic Dimensions*, The Institute for Research on Public Policy, Montreal.

Balthazar, Louis (1984), 'Quebec's Policies Toward the United States', in Alfred O. Hero, Jr. and Marcel Daneau, *Problems and Opportunities in the United States and Quebec Relations*, Westview Press, Boulder.

Barlow, Maude (1990), *Parcel of Rogues*, Key Porter Books, Toronto.

Brecher, Irving (1987), 'The Free Trade Initiative, On Course or Off', in A.R. Riggs and Tom Velk, *Canadian-American Free Trade: Historical, Political and Economic Dimensions*, The Institute for Research in Public Policy, Montreal.

Cameron, Duncan and Watkins, Mel (1993), *Canada Under Free Trade*, James Lorimer & Co., Toronto.

Campbell, Bruce (1992), *We Need Free Trade Abrogation to Rebuild the Nation*, Canadian Centre for Policy Alternatives, Ottawa.

Campbell, Bruce (1993), *Free Trade, Destroyer of Jobs*, Canadian Centre for Policy Alternatives, Ottawa.

Canada–United States Free Trade Agreement, 1989.

Chartier, Armand (1984), 'Franco-Americans and Quebec', in Alfred O. Hero, Jr. and Marcel Daneau, *Problems and Opportunities in the United States and Quebec Relations*, Boulder: Westview Press, Boulder.

Creighton, Donald (1970), *The Empire of the St. Lawrence*, Macmillan, Toronto.

D'Aquino, Thomas (1987), 'Truck and Trade with the Yankees, The Case for a Canada-U.S. Comprehensive Trade Agreement', in A.R. Riggs and Tom Velk, *Canadian-American Free Trade: Historical, Political and Economic Dimensions*, The Institute for Research on Public Policy, Montreal.

Davenport, Paul (1988), 'L'Economie Politique du Libre Echange, Un Survol', in A.R. Riggs and Tom Velk, *Canadian-American Free Trade: (The Sequel) Historical, Political and Economic Dimensions*, The Institute for Research on Public Policy, Montreal.

Dinsmore, John (1975), 'Elements d'une position du Québec dans les relations économiques avec les Etats-Unis', in *Choix*, Centre Québécois de Relations Internationales, Laval.

Easterbrook, W.T. and Aitken, Hugh (1976), *Canadian Economic History*, Macmillan, Toronto.

Faucher, Albert and Lamontagne, Maurice (1953), 'The History of Industrial Development', in Jean-Claude Falardeau, *Essays on Contemporary Quebec*, Les Presses Universitaires Laval, Québec.

Fry, Earl (1987), 'Trends in Canada-U.S. Free Trade Discussions', in A.R. Riggs and Tom Welk, *Canadian-American Free Trade: Historical, Political and Economic Dimensions*, The Institute for Research in Public Policy, Montreal.

General Agreement on Tariffs and Trade.

Government of Canada (1993), *The North American Free Trade Agreement At A Glance*, Ottawa.

Government of Canada (2002), *NAFTA at Eight*, Department of Foreign Affairs, Ottawa.

Government of Quebec, Ministère des Affaires Internationales (1993), *Quebec and the North American Free Trade Agreement*, Québec.

Government of Quebec, Ministère des Affaires Internationales, de l'Immigration et des Communautés Culturelles du Québec (1994), *Commerce International du Québec, Etats-Unis, Jan-Juin, 1993-1994*, Quebec.

Government of Quebec, Ministère des Affaires Internationales, de l'Immigration et des Communautés Culturelles du Québec (1994), *Commerce International du Québec, Etats-Unis, 1992-1993*, Quebec.

Griffin Cohen, Marjorie (1987), *Free Trade and the Future of Women's Work, Manufacturing and Service Industries*, Garamond Press, Toronto.

Guindon, Hubert (1988), *Quebec Society: Tradition, Modernity, and Nationhood*, University of Toronto Press, Toronto.

Hamelin, Jean (1976), *Histoire du Québec*, Edisem, St. Hyacinthe.

Hamelin, Jean and Roby, Yves (1971), *Histoire Economique du Québec 1851-1896*, Fides, Montreal.

Harris, Richard (1988), 'Some Observations on the Canada-U.S. Free Trade Deal', in A.R. Riggs and Tom Velk, *Canadian-American Free Trade: (The Sequel) Historical, Political and Economic Dimensions*, The Institute for Research on Public Policy, Montreal.

Hazledine, Tim (1987), 'What do Economists Know about Free Trade', in A.R. Riggs and Tom Velk, *Canadian-American Free Trade: Historical, Political and Economic Dimensions*, The Institute for Research in Public Policy, Montreal.

Hero, Alfred and Balthazar, Louis (1988), *Contemporary Quebec and the United States 1960-1985*, University Press of America, Boston.

Hurtig, Mel (1991), *The Betrayal of Canada*, Stoddart Publishing, Toronto.

Innis, Harold (1995), *Staples, Markets and Cultural Change*, McGill Queen's University Press, Montreal.

Jones, Robert, 'Agriculture in Lower Canada, 1792-1815', *The Canadian Historical Review*, Vol.27, 1946, p.33.

Kennedy, President John F.

Laun, Louis (1987), 'U.S.-Canada Free Trade Negotiations: Historical Opportunities', in A.R. Riggs and Tom Velk, *Canadian-American Free Trade: Historical, Political and Economic Dimensions*, The Institute for Research in Public Policy, Montreal.

Lavoie, Yolande (1981), *L'Emigration des Québécois aux Etats-Unis de 1840-1930*, Editeur Officielle du Québec.

Layton, Robert (1987), 'Why Canada Needs Free Trade', in A.R. Riggs and Tom Velk, *Canadian-American Free Trade: Historical, Political and Economic Dimensions*, The Institute for Research in Public Policy, Montreal.

Lipsey, Richard (1987), 'Canada's Trade Options', in A.R. Riggs and Tom Velk, *Canadian-American Free Trade: Historical, Political and Economic Dimensions*, The Institute for Research in Public Policy, Montreal.

Lisée, Jean-Francois (1990), *Dans l'Oeil de L'Aigle*, Boreal, Montreal.

Little, J.I. (1989), *Nationalism, Capitalism and Colonization*, McGill Queen's University Press, Kingston.

Lyon, Peyton (1987), 'CUFTA and Canadian Independence', in A.R. Riggs and Tom Velk, *Canadian-American Free Trade: Historical, Political and Economic Dimensions*, The Institute for Research in Public Policy, Montreal.

Marr, William and Paterson, Donald (1980), *Canada: An Economic History*, Gage, Toronto.

Masters, Donald (1963), *The Reciprocity Treaty of 1854*, McClelland & Stewart Ltd., London.
McPhail, Brenda (1985), *NAFTA Now*, University Press of America, Lanham.
Merrett, Christopher (1996), *Free Trade, Neither Free Nor About Trade*, Black Rose Books, New York.
Mexican Investment Board (1994), *Mexico Your Partner for Growth, Regulatory Reform and Competition Policy, Setting the Incentives for an Efficient Economy*, Mexico.
Nader, Ralph (1993), *The Case Against Free Trade*, Earth Island Press, San Francisco.
Neufeld, E.P. (1987), 'Financial and Economic Dimensions of Free Trade', in A.R. Riggs and Tom Velk, *Canadian-American Free Trade: Historical, Political and Economic Dimensions*, The Institute for Research on Public Policy, Montreal.
Niles, Thomas (1987), 'Address', in A.R. Riggs and Tom Velk, *Canadian-American Free Trade: Historical, Political and Economic Dimensions*, The Institute for Research on Public Policy, Montreal.
North American Agreement on Labor Cooperation, 1994.
North American Free Trade Agreement, 1991.
Oliver, Michael (1991), *The Passionate Debate*, Vehicule Press, Montreal.
Papillon, Benoit (1987), 'Bankruptcy Law, Free Trade and Economic Adjustments, Preliminary Considerations', in A.R. Riggs and Tom Velk, *Canadian-American Free Trade: Historical, Political and Economic Dimensions*, The Institute for Research on Public Policy, Montreal.
Raynauld, Andre (1987), 'Looking Outward Again', in A.R. Riggs and Tom Velk, *Canadian-American Free Trade: Historical, Political and Economic Dimensions*, The Institute for Research on Public Policy, Montreal.
Riggs, A.R. and Velk, Tom (1987), *Canadian-American Free Trade: Historical, Political and Economic Dimensions*, The Institute for Research on Public Policy, Montreal.
Riggs, A.R. and Velk, Tom (1988), *Canadian-American Free Trade: (The Sequel) Historical, Political and Economic Dimensions*, The Institute for Research on Public Policy, Montreal.
Ritchie, Gordon (1988), 'The Free Trade Agreement', in A.R. Riggs and Tom Velk, *Canadian-American Free Trade: (The Sequel) Historical, Political and Economic Dimensions*, The Institute for Research on Public Policy, Montreal.
Skud, Tim (1988), 'Free Trade, What Now for the U.S.', in A.R. Riggs and Tom Velk, *Canadian-American Free Trade: (The Sequel) Historical, Political and Economic Dimensions*, The Institute for Research on Public Policy, Montreal.
Soldatos, P (1988), 'Canada's Foreign Policy in Search of a Fourth Option: Continuity and Change in Orientation Towards the U.S.', in A.R. Riggs and Tom Velk (1988), *Canadian-American Free Trade: (The Sequel) Historical, Political and Economic Dimensions*, The Institute for Research on Public Policy, Montreal.
Stevens, Paul (1987), Reciprocity 1911: The Canadian Perspective, in A.R. Riggs and Tom Velk, *Canadian-American Free Trade: Historical, Political and Economic Dimensions*, The Institute for Research on Public Policy, Montreal.
Stone, Frank (1987), 'Removing Barriers to Canada', in A.R. Riggs and Tom Velk, *Canadian-American Free Trade: Historical, Political and Economic Dimensions*, The Institute for Research on Public Policy, Montreal.
Surrey, David (1982), *Choice of Conscience Vietnam Era and Draft Resisters in Canada*, Praeger, New York.
Thompson, Mark (1975), 'Le Syndicalisme Québecois dans le contexte Nord-Americain', in *Choix*, Centre Québécois de Relations Internationales, Laval.
Velk, Tom and Riggs, A.R. (1987), 'The Men that Corrupted Everyburg, American Farmers and the Free Trade Initiative 1911', in A.R. Riggs and Tom Velk, *Canadian-*

American Free Trade: Historical, Political and Economic Dimensions, The Institute for Research on Public Policy, Montreal.

Velk, Tom and Riggs, A.R. (1987), 'The Ongoing Debate Over Free Trade', in A.R. Riggs and Tom Velk, *Canadian-American Free Trade: Historical, Political and Economic Dimensions*, The Institute for Research on Public Policy, Montreal.

Watkins, Mel, *Alternatives to Free Trade*, Centre for Policy Alternatives, Ottawa.

Watkins, Mel (1989), 'The Political Economy of Growth', in Wallace Clement and Glen Williams, *The New Canadian Political Economy*, McGill-Queen's University Press, Kingston.

Watson, William, 'The Draft Agreement, Cohabitation Worth a Try', in A.R. Riggs and Tom Velk (1988), *Canadian-American Free Trade: (The Sequel) Historical, Political and Economic Dimensions*, The Institute for Research on Public Policy, Montreal.

White, Randall (1988), *Fur Trade to Free Trade: Putting the Canada-U.S. Trade Agreement in Historical Perspective*, Dundurn Press, Toronto.

Wigle, Randall (1987), 'The Received Wisdom of the Canada-U.S. Free Trade, Qualifications', in A.R. Riggs and Tom Welk, *Canadian-American Free Trade: Historical, Political and Economic Dimensions*, The Institute for Research in Public Policy, Montreal.

Young, Robert (1987), 'Canada-U.S. Free Trade, Economic Realities and Political Choices', in A.R. Riggs and Tom Velk, *Canadian-American Free Trade: Historical, Political and Economic Dimensions*, The Institute for Research on Public Policy, Montreal.

Chapter 8

Gender Injustice in the United Kingdom and Ireland

Introduction

This chapter will examine Gender Injustice in the United Kingdom and Ireland. It will initially look at the Commonwealth, then go on to examine Great Britain, namely England, Scotland and Wales, and finally as a means of comparison, it will look at Northern Ireland and the Republic of Ireland.

The Commonwealth

There is a need for intervention in the area of public/private distinctions in the application of international human rights law. The State's accountability for violations committed by private actors has long been an important debate. Recent jurisprudence holds the states to a due diligence standard with regard to preventing and prosecuting crimes against women. This will be of critical relevance to Commonwealth governments and the Secretariat as part of their continuing priority work in the area of democracy, rule of law, and human rights. The increased participation of women at decision-making levels in conflict prevention, mediation and resolution is vital.

Gender refers to the socially determined difference between women and men such as roles, attitudes, behaviors and values, according to the 1995 Commonwealth Plan.[1] Gender identifies the biological differences between women and men. While sex is genetically determined, gender roles vary across cultures and over time, and are amenable to change. Gender is a relational term based on the fact that women and men have different life courses, and development policies affect them differently. Gender mainstreaming addresses these differences by making gender equality integral to the process of policy-making, planning and program delivery at all levels and in all sectors, focusing less on providing equal treatment for women and men, since equal treatment does not necessarily result in equal outcomes, and more on taking whatever steps are necessary to ensure equal outcomes. Gender mainstreaming is everyone's business and involves all social actors, including governments, civil society and the private sector.

The strategy to advance the Commonwealth agenda to 2005 maintains the two-level approach of the 1995 Plan, namely action related to policy priorities such as human rights, peace and political participation, and macroeconomics and social development; and action related to mechanisms for gender mainstreaming within both governments and the Secretariat. To achieve these goals, Commonwealth governments are committed to:

(a) promote and protect women's human rights, promote women's awareness of their human rights, and also involve men in awareness raising through education about the human rights of women. Eliminate violence against women especially through the ratification and implementation of human rights conventions, promotion and adoption of model legislation and integrated approaches to violence against women, provision of training for the criminal justice system, provision of support services, in particular, services for victims of violence, and documenting the economic costs of violence against women;
(b) support international efforts for strengthening mechanisms for promoting women's human rights, elimination of trafficking of women and children, and violence against women in armed conflict; promote the effective implementation of the Convention on the Elimination of All Forms of Discrimination against Women (CEDAW), international trafficking conventions and Protocols, the Statutes and decisions of the International Criminal Court and International War Crimes Tribunals with regard to sexual violence crimes committed during armed conflict;
(c) introduce and promote equal opportunities legislation, policies and practices in public and private sector employment, formal and non-formal education and ongoing vocational training. Introduce legal structures to provide effective and practical redress in cases of discrimination;
(d) promote and increase women's participation in politics and decision-making by adopting measures to achieve the Commonwealth target of having women number no less than a third of decision-makers in the political, public and private sectors by the year 2005. Countries and political parties which have achieved this goal should be used as examples of success, with appropriate exploration and sharing of current models;
(e) enhance the capacity of women parliamentarians and parliamentary candidates so that they can contribute more effectively to the democratic processes, incorporate a gender perspective into debates and introduce critical gender equality issues into the political agenda. Enhance the capacity of women for leadership in the public and private sectors, especially in areas with economic planning and budgeting;
(f) promote measures to develop a more articulate and gender-aware electorate to ensure that women's priorities are effectively represented and addressed as part of mainstream political agendas;
(g) increase women's participation in senior-level decision-making processes on peace, conflict prevention and resolution, and in post-conflict reconstruction, and protect the human rights of women and children who are refugees and victims in situations of armed conflict or foreign occupation;
(h) encourage the participation of women and women's organizations in the development of professional guidelines and codes of conduct or other

appropriate self-regulatory mechanisms to promote balanced and non-stereotyped portrayals of women by the media; and

(i) work towards more effective collaboration and partnership with Non-Governmental Organizations (NGOs) and the private sector in the achievement of the goals of human rights, peace and political participation.[2]

Therefore, Commonwealth governments undertake to:

(a) monitor and analyze the different impact of macroeconomic policy and economic reform programs on women and men, and develop strategies, mechanisms, and corrective measures to address gender imbalances in key areas, including national economic reforms and budgetary processes;
(b) implement strategies, mechanisms and processes to ensure the ongoing collection and dissemination of sex-disaggregated data for use in economic and social impact assessments and policy development. Produce and maintain statistics relevant to the recognition of the contribution of women as proactive agents, investors and producers in the economic sector and the economic recovery process; the socio-political dimension of the retrenchment of basic services and the 'feminization' of poverty; counting of unremunerated work; and provide a mechanism for quantifying and recording the money value of such work;
(c) monitor and analyze the differential economic and social impact of current globalization trends to identify opportunities for and challenges to equal gender participation in micro- and small-scale enterprise, and in formal and informal economy; and develop strategies and policy frameworks, programs and corrective measures to address gender imbalances;
(d) support vocational and information technology skills training to ensure equal access to emerging employment opportunities; and
(e) integrate gender analysis in national planning and in the development and provision of social services and social safety nets.[3]

Gender mainstreaming is an essential element of good governance. It requires the implementation by sector of women-specific activities and projects. Recognizing that gender mainstreaming is essentially an issue of good governance, Commonwealth governments will endeavor to strengthen the institutional capacity for gender mainstreaming, including placing the National Women's Machineries (NWMs) at a more strategic level, providing adequate human and financial resources, strengthening linkages between the NWMs and other sectoral ministries and social partners, and developing capacity within sectoral ministries for gender planning, analysis and mainstreaming; develop processes and mechanisms to mainstream gender through the collection and utilization of sex-disaggregated data, gender analysis, policy research, gender planning and gender training. These processes should be developed in all sectors and at all levels, and advance the processes of gender mainstreaming through the development of national action plans for gender equality, enhancing the capacity for integrating gender in the national development planning process and sectoral ministries.

In a number of Commonwealth countries, the process of gender mainstreaming is far advanced through a strategy based on gender analysis. When applied at all stages of policy or project development, gender analysis leads to an improved understanding of the differential impacts and opportunities that policies and activities may have on women and men. The gender analysis strategy is complemented by the provision of training, the development of guidelines and materials, models of gender analysis and planning in various sectors, statistical indicators and accountability measures. Many countries face constraints in terms of resources, including local expertise to develop gender analysis and monitoring skills.

The Fifth Meeting of Ministers Responsible for Women's Affairs recommended that countries should achieve a target of no less than 30 per cent of women in decision-making by the year 2005 and that those already close to achieving this target should strive for parity, and further called on governments to develop equal employment opportunities policies. A number of obstacles continue to affect women's ability to participate fully and equally in decision-making in the political, public and private sectors. Traditional perceptions often limit the role of women to the household. Socio-economic impediments affecting women in many countries include women's limited access to formal education, and the streaming of girls and women in traditional subject areas with the result that they are concentrated in low waged, low status occupational groups such as clerks, sales and personnel services. In most countries, girls' access to education to science and technology still lags behind that of boys. The political framework acts to inhibit the equal participation of women with the result of the lack of family-friendly policies, bias toward male candidates, and lack of funding, of training and of support in elections. More effort is required to address impediments to women's involvement in the political process such as family responsibilities, and to encourage women to transcend cultural barriers. Education systems have a role to play in providing encouragement for women's leadership and critical thinking skills.

As well, areas relating to the promotion, protection and respect of women's rights as human rights, the elimination of violence against women, including the trafficking of women and girls, and the protection of the rights of the girl-child remain key priorities for Commonwealth governments and the Secretariat. With respect to involvement in processes of conflict prevention, mediation and resolution, women's activities are often limited to peace building at the community level. Where women have been involved in mediating major national conflicts, they do not tend to be appointed by governments as peace negotiators or special envoys. It is recommended that women be involved in peace processes at the highest levels, and that governments take into account gender considerations in the design of programs for victims of conflicts, including refugees and displaced persons.

Commonwealth action on a limited number of critical issues in the areas of political and human rights, and economic and social development is one of the priority areas. In the area of macroeconomic policy, efforts need to be made to address gender equality issues within structural adjustment and poverty alleviation programs, in particular the 'feminization of poverty', and economic empowerment, since limited progress has been achieved in integrating gender considerations in macroeconomic policies. Where a degree of integration has been achieved, the involvement of NWMs and the application of gender analysis at the early stages as well as throughout the policy development process have been instrumental.

Tradition, religious and cultural values and practices have presented serious constraints in the advancement of gender equality. As well, there is a need to enhance the awareness of the media to gender issues, and to use the media more effectively to raise the level of gender awareness among the population at large as well as disseminating strategic information to influence decision-making.

In looking at Gender and Globalization: Trade and Employment issues, at the Sixth Meeting of Ministers Responsible for Women's Affairs (6WAMM) in 2000, the interrelationship between structural adjustment, trade liberalization and globalization was noted, as was the impact of privatization on health care, education and employment. Globalization has had negative effects on rising unemployment, poverty and the difficulty of providing social safety nets in weak and vulnerable economies especially effecting women and children.

A Gender Management System is defined as 'a network of processes, mechanisms and structures to guide, monitor and evaluate' gender mainstreaming activities, and may be used in a sector or in an institution to address a particular issue. For effective Gender Mainstreaming, the following strategies need to be applied, namely strengthening the political will at the local, national and global levels are essential for effective gender mainstreaming; changing policy, resource allocation and planning to make them gender sensitive within organizations; collecting gender-disaggregated data to greatly benefit the process of gender mainstreaming as an excellent advocacy tool showing how policies impact differently on men and women; increasing the number of women and ultimately ensuring an equal amount of men and women in decision-making positions in the Government and all other sectors; providing all decision-makers with training and tools for gender awareness, analysis and planning; and successful mainstreaming for dynamic links to be forged between stakeholders, Government, private sector, civil society, Non-Governmental Organizations (NGOs), to ensure major advocacy efforts and a coordination of resources.

Some Practical Tips to Mainstream Gender include ensuring that gender is part of the planning process at the early stages of policy development can bring in tremendous gains as it avoids the process of 'adding on gender' at a later stage; integrating gender into areas of policy such as structural adjustment, poverty alleviation, trade and industry, and employment, not only in the social services sectors, that is health, family planning, and education; obtaining political and social commitments from sectors of public, private and civil society; overcoming capacity and delivery issues by contacts with people from other organizations that have the necessary authority, skills and resources; and networking and sharing of experiences at workshops, conferences and websites so that others may learn strategies to overcome certain obstacles to mainstreaming gender.

The United Kingdom's Global Platform for Action is a key driving force for action and sets important standards.[4] A vast amount of talent and human potential is wasted when women are denied full and equal citizenship.

Organizations that represent women, Non-Governmental Organizations (NGOs), trade unions and employers all have an important part to play in empowering women to reach their potential and claim their rights. There are still gross inequalities between the sexes. Millions of women still have to work harder than men to make a living, and many still shoulder the full responsibility for caring. They still have less control over income and assets, are subject to violence and intimidation, and often have no real say in important decisions that affect them. It is a situation that is not only unfair, but also lacks vision. It is in everyone's interests to realize the immense potential of women, since they have unique talents, skills, knowledge and insights. As technology continues to make the world a smaller more interconnected place, women have what it takes to flourish in this new economy.

Great Britain

The Role of Women in British Society

Overall, in 2001, there were around 30.4 million women and 29.6 million men in Britain, with women accounting for 51 per cent of the population.[5] In terms of the gender pay gap in Great Britain, female employees who work full-time earn 81 per cent of the average gross hourly earnings of male full-time employees.[6] The gender pay gap in hourly earnings is 19 per cent. It is wider than this in weekly earnings at 25 per cent, because men worked longer hours than women on average and are more likely to receive overtime and other additional payments. Men receive £54 per week from additional payments on average, but women only £20 per week.

Women working part-time have lower average hourly earnings than women who work full-time. There is a particularly large difference between the average hourly earnings of women who work part-time and men who work full-time, resulting in a gender pay gap of 41 per cent. If full-time and part-time employees are combined, the gender pay gap in hourly earnings is wider than for full-time employees, since more women than men work part-time. In 2002, 230,000 women, compared with only 110,000 men, were employed in jobs which paid below the National Minimum Wage.

In comparison, the gender pay gap is narrower in Wales for hourly, weekly and annual earnings than in England and Scotland. The main reason for this is the low average male earnings in Wales; 18 per cent of male full-time employees in Wales earn less than £250 per week, compared with 12 per cent in Britain overall. The gap between the hourly earnings of women who work part-time and men who work full-time is also wider in England at 42 per cent than in Scotland at 37 per cent or Wales at 34 per cent.

In terms of sectors and industries, average weekly earnings are higher for men in the private sector than the public sector, but are higher for women in the public sector. Consequently, the gender pay gap is much wider in the private sector at 29 per cent, than in the public sector at 16 per cent. Within the public sector, the gap is wider in central government at 20 per cent, than in public corporations at 16 per cent, and local government at 15 per cent. A key explanation for the wider gender pay gap in the private sector is likely to be the differing representation of women in the three highest paid occupational groups, that is managers and administrators, professional occupations, and associate professional and technical occupations, in the two sectors. In the public sector, women comprise 53 per cent of full-time employees in these groups combined, and in the private sector, only 27 per cent.

Among the nine major occupational groups, average hourly earnings of full-time employees are highest for men working as managers and administrators, and for women in professional occupations. Men have higher average hourly earnings than women in all nine groups, but the extent of the gender pay gap varies, with managers and administrators at 30 per cent, sales occupations at 28 per cent, and clerical and secretarial occupations at 2 per cent. Men make up the majority of employees in the five highest paid occupations, but women predominate in four of the five lowest paid.

Women comprise around 27 per cent of the 3.5 million self-employed.[7] The rate of female self-employment has more than doubled over the last 20 years. Women start up one-third of new businesses and own 13 per cent of all businesses. Women's participation in self-employment and business ownership in the UK is on a par with that of most northern European countries but lower than in the United States. The UK has the fourth highest female employment rate of all European Union countries, just behind Denmark, Sweden and Finland.

In looking at the role of women in senior management, of the 100 FTSE firms, only 7.2 per cent of directorships are held by women. Women comprise just 24 per cent of managers. In looking at women in the important sphere of the Judiciary, only 5 per cent of High Court Judges are women.[8]

In terms of marital and parental status, women who are single have lower average hourly earnings than those who are either married/cohabiting or separated, divorced or widowed, and the pattern for men is the same.[9] However, the gender gap for all employees is widest in the married/cohabiting group at 27 per cent, and the gap is wider than for full-time employees because a high proportion of married/cohabiting women work part-time, having lower earnings on average. The gender pay gap for all employees is higher for those with dependent children at 31 per cent, than without at 18 per cent. Among those with dependent children, the pay gap is at 22 per cent for parents of 0 to 2 year olds, and 35 per cent for parents of dependent children aged 11 or over.

In terms of qualification levels, average hourly earnings increase steadily for both women and men as highest qualifications rise. Among full-time employees, there were similar gender pay gaps for each qualification level, that is the gender pay gap for full-time employed graduates with a degree or equivalent is 19 per cent, while the gap for those with no qualifications is at 18 per cent. Women with a degree or equivalent qualification have double the average hourly earnings of those with no qualifications, and the pattern was the same for men.

Unequal income is a major source of gender inequality which can result in women having reduced economic independence and a greater likelihood of poverty than men in old age. Income has seven component elements: earnings, self-employment income, occupational pensions and annuities, investment income, tax credits, benefit income and other income. Overall, the gender income gap is much wider than the gender pay gap. Women's average income in 2001 was £191 per week and men's was £368 per week. Women received only 52 per cent of men's income on average and the gender income gap was 48 per cent. Income levels are highest for both women and men in England, lower in Scotland, and lowest in Wales. The gender income gap is widest in England at 49 per cent and narrowest in Wales at 39 per cent, and in Scotland, it is 46 per cent.

In terms of the labor force in Great Britain, 67 per cent of women and 79 per cent of men aged 16 to 64 are in employment.[10] People aged 25 to 44 have the highest employment rates, that is 73 per cent for women and 88 per cent for men. Only 9 per cent of male employees work part-time, compared with 43 per cent of female employees, and the largest group of male part-time employees is aged under 25. In terms of occupations, women form over 69 per cent of administrative and secretarial, personal service, and sales and customer service occupations, while men make up over 69 per cent of managers and senior officials, skilled trades, and process, plant and machine operatives.

In looking at equal pay, female employees working full-time earn on average 18.8 per cent less than the average hourly earnings of male full-time employees. Women's gross individual income, including income from employment, pensions, benefits and investments, is on average 51 per cent less than men's gross individual income.

In examining work/life balance, employment rates for women and men without dependent children are 67 per cent and 74 per cent respectively. In comparison, there is a wide gap between mothers and fathers with dependent children, where employment rates are 65 per cent and 89 per cent respectively. Women whose youngest child is aged under five have an employment rate of 53 per cent, and those whose youngest child is five or over have an employment rate of 73 per cent.

In terms of the labor force in Scotland, overall, 66 per cent of women and 76 per cent of men aged 16 to 64 are in employment.[11] People aged 25 to 44 have the highest employment rates, that is 75 per cent for women and 85 per cent for men. Only 9 per cent of male employees aged 16 and over work part-time, compared with 42 per cent of female employees, and nearly half the male part-time employees are aged under 25. In terms of occupations, women form over 70 per cent of administrative and secretarial, personal service, and sales and customer service occupations, while men make up over 80 per cent in skilled trades, and process, plant and machine operatives.

In looking at equal pay, female employees working full-time earn on average 18.6 per cent less than the average hourly earnings of male full-time employees. Women's gross individual income, including income from employment, pensions, benefits and investments, is on average 46 per cent less than men's gross individual income.

In examining work/life balance, employment rates for women and men without dependent children are 65 per cent and 70 per cent respectively. In comparison, there is a wide gap between mothers and fathers with dependent children, where employment rates are 69 per cent and 89 per cent respectively. Over a quarter, that is 26 per cent of women employees and 19 per cent of men employees have at least one type of flexible working arrangement.

In terms of the labor force in Wales, 59 per cent of women and 74 per cent of men aged 16-64 are in employment.[12] People aged 25 to 44 have the highest employment rates, that is 72 per cent for women and 85 per cent for men. Only 9 per cent of male employees aged 16 and over work part-time, compared with 46 per cent of female employees. In terms of occupations, women form 69 per cent or more of administrative and secretarial, personal service, and sales and customer service occupations, while men make up over 80 per cent of skilled trades, and process, plant and machine operatives.

In looking at equal pay, female employees working full-time earn on average 13.4 per cent less than the average hourly earnings of male full-time employees. Women's gross individual income, including income from employment, pensions, benefits and investments, is on average 42 per cent less than men's gross individual income.

In examining work/life balance, employment rates for women and men without dependent children are 56 per cent and 67 per cent respectively. In comparison, there is a wide gap between mothers and fathers with dependent children, where employment rates are 64 per cent and 87 per cent respectively. Women whose youngest child is aged under 5 have the lowest employment rate of 49 per cent, and those whose dependent children are 5 or over have an employment rate of 72 per cent.

Legislation

The relevant domestic law is contained in the Equal Pay Act 1970 (as amended), the Sex Discrimination Act 1975 (as amended), and the Pensions Act 1995. The Equal Pay Act covers all contractual terms and not simply those relating to pay; the Sex Discrimination Act covers claims, which do not relate to contractual issues. Claims under both Acts are taken initially to an Industrial Tribunal. The courts have established that a woman may bring a complaint under the Equal Pay Act in relation to any term or condition contained in her contract whether or not it relates to money. This Act excludes non-contractual benefits, even if they relate to money, but these may be taken under the Sex Discrimination Act. The Pensions Act allows claims in relation to the terms of, and access to, occupational pension schemes. There is no overlap between an individual's rights under the Equal Pay Act and those under the Sex Discrimination Act. All complaints of discrimination about access to jobs and matters not included in a contract of employment and about contractual matters other than those relating to the payment of money in situations not covered by the Equal Pay Act are dealt with under the Sex Discrimination Act.

The Equal Pay Act 1970 (EPA) According to the Equal Pay Act 1970 (as amended), there is a requirement of equal treatment for men and women in same employment, guaranteed in Section 1(1):

> 1(1) If the terms of a contract under which a woman is employed at an establishment in Great Britain do not include...an equality clause they shall be deemed to include one.[13]

However, a genuine occupational qualification is recognized in Section 1(3):

> 1(3) An equality clause shall not operate in relation to a variation between the woman's contract and the man's contract if the employer proves that the variation is genuinely due to a material factor which is not the difference of sex....[14]

The concepts of like-work and equal value are contained in Section 1(4) and (5) respectively:

> 1(4) A woman is to be regarded as employed on like work with men if, but only if, her work and theirs is of the same or a broadly similar nature, and the differences (if any) between the things she does and the things they do are not of practical importance in relation to terms and conditions of employment; and accordingly in comparing her work with theirs regard shall be had to the frequency or otherwise with which any such differences occur in practice as well as to the nature and extent of the differences.[15]

> 1(5) A woman is to be regarded as employed on work rated as equivalent with that of any men if, but only if, her job and their job have been given an equal value, in terms of the demand made on a worker under various headings (for instance effort, skill, decision), on a study undertaken with a view to evaluating in those terms the jobs to be done by all or any of the employees in an undertaking or group of undertakings, or would have been given an equal value but for the evaluation being made on a system setting different values for men and women on the same demand under any heading.[16]

Finally, Section 2(1) guarantees the important right of tribunal recourse for redress:

> 2(1) Any claim in respect of the contravention of a term modified or included by virtue of an equality clause, including a claim for arrears of remuneration or damages in respect of the contravention, may be presented by way of a complaint to an employment tribunal.[17]

The Equal Pay Act 1970 gives an individual a right to the same contractual pay and benefits as a person of the opposite sex in the same employment, where the man and the woman are doing Like work; or Work rated as equivalent under an analytical job evaluation study; or Work that is proved to be of equal value. The employer will not be required to provide the same pay and benefits if it can be proven that the difference in pay or benefits is genuinely due to a reason other than one related to sex.

The EPA covers direct and indirect sex discrimination, that is where the pay difference is due to a condition or practice which applies to men and women but which adversely affects a considerably larger proportion of one sex than the other and it is not justifiable, irrespective of sex, to apply that condition or practice. The EPA applies to people who are 'employees' but also to other people who are engaged under a contract personally to execute work or labor. The EPA does not apply to occupational pensions, but rights to equal treatment are contained in the Pensions Act 1995.

Claims under the Equal Pay Act can be taken at any time up to 6 months after leaving the employment to which the claim relates. If a claim is successful under the EPA, the complainant will be entitled to the same level of pay or benefits as the comparator for the future, if the complainant is still in the same job, and backpay representing the difference in pay subject to a limit with interest. However, the EPA contains a limit on back pay of up to two years before commencement of proceedings.

The Sex Discrimination Act 1975 (SDA) According to the Sex Discrimination Act 1975 (as amended), in guarding against gender discrimination, direct and indirect discrimination is defined in Section 1:

> 1(1) In any circumstances relevant for the purposes of any provision of this Act …, a person discriminates against a woman if:
> (a) on the ground of her sex he treats her less favourably than he treats or would treat a man, or
> (b) he applies to her a requirement or condition which he applies or would apply equally to a man but:
> (i) which is such that the proportion of women who can comply with it is considerably smaller than the proportion of men who can comply with it, and
> (ii) which he cannot show to be justifiable irrespective of the sex of the person to whom it is applied, and
> 1(1)(b)(iii) which is to her detriment because she cannot comply with it.[18]

In terms of sex discrimination against men, Section 2 holds that Section 1 is to be read as applying equally to the treatment of men, and for that purpose shall have effect with such modifications as are required.[19]

In looking at discrimination in the pre-employment stage, Section 6(1) states:

> 6(1) It is unlawful for a person, in relation to employment by him at an establishment in Great Britain, to discriminate against a woman
> (a) in the arrangements he makes for the purpose of determining who should be offered that employment, or
> (b) in the terms on which he offers her that employment, or
> (c) by refusing or deliberately omitting to offer her that employment.[20]

In looking at discrimination in the employment stage, Section 6(2) states:

> 6(2) It is unlawful for a person, in the case of a woman employed by him at an establishment in Great Britain, to discriminate against her

> (a) in the way he affords her access to opportunities for promotion, transfer or training, or to any other benefits, facilities or services, or by refusing or deliberately omitting to afford her access to them, or
> (b) by dismissing her, or subjecting her to any other detriment.[21]

There is an exception to the rule where sex is a genuine occupational qualification, which is contained in Section 7:

> 7(1) In relation to sex discrimination
> (a) section 6(1)(a) or (c) does not apply to any employment where being a man is a genuine occupational qualification for the job.
> 7(2) Being a man is a genuine occupational qualification for a job only where
> (a) the essential nature of the job calls for a man for reasons of physiology (excluding physical strength or stamina) or, in dramatic performances or other entertainment, for reasons of authenticity, so that the essential nature of the job would be materially different if carried out by a woman, or
> (b) the job needs to be held by a man to preserve decency or privacy…, or
> (c) the nature or location of the establishment makes it impracticable for the holder of the job to live elsewhere than in premises provided by the employer…,
> (d) the nature of the establishment, or of the part of it within which the work is done, requires it to be held by a man…, or
> (e) the holder of the job provides individuals with personal services promoting their welfare or education, or similar personal services, and those services can most effectively be provided by a man, or
> (f) the job needs to be held by a man because of restrictions imposed by the laws regulating the employment of women, or
> (g) the job needs to be held by a man because it is likely to involve the performance of duties outside the United Kingdom in a country whose laws or customs are such that the duties could not, or could not effectively, be performed by a woman, or
> (h) the job is one of two to be held by a married couple.[22]

Section 48 allows for positive action by employers to overcome the effects of past discrimination, in terms of training and encouragement where few or no members of one sex have been doing particular work in the preceding 12 months.[23] The Equal Opportunity Employment Commission is recognized in Section 53:

> 53(1) There shall be a body of Commissioners named the Equal Opportunities Commission…, which shall have the following duties
> (a) to work toward the elimination of discrimination,
> (b) to promote equality of opportunity between men and women generally, and
> (c) to keep under review the working of this Act and the Equal Pay Act 1970 and, when they are so required by the Secretary of State or otherwise think it necessary, draw up and submit to the Secretary of State proposals for amending them.[24]

The Sex Discrimination Act makes it unlawful to discriminate on the grounds of sex or marital status. It applies to both males and females, and makes gender discrimination unlawful in employment, vocational training, education, provision of goods, facilities and services, and housing. Failure to observe the Codes of Practice issued by the Equal Opportunities Commission may result in breaches of the law. The 1986 Amendment removes certain restrictions applying to the working hours and working conditions of women. A further recent amendment places the burden of proof with the employer, in line with the European Directives.

The SDA prohibits sex discrimination against individuals in the areas of employment and education, in the provision of goods, facilities and services, and in the disposal or management of premises. It applies to women and men of any age, including children, and discriminatory advertisements are unlawful. There are some general exceptions to when gender discrimination is unlawful, namely when a charity is providing a benefit to one sex only, in accordance with its charitable instrument; when people are competing in a sport in which the average woman is at a disadvantage to the average man because of physical strength, stamina or physique; and in insurance, where the discriminatory treatment reasonably relates to actuarial or other data.

Importantly, the SDA prohibits direct and indirect sex discrimination. Direct sex discrimination is where a woman or man is treated less favorably than a person of the opposite sex in comparable circumstances is, or would be, because of their gender. The test is: was the treatment less favorable than the treatment which was or would be accorded to a person of the opposite sex?; and was the treatment less favorable because of the gender of the person involved? Indirect sex discrimination is where a condition or practice is applied to both sexes but it adversely affects a considerably larger proportion of one sex than the other, and it is not justifiable, irrespective of sex, to apply that condition or practice. Concerning discrimination in the field of employment, it is unlawful for an employer to discriminate directly or indirectly on grounds of gender or marriage in recruitment, although sex discrimination will be lawful if there is a genuine occupational requirement. Objective justification will be shown if the provision, criterion or practice corresponds to a real need on the part of the employer, and is appropriate and necessary to achieving that objective.

There are also special provisions prohibiting discrimination by firms against partners or potential partners, by trade unions and employers' organizations against members or potential members, by authorities or bodies in conferring authorizations or qualifications needed for or facilitating engagement in a particular profession or trade, by people providing vocational training, by employment agencies, and by or in relation to barristers or advocates. The SDA also protects people engaged under a contract personally to execute work or labor, and contract workers whose labor is supplied by their employer to another person, the principal, are protected against discrimination by the principal.

In general, positive discrimination to favor one sex is not lawful. There are limited exceptions allowing discrimination in training, or encouragement to apply for particular work in which members of the relevant sex are under-represented, and these lawful exceptions are often referred to as positive action.

In a claim of sex discrimination presented to an employment tribunal, it is first up to the applicant to establish facts, which constitute a 'prima facie' case of discrimination. The burden of proof is initially on the employee to show on the balance of probabilities that her male comparator is doing the same or broadly similar work, or that her work has been rated as equivalent to his, or that her work is of equal value, and that his contract contains a more favorable term. The burden of proof then shifts from the applicant to the employer to show that there is a nondiscriminatory reason for their actions, that is the difference between the contracts is genuinely due to a material factor which is not the difference of gender. The material factor defense is the reason put forward by the employer to explain why the comparator, although doing equal work, is paid more than the applicant. To be successful, this factor must be significant and relevant; that is, it must be an important cause of the difference and apply to the jobs in question. The difference in pay must be genuinely due to the material factor which must not be tainted by gender discrimination. If the reason given for paying the comparator more is that he has certain skills which the applicant does not have, then the employer would have to demonstrate that these skills are necessary for the job, and genuinely applied during the performance of the job, and are not simply rewarded because past pay agreements recognized and rewarded skills which are no longer applicable. To succeed in a defense, the employer needs to show that the material factor accounts for the whole of the difference in pay.

Employment related claims are brought in the employment tribunal. Other claims are brought in a county court in England and Wales or in a sheriff court in Scotland. Strict time limits apply, that is three months less one day from the act of discrimination for employment tribunal claims and six months less one day for other claims. Special provisions apply to claims about discrimination in the state education sector. Possible remedies for unlawful discrimination include a declaration that unlawful discrimination has occurred; compensation for financial loss, injury to feelings and injury to health with interest; in employment tribunals, a recommendation that the employer take action which will reduce the effect of discrimination on the complainant; and in a county court in England and Wales, or sheriff court in Scotland, an order that the discriminator stop the discrimination.

As well as the Sex Discrimination Act and the Equal Pay Act, the following legislative provisions apply in England, Wales and Scotland and may be relevant to cases of gender discrimination or equal pay:

The Disability Discrimination Act 1995 It deals with discrimination against disabled people in the areas of employment, the provision of goods, facilities and services and premises, education and public transport.[25]

The Employment Act 1989 It includes an exemption from the operation of the Sex Discrimination Act for acts done in connection with employment or vocational training to comply with certain specified statutory provisions relating to the protection of women at work.[26]

The Employment Relations Act 1999 It includes a right to be accompanied at disciplinary or grievance hearings by a trade union official or another of the employer's workers.[27]

The Employment Rights Act 1996 It includes the right not to be unfairly dismissed on the grounds of pregnancy.[28]

The Employment Tribunals (Interest on Awards in Discrimination Cases) Regulations 1996 They provide for tribunals to award interest on backpay in Equal Pay Act cases and compensation awards made under the Sex Discrimination Act 1975, the Race Relations Act 1976 and the Disability Discrimination Act 1995.[29]

The Equal Pay (Complaints to Employment Tribunals) (Armed Forces) Regulations 1997 They allow individuals serving in the armed forces to bring equal pay claims in the employment tribunal provided a complaint has been made about the same matter under the service redress procedures which has not been withdrawn.[30]

The Health and Safety at Work Act 1974 It places a duty on employers to ensure, so far as is reasonably practicable, the health, safety and welfare at work of all their employees.[31]

The Human Rights Act 1998 It incorporates rights under the European Convention of Human Rights into domestic law, and individuals can bring claims under the HRA against public authorities for breaches of Convention rights, which include a right not to be discriminated against on nonexhaustive grounds, such as gender.[32]

The Management of Health and Safety at Work Regulations 1999 They require employers to carry out risk assessments, with specific obligations on employers to assess risk where there are women of childbearing age at work.[33]

The Maternity and Parental Leave Regulations 1999 They contain the detail of the rights to maternity and parental leave contained in the Employment Rights Act 1996 (ERA), and also prescribe the circumstances in which a dismissal will be automatically unfair for the purposes of the ERA if the dismissal is for a reason related to pregnancy, childbirth, maternity leave, parental leave, or time off for dependants.[34]

The National Minimum Wage Act 1998 It provides that workers shall not be paid less than a designated minimum rate per hour.[35]

The National Minimum Wage Regulations 1999 They contain detailed rules as to who qualifies for the national minimum wage and what counts as working time and remuneration for these purposes.[36]

The Occupational Pension Schemes (Equal Treatment) Regulations 1995 They set out how claims may be made to enforce rights to equal treatment in occupational pension schemes.[37]

The Part-Time Workers Regulations 2000 They give part-time workers the right not to be treated less favorably than comparable full-time workers unless the difference in treatment is objectively justifiable.[38]

The Pensions Act 1995 It requires occupational pension schemes to observe the principle of equal treatment between men and women.[39]

The Protection from Harassment Act 1997 It creates a criminal offence of harassment and also creates a civil claim, allowing individuals who are harassed to claim damages and seek a court order to stop the harasser from continuing the harassment.[40]

The Race Relations Act 1976 It prohibits discrimination on racial grounds in the areas of employment, education, and the provision of goods, facilities and services and premises, with the Race Relations (Amendment) Act 2000 imposing a positive duty on public authorities to eliminate unlawful discrimination and promote equality of opportunity.[41]

The Sex Discrimination (Complaints to Employment Tribunals) (Armed Forces) Regulations 1997 They allow individuals serving in the armed forces to bring sex discrimination claims in the employment tribunal provided a complaint has been made about the same matter under the service redress procedures which has not been withdrawn.[42]

The Sex Discrimination (Questions and Replies) Order 1975 It prescribes the forms to be used to obtain information in accordance with Section 74 Sex Discrimination Act 1975 and also sets out the time limits and methods for service of these questionnaires.[43]

The Social Security Contributions and Benefits Act 1992.[44] It contains guidelines for Social Security Contributions and Benefits.

The Statutory Maternity Pay (General) Regulations 1986,[45] and *The Statutory Maternity Pay (General) (Modification and Amendment) Regulations 2000* They contain the provisions relating to entitlement to Statutory Maternity Pay.[46]

The Working Time Regulations 1998 They contain provisions regulating working time including a limit of average 48 hours work per week with exceptions, daily and weekly rest entitlements and rest breaks, a right to four weeks paid annual leave and to be paid for accrued but untaken leave on termination of employment, and special provisions relating to night work.[47]

The Equal Opportunities Commission (EOC) and the Code of Practice on Equal Pay The Equal Opportunities Commission (EOC) was set up under the Sex Discrimination Act 1975 (as amended) and is empowered to issue Codes of Practice under Section 58(A)(1). The EOC is charged with the duty to work towards the elimination of sex discrimination, to promote equality of opportunity between men and women generally, and to keep under review the working of the Sex Discrimination Act 1975 and the Equal Pay Act 1970 (each as amended). The Commission fulfills its duties in various ways, including providing advice and assistance to employers, employees, trade unions and other interested parties, about rights and obligations under the law.

The Code of Practice on Equal Pay was issued by the Equal Opportunities Commission and was brought into force on March 26, 1997.[48] It aims to provide practical guidance and to recommend good practice to those with responsibility for or interest in the pay arrangements within a particular organization. It is grounded in the concept that a right to equal pay free of sex bias is conferred under both domestic and European legislation. In addition to the need to meet the legal requirements, there are sound business reasons for implementing equal pay, since pay systems which are transparent and value the entire workforce send positive messages about an organization's values and ways of working. Fair and non-discriminatory systems represent good management practice and contribute to the efficient achievement of business objectives by encouraging maximum productivity from all employees.

Gender segregation involves a form of labor market rigidity that prevents the allocation of the most appropriate worker to any given job slot, and is a failure of the market to allocate people to their most productive location. Gender discrimination in pay occurs primarily because women and men tend to do different jobs or to have different work patterns. As a result it is easy to undervalue the demands of work performed by one sex compared with the demands associated with jobs typically done by the other. Such differences can be reinforced by discriminatory recruitment, training, selection and promotion procedures which may restrict the range of work each sex performs. Gender segregation in employment is often historical, and consequently, it may be difficult to recognize the discriminatory effects of past pay and grading decisions based on traditional values ascribed to 'male' and 'female' work. Career progression and promotion in all sectors are mechanisms, which sustain and even widen the gender pay gap.

Past discriminatory assumptions about the value of what has been regarded as men's or women's work may be reflected in current grading schemes. Men and women may be doing the same or very similar work but have different job titles and consequently be in separate grades, with the women's jobs being graded lower. They may also be doing different jobs, which are actually of equal value though the women are in lower grades. The grading scheme could fail to value the actual work done and result in discrimination.

There has been a tendency for payment systems to be designed to reward work patterns traditionally associated with men's employment and fail to recognize the different pattern of 'female' work. Most of the discrimination in pay systems takes the form of indirect or hidden discrimination. This occurs where pay rules and agreements appear to be neutral between men and women, but the effect of their application is to disadvantage substantially more of one sex than the other.

The Code of Practice on Equal Pay is the main source of advice on implementing equal pay in the workplace and was issued by the Equal

Opportunities Commission (EOC) in 1997. The Code has been approved by Parliament and is admissible in evidence in any proceedings under the Equal Pay Act 1970 or the Sex Discrimination Act 1975 (each as amended) before an employment tribunal. It is unlawful to offer different pay and different working conditions where women and men are doing the same or like work or rated as equivalent in the same employment, that is work of equal value in terms of the demands that it makes. Employers must include an equality clause into individual contracts of employment.

The Equal Opportunities Commission's Code of Practice on Equal Pay recommends that employers introduce an equal pay policy and review, and monitor their pay systems for gender bias. A failure on the part of any person to observe any provision of a code of practice shall not of itself render him liable to any proceedings, but in any proceedings under this Act before an employment tribunal, any code of practice issued shall be admissible in evidence, and if any provision of such a code appears to the tribunal, to be relevant to any question arising in the proceedings, it shall be taken into account in determining that question.

The EOC issued a Code of Practice for the purposes of the elimination of discrimination in employment; for guidance as to what steps it is reasonably practicable for employers to take to ensure that their employees do not in the course of their employment act unlawfully contrary to the Sex Discrimination Act (SDA); and for the promotion of equality of opportunity between men and women in employment. The Code gives guidance to employers, trade unions and employment agencies on measures that can he taken to achieve equality. The primary responsibility at law rests with each employer to ensure that there is no unlawful discrimination.

A full equal pay review, such as is outlined in the Code of Practice on Equal Pay, involves determining which women and men in an organization are performing equal work, then analyzing and comparing all aspects of their pay, including full and part-time employees. Employers should ensure that any differences between the pay of women and men can be objectively justified by factors unrelated to sex, and if not, steps should be taken to equalize pay.

The Code recommends the establishment and use of consistent criteria for selection, training, promotion, redundancy and dismissal that are made known to all employees, as part of good employment practices in eliminating gender discrimination. It is recommended that each individual should be assessed according to his personal capability to carry out a given job.

There are very few instances in which a job will qualify for Genuine Occupational Qualification (GOQ) on the ground of sex. It is recommended that a job for which a GOQ was used in the past should be re-examined if the post falls vacant to see whether the GOQ still applies, since circumstances may well have changed, rendering the GOQ inapplicable.

Unless the job is covered by an exception, it is unlawful for employers to discriminate directly or indirectly on the grounds of sex in the way they afford access to opportunities for promotion, transfer or training. It is recommended that where an appraisal system is in operation, the assessment criteria should be examined to ensure that they are not unlawfully discriminatory and the scheme monitored to assess how it is working in practice, and promotion and career development patterns should be reviewed to ensure that the traditional qualifications are justifiable requirements for the job to be done.

It is unlawful to victimize an individual for a complaint or grievance made in good faith about sex discrimination or for giving evidence about such a complaint. It is recommended that particular care is taken to ensure that an employee who has in good faith taken action under the Equal Pay Act or the Sex Discrimination Act does not receive less favorable treatment than other employees.

It is unlawful to discriminate directly or indirectly on grounds of sex in dismissals, redundancies or by treating an employee unfavorably in any other way. It is recommended that care is taken that members of one sex are not disciplined or dismissed for performance or behavior which would be overlooked or condoned in the other sex, and redundancy procedures affecting a group of employees predominantly of one sex should be reviewed, so as to remove any effects which could be disproportionate and unjustifiable.

Although selection for recruitment or promotion must be on merit, irrespective of sex, the Sex Discrimination Act does allow certain steps to redress the effects of previous unequal opportunities, in terms of positive action. Employers may wish to consider training their own employees for work which is traditionally the preserve of the other sex; positive encouragement to women to apply for management posts; and advertisements which encourage applications from the minority sex, but selection made on merit without reference to gender.

The Equal Opportunities Commission recommends that a pay systems review should involve the following stages:

> Stage One. Undertake a thorough analysis of the pay system to produce a breakdown of all employees, which covers gender, job title, grade, whether part-time or full-time, with basic pay, performance ratings and all other elements of remuneration.
> Stage Two. Examine each element of the pay system against the data obtained in stage one.
> Stage Three. Identify any elements of the pay system that the review indicates may be the source of any discrimination.
> Stage Four. Change any rules or practices, including those in collective agreements, which stages 1 to 3 have identified as likely to give rise to discrimination in pay, in consultation with employees, trade unions or staff representatives where appropriate. Stages 1 to 3 may reveal that practices and procedures in relation to recruitment, selection and access to training have contributed to discrimination in pay, and these should be addressed.
> Stage Five. Analyze the likely effects of any proposed changes in practice to the pay system before implementation, to identify and rectify any discrimination that could be caused.
> Stage Six. Give equal pay to current employees. Where the review shows that some employees are not receiving equal pay for equal work and the reasons cannot be shown to be free of sex bias, then a plan must be developed for dealing with this.
> Stage Seven. Set up a system of regular monitoring to allow checks to be made to pay practices.

Stage Eight. Draw up and publish an equal pay policy with provision for assessing the new pay system or modification to a system in terms of sex discrimination.[49]

The following is a suggested equal pay policy statement:

'Action to implement policy
In order to put our commitment to equal pay into practice we will:
examine our existing and future pay practices for all our employees including those in non-standard employment and those who are absent on pregnancy and maternity leave.
carry out regular monitoring of the impact of our practices.
inform employees of how these practices work and how their own pay is arrived at.
provide training and guidance for managers and supervisory staff involved in decisions about pay and benefits.
discuss and agree the equal pay policy with employees, trade unions or staff representatives where appropriate.
We intend through the above action to avoid unfair discrimination, to reward fairly the skills, experience and potential of all staff and thereby to increase efficiency, productivity and competitiveness and enhance the organisation's reputation and image'.[50]

The Code provides guidance on drawing up an equal pay policy and a suggested equal pay policy. However, there is no legal obligation on employers to carry out a pay systems review or to adopt an equal pay policy.

Northern Ireland

Legislation

Although there are various regulations, European Directives and case law on the area of gender discrimination in employment, there are two main pieces of legislation on sex discrimination in Northern Ireland, namely the Equal Pay Act (Northern Ireland) 1970, which makes discrimination on the grounds of gender unlawful in the area of pay; and the Sex Discrimination (Northern Ireland) Order 1976 (as amended), which applies to both women and men, and makes discrimination on grounds of both sex and marital status unlawful in the various areas, such as employment; vocational training; education; the provision of goods, facilities and services; and housing. In Northern Ireland, the gender pay gap owes more to the 'unequal treatment' of women than to differences between men and women in their labor market characteristics.[51] To be discriminated against means to be treated less favorably than others, and sex discrimination is less favorable treatment on the grounds of sex or marital status.

The Equal Pay Act (Northern Ireland) 1970 (EPA) The Equal Pay Act of Northern Ireland, entitled an Act to prevent discrimination as regards terms and conditions of employment between men and women, outlines the equality clause provision in Article 1:

> 1(1) If the terms of a contract under which a woman is employed at an establishment in Northern Ireland do not include (directly or by reference to a collective agreement or otherwise) an equality clause they shall be deemed to include one.
> (2) An equality clause is a provision which relates to terms (whether concerned with pay or not) of a contract under which a woman is employed (the 'woman's contract'), and has the effect that
> (a) where the woman is employed on like work with a man in the same employment
> (i) if (apart from the equality clause) any term of the woman's contract is or becomes less favourable to the woman than a term of a similar kind in the contract under which that man is employed, that term of the woman's contract shall be treated as so modified as not to be less favourable, and
> (ii) if (apart from the equality clause) at any time the woman's contract does not include a term corresponding to a term benefiting that man included in the contract under which he is employed, the woman's contract shall be treated as including such a term;
> (b) where the woman is employed on work rated as equivalent with that of a man in the same employment
> (i) if (apart from the equality clause) any term of the woman's contract determined by the rating of the work is or becomes less favourable to the woman than a term of a similar kind in the contract under which that man is employed, that term of the woman's contract shall be treated as so modified as not to be less favourable, and,
> (ii) if (apart from the equality clause) at any time the woman's contract does not include a term corresponding to a term benefiting that man included in the contract under which he is employed and determined by the rating of the work, the woman's contract shall be treated as including such a term.
> (3) An equality clause shall not operate in relation to a variation between the woman's contract and the man's contract if the employer proves that the variation is genuinely due to a material difference (other than the difference of sex) between her case and his.[52]

In terms of enforcement of equal treatment, Article 2 establishes that any claim in respect of the contravention of a term modified or included by virtue of an equality clause, including a claim for arrears of remuneration or damages in respect of the contravention, may be presented by way of a complaint to an industrial tribunal.[53]

The Equal Pay Act provides for equal pay between men and women by giving a woman the right to equality in the terms of the contract of employment where employed on like work to that of a man, work rated as equivalent to that of a man, or work of equal value to that of a man. The Act applies equally to men and women of all ages, and its purpose is to eliminate discrimination between men and women in pay and other terms of the contracts of employment such as piecework, output and bonus payments, holidays, free accommodation and sick leave.

In practice, any term which is in the man's contract but missing from the woman's is to be treated as if it is in her contract. In addition, any term in the woman's contract which is less favorable than the same term in the man's contract is improved so that they are equal. The Act applies to all employees whether on full-time, part-time, casual or temporary contracts, regardless of length of service; other workers, including self-employed, whose contracts require personal performance of the work; and employment carried out wholly or mainly in Northern Ireland. The equal pay law is meant to help insure that women and men in the same employment are treated equally in pay and other terms and conditions of employment. The law allows an employer to defend an equal pay case by showing that the difference in pay between male and female employees is genuinely due to some material factor other than the difference of sex.

The Sex Discrimination (Northern Ireland) Order 1976 (SDO) The Sex Discrimination Order of Northern Ireland prohibits sex discrimination against women in Article 3:

> 3(1) A person discriminates against a woman in any circumstances relevant for the purposes of any provision of this Order if
> (a) on the ground of her sex he treats her less favourably than he treats or would treat a man, or
> (b) he applies to her a requirement or condition which he applies or would apply equally to a man but
> (i) which is such that the proportion of women who can comply with it is considerably smaller than the proportion of men who can comply with it, and
> (ii) which he cannot show to be justifiable irrespective of the sex of the person to whom it is applied, and
> (iii) which is to her detriment because she cannot comply with it.[54]

As well, sex discrimination against men is prohibited in Article 4:

> 4(1) Article 3 and the provisions of Parts III and IV relating to sex discrimination against women, are to be read as applying equally to the treatment of men, and for that purpose shall have effect with such modifications as are requisite.
> (2) In the application of paragraph (1) no account shall be taken of special treatment afforded to women in connection with pregnancy or childbirth.[55]

In terms of discrimination against applicants and employees, Article 8 states:

> 8(1) It is unlawful for a person, in relation to employment by him at an establishment in Northern Ireland, to discriminate against a woman
> (a) in the arrangements he makes for the purpose of determining who should be offered that employment, or
> (b) in the terms on which he offers her that employment, or
> (c) by refusing or deliberately omitting to offer her that employment.

(2) It is unlawful for a person, in the case of a woman employed by him at an establishment in Northern Ireland, to discriminate against her

(a) in the way he affords her access to opportunities, for promotion, transfer or training, or to any other benefits, facilities or services, or by refusing or deliberately omitting to afford her access to them, or

(b) by dismissing her, or subjecting her to any detriment.[56]

An exception to discrimination where sex is a genuine occupational qualification is contained in Article 10:

10(1) In relation to sex discrimination

(a) Article 8(1)(a) or (c) does not apply to any employment where being a man is a genuine occupational qualification for the job, and

(b) Article 8(2)(a) does not apply to opportunities for promotion or transfer to, or training for, such employment.

(2) Being a man is a genuine occupational qualification for a job only where

(a) the essential nature of the job calls for a man for reasons of physiology (excluding physical strength or stamina) or, in dramatic performances or other entertainment, for reasons of authenticity, so that the essential nature of the job would be materially different if carried out by a woman, or

(b) the job needs to be held by a man to preserve decency or privacy because

(i) it is likely to involve physical contact with men in circumstances where they might reasonably object to its being carried out by a woman, or

(ii) the holder of the job is likely to do his work in circumstances where men might reasonably object to the presence of a woman because they are in a state of undress or are using sanitary facilities, or

(c) the nature or location of the establishment makes it impracticable for the holder of the job to live elsewhere than in a premises provided by the employer, and

(i) the only such premises which are available for persons holding that kind of job are lived in, or normally lived in by men and are not equipped with separate sleeping accommodation for women and sanitary facilities which could be used by women in privacy from men, and

(ii) it is not reasonable to expect the employer either to equip those premises with such accommodation and facilities or to provide other premises for women, or

(d) the nature of the establishment, or of part of it within which the work is done, requires the job to be hold by a man because

(i) it is, or is part of, a hospital, prison or other establishment for persons requiring special supervision, attention or care and

(ii) those persons are all men (disregarding any woman whose presence is exceptional) and

(iii) it is reasonable, having regard to the essential character of the establishment or that part, that the job should not be held by a woman, or

(e) the holder of the job provides individuals with personal services promoting their welfare or education, or similar personal services, and those services can most effectively be provided by a man, or

(f) the job needs to be held by a man because of restrictions imposed by the laws regulating the employment of women, or
(g) the job needs to be held by a man because it is likely to involve the performance of duties outside the United Kingdom or a country whose laws or customs are such that the duties could not, or could not effectively, be performed by a woman, or
(h) the job is one of two to be held by a married couple.[57]

Article 54 establishes that there shall be a body of Commissioners named the Equal Opportunities Commission for Northern Ireland, which shall have the following duties to work towards the elimination of discrimination, to promote equality of opportunity between men and women generally, and to keep under review the working of this Order and the Equal Pay Act and, when the Commission is so required by the Department or otherwise thinks it necessary, draw up and submit to the Department proposals for amending them.[58]

The Sex Discrimination Order makes it unlawful to discriminate against an individual on the grounds of gender in the fields of employment, training and service provision. It outlines three types of discrimination, namely direct discrimination where someone is treated less favorably than others in the same or similar position and the grounds for that treatment is sex or marital status; indirect discrimination in employment where an apparently neutral provision, criterion or practice disadvantages a considerably larger proportion of the members of one sex and cannot be justified by objective factors unrelated to sex; and victimization where someone is treated less favorably than others because they have, for instance, complained of sexual discrimination or have assisted someone else to do so. The employment provisions of the Order do not apply where being a woman or a man is a genuine occupational qualification for a job.

Complaints of discrimination in employment must be made within three months of the act complained of, and are dealt with by an industrial tribunal. Where a tribunal decides in favor of the complainant, it may award an order declaring the rights of the parties, an order requiring the respondent to pay compensation to the complainant, or a recommendation that the respondent takes remedial action to obviate or reduce discrimination. It is unlawful for an employer to discriminate in the recruitment and selection including the terms of an offer of employment; in the terms and conditions of employment and in relation to access to benefits including opportunities for promotion, transfer and training and any other benefits or the refusal of those opportunities; and in the dismissal of an employee or any other detriment.

The Equality Commission for Northern Ireland has responsibility for enforcing the Equal Pay (Northern Ireland) Act 1970 and the Sex Discrimination Order 1976 (as amended).[59] It is also under a duty to work towards the elimination of sex discrimination, to promote equality of opportunity between the sexes and to keep the workings of the legislation under review.

Ireland

Legislation

In looking at gender equality in the Republic of Ireland, the two main pieces of legislation are the Employment Equality Act, 1998 and the Equal Status Act, 2000.

Employment Equality Act, 1998 The Employment Equality Act of Ireland outlines the concept of discrimination in Article 6:

> 6(1) For the purposes of this Act, discrimination shall be taken to occur where, on any of the grounds in subsection (2) (in this Act referred to as 'the discriminatory grounds'), one person is treated less favourably than another is, has been or would be treated.
> (2) As between any 2 persons, the discriminatory grounds (and the descriptions of those grounds for the purposes of this Act) are
> (a) that one is a woman and the other is a man (in this Act referred to as 'the gender ground').[60]

Article 7(1) establishes equal work:

> 7(1) ...for the purposes of this Act, in relation to the work which one person is employed to do, another person shall be regarded as employed to do like work if
> (a) both perform the same work under the same or similar conditions, or each is interchangeable with the other in relation to the work,
> (b) the work performed by one is a similar nature to that performed by the other and any differences between the work performed or the conditions under which it is performed by each either are of small importance in relation to the work as a whole or occur with such irregularity as not to be significant to the work as a whole, or
> (c) the work performed by one is equal in value to the work performed by the other, having regard to such matters as skill, physical or mental requirements, responsibility and working conditions.[61]

Further, Article 7(3) establishes equal pay:

> 7(3) In any case where
> (a) the remuneration received by one person ('the primary worker') is less than the remuneration received by another ('the comparator'), and
> (b) the work performed by the primary worker is greater in value than the work performed by the comparator...,
> then,...the work performed by the primary worker shall be regarded as equal in value to the work performed by the comparator.[62]

In terms of discrimination in specific areas, Article 8(1) states that in relation to access to employment, conditions of employment, training or experience for or in relation to employment, promotion or re-grading, or classification of posts, an employer shall not discriminate against an employee or prospective employee.[63]

In terms of access to employment, Article 8(5) states that an employer shall be taken to discriminate against an employee or prospective employee in relation to access to employment if the employer discriminates against the employee or prospective employee in any arrangements the employer makes for the purpose of deciding to whom employment should be offered, or by specifying, in respect of one person or class of persons, entry requirements for employment which are not specified in respect of other persons or classes of persons, where the circumstances in which both such persons or classes would be employed are not materially different.[64]

In terms of conditions of employment, Article 8(6) states that an employer shall be taken to discriminate against an employee or prospective employee in relation to conditions of employment if, on any of the discriminatory grounds, the employer does not offer or afford to that employee or prospective employee or to a class of persons of whom he or she is one the same terms of employment other than the remuneration and pension rights, the same working conditions, and the same treatment in relation to overtime, shift work, short time, transfers, lay-offs, redundancies, dismissals and disciplinary measures, as the employer offers or affords to another person or class of persons, where the circumstances in which both such persons or classes are or would be employed are not materially different.[65]

In terms of training, Article 8(7) states that an employer shall be taken to discriminate against an employee in relation to training or experience for, or in relation to, employment if, on any of the disciplinary grounds, the employer refuses to offer or afford to that employee the same opportunities or facilities for employment counselling, training whether on or off the job and work experience as the employer offers or affords to other employees, where the circumstances in which that employee and those employees are employed are not materially different.[66]

In terms of promotion, Article 8(8) states that an employer shall not be taken to discriminate against an employee in relation to promotion if, on any of the discriminatory grounds the employer refuses or deliberately omits to offer or afford the employee access to opportunities for promotion in circumstances in which another eligible and qualified person is offered or afforded such access, or the employer does not in those circumstances offer or afford the employee access in the same way to those opportunities.[67]

Equal remuneration is established under Article 19 and 20:

> 19(1) It shall be a term of the contract under which A is employed that, subject to this Act, A shall at any time be entitled to the same rate of remuneration for the work which A is employed to do as B who, at that or any relevant time, is employed to do like work by the same or an associated employer.[68]
>
> 20(1) Where a person is employed under a contract which does not include (expressly or by reference to a collective agreement or otherwise) a term satisfying

subsection (1) of section 19, the contract shall be taken to include a term giving effect to that subsection; and, if such an implied term conflicts with an expression term, it shall over-ride the express term.[69]

Further, a gender equality clause is guaranteed under Article 21:

21(1) If and so far as the terms of a contract of employment do not include (expressly or by reference to a collective agreement or otherwise) a gender equality clause, they shall be taken to include one.
(2) A gender equality clause is a provision relating to the terms of a contract of employment, other than a term relating to remuneration or pension rights, which has the effect that if

(a) A is employed in circumstances where the work done by A is not materially different from that done by B in the same employment, and
(b) at any time A's contract of employment would (but for the gender equality clause)

(i) contain a term which is or becomes less favourable to A than a term of a similar kind in B's contract of employment, or
(ii) not include a term corresponding to a term in B's contract of employment which benefits B,

then the terms of A's contract of employment shall be treated as modified so that the term in question is not less favourable to A or, as the case may be, so that they include a similar term benefiting A.
(3) A gender equality clause shall not operate in relation to a difference between A's contract of employment and B's contract of employment if the employer proves that the difference is genuinely based on grounds other than the gender ground.[70]

Indirect discrimination is prohibited under Article 22:

22(1) Where a provision (whether in the nature of a requirement, practice or otherwise) which relates to any of the matters specified in...section 8(1)...

(a) applies to both A and B,
(b) is such that the proportion of persons who are disadvantaged by the provisions is substantially higher in the case of those of the same sex as A than in the case of those of the same sex as B, and
(c) cannot be justified by objective factors unrelated to A's sex,

then, for purposes of this Act, A's employer...shall be regarded as discriminating against A on the gender ground contrary to section 8....[71]

Positive action is established under Article 24 in that the provisions of this Act are without prejudice to measures to promote equal opportunity for men and women, in particular by removing existing inequalities which affect women's opportunities in the areas of access to employment, vocational training and promotion, and working conditions.[72]

The exclusion of discrimination in certain employment is allowed by way of a bona fide occupational qualification as outlined in Article 25:

> 25(1) Nothing in this Part of Part II applies to discrimination against A in respect of employment in a particular post if the discrimination results from preferring B on the ground that, by reference to one or more of subsections (2) to (4) the sex of B is or amounts to an occupational qualification for the post in question.
> (2) For the purposes of this section, the sex of B shall be taken to be an occupational qualification for a post where, on grounds of physiology (excluding physical strength or stamina) or on grounds of authenticity for the purpose of entertainment, the nature of the post
> (a) requires a person of the same sex as B, and
> (b) would be materially different if filled by a person of the same sex as A.
> (3) For the purposes of this section, the sex of B shall be taken to be an occupational qualification for a post where it is necessary that the post should be held by B because it is likely to involve the performance of duties outside the State in a place where the laws or customs are such that those duties could not reasonably be performed by a person who is of the same sex as A.
> (4) For the purposes of this section, the sex of B shall be taken to be an occupational qualification for a post
> (a) where the duties of the post involve personal services and it is necessary to have persons of both sexes engaged in such duties, or
> (b) where, because of the nature of the employment it is necessary to provide sleeping and sanitary accommodation for employees on a communal basis and it would be unreasonable to expect the provision of separate accommodation of that nature or impracticable for an employer so to provide.[73]

The functions of the Equality Authority are outlined under Article 39 as to work towards the elimination of discrimination in relation to employment; to promote equality of opportunity in relation to the matters to which this Act applies; to provide information to the public on and to keep under review the working of this Act, the Maternity Protection Act, 1994, and the Adoptive Leave Act, 1995, and, whenever it thinks necessary, to make proposals to the Minister for amending any of those Acts; and to keep under review the working of the Pensions Act, 1990, as regards the principle of equal treatment and, whenever it thinks necessary, to make proposals to the Minister for Social, Community and Family Affairs for amending that Act.[74]

In Ireland, the gender pay gap stands at 84.5 per cent.[75] The Employment Equality Act makes the principle of 'equal pay for like work' a term of every employment contract. Proving 'like work' means showing that the work of the person claiming equal pay, the claimant, is the same, similar or equal in value to the work of the appropriate comparator, the person with whom the claimant is comparing themselves. The comparator must, among other things, be employed by the same or an associated employer, at the same time or during the previous or following three years.

The Equality Authority has important legal powers, not to decide on disputes but to work generally for the elimination of discrimination and the promotion of equal opportunities. It can develop Codes of Practice, carry out equality reviews in particular employment, draw up Equality Action Plans, and serve Substantive Notices. The Authority has broad powers to ensure the development of a proactive, equality-conscious approach to equal opportunities in the workplace. The Act also establishes the Office of the Director of Equality Investigations, and if the Director decides there has been discrimination, he may order equal pay and a maximum compensation of three years' pay. The Director's decision can be appealed to the Labour Court within 42 days. Complainants of gender equality cases can go directly to the Circuit Court, as an alternative, and Circuit Court decisions, like Labour Court determinations, can be appealed to the High Court on points of law.

Equal Status Act, 2000 The Equal Status Act of Ireland prohibits discrimination in Article 3:

> 3(1) For the purposes of this Act, discrimination shall be taken to occur where
> (a) on any grounds specified in subsection (2) (in this Act referred to as 'the discriminatory grounds') which exists at present or previously existed but no longer exists or may exist in the future, or which is imputed to the person concerned, a person is treated less favourably than another person is, has been or would be treated.
> (b) (i) a person who is associated with another person is treated, by virtue of that association, less favourably than a person who is not so associated is, has been or would be treated, and
> (ii) similar treatment of that other person on any of the discriminatory grounds would, by virtue of paragraph (a), constitute discrimination,
> (2) As between any two groups of persons, the discriminatory grounds (and the descriptions of those grounds for the purposes of this Act) are:
> a) that one is male and the other is female (the 'gender ground').[76]

Positive action is permitted under Article 14:

> 14. Nothing in this Act shall be construed as prohibiting
> (b) preferential treatment or the taking of positive measures which are bona fide intended to –
> (i) promote equality of opportunity for persons who are, in relation to other persons, disadvantaged or who have been or are likely to be unable to avail themselves of the same opportunities as those other persons.[77]

Conclusion

Overall, more emphasis needs to be given to encouraging female career development and to 'gender proofing' systems of promotion and higher level recruitment in the United Kingdom and Ireland. As gender monitoring of posts, recruitment and promotion would be useful, action is needed both to encourage women to develop their careers and to remove obstacles in their paths.[78] In order for gender mainstreaming processes and activities to be effective, a comprehensive, cross-cutting and gender-aware approach is very important, as a long-term strategy to redress the existing and emerging inequalities between women and men. The principle is that redressing this inequality is a shared responsibility by all aspects of government stakeholders in gender analysis, gender planning and gender training. Women today have more independence and freedom of action than ever before. Given the chance, they can transform their own lives and the lives of others.

Notes

1 Commonwealth Office, *Advancing the Commonwealth Agenda for Gender Equality into the New Millennium (2000-2005).*
2 Commonwealth Secretariat, *1995 Commonwealth Plan.*
3 *Ibid.*
4 Government of the United Kingdom, *Equality in Practice*, 2002.
5 Women and Equality Unit, *Key indicators of women's position in Britain*, 2002.
6 Equal Opportunities Commission, *Women and Men in Britain, Pay and Income*, 2003.
7 Department of Trade and Industry, Great Britain, *Key Facts about Women in the Labour Market*, 2003.
8 *Supra* note 4.
9 Equal Opportunities Commission, *Women and Men in Britain, Pay and Income*, 2003.
10 Equal Opportunities Commission, *Facts About Women and Men in Great Britain*, 2003.
11 Equal Opportunities Commission, *Facts About Women and Men in Scotland*, 2003.
12 Equal Opportunities Commission, *Facts About Women and Men in Wales*, 2003.
13 Equal Pay Act 1970 (As amended), Great Britain, Section 1(1).
14 *Ibid.*, at Section 1(3).
15 *Ibid.*, at Section 1(4).
16 *Ibid.*, at Section 1(5).
17 *Ibid.*, at Section 2(1).
18 Sex Discrimination Act 1975 (As amended), Great Britain, Section 1.
19 *Ibid.*, at Section 2.
20 *Ibid.*, at Section 6(1).
21 *Ibid.*, at Section 6(2).
22 *Ibid.*, at Section 7.
23 *Ibid.*, at Section 48.
24 *Ibid.*, at Section 53.
25 Disability Discrimination Act, Great Britain.
26 Employment Act, Great Britain.
27 Employment Relations Act, Great Britain.
28 Employment Rights Act, Great Britain.
29 Employment Tribunals (Interest on Awards in Discrimination Cases) Regulations, Great Britain.
30 Equal Pay (Complaints to Employment Tribunals) (Armed Forces) Regulations, Great Britain.
31 Health and Safety at Work Act, Great Britain.
32 Human Rights Act, Great Britain.
33 Management of Health and Safety at Work Regulations, Great Britain.
34 Maternity and Parental Leave Regulations, Great Britain.
35 National Minimum Wage Act, Great Britain.
36 National Minimum Wage Regulations, Great Britain.
37 Occupational Pension Schemes (Equal Treatment) Regulations, Great Britain.
38 Part-Time Workers Regulations, Great Britain.
39 Pensions Act, Great Britain.

[40] Protection from Harassment Act, Great Britain.
[41] Race Relations Act 1976.
[42] Sex Discrimination (Complaints to Employment Tribunals) (Armed Forces) Regulations 1997.
[43] Sex Discrimination (Questions and Replies) Order 1975.
[44] Social Security Contributions and Benefits Act 1992.
[45] Statutory Maternity Pay (General) Regulations 1986.
[46] Statutory Maternity Pay (General) (Modification and Amendment) Regulations 2000.
[47] Working Time Regulations 1998.
[48] Equal Opportunities Commission, *Code of Practice on Equal Pay*.
[49] *Ibid.*
[50] *Ibid.*
[51] Department of Justice, Equality & Law Reform, *Developing Sectoral Strategies to Address Gender Pay Gaps*, 2003.
[52] Equal Pay Act (Northern Ireland), Article 1.
[53] *Ibid.*, at Article 2.
[54] Sex Discrimination (Northern Ireland) Order, Article 3.
[55] *Ibid.*, at Article 4.
[56] *Ibid.*, at Article 8.
[57] *Ibid.*, at Article 10.
[58] *Ibid.*, at Article 54.
[59] Equality Commission for Northern Ireland, *Sex Discrimination and Equal Pay in Northern Ireland.*
[60] Employment Equality Act, Ireland, Article 6.
[61] *Ibid.*, at Article 7(1).
[62] *Ibid.*, at Article 7(3).
[63] *Ibid.*, at Article 8(1).
[64] *Ibid.*, at Article 8(5).
[65] *Ibid.*, at Article 8(6).
[66] *Ibid.*, at Article 8(7).
[67] *Ibid.*, at Article 8(8).
[68] *Ibid.*, at Article 19.
[69] *Ibid.*, at Article 20.
[70] *Ibid.*, at Article 21.
[71] *Ibid.*, at Article 22.
[72] *Ibid.*, at Article 24.
[73] *Ibid.*, at Article 25.
[74] *Ibid.*, at Article 39.
[75] *Supra* note 51.
[76] Equal Status Act, Ireland, Article 3.
[77] *Ibid.*, at Article 14.
[78] *Supra* note 51.

References

Commonwealth Office, *Advancing the Commonwealth Agenda for Gender Equality into the New Millennium (2000-2005).*

Commonwealth Secretariat, *1995 Commonwealth Plan.*

Department of Justice, Equality & Law Reform (2003), *Developing Sectoral Strategies to Address Gender Pay Gaps*.
Disability Discrimination Act, Great Britain, 1995.
Department of Trade and Industry, Great Britain (2003), *Key Facts about Women in the Labour Market*.
Employment Act, Great Britain, 1989.
Employment Equality Act, Ireland, 1998.
Employment Relations Act, Great Britain, 1999.
Employment Rights Act, Great Britain, 1996.
Employment Tribunals (Interest on Awards in Discrimination Cases) Regulations, Great Britain, 1996.
Equal Opportunities Commission, *Code of Practice on Equal Pay*.
Equal Opportunities Commission (2003), *Facts About Women and Men in Great Britain*.
Equal Opportunities Commission (2003), *Facts About Women and Men in Scotland*.
Equal Opportunities Commission (2003), *Facts About Women and Men in Wales*.
Equal Opportunities Commission (2003), *Women and Men in Britain, Pay and Income*.
Equal Pay Act 1970 (As amended), Great Britain.
Equal Pay Act (Northern Ireland) 1970.
Equal Pay (Complaints to Employment Tribunals) (Armed Forces) Regulations, Great Britain, 1997.
Equal Status Act, Ireland, 2000.
Equality Commission for Northern Ireland, *Sex Discrimination and Equal Pay in Northern Ireland*.
Government of the United Kingdom (2002), *Equality in Practice*.
Health and Safety at Work Act, Great Britain, 1974.
Human Rights Act, Great Britain, 1998.
Management of Health and Safety at Work Regulations, Great Britain, 1999.
Maternity and Parental Leave Regulations, Great Britain, 1999.
National Minimum Wage Act, Great Britain, 1998.
National Minimum Wage Regulations, Great Britain, 1999.
Occupational Pension Schemes (Equal Treatment) Regulations, Great Britain, 1995.
Part-Time Workers Regulations, Great Britain, 2000.
Pensions Act, Great Britain, 1995.
Protection from Harassment Act, Great Britain, 1997.
Race Relations Act, Great Britain, 1976.
Sex Discrimination Act 1975 (As amended), Great Britain
Sex Discrimination (Complaints to Employment Tribunals) (Armed Forces) Regulations, Great Britain, 1997.
Sex Discrimination (Northern Ireland) Order 1976.
Sex Discrimination (Questions and Replies) Order, Great Britain, 1975.
Social Security Contributions and Benefits Act, Great Britain, 1992
Statutory Maternity Pay (General) Regulations, Great Britain, 1986.
Statutory Maternity Pay (General) (Modification and Amendment) Regulations, Great Britain, 2000.
Women and Equality Unit (2002), *Key indicators of women's position in Britain*.
Working Time Regulations, Great Britain, 1998.

Chapter 9

Gender Injustice and the European Union

Introduction

This Chapter will examine Gender Injustice and the European Union (EU). It will initially look at the role of women in European society. It will then examine the European Community treaties from their inception, and will then look at the European Court of Justice (ECJ), the European Convention for the Protection of Human Rights and Fundamental Freedoms (ECHR) and the European Social Charter with their impact on equality. Finally, important EU Directives affecting women will be analyzed. The European Union has provided important contributions to the ending of gender discrimination in the coming together of people of different Nations. Equal pay and equal treatment are real commitments for the Member States.

In recent years, the promotion of gender equality between men and women, particularly in the areas of economic and social life, has come to the forefront of the public policy agenda in the EU.[1] As more and more women enter the labor market in all countries across the European Union, ensuring that men and women receive equal treatment in the workplace becomes all the more important. The position of women relative to men in the labor market has improved greatly over the last few decades and this has included a narrowing of the gender pay gap. Employment equality legislation has played an important part. As well, economic and social factors have had an effect, as there are now an increasing number of women entering what were traditionally viewed as male-dominated occupations and an increasing proportion of women entering senior management positions. In addition, there has been an increase in the participation of women in third level education, which has thus increased the overall average level of education of the female workforce. However, in terms of the gender pay gap in the EU, women on average earn less than men in all EU Member States, as women's earnings as a percentage of men's stands at around 83 per cent.

The Role of Women in European Society

In Europe, there are 365,736,000 people, with 178,144,000 males and 187,592,000 females, according to the latest statistics.[2] The European Union's share of the world population is falling, and as such, the EU ranks third in the world population behind China and India.[3] If current trends for fertility, mortality and migration continue, the EU population will peak in the year 2025 and revert to its current level in the year 2050. In the labor force, there are 73,298,000 women and 96,404,000 men, with women accounting for roughly 40 per cent of the work force, up significantly from ten years ago. The employment rate is at 52.6 per cent for women and at 71.6 per cent for men. In terms of part-time employment as a percentage of all employment, 33.5 per cent of women and only 6.2 per cent of men work part-time. Therefore, part-time employment continues to be more important for women. In terms of employment sectors, men and women continue to pursue careers in different occupations and to occupy different positions. The agricultural sector has 2,297,000 women and 4,601,000 men, the industrial sector 10,269,000 women and 35,130,000 men, and the services sector 52,999,000 women and 49,692,000 men.

The unemployment rate is at 8,018,000 for women and at 7,746,000 for men. Further, in terms of the rate for men and women by educational level, men account for 4.3 per cent and women for 6.3 per cent of unemployment in the higher education level, 6.5 per cent and 9.3 per cent respectively in the upper secondary and post secondary education level, and 10 per cent and 13.8 per cent respectively in the pre-primary, primary and lower secondary level. Thus, women continue to outnumber men in the unemployment figures. In terms of long-term unemployment defined as 12 months or longer, women account for 47.3 per cent and men for 44.7 per cent. Further, women account for 34 per cent and men for 53.4 per cent of those considered not in the labor market.

In most European countries, women are still more likely than men to be unemployed. In fact, there is a widening of unemployment rates. Women feel threatened, because of their lack of qualifications, their position in nonsecure jobs, and the difficulty in professional re-entry. Over the last few years, the number of men in employment has fallen markedly, while the number of women in employment has gone down only marginally.[4] However, despite the larger job losses suffered by men, the rate of unemployment for women remains higher, with women at 10.9 per cent and men at 7.9 per cent.[5]

Women continue to earn less than their male counterparts. A wide pay gap persists between women and men in all European Union Member States, and in addition to the gap arising from a variety of factors, there is an unexplained difference in wages, which is presumed to be due to discrimination. The earnings of women as a percentage of men's varies from a low of 61.2 per cent for the United Kingdom to a high of 82.4 per cent in Sweden.[6] In the EU as a whole, women doing the same work as men are paid only 76 per cent of the gross hourly wage men earn, and the employment rate for women is 51.2 per cent, compared to 70.8 per cent for men, with 83 per cent of part-time workers being women.

Gender differences in salaries persist and even have increased in some countries, despite the economic activity of women and egalitarian legislation.[7] The significant trends show that pay differentials between men and women are narrow for young people, grow with time, and peak at the middle and at the end of careers.[8] As well, in a number of countries, pay differentials are widest at the extremes of the educational scale, that is little education and extensive education.

Although women who spend a long time with an individual employer appear to gain a greater financial return as a consequence than do men, especially during the initial years of their working careers, the relationship between the overall length of the working career and the financial rewards for staying in the labor market is more favorable for men than for women, as periods out of the labor market do adversely affect earnings. In the EU, men obtain a higher return on educational attainment levels and specific skills than women in all Member States. In looking at family status and caring, men who are married with children tend to have higher wages than single men without children. However, women do not benefit from a similar pay premium, and in fact married women with children have lower average wages than those of single women without children, with the number of children a woman has often impacting on her earnings.[9]

As for sectors and occupations, the gap between the wages of men in supervisory and managerial positions and those in subordinate positions is much greater than for women. Men gain more from promotion than do women. It is likely that men when promoted are promoted to higher levels than are women so that gender differences in career progression are likely to exacerbate the gender pay gap. Significant differences in earnings between men and women remain within sectors. In sectors with a relatively high share of female employment, earnings for both men and women are below the national average, and female dominated sectors are low paid sectors. The most important factors contributing to the gender pay gap in the EU are earnings differences between men and women with children; a high concentration of women in low paying sectors and occupations; and lower earnings for women in female-dominated sectors and occupations that cannot be explained by productivity differences between sectors and occupations.[10]

In terms of education, recent trends have brought about an increase in the level of education for women, but the types of fields chosen do not lend themselves to profitable job prospects. However, education is proven to help overcome some discrimination. Further, Europe has experienced an increased divorce rate, a falling birth rate, a longer life expectancy and a positive net balance of migration.[11] Marriage and children are no longer the sole limits to women. Due to the various characteristics of the different States, the birth of children has had a different effect on women's level of participation in the workforce, namely no influence (Denmark), a minimal impact (France), part-time work (Germany, United Kingdom), and a drop with the advent of the first child (Netherlands, Ireland).[12] Interestingly, less than half of all women in the EU have children, and over a quarter of women are heads of households.[13]

Overall, in looking at the statistics, we can see a number of important trends impacting women in Europe. The majority of women between the ages of 25 and 49 now work, despite having young children.[14] This is a major difference from the once strict family imperatives, showing that women have made a bid for more autonomy in their lives and their careers. Now, 80 per cent of women are employees and no longer work in family firms. Further, of the roughly 24 million employed part-time, roughly 80 per cent of these are women.[15] Interestingly, in the entrepreneur area, of the 19.8 million who are self-employed, 22.1 per cent are women.[16]

This integration into the labor force allows women to encounter a different universe from the family unit. In the industries which have expanded to adjust for the employment of women, an increasing proportion of these jobs have been part-time, lending themselves to the realities of many women who combine work and family. The share of women in employment has increased everywhere in the European Union, even in countries where part-time work is relatively unimportant. However, women find themselves most often in small non-unionized businesses, and are thus more vulnerable to wage inequity. As well, they predominate in the tertiary service sector, which accounts for 54 per cent of male employment and 79 per cent of female employment.[17]

It is important that equality for women be achieved in securing access to jobs, which are commensurate with skill levels. Women are still lagging behind due to horizontal segregation, with a concentration in feminine jobs, and vertical segregation, with difficulty acceding to higher positions in the occupational hierarchy. The system has failed to reward women's skills, and even provides guises for discrimination.

The demographic changes on the horizon will bring about a further need for qualified workers, including women. However, women remain under-utilized, and are still considered as reserve labor. This attitude is a barrier to progressive legislation. Although European laws have gone a long way to improving the plight of women in the EU, in reality, women have yet to enjoy the equality they are entitled to in theory.

Toward the European Union

Initially, many centuries ago, Europe was united within the Roman Empire. Throughout its history, the European continent has naturally been restless, fragile, contradictory, competitive and pluralistic, divided by language and religion. National ambitions and self-interest have been the predominant political forces throughout the 20th century. However, with the two World Wars and the threat of the Cold War, European integration by peaceful methods was seriously reconsidered as an alternative to the independent and aggressive Nation State. Political integration is the peaceful creation of a larger political unit out of several separate ones, which voluntarily give up some powers to a central authority and renounce the use of force toward the other units.[18] In Europe, a political structure at a supranational level exists. Only continental wide superpowers can think of solving their major problems at the national level, but for smaller powers like Western Europe, it requires wider alliance decisions. It is a multitiered approach to government and decision-making.

Prior to the development of the European Union, there had been a growing disparity between European and American industrial growth. In the United States, industrial production had increased by 163 per cent between 1900 and 1938.[19] In contrast, while Western Europe had produced one half of the world's industrial goods in 1913, this had dropped to merely a quarter only forty years later. Thus, the European Community was set up so as to be the only one which removed countervailing duties, having a supranational mechanism called the European Court, which disciplined the use of subsidies. Prior to the European Community, there was little experience in regional trade arrangements for disputes over subsidies, and countervailing duties for services and investments. The 1950s and 1960s saw the formation of the European Community. This allowed the expansion of interindustry and intraindustry trade, with no major dislocations of individual industries, and brought about more specialization and production. The 1970s saw open trade in the European Community with both small-scale and large-scale economic growth.[20]

With democratic governments reinstated in liberated Europe in the post-war era, the restructuring of the region was begun. A Congress of Europe was held in the Hague in May 1948, bringing together leading figures from France, Britain, the Netherlands, Belgium, Germany, Italy and elsewhere. Britain's Prime Minister Churchill referred to the idea of a setting up of 'a kind of United States of Europe', which made a powerful impact.[21]

The Treaty of Paris

The advocates of integration sought to escape from national rivalries. Thus came the flagship of European integration, the European Communities. The first of these was the Coal and Steel Community, also known as the Treaty of Paris signed on April 18, 1951, entered into force on July 23, 1952, and expired on July 23, 2002. It removed the Coal and Steel industries from full national control to a supranational stewardship. The High Authority, which it created, was presided over by Jean Monnet and comprised delegates from the Member States, making decisions in consultation with the Assembly. The Treaty of Paris was regarded only as a starting point, with the success foreseen in this sector expected to spread to others. The preamble of the Treaty wrote of safeguarding world peace, establishing an economic community, and substituting essential interests for age-old rivalries and conflicts.[22] Monnet, the most influential of the founding fathers of the European Economic Community, insisted on cooperation across national frontiers in a sector by sector approach. He persuaded the foreign ministers of the six countries involved to meet at Messina on June 1, 1955. They resolved that the moment had come to go a step further towards the construction of Europe. The Messina Conference set up a committee of government representatives, who wanted to proceed to a customs union with no internal tariff barriers, but only a common external tariff.

The Treaty of Rome

The Treaty of Rome was signed by France, Italy, West Germany, Luxembourg, the Netherlands and Belgium on March 25, 1957, and entered into force on January 1, 1958, creating the European Economic Community (EEC). The European Community was set up by the Treaty of Rome to maintain peace in Europe and to foster prosperity through cooperation. With the Treaty of Rome, the European Economic Community States transferred to the Community the power to conclude treaties with international organizations and with non-member countries.[23] Lord Denning, a leading constitutional expert, stated 'the Treaty of Rome is like an incoming tide. It flows into the estuaries and up the rivers. It cannot be held back'.[24] The Member States agreed to work together for an integrated multinational economy for the free movement of labor and capital in the Community, while having joint institutions and common policies toward underdeveloped regions of the Community and toward those outside the Community. The Treaty gave the community institutions power to take the necessary steps to adjust national legal rules through harmonization procedures. This was required in order to remove national, technical or legal arrangements inhibiting the free movement of products, people and resources.

The larger market allowed for a more rational use of resources and provided for higher productivity. By July 1, 1968, all internal tariffs had been abolished among the Member States for a community wide production and distribution of products and services.[25] The abolition of tariffs encouraged mutual trade so that by 1969, intraCommunity trade in manufactured products was about 50 per cent higher than previously. The long term implications of the Treaty of Rome were a system of majority voting among the representatives of the national governments in the Council, a supranational bureaucracy over which national governments would have little control, a directly elected European Parliament, and a commitment by the Member States to work for a closer union.

In accordance with Article 3, the activities of the Community include:

> 3(a) the elimination as between Member States, of customs duties and quantitative restrictions on the import and export of goods, and of all other measures having equivalent effect;
> (b) a common commercial policy;
> (c) an internal market characterized by the abolition, as between Member States, of obstacles to the free movement of goods, persons, services and capital;
> (d) Measures concerning the entry and movement of persons in the internal market…;
> (e) a common policy in the sphere of agriculture and fisheries;
> (f) a common policy in the sphere of transport;
> (g) a system ensuring that competition in the common market is not distorted;
> (h) the approximation of the laws of the Member States to the extent required for the functioning of the common market;
> (i) a policy in the social sphere comprising a European Social Fund;
> (j) the strengthening of economic and social cohesion;
> (k) a policy in the sphere of the environment;
> (l) the strengthening of the competitiveness of Community industry;
> (m) the promotion of research and technological development;
> (n) encouragement for the establishment and development of trans-European networks;
> (o) a contribution to the attainment of a high level of health protection;
> (p) a contribution to education and training of quality and to the flowering of the cultures of the Member States;

(q) a policy in the sphere of development cooperation;
(r) the association of the overseas countries and territories in order to increase trade and promote jointly economic and social development;
(s) a contribution to the strengthening of consumer protection;
(t) measures in the spheres of energy, civil protection and tourism.[26]

In terms of equal pay, Article 119 of the Treaty of Rome states:

> Each Member State shall during the first stage ensure and subsequently maintain the application of the principle that men and women should receive equal pay for equal work.
> For the purpose of this Article, 'pay' means the ordinary basic or minimum wage or salary and any other consideration, whether in cash or in kind, which the worker receives, directly or indirectly, in respect of his employment from his employer.
> Equal pay without discrimination based on sex means:
> (a) that pay for the same work at piece rates shall be calculated on the basis of the same unit of measurement;
> (b) that pay for work at time rates shall be the same for the same job.[27]

The Maastricht Treaty

The Maastricht Treaty was signed on February 7, 1992 and entered into force on November 1, 1993, creating the European Union (EU). The EU became an internal market of over 340 million people providing for the free movement of goods, capital, services and citizens of Member States. The Maastricht Treaty affirms that it marks a new stage in the process of European integration undertaken with the establishment of the European Communities. The Treaty was designed to create a firm basis for the construction of the future of Europe, by deepening the solidarity between peoples while respecting the different histories, cultures and traditions. Further, the Maastricht Treaty espoused the desire to enhance the democracy and efficient functioning of the institutions so as to enable them better to carry out, within a single institutional framework, the tasks entrusted to them. The foundations for a united Europe were laid on fundamental values including peace, unity, equality, freedom, solidarity and security, through intergovernmental cooperation and the creation of the three pillars of EC society. By the Maastricht Treaty, the European Union confirms its 'attachment to the principles of liberty, democracy and respect for human rights and fundamental freedoms and of the rule of law'.

According to Article A, the Treaty 'marks a new stage in the process of creating an ever closer union among the peoples of Europe, in which decisions are taken as closely as possible to the citizen'.[28] Further, Article B states:

> The Union shall set itself the following objectives:
> to promote economic and social progress which is balanced and sustainable, in particular through the creation of an area without internal frontiers, through the strengthening of economic and social cohesion and through the establishment of

> economic and monetary union, ultimately including a single currency in accordance with the provisions of this Treaty;
> to assert its identity on the international scene, in particular through the implementation of a common foreign and security policy including the eventual framing of a common defence policy, which might in time lead to a common defence;
> to strengthen the protection of the rights and interests of the nationals of its Member States through the introduction of a citizenship of the Union;
> to develop close cooperation on justice and home affairs;
> to maintain in full the 'acquis communautaire' and build on it with...the aim of ensuring the effectiveness of the mechanisms and the institutions of the Community.[29]

The Treaty of Amsterdam

The Treaty of Amsterdam, amending the Treaty on European Union, the Treaties establishing the European Communities and Related Acts, amending and renumbering the EU and EC treaties, was signed on October 2, 1997 and entered into force on May 1, 1999.[30]

Article 141 of the Treaty of Amsterdam, amending Article 119 of the Treaty of Rome, states:

> 1. Each Member State shall ensure that the principle of equal pay for male and female workers for equal work or work of equal value is applied.
> 2. For the purpose of this Article, 'pay' means the ordinary basic or minimum wage or salary and any other consideration, whether in cash or in kind, which the worker receives directly or indirectly, in respect of his employment, from his employer.
> Equal pay without discrimination based on sex means:
> (a) that pay for the same work at piece rates shall be calculated on the basis of the same unit of measurement;
> (b) that pay for work at time rates shall be the same for the same job.
> 3. The Council, acting in accordance with the procedure referred to in Article 251, and after consulting the Economic and Social Committee, shall adopt measures to ensure the application of the principle of equal opportunities and equal treatment of men and women in matters of employment and occupation, including the principle of equal pay for equal work or work of equal value.
> 4. With a view to ensuring full equality in practice between men and women in working life, the principle of equal treatment shall not prevent any Member State from maintaining or adopting measures providing for specific advantages in order to make it easier for the under-represented sex to pursue a vocational activity or to prevent or compensate for disadvantages in professional careers.

The extension of civil rights is a step toward European integration. The concept of citizenship is based on the principle that nationals of Member States have certain rights to move freely across national borders in the common market. Freedom of movement, under the Treaty of Rome, applied only to certain economic categories of workers, the self-employed and service providers. This, however, was expanded by the Treaty of Amsterdam and the European Court of

Justice, which had a profound impact on employment. Where EU law has direct effect, it will take precedence over domestic law in such cases as equal pay.

Equal pay for men and women is one of the principles enshrined in EU legislation since its origins. Article 119 of the Treaty of Rome holds that men and women should receive equal pay for equal work, calling for pay equality and the abolishment by Member States of gender discrimination in employment. Article 141 of the Amsterdam Treaty, which amends and replaces Article 119 of the Treaty of Rome, provides that men and women should receive equal pay and guarantees that each Member State shall ensure that the principle of equal pay for male and female workers for equal work or work of equal value is applied. The concept of pay is defined as the ordinary basic or minimum wage or salary and any other consideration, whether in cash or in kind, which the worker receives directly or indirectly, in respect of his employment from his employer. The Treaty of Amsterdam made a significant change to the former Article 119 in two respects: it placed a legal obligation on the Community to adopt measures to ensure the application of the principle of equal opportunities and equal treatment of men and women in matters of employment and occupation, and it allows for the implementation of positive action measures by the Members States. It is therefore the Community's task to promote equality between men and women.

According to the rulings of the European Court of Justice in conjunction with the spirit of the law, Article 141 of the Treaty of Amsterdam calls for Member States to ensure and maintain the application of the principle that men and women should receive equal pay for equal work. It is directly applicable where unequal pay for equal work is carried out in the same establishment or service, whether public or private. Further, the concept of equal work for equal value forbids the payment of a lower salary to workers of one gender, who are engaged in work of equal value to the opposite gender, and a fortiori, it also prohibits different pay at a lower rate for higher valued work. The contrary would render equal pay laws ineffective, and would allow an employer to circumvent the law by assigning additional duties to one gender in order to pay them lower. Therefore, national courts must take into account Article 141 as a constituent part of community law. This provision helps to ensure equal pay for equal work, and equal pay for work of equal value.

Under national law, the national court of the Member State is within its limits of discretion, when interpreting domestic law. However, domestic law must be in accord with the requirements of community law, and if this is not possible, then domestic law is inapplicable. This, therefore, is a strong incentive for national courts to rule against gender discrimination. Article 141 must be applied by the national court to ensure that free competition at work is not distorted, guarding against the employment of women at lower rates than men, when doing the same job. The Treaty of Amsterdam can preempt any inconsistent national provision. Its prohibition of sex discrimination binds State authorities, and extends to contracts and collective bargaining agreements with different pay provisions, as de facto discrimination. Therefore, the European Court of Justice pushes member countries into passing equality laws.[31]

Community legislation establishes that a citizen of the European Union should not be discriminated against in the workplace on the basis of gender, and in fact enjoys a right to equal pay for equal work or work of equal value regardless of gender. Discrimination can occur in two ways: direct discrimination occurs when men and women are treated differently, such as in terms of pay, solely on the basis of their gender; and indirect discrimination occurs when men and women are treated differently because an apparently neutral provision, criterion or practice determining recruitment, pay, working conditions, dismissal, and social security in practice disadvantages a substantially higher proportion of the members of one gender. Such provisions, criteria or practices are prohibited under Community law, unless it is proven that they are justified by objective reasons in no way related to any gender discrimination. The linkage of certain types of benefits to criteria such as marital or family status, the notion of head of household or 'breadwinner', and part-time work can result in indirect discrimination.

In terms of equal treatment in the workplace and access to employment, employers should not discriminate between men and women when recruiting workers. Employers are not permitted to apply different working conditions to men and women doing the same job. Further, looking at vertical mobility, employers should not discriminate when deciding which employees to promote, and must consider workers in terms of aspects such as skills, education, performance and seniority, and not gender. Finally, employers are not allowed to use gender as a ground for employee dismissal.

In the European Court of Justice, the Plaintiff has the burden of showing, in indirect cases, that a sexually neutral policy has a disproportionate impact (Teuling v. Bredrijfsvereniging [1987] ECR 2497).[32] The burden is then shifted to the Defendant who must justify this by objective reasons other than gender. The Plaintiff must then show that the explanation is not effective for the purpose, or that there is an alternative provision to accomplish it in a manner that has a less discriminatory impact. Equal pay without discrimination based on gender means that pay for work at time rates shall be the same for the same job. Otherwise, if there is a difference in treatment, it must be justified by objective factors other than gender. If a provision is neutral on its terms, but factually disadvantages a particular gender, an employer bears the burden of justification. The European Court of Justice requires a showing of objective justification as a defence to gender discrimination. Overall, there have been a number of landmark rulings in this area by the European Court of Justice in cases referred by national courts and successful cases have encouraged employers to be proactive in examining pay systems and review their grading systems.

In examining positive action, community law allows EU countries and companies to undertake several initiatives to counter gender discrimination. While there is no official definition of positive action, it does include all measures which are designed to counter the effects of past disadvantages and existing discrimination, and to promote equality of opportunity between men and women in the field of employment. Positive measures can take different forms of action, namely to eliminate the causes of the underemployment and reduced career opportunities for either sex, such as by intervening early on when career choices are made and in vocational training; to achieve a better balance between family and work responsibilities, and the more even distribution of these between the two sexes, such as developing childcare infrastructures or introducing career breaks; and to counter past disadvantages with affirmative action or preferential treatment, which can be prescribed in favor of certain categories of persons. In the context of those initiatives, one gender may be treated differently from the other, but since the aim is to promote equality, such initiatives can be considered to be compatible with the principle of equal treatment between men and women.

Positive action is needed not only to help guarantee equality, but also to combat the perpetuation of traditional discriminatory attitudes so as to ensure access to equal opportunities for all. It thereby helps to correct the discriminatory situation, which prevents women from seeking the same jobs as men. Historically, there have been discriminatory policies directly on their face or indirectly, applied to either gender. However, in practice, these affect women more heavily. In order to correct de facto inequalities, to promote women in all professions at all levels and to eliminate occupational segregation, personnel procedures and practices have to be changed in the initial allocation of work, the rules of transfer and promotion, and the conditions of employment.

Apart from legislation at the European and national level, the issue of the gender pay gap has been at the center of employment and equality policies, so much so that the European Commission published a code of practice on the Implementation of equal pay for work or equal value for men and women in 1996, which, although not binding, aims to provide concrete advice for employers and collective bargaining partners to ensure that the principle of equality between women and men performing work of equal value is applied to all aspects of pay. In particular, it aims to eliminate gender discrimination whenever pay structures are based on job classification and evaluation systems. The code proposes that: Employers and trade union negotiators at all levels who are involved in the setting of pay systems should carry out an analysis of these systems and pin-point any signs of gender discrimination so that remedies can be found; and a follow-up plan should be drawn up and implemented to eliminate any gender discrimination evident in the pay structures.

The Member States and the social partners must promote equal pay for equal work or work of equal value and must take steps to minimize gender related pay differentials. Three dimensions of legislative action to tackle the gender pay gap exist: 1. Equal pay legislation focused on outright discrimination of women being paid less than men for the same job; 2. Legislation to enforce the principle of equal pay for work of equal value; and 3. Legislation to improve child care support and to encourage flexible working to enable women to be more competitive and productive in the workplace and thus to improve their relative earnings, addressing factors which may prevent women accumulating or using human capital.

The Fourth European Ministerial Conference on Equality between Men and Women outlined an action plan to help create fairer, more democratic conditions, namely governments to enact and enforce laws that guarantee women's right to equal pay; provision of childcare; adoption of adequate paternal and maternal leave schemes; prohibition of references to pregnancy in recruitment procedures; adoption of laws and incentives to encourage equal sharing of parental responsibilities, such as flexible working patterns; firms to view men's role as fathers as positive in work terms; employers to contribute to childcare and family facilities for employees; trade unions, employers and other organizations to provide systems of benefits for temporary child care; more suitable meeting times to suit families; and revision of selection and nomination procedures to remove any direct or indirect discrimination against women.

The European Commission chose equal pay as the priority topic of the new Program relating to the Community Support Framework Strategy on Gender Equality (2001-2005), which forms part of the Framework Strategy that combines specific measures designed to foster gender equality with the mainstreaming approach to ensure that all Community policies take gender into account.

The European Union and the European Court of Justice (ECJ)

There are five European Union (EU) institutions, each playing a specific role, namely the European Parliament, which is elected by the citizens of the Member States; the Council of the European Union, which represents the governments of the Member States; the European Commission, which is the driving force and is the executive body; the European Court of Justice, which ensures compliance with the law; and the Court of Auditors, which controls sound and lawful management of the EU budget. There are five other important bodies, namely the European Economic and Social Committee, which expresses the opinions of organised civil society on economic and social issues; the Committee of the Regions, which expresses the opinions of regional and local authorities; the European Central Bank, which is responsible for monetary policy and managing the euro; the European Ombudsman, which deals with citizens' complaints about maladministration by any EU institution or body; and the European Investment Bank, which helps achieve EU objectives by financing investment projects. A number of agencies and other bodies complete the system.

The Commission is responsible for making legislative proposals, executing policies and monitoring the compliance of Member States with their obligations. It is the driving force behind European integration by its right of initiative. It is also the guardian of the treaties by its right to intervene with Member States and to demand compliance with their obligations. If Member States breach their treaty obligations, they will face Commission action, and possible legal proceedings in the European Court of Justice. As assistance to the European Court of Justice, the Commission is the Community watchdog for the observance of the treaties. It originates and administers Community law. The Council of Ministers is composed of representatives of Member State governments, and decides on Commission proposals. It is the Union's legislator, with all decisions involving new policies requiring unanimity. The Assembly is charged with proposing, to the Council, arrangements for universal direct elections. The Council, in turn, commends them to the Member States for adoption under constitutional procedures. The Assembly is consultative and can, if it has a sufficient majority, express its non-confidence in the commission by dismissing it.

The Community can legislate directly through regulations, which are binding in law and are automatically incorporated into the national legal systems of Member States, without the need for specific individual ratification. The Community can also work through the legal systems of the Member States, by the use of the Commission, which implements directives with broad objectives. Although directives require some legal action, such as legislation, by the Member States before they become national law, they are laws transposed into Member States' legislation to enforce treaty principles. Decisions by the ECJ are binding as force of law, whereas recommendations and opinions by the Council of Ministers or the Commission are not.

The European Court of Justice (ECJ) is the EU's supreme constitutional authority. It renders judgments on the obligations of the institutions, Member States and citizens. The very existence of the European Union is conditional on the recognition of the binding nature of its rules, by the Member States, by the institutions, and by individuals. Community law has successfully embedded itself thoroughly in the legal life of the Member States through the supervision of the European Court of Justice. The founding European Treaties are the primary source of Community law, and therein is found the central jurisdiction of the European Court of Justice. Community law involves primary law, namely treaties, and secondary law, namely legislative acts, both of which are binding on national governments, and take precedence over national law. The nature of the EU, its existence and its functions, demand a consistent application of Community law between Member States.

The European Court of Justice was to provide the legal sanctions for the carrying out of the Treaties. Before the European Community and the European Union, courts operating beyond national boundaries were set up by international agreement, such as the International Court of Justice. In essence, European Union citizens are affected by two legal systems, national and Community law. The courts of law must apply both systems of law where relevant, and if there is a conflict, the Community law takes precedence. The supremacy of Community law is implicit in the nature of the Communities, since their existence and functioning require its application. This surrender of sovereignty cannot be reversed by measures taken by national authorities in conflict with Community law. Community law is directly applicable to Member States, and there is no requirement that it be passed into national law for its validity, since the rights and obligations accrue directly to EU citizens.[33]

The primacy of Community law and its direct applicability are distinctive features of the European Union, turning freedoms into rights. European Community law is a system of laws, which is directly applicable to people and institutions in Member States, and is invoked in national courts. Community law touches on many aspects of national life, including immigration, control of foreign workers, and matters relating to equality between the sexes. National law has been challenged or influenced by Community law, which is enforced and overseen by the European Court of Justice. This is a loss of sovereignty by the Member States, surrendering far-reaching powers to an independent legal order, which binds Member States.

Points of law and the interpretation of treaties are decided by the European Court of Justice, the community's judicial institution having jurisdiction over disputes concerning the Member States. Often, the national court is faced with issues, such as the interpretation of a treaty, the validity of acts, or the lack of a judicial remedy under national law. If a Nation State's court decides that a question of community law needs to be answered before it can render a judgment, it can go before the European Court of Justice for the ruling. The EU Treaties are part of the domestic law of the State. As such, they impinge on the finality of national court decisions.

Two types of cases may be brought before the European Court of Justice, namely direct actions, brought directly before the Court by the Commission, other Community institutions or a Member State, or preliminary rulings, requested by courts or tribunals in the Member States on a question of Community Law. The European Court of Justice may hear a variety of cases involving: annulment of binding legal acts; failure to act; infringement of the EU treaties, under Article 33, in order to have Commission decisions or recommendations declared void for lack of competence, infringement of an essential procedural requirement, the Treaty or any rule of law relating to its application, or misuse of powers; preliminary rulings, in which national courts petition the Court of Justice for a ruling on a point of Community law, binding in the case; damages; and application of Staff Regulations. The Treaties state that the Community's legal system, which must not be impeded by any State, applies throughout the EU.

The European Court of Justice is at the heart of the legal system, and ensures that Community law is observed in the interpretation and application of the treaties. Its judgments are binding on Member States. The court reviews the lawfulness of acts of Council, the Commission, the Member State's governments and citizens. National laws in conflict with Community law may be declared invalid by the European Court of Justice. Appeals against acts of an institution or a Member State can be lodged by any other institution, government, firm or individual citizen directly affected.

The legal order is called the 'originality' of the European Union, which is the jurisdiction of the constitutional court, the European Court of Justice. The Court's decisions are made by majority vote, presented in open court. The judgments are directly applicable to Member States and are enforceable through the national courts. The Court of Justice located in Luxembourg may sit in plenary session, when a Member State or an EU institution is a party to the proceeding and so requests or when a case is considered complex and important, or may sit in chamber. Since all the official languages of the EU are used at some point, the Court provides for a large translation and interpretation service. The Court is also assisted by an Advocate General, as amici curiae acting as an independent judicial observer representing the public interest, who makes a reasoned presentation of the case before the Court, gives a summary of the submissions of the parties, puts forth observations of oral hearings, statute law and previous cases, and offers an opinion, which although published is not binding on the Court. In order to enable the Court of Justice to concentrate its activities on the fundamental task of ensuring uniform interpretation of Community law, a Court of First Instance was established in 1989, which has jurisdiction over actions brought by individuals and companies against decisions of the EU institutions and agencies, and these judgments are in turn subject to appeal before the Court of Justice on a point of law.

As the arbiter of Community law, the European Court of Justice, with its power, has strengthened the European Union as a political system. Defiance of its rulings has been exceptional. By creating a body of independent Community law, the EU has promoted its survival, by requiring harmonization of the laws of the Member States. The national courts are, therefore, responsible for aligning national law with Community law. The treaties are a comprehensive code of law, which set out the rights and duties of governments and individuals, and from which rights and remedies can be deduced. For the European Court of Justice, the EU's common aims count more than a literal construction of legal texts. The legal character of the EU is also concerned with influencing, shaping and controlling the legislative output of the Community.

Fundamental rights are part of the bedrock of the Community's legal order. The European Court of Justice held that the protection of such rights, while inspired by the constitutional traditions common to Member States, must be ensured within the framework of the structure and objectives of the Community (Internationale Handelsgesellschaft [1970] ECR 1125, [1972] CMLR 255).[34] Importantly, in a seminal case, the European Court of Justice stated:

> The integration into the laws of each Member State of provisions which derive from the Community, and more generally the terms and the spirit of the Treaty, make it impossible for the States, as a corollary, to accord precedence to a unilateral and subsequent measure over a legal system accepted by them on a basis of reciprocity....The executive force of Community law cannot vary from one State to another...without jeopardising the attainment of the object of the Treaty....It follows from all these observations that the law stemming from the treaty, an independent source of law, could not, because of its special and original nature, be overridden by domestic legal provisions, however framed, without being deprived of its character as Community law and without the legal basis of the Community itself being called into question (Costa v. ENEL [1964] CMLR 425).[35]

The European Convention for the Protection of Human Rights and Fundamental Freedoms (ECHR) and the European Social Charter

The European Convention for the Protection of Human Rights and Fundamental Freedoms (ECHR)

The European Convention for the Protection of Human Rights and Fundamental Freedoms came into being on November 4, 1950, which afforded protection against discrimination. In the Preamble, the Governments signatory hereto, being Members of the Council of Europe, undertake the agreement:

Considering the Universal Declaration of Human Rights proclaimed by the General Assembly of the United Nations on 10 December 1948;

Considering that this Declaration aims at securing the universal and effective recognition and observance of the Rights therein declared;

Considering that the aim of the Council of Europe is the achievement of greater unity between its Members and that one of the methods by which the aim is to be pursued is the maintenance and further realisation of Human Rights and Fundamental Freedoms;

Reaffirming their profound belief in those Fundamental Freedoms which are the foundation of justice and peace in the world and are best maintained on the one hand by an effective political democracy and on the other by a common understanding and observance of the Human Rights upon which they depend;

Being resolved, as the Governments of European countries which are like-minded and have a common heritage of political traditions, ideals, freedom and the rule of law to take the first steps for the collective enforcement of certain of the Rights stated in the Universal Declaration.

ARTICLE 1
The High Contracting Parties shall secure to everyone within their jurisdiction the rights and freedoms defined....[36]

Importantly, in the European Convention for the Protection of Human Rights and Fundamental Freedoms (ECHR) as amended by Protocol No. 11, the prohibition of discrimination is guaranteed under Article 14:

14. The enjoyment of the rights and freedoms set forth in this Convention shall be secured without discrimination on any ground such as sex, race, colour, language, religion, political or other opinion, national or social origin, association with a national minority, property, birth or other status.[37]

Article 13 recognizes that everyone whose rights and freedoms as set forth in this Convention are violated shall have an effective remedy before a national authority notwithstanding that the violation has been committed by persons acting in an official capacity.[38]

The European Court of Human Rights is established under Article 19:

19. To ensure the observance of the engagements undertaken by the High Contracting Parties in the Convention and the Protocols thereto, there shall be set up a European Court of Human Rights, hereinafter referred to as 'the Court'. It shall function on a permanent basis.[39]

In terms of jurisdiction, Article 32 establishes that the jurisdiction of the Court shall extend to all matters concerning the interpretation and application of the Convention and the protocols thereto, which are referred to it.[40] Under Article 34, the Court may receive applications from any person, Non-Governmental

Organization (NGO) or group of individuals claiming to be the victim of a violation by one of the High Contracting Parties of the rights set forth in the Convention or the protocols thereto, and the High Contracting Parties undertake not to hinder in any way the effective exercise of this right.[41]

Pursuant to Article 35's admissibility criteria, the Court may only deal with the matter after all domestic remedies have been exhausted, according to the generally recognized rules of international law, and within a period of six months from the date on which the final decision was taken.[42] Under Article 38, if the Court declares the application admissible, it shall pursue the examination of the case, together with the representatives of the parties, and if need be, undertake an investigation, for the effective conduct of which the States concerned shall furnish all necessary facilities, and place itself at the disposal of the parties concerned with a view to securing a friendly settlement of the matter on the basis of respect for human rights as defined in the Convention and the protocols thereto.[43]

Importantly, Article 41 holds that if the Court finds that there has been a violation of the Convention or the protocols thereto, and if the internal law of the High Contracting Party concerned allows only partial reparation to be made, the Court shall, if necessary, afford just satisfaction to the injured party.[44] According to Article 44, the judgment of the Grand Chamber shall be final,[45] and according to Article 45, reasons shall be given for judgments as well as for decisions declaring applications admissible or inadmissible.[46]

Further, in the Preamble of the Protocol No. 12 to the European Convention for the Protection of Human Rights and Fundamental Freedoms, the Member States of the Council of Europe signatory hereto, undertake the agreement:

> Having regard to the fundamental principle according to which all persons are equal before the law and are entitled to the equal protection of the law;
>
> Being resolved to take further steps to promote the equality of all persons through the collective enforcement of a general prohibition of discrimination by means of the Convention for the Protection of Human Rights and Fundamental Freedoms signed at Rome on 4 November 1950 (hereinafter referred to as 'the Convention');
>
> Reaffirming that the principle of non-discrimination does not prevent States Parties from taking measures in order to promote full and effective equality, provided that there is an objective and reasonable justification for those measures.[47]

Article 1 outlines the general prohibition against discrimination:

> 1(1) The enjoyment of any right set forth by law shall be secured without discrimination on any ground such as sex, race, colour, language, religion, political or other opinion, national or social origin, association with a national minority, property, birth or other status.
> (2) No one shall be discriminated against by any public authority on any ground such as those mentioned in paragraph 1.[48]

The European Social Charter

The European Social Charter (revised) of May 3, 1996 promotes the right for workers to equal opportunities and equal treatment in matters of employment and occupation without discrimination on the ground of gender. The Charter espouses the notion of 'equal pay for work of equal value' for male and female workers. It also provides for the equal treatment with regard to access to employment, vocational training, promotion and working conditions, aimed at eliminating all discrimination, both direct and indirect, in the world of work, and provides for opportunities for positive measures.

In the Preamble to the European Social Charter, the governments signatory hereto, being members of the Council of Europe, undertake the agreement:

> Considering that the aim of the Council of Europe is the achievement of greater unity between its members for the purpose of safeguarding and realising the ideals and principles which are their common heritage and of facilitating their economic and social progress, in particular by the maintenance and further realisation of human rights and fundamental freedoms;
> Considering that in the Convention for the Protection of Human Rights and Fundamental Freedoms signed at Rome on 4 November 1950, and the Protocols thereto, the member States of the Council of Europe agreed to secure to their populations the civil and political rights and freedoms therein specified;
> Considering that in the European Social Charter opened for signature in Turin on 18 October 1961 and the Protocols thereto, the member States of the Council of Europe agreed to secure to their populations the social rights specified therein in order to improve their standard of living and their social well-being;
> Recalling that the Ministerial Conference on Human Rights held in Rome on 5 November 1990 stressed the need, on the one hand, to preserve the indivisible nature of all human rights, be they civil, political, economic, social or cultural and, on the other hand, to give the European Social Charter fresh impetus;
> Resolved, as was decided during the Ministerial Conference held in Turin on 21 and 22 October 1991, to update and adapt the substantive contents of the Charter in order to take account in particular of the fundamental social changes which have occurred since the text was adopted;
> Recognising the advantage of embodying in a Revised Charter, designed progressively to take the place of the European Social Charter, the rights guaranteed by the Charter as amended, the rights guaranteed by the Additional Protocol of 1988 and to add new rights.[49]

Article E defines Non-Discrimination as the enjoyment of the rights set forth in this Charter secured without discrimination on any ground such as race, color, sex, language, religion, political or other opinion, national extraction or social origin, health, association with a national minority, birth or other status.[50]

Article 4 guarantees the right to a fair remuneration and equal pay:

> 4. With a view to ensuring the effective exercise of the right to a fair remuneration, the Parties undertake:

> (3) to recognise the right of men and women workers to equal pay for work of equal value....[51]

Under Article 8, with a view to ensuring the effective exercise of the right of employed women to the protection of maternity, the Parties undertake to provide either by paid leave, by adequate social security benefits or by benefits from public funds for employed women to take leave before and after childbirth up to a total of at least fourteen weeks; and to consider it as unlawful for an employer to give a woman notice of dismissal during the period from the time she notifies her employer that she is pregnant until the end of her maternity leave, or to give her notice of dismissal at such a time that the notice would expire during such a period.[52] Further, Article 18 ensures the effective exercise of the right to engage in a gainful occupation in the territory of any other Party.[53]

According to Article 27, with a view to ensuring the exercise of the right to equality of opportunity and treatment for men and women workers with family responsibilities, the Parties undertake to take appropriate measures to enable workers with family responsibilities to enter and remain in employment, as well as to reenter employment after an absence due to those responsibilities, including measures in the field of vocational guidance and training; to take account of their needs in terms of conditions of employment and social security; and to develop or promote services, public or private, in particular child daycare services and other childcare arrangements. Further, they undertake to provide a possibility for either parent to obtain, during a period after maternity leave, parental leave to take care of a child, the duration and conditions of which should be determined by national legislation, collective agreements or practice; and to ensure that family responsibilities shall not, as such, constitute a valid reason for termination of employment.[54]

Article 20 guarantees the right to equal opportunities and equal treatment in matters of employment and occupation without discrimination on the grounds of gender:

> 20. With a view to ensuring the effective exercise of the right to equal opportunities and equal treatment in matters of employment and occupation without discrimination on the grounds of sex, the Parties undertake to recognise that right and to take appropriate measures to ensure or promote its application in the following fields:
>
> a. access to employment, protection against dismissal and occupational reintegration;
> b. vocational guidance, training, retraining and rehabilitation;
> c. terms of employment and working conditions, including remuneration;
> d. career development, including promotion.[55]

Pursuant to Article 22, the Parties undertake to adopt or encourage measures enabling workers or their representatives, in accordance with national legislation and practice, to contribute to the determination and the improvement of the working conditions, work organization and working environment; to the protection of health and safety within the undertaking; to the organization of social and socio-cultural services and facilities within the undertaking; and to the supervision of the observance of regulations on these matters.[56]

Under Article 26, with a view to ensuring the effective exercise of the right of all workers to the protection of their dignity at work, the Parties undertake, in consultation with employers' and workers' organizations to promote awareness, information and prevention of sexual harassment and of recurrent reprehensible or distinctly negative and offensive actions directed against individual workers in the workplace or in relation to work and to take all appropriate measures to protect workers from such conduct.[57]

Directives

When women became more militant in the 1970s, the Community began to adopt a more positive attitude toward women's rights. Community legislation, through Council Directives, reinforced the general legal provisions for equal pay and equal treatment. A series of directives have been adopted aimed at ensuring equal opportunities and treatment for men and women. The Council Directives require the Member States to realign their national laws in providing recourse to the courts, and importantly prohibit any possible retribution against those who pursue a judicial action:

> Member States shall introduce into their national legal systems such measures as are necessary to enable all persons who consider themselves wronged by failure to apply them the principle...to pursue their claims by judicial process after possible recourse to other competent authorities.
> Member States shall take the necessary measures to protect employees against dismissal by the employer as a reaction to a complaint within the undertaking or to any legal proceedings aimed at enforcing compliance with the principle.[58]

Council Directive 75/117/EEC of 10 February 1975 on the approximation of the laws of the Member States relating to the application of the principle of equal pay for men and women

Directive 75/117/EEC known as the Equal Pay Directive calls for the approximation of laws of Member States to the application of equal pay between men and women, in order to further reinforce the equality provisions of Article 119 of the Treaty of Rome. The Directive establishes that the principle of equal pay refers to work which is the same or which is judged to be of equal value, and requires Member States to introduce appropriate legal mechanisms for the redress of all discrimination on the grounds of gender with regard to all aspects and conditions of remuneration.

In the Preamble of the directive, it is stated:

> The Council of the European Communities,...

> Whereas implementation of the principle that men and women should receive equal pay contained in Article 119 of the Treaty is an integral part of the establishment and functioning of the common market;
> Whereas it is primarily the responsibility of the Member States to ensure the application of this principle by means of appropriate laws, regulations and administrative provisions;
> Whereas the Council resolution of 21 January 1974 concerning a social action programme, aimed at making it possible to harmonize living and working conditions while the improvement is being maintained and at achieving a balanced social and economic development of the Community, recognized that priority should be given to action taken on behalf of women as regards access to employment and vocational training and advancement, and as regards working conditions, including pay;
> Whereas it is desirable to reinforce the basic laws by standards aimed at facilitating the practical application of the principle of equality in such a way that all employees in the Community can be protected in these matters;
> Whereas differences continue to exist in the various Member States despite the efforts made to apply the resolution of the conference of the Member States of 30 December 1961 on equal pay for men and women and whereas, therefore, the national provisions should be approximated as regards application of the principle of equal pay,
> Has adopted this Directive.[59]

Article 1 defines equal pay:

> The principle of equal pay for men and women outlined in Article 119 of the Treaty, hereinafter called 'principle of equal pay', means, for the same work or for work to which equal value is attributed, the elimination of all discrimination on grounds of sex with regard to all aspects and conditions of remuneration. In particular, where a job classification system is used for determining pay, it must be based on the same criteria for both men and women and so drawn up as to exclude any discrimination on grounds of sex.[60]

Article 3 calls on Member States to abolish all discrimination between men and women arising from laws, regulations or administrative provisions which is contrary to the principle of equal pay.[61] Further, Article 4 provides that Member States shall take the necessary measures to ensure that provisions appearing in collective agreements, wage scales, wage agreements or individual contracts of employment which are contrary to the principle of equal pay shall be, or may be declared, null and void or may be amended.[62]

In terms of the judicial process to correct gender inequality, Article 2 holds that Member States shall introduce into their national legal systems such measures as are necessary to enable all employees who consider themselves wronged by failure to apply the principle of equal pay to pursue their claims by judicial process after possible recourse to other competent authorities.[63] Finally, Article 5 guarantees that Member States shall take the necessary measures to protect employees against dismissal by the employer as a reaction to a complaint within the undertaking or to any legal proceedings aimed at enforcing compliance with the principle of equal pay.[64]

Council Directive 76/207/EEC of 9 February 1976 on the implementation of the principle of equal treatment for men and women as regards access to employment, vocational training and promotion, and working conditions

Directive 76/207/EEC known as the Equal Treatment Directive provides that there should be no discrimination on grounds of gender, either directly or indirectly, nor by reference to marital or family status, in access to employment, training, working conditions, promotion or dismissal, but allows exceptions for occupational activities/training where a worker's sex is a determining factor. Member States must eradicate any discriminatory laws, policies or provisions.

In the Preamble of the directive, it is stated:

> The Council of the European Communities,...
> Whereas the Council, in its resolution of 21 January 1974 concerning a social action programme, included among the priorities action for the purpose of achieving equality between men and women as regards access to employment and vocational training and promotion and as regards working conditions, including pay;
> Whereas, with regard to pay, the Council adopted on 10 February 1975 Directive 75/117/EEC on the approximation of the laws of the Member States relating to the application of the principle of equal pay for men and women;
> Whereas Community action to achieve the principle of equal treatment for men and women in respect of access to employment and vocational training and promotion and in respect of other working conditions also appears to be necessary; whereas, equal treatment for male and female workers constitutes one of the objectives of the Community, in so far as the harmonization of living and working conditions while maintaining their improvement are inter alia to be furthered; whereas the Treaty does not confer the necessary specific powers for this purpose;
> Whereas the definition and progressive implementation of the principle of equal treatment in matters of social security should be ensured by means of subsequent instruments,
> Has adopted this Directive.[65]

According to Article 1(1), the purpose of this Directive is to put into effect in the Member States the principle of equal treatment for men and women as regards access to employment, including promotion, and to vocational training and as regards working conditions and social security.[66] Article 2 defines equal treatment and allows for affirmative action:

> 2. 1. For the purposes of the following provisions, the principle of equal treatment shall mean that there shall be no discrimination whatsoever on grounds of sex either directly or indirectly by reference in particular to marital or family status.
> 2. This Directive shall be without prejudice to the right of Member States to exclude from its field of application those occupational activities and, where appropriate, the training leading thereto, for which, by reason of their nature or the context in which they are carried out, the sex of the worker constitutes a determining factor.[67]

Further, Article 3 holds:

3. 1. Application of the principle of equal treatment means that there shall be no discrimination whatsover on grounds of sex in the conditions, including selection criteria, for access to all jobs or posts, whatever the sector or branch of activity, and to all levels of the occupational hierarchy.
2. To this end, Member States shall take the measures necessary to ensure that:
(a) any laws, regulations and administrative provisions contrary to the principle of equal treatment shall be abolished;
(b) any provisions contrary to the principle of equal treatment which are included in collective agreements, individual contracts of employment, internal rules of undertakings or in rules governing the independent occupations and professions shall be, or may be declared, null and void or may be amended;
(c) those laws, regulations and administrative provisions contrary to the principle of equal treatment when the concern for protection which originally inspired them is no longer well founded shall be revised ; and that where similar provisions are included in collective agreements labour and management shall be requested to undertake the desired revision.[68]

Directive 2002/73/EC of the European Parliament and of the Council of 23 September 2002 amending Council Directive 76/207/EEC on the implementation of the principle of equal treatment for men and women as regards access to employment, vocational training and promotion, and working conditions

Directive 2002/73/EC recognizes that the right to equality before the law and protection against discrimination for all persons constitutes a universal right recognized by the Universal Declaration of Human Rights, the United Nations Convention on the Elimination of all forms of Discrimination Against Women, the International Convention on the Elimination of all Forms of Racial Discrimination and the United Nations Covenants on Civil and Political Rights and on Economic, Social and Cultural Rights and by the Convention for the Protection of Human Rights and Fundamental Freedoms, to which all Member States are signatories; that Article 141 of the Treaty, in particular paragraph 3, addresses specifically equal opportunities and equal treatment of men and women in matters of employment and occupation; and that Council Directive 76/207/EEC does not define the concepts of direct or indirect discrimination. The principle of equal pay for men and women constitutes an essential and indispensable part of the acquis communautaire concerning sex discrimination.[69]

Article 1 of Directive 76/207/EEC is amended by Article 1 of 2002/73/EC which holds that Member States shall actively take into account the objective of equality between men and women when formulating and implementing laws, regulations, administrative provisions, policies and activities in the areas.[70] Further, Article 2 of Directive 76/207/EEC is replaced by Article 2 of 2002/73/EC:

2. 1. For the purposes of the following provisions, the principle of equal treatment shall mean that there shall be no discrimination whatsoever on grounds of sex either directly or indirectly by reference in particular to marital or family status.
2. For the purposes of this Directive, the following definitions shall apply:
direct discrimination: where one person is treated less favourably on grounds of sex than another is, has been or would be treated in a comparable situation,

> indirect discrimination: where an apparently neutral provision, criterion or practice would put persons of one sex at a particular disadvantage compared with persons of the other sex, unless that provision, criterion or practice is objectively justified by a legitimate aim, and the means of achieving that aim are appropriate and necessary,
> harassment: where an unwanted conduct related to the sex of a person occurs with the purpose or effect of violating the dignity of a person, and of creating an intimidating, hostile, degrading, humiliating or offensive environment,
> sexual harassment: where any form of unwanted verbal, non-verbal or physical conduct of a sexual nature occurs, with the purpose or effect of violating the dignity of a person, in particular when creating an intimidating, hostile, degrading, humiliating or offensive environment.[71]

Council Directive 97/80/EC of 15 December 1997 on the burden of proof in cases of discrimination based on sex

Directive 97/80/EC known as the Burden of Proof Directive requires any necessary changes in Member States' judicial systems to ensure more effective implementation of the principle of equal treatment.[72] According to Article 1, the aim of this Directive shall be to ensure that the measures taken by the Member States to implement the principle of equal treatment are made more effective, in order to enable all persons who consider themselves wronged because the principle of equal treatment has not been applied to them to have their rights asserted by judicial process after possible recourse to other competent bodies.[73]

Article 2 defines equal treatment and indirect discrimination:

> 2. 1. For the purposes of this Directive, the principle of equal treatment shall mean that there shall be no discrimination whatsoever based on sex, either directly or indirectly.
> 2. For purposes of the principle of equal treatment referred to in paragraph 1, indirect discrimination shall exist where an apparently neutral provision, criterion or practice disadvantages a substantially higher proportion of the members of one sex unless that provision, criterion or practice is appropriate and necessary and can be justified by objective factors unrelated to sex.[74]

In terms of the burden of proof, Article 4 holds:

> 4. 1. Member States shall take such measures as are necessary, in accordance with their national judicial systems, to ensure that, when persons who consider themselves wronged because the principle of equal treatment has not been applied to them establish, before a court or other competent authority, facts from which it may be presumed that there has been direct or indirect discrimination, it shall be for the respondent to prove that there has been no breach of the principle of equal treatment.
> 2. This Directive shall not prevent Member States from introducing rules of evidence which are more favourable to plaintiffs.[75]

Directives 75/117, 97/80 and 2002/73 explicitly deal with the issue of equal pay for men and women. Directive 75/117 builds on the principle of equal pay outlined in Article 119 of the Treaty of Rome by introducing the concept of equal pay for the same work or for work to which equal value is attributed. Further, Directive 76/207, the equal treatment directive, is also significant for the gender pay gap as it prohibits direct and indirect discrimination on the grounds of sex in relation to employment for areas other than pay. Prior to the implementation of Directive 97/80, if a woman took a case against her employer, believing she was being discriminated against in terms of pay based on gender, the woman would usually have to assume the burden of proof. However, Directive 97/80 shifts the burden of proof to employers once a prima facie case of discrimination has been established, and Directive 2002/73 updates and improves Directive 97/80 by virtue of Article 141 of the Treaty of Amsterdam.

Other Directives and Recommendations

As well as the aforementioned directives, the following directives may be relevant to cases of gender discrimination:

Council Directive 79/7/EEC of 19 December 1978 on the progressive implementation of the principle of equal treatment for men and women in matters of social security. The Social Security Directive requires equal treatment of men and women in statutory schemes providing protection against sickness, invalidity, old age, accidents at work and occupational diseases and unemployment, but does not require equalization of pension ages.[76]

Council Directive 86/378/EEC of 24 July 1986 on the implementation of the principle of equal treatment for men and women in occupational social security schemes The Occupational Social Security Directive aims to implement the principle of equal treatment for men and women in occupational social security schemes.[77]

Council Directive 86/613/EEC of 11 December 1986 on the application of the principle of equal treatment between men and women engaged in an activity, including agriculture, in a self-employed capacity, and on the protection of self-employed women during pregnancy and motherhood The Directive covers self-employed workers, that is all persons pursuing a gainful activity for their own account, under the conditions laid down by national law, and defines the principle of equal treatment as implying the absence of all discrimination on grounds of sex, either directly or indirectly, by reference in particular to marital or family status.[78]

Council Directive 92/85/EEC of 19 October 1992 on the introduction of measures to encourage improvements in the safety and health at work of pregnant workers and workers who have recently given birth or are breastfeeding The Pregnant Workers Directive requires minimum measures to improve the safety and health at work of pregnant women, and women who have recently given birth or are breastfeeding, including a right to maternity leave. It extends the rights of all pregnant women to at least 14 weeks' maternity leave, regardless of length of service, with all contractual rights and benefits maintained during the maternity leave period, and employment protection throughout pregnancy and maternity leave.[79]

Council Directive 93/104/EC of 23 November 1993 concerning certain aspects of the organization of working time The Working Time Directive provides for minimum health and safety requirements for the organization of working time. It requires minimum periods of daily and weekly rest and annual leave, breaks and maximum weekly working time, and contains provisions relating to night work, shift work and other patterns of work.[80]

Council Directive 96/34/EC of 3 June 1996 on the framework agreement on parental leave concluded by UNICE, CEEP and the ETUC The Parental Leave Directive provides for all parents of children up to a given age to be defined by Member States, to be given up to three months' unpaid parental leave, and for individuals to take unpaid time off when a dependant is ill or injured.[81]

Council Directive 2000/78/EC of 27 November 2000 establishing a general framework for equal treatment in employment and occupation The directive establishes a general framework for combating discrimination on the grounds of religion or belief, disability, age or sexual orientation as regards employment and occupation, with a view to putting into effect in the Member States the principle of equal treatment, recognizing that women are often the victims of multiple discrimination.[82]

Council Recommendation 84/635/EEC of 13 December 1984 on the promotion of positive action for women Article 1 of the Council Recommendation states:

> 1. To adopt a positive action policy designed to eliminate existing inequalities affecting women in working life and to promote a better balance between the sexes in employment,
> (a) to eliminate or counteract the prejudicial effects on women in employment or seeking employment which arise from existing attitudes, behaviours and structures based on the idea of a traditional division of roles in society between men and women;
> (b) to encourage the participation of women in various occupations in those sectors of working life where they are at present under-represented, particularly in the sectors of the future, and at higher levels of responsibility in order to achieve better use of all human resources.[83]

Further, Article 4 goes on to enumerate positive action measures:

> 4. To take steps to ensure that positive action includes as far as possible actions having a bearing on the following aspects:
> informing and increasing the awareness of both the general public and the working world of the need to promote equality of opportunity for working women,
> respect for the dignity of women at the workplace,

qualitative and quantitative studies and analyses of the position of women on the labour market,
diversification of vocational choice, and more relevant vocational skills, particularly through appropriate vocational training, including the implementation of supporting measures and suitable teaching methods,
measures necessary to ensure that placement, guidance and counselling services have sufficient skilled personnel to provide a service based on the necessary expertise in the special problems of unemployed women,
encouraging women candidates and the recruitment and promotion of women in sectors and professions and at levels where they are underrepresented, particularly as regards positions of responsibility,
adapting working conditions; adjusting the organization of work and working time,
encouraging supporting measures such as those designed to foster greater sharing of occupational and social responsibilities,
active participation by women in decision making bodies, including those representing workers, employers and the self-employed.[84]

Commission Recommendation 92/131/EEC of 27 November 1991 on the protection of the dignity of women and men at work The European Commission Recommendation and Code of Practice on the protection of the dignity of women and men at work contains recommendations for employers, trade unions and employees on avoiding and dealing with sexual harassment. The Code gives practical guidance to employers, trade unions and employees on the protection of dignity at work in the public and private sector. The aim of the Code is to ensure sexual harassment does not occur and, if it does, to ensure that adequate procedures are readily available to deal with the problem and prevent its recurrence. The Code can be taken into account in proceedings to determine a relevant question.[85]

Conclusion

In essence, Europe is now the biggest frontier-free market in the world. The single market removed three types of barriers to free movement, namely physical, technical and fiscal. The four freedoms of the Union, for goods, services, people and capital, have become a reality. Further, the new single currency, the euro was introduced as legal tender on January 1, 1999, and replaced the currencies of those Member States in agreement on January 1, 2002. The criteria used for a nation to secure membership in the European Union are: 1. Democratic institutions and the rule of law, with respect for human rights and minorities within the borders; 2. A functioning market economy capable of competing within the union's single market; and 3. The acceptance of obligations of membership, signing onto the union's body of rules. The latter is perhaps the most important criteria for equal rights and their enforcement.

Currently, the Member States of the European Union are: Austria, Belgium, Denmark, Finland, France, Germany, Greece, Ireland, Italy, Luxembourg, the Netherlands, Portugal, Spain, Sweden and the United Kingdom.

On May 1, 2004, the EU will be expanded from 15 to 25 Member States, with ten countries having been invited to join, namely Cyprus (Greek part), the Czech Republic, Estonia, Hungary, Latvia, Lithuania, Malta, Poland, Slovakia and Slovenia. The European Union Member States are now looking to formulate a Constitution for Europe. The EU is at a crossroads, challenged to adapt the vision of the 'founding fathers' first designed for six Member States to a future union of over twenty States.

The European Union is a political structure, which emerged out of a general act of will of heterogeneous States. It is ultimately dependent on statements of general principle. Therefore, Community law is the motor to enable the European Union to move toward its ultimate aim, the 'ever closer union'. The EU's action program has several main components, namely a fair deal in rights at work involving equality legislation and court cases; better opportunities to earn a living involving the promotion of jobs, education and entrepreneurship; getting women in positions of power involving equal opportunities in employment; and community-wide networks involving training, expanding subjects in school and reinforcing a positive image of women.[86] Relations between the institutions of the European Union are based on partnership, cooperation and mutual dependence.

All Member States within the EU have legislation prohibiting direct or indirect pay discrimination on the grounds of gender. Despite this, there still exists a gap between the earnings of men and women. As a result, amendments have been made to the existing legislation in an effort to enhance gender pay equality, though these have tended to focus on more indirect methods such as ruling out gender discrimination in hiring, promotion and training. The concern is to enhance the social, economic and cultural welfare of all citizens in an atmosphere of peace. This, thereby, advances the cause for gender equality in stamping out discrimination of any kind, including gender injustice, through the effective use of laws and the courts.

Notes

1 Department of Justice, Equality & Law Reform, *Developing Sectoral Strategies to Address Gender Pay Gaps*, 2003.
2 United Nations (1997), *Demographic Yearbook.*
3 Eurostat (2001), *Yearbook, 1989-1991, Statistical Guide to Europe*, Brussels.
4 Commission of the European Communities, *Employment in Europe*, Brussels, 1995.
5 *Supra* note 3, at p.133.
6 *Ibid.*
7 Commission of the European Communities, *The Position of Women on the Labour Market*, 1991, p.52.
8 *Ibid.*
9 *Supra* note 1.
10 *Ibid.*
11 *Ibid.*
12 *Supra* note 7.

13 Commission of the European Communities, *Equal Opportunities for Women in the Community*, Brussels, 1993.
14 Eurostat, *Statistics in Focus*, Brussels, 1996.
15 Commission of the European Communities, *Europe*, Brussels, 1994.
16 *Ibid.*, at p.1.
17 *Ibid.*
18 Daltrop, Anne (1982), *Political Realities, Politics and the European Community*, Longman, London, 1982, p.2.
19 Ibid., at p.7.
20 Smith, Murray, 'Free Trade and the European Experience', in A.R. Riggs and Tom Velk (1988), *Canadian-American Free Trade: (The Sequel) Historical, Political and Economic Dimensions*, The Institute for Research on Public Policy, Montreal, 1988, p.4.
21 Nicoll, William and Salmon, Trevor, *Understanding the New European Community*, 1994, p.11.
22 *Ibid.*, at p.13.
23 *Ibid.*, at p.20.
24 *Ibid.*, at p.99.
25 *Supra* note 18, at p.18.
26 Treaty of Rome, Article 3.
27 *Ibid.*, at Article 119.
28 Maastricht Treaty, Article A.
29 *Ibid.*, at Article B.
30 Treaty of Amsterdam, Article 141.
31 Commission of the European Communities (1996), *Burden of Proof in Sex Discrimination Cases*, Brussels, p.1.
32 Teuling v. Bredrijfsvereniging [1987] ECR 2497.
33 *Supra* note 21, at p.97.
34 Internationale Handelsgesellschaft [1970] ECR 1125, [1972] CMLR 255.
35 Costa v. ENEL [1964] CMLR 425.
36 European Convention for the Protection of Human Rights and Fundamental Freedoms (ECHR), the Preamble.
37 European Convention for the Protection of Human Rights and Fundamental Freedoms as amended by Protocol No. 11, Article 14.
38 *Ibid.*, at Article 13.
39 *Ibid.*, at Article 19.
40 *Ibid.*, at Article 32.
41 *Ibid.*, at Article 34.
42 *Ibid.*, at Article 35.
43 *Ibid.*, at Article 38.
44 *Ibid.*, at Article 41.
45 *Ibid.*, at Article 44.
46 *Ibid.*, at Article 45.
47 European Convention for the Protection of Human Rights and Fundamental Freedoms as amended by Protocol No. 12, the Preamble.
48 *Ibid.*, at Article 1.
49 European Social Charter (revised), at Preamble.
50 *Ibid.*, at Article E.
51 *Ibid.*, at Article 4.
52 *Ibid.*, at Article 8.
53 *Ibid.*, at Article 18.
54 *Ibid.*, at Article 27.

[55] *Ibid.*, at Article 20.
[56] *Ibid.*, at Article 22.
[57] *Ibid.*, at Article 26.
[58] Council Directives.
[59] Council Directive 75/117/EEC of 10 February 1975 on the approximation of the laws of the Member States relating to the application of the principle of equal pay for men and women [OJ L 045, 19/02/1975 P. 0019–0020], the Preamble.
[60] *Ibid.*, at Article 1.
[61] *Ibid.*, at Article 3.
[62] *Ibid.*, at Article 4.
[63] *Ibid.*, at Article 2.
[64] *Ibid.*, at Article 5.
[65] Council Directive 76/207/EEC of 9 February 1976 on the implementation of the principle of equal treatment for men and women as regards access to employment, vocational training and promotion, and working conditions [OJ L 039, 14/02/1976 P. 0040–0042], the Preamble.
[66] *Ibid.*, at Article 1(1).
[67] *Ibid.*, at Article 2.
[68] *Ibid.*, at Article 3.
[69] Directive 2002/73/EC of the European Parliament and of the Council of 23 September 2002 amending Council Directive 76/207/EEC on the implementation of the principle of equal treatment for men and women as regards access to employment, vocational training and promotion, and working conditions [OJ L 269, 05/10/2002 P. 0015–0020].
[70] *Ibid.*, at Article 1.
[71] *Ibid.*, at Article 2.
[72] Council Directive 97/80/EC of 15 December 1997 on the burden of proof in cases of discrimination based on sex [OJ L 014, 20/01/1998 P. 0006–0008].
[73] *Ibid.*, at Article 1.
[74] *Ibid.*, at Article 2.
[75] *Ibid.*, at Article 4.
[76] Council Directive 79/7/EEC of 19 December 1978 on the progressive implementation of the principle of equal treatment for men and women in matters of social security [OJ L 006, 10/01/1979 P. 0024–0025].
[77] Council Directive 86/378/EEC of 24 July 1986 on the implementation of the principle of equal treatment for men and women in occupational social security schemes [OJ L 225, 12/08/1986 P. 0040–0042].
[78] Council Directive 86/613/EEC of 11 December 1986 on the application of the principle of equal treatment between men and women engaged in an activity, including agriculture, in a self-employed capacity, and on the protection of self-employed women during pregnancy and motherhood [OJ L 359, 19/12/1986 P. 0056–0058].
[79] Council Directive 92/85/EEC of 19 October 1992 on the introduction of measures to encourage improvements in the safety and health at work of pregnant workers and workers who have recently given birth or are breastfeeding (tenth individual Directive within the meaning of Article 16 (1) of Directive 89/391/EEC) [OJ L 348, 28/11/1992 P. 0001–0008].
[80] Council Directive 93/104/EC of 23 November 1993 concerning certain aspects of the organization of working time [OJ L 307, 13/12/1993 P. 0018–0024].
[81] Council Directive 96/34/EC of 3 June 1996 on the framework agreement on parental leave concluded by UNICE, CEEP and the ETUC [OJ L 145, 19/06/1996 P. 0004-0009 CONSLEG 96L0034 16/01/1998 11 P].

82 Council Directive 2000/78/EC of 27 November 2000 establishing a general framework for equal treatment in employment and occupation [OJ L 303, 02/12/2000 P. 0016–0022].

83 Council Recommendation 84/635/EEC of 13 December 1984 on the promotion of positive action for women [OJ L 331, 19/12/1984 P. 0034–0035], Article 1.

84 *Ibid.*, at Article 4.

85 Commission Recommendation 92/131/EEC of 27 November 1991 on the protection of the dignity of women and men at work [OJ L 049, 24/02/1992 P. 0001–0008].

86 Commission of the European Communities, *Equal Opportunity for Women and Men*, Brussels, p.5.

References

Borchardt, Klaus-Dieter (1993), *The ABC of Community Law*, Official Publications of the European Communities, Luxembourg.

Brecher, Irving (1988), 'Free at Last', in A.R. Riggs and Tom Velk, *Canadian-American Free Trade: (The Sequel) Historical, Political and Economic Dimensions*, The Institute for Research on Public Policy, Montreal.

Commission of the European Communities, *Equal Opportunity for Women and Men*, Brussels.

Commission of the European Communities, *Promotion of Positive Action*, Brussels.

Commission of the European Communities (1991), *The Position of Women on the Labour Market*, Brussels.

Commission of the European Communities (1992), *From Single Market to European Union*, Brussels.

Commission of the European Communities (1992), *Women's Information Service*, Brussels.

Commission of the European Communities (1993), *Equal Opportunities for Women in the Community*, Brussels.

Commission of the European Communities (1994), *Europe*, Brussels.

Commission of the European Communities (1995), *Employment in Europe*, Brussels.

Commission of the European Communities (1996), *Burden of Proof in Sex Discrimination Cases*, Brussels.

Commission of the European Communities (1996), *Serving the European Community*, Brussels.

Commission Recommendation 92/131/EEC of 27 November 1991 on the protection of the dignity of women and men at work [OJ L 049, 24/02/1992 P. 0001–0008].

Costa v. ENEL [1964] CMLR 425.

Council Directive 75/117/EEC of 10 February 1975 on the approximation of the laws of the Member States relating to the application of the principle of equal pay for men and women [OJ L 045, 19/02/1975 P. 0019–0020].

Council Directive 76/207/EEC of 9 February 1976 on the implementation of the principle of equal treatment for men and women as regards access to employment, vocational training and promotion, and working conditions [OJ L 039, 14/02/1976 P. 0040–0042].

Council Directive 79/7/EEC of 19 December 1978 on the progressive implementation of the principle of equal treatment for men and women in matters of social security [OJ L 006, 10/01/1979 P. 0024–0025].

Council Directive 86/378/EEC of 24 July 1986 on the implementation of the principle of equal treatment for men and women in occupational social security schemes [OJ L 225, 12/08/1986 P. 0040–0042].

Council Directive 86/613/EEC of 11 December 1986 on the application of the principle of equal treatment between men and women engaged in an activity, including agriculture, in a self-employed capacity, and on the protection of self-employed women during pregnancy and motherhood [OJ L 359, 19/12/1986 P. 0056–0058].

Council Directive 92/85/EEC of 19 October 1992 on the introduction of measures to encourage improvements in the safety and health at work of pregnant workers and workers who have recently given birth or are breastfeeding [OJ L 348, 28/11/1992 P. 0001–0008].

Council Directive 93/104/EC of 23 November 1993 concerning certain aspects of the organization of working time [OJ L 307, 13/12/1993 P. 0018–0024].

Council Directive 96/34/EC of 3 June 1996 on the framework agreement on parental leave concluded by UNICE, CEEP and the ETUC [OJ L 145, 19/06/1996 P. 0004-0009 CONSLEG 96L0034 16/01/1998 11 P].

Council Directive 97/80/EC of 15 December 1997 on the burden of proof in cases of discrimination based on sex [OJ L 014, 20/01/1998 P. 0006–0008].

Council Directive 2000/78/EC of 27 November 2000 establishing a general framework for equal treatment in employment and occupation [OJ L 303, 02/12/2000 P. 0016–0022].

Council Recommendation 84/635/EEC of 13 December 1984 on the promotion of positive action for women [OJ L 331, 19/12/1984 P. 0034–0035].

Daltrop, Anne (1982), *Political Realities, Politics and the European Community*, Longman, London.

Department of Justice, Equality & Law Reform, *Developing Sectoral Strategies to Address Gender Pay Gaps*, 2003.

Directive 2002/73/EC of the European Parliament and of the Council of 23 September 2002 amending Council Directive 76/207/EEC on the implementation of the principle of equal treatment for men and women as regards access to employment, vocational training and promotion, and working conditions [OJ L 269, 05/10/2002 P. 0015–0020].

Duff, Andrew, Pinder, John, and Pryce, Roy (1994), Maastricht and Beyond, Routledge, London.

European Charter of Fundamental Social Rights, 1989.

European Convention for the Protection of Human Rights and Fundamental Freedoms, 1950.

European Convention for the Protection of Human Rights and Fundamental Freedoms as amended by Protocol No. 11.

European Convention for the Protection of Human Rights and Fundamental Freedoms as amended by Protocol No. 12.

European Social Charter (revised).

Eurostat (1995), *Statistics*, Brussels.

Eurostat (1996), *Statistics in Focus*, Brussels.

Eurostat (2001), *Yearbook, 1989-1991, Statistical Guide to Europe*, Brussels.

Internationale Handelsgesellschaft, [1970] ECR 1125, [1972] CMLR 255.

Kelly, J.M. (1984), *The Irish Constitution*, Leinster Leader, Ireland.

Kokott, Juliane, 'European Communities, Equal Pay for Men and Women, DeFacto Discrimination', *American Journal of International Law*, Vol.86, N.2, 1991, p.348.

Maastricht Treaty, 1992.

Nicoll, William and Salmon, Trevor (1994), *Understanding the New European Community.*

Smith, Murray (1988), 'Free Trade and the European Experience', in A.R. Riggs and Tom Velk, *Canadian-American Free Trade: (The Sequel) Historical, Political and Economic Dimensions*, The Institute for Research on Public Policy, Montreal.

Teuling v. Bredrijfsvereniging [1987] ECR 2497.

Treaty of Amsterdam, 1997.

Treaty of Paris, 1951.

Treaty of Rome, 1957.

United Nations (1997), *Demographic Yearbook.*

White, Gerry, 'Report of the Revision Group on the Treatment of Households in the Social Welfare Code', *Administration*, Vol.40, N.3, 1992.

Chapter 10

Conclusion to Gender Injustice

Gender is the articulation in specific contexts of the social understandings of sexual differences, and is of a classifying phenomenon based on a socially agreed upon system of distinctions rather than an objective description of inherent traits and relations among categories.[1] Gender identity has been socially constructed around biological differences. The very notion of gender is a constitutive element of social relationships based on perceived differences between the sexes and is a primary way of signifying relationships of power.[2] Therefore, in examining gender, no law can adequately concretize the equal right to autonomous freedom in the private sphere, unless it simultaneously strengthens the position of women in the public sphere and augments their participation in the communication for equal status, so that all facets of life are covered.

Despite concerns that focusing on gender equality will deter in the struggle for general human equality, the necessity exists more than ever to go beyond the invisible differences to those visible differences such as gender. Our patriarchal society has served to produce superordinates and subordinates. Although not all men occupy positions of power and not all women occupy positions of servitude, it is realistic, however, to see that society's laws rest on masculinist false universals.

Women have not achieved total equality, despite all efforts. Over the years, there has been a feminization of poverty, with women poorer than men across class, race, national, economic and ethnic lines.[3] The position of women throughout the industrialized world is very much alike, with women occupying a very fragile position despite institutions and laws to promote their rights. High unemployment in general does not help the cause of equality, since gender discrimination is still not seen as a priority. Contrary to popular belief, the net effect on discrimination is close to zero, because of the way the laws are written, interpreted and enforced by hostility or indifference. Thus, there continues to be employment segregation and income gaps, with women's economic mobility limited by gender discrimination.

The effect of cultural liberalism, hedonism and anti-authoritarian attitudes has made a difference for women. Women with these new values have the potential to bring about change through their influence on their colleagues, their friends and their children, who in turn become less sexist. However, although women have made some progress into the higher echelons, they often have to start out in part-time work, that is not always chosen or that does not afford opportunities for promotion. Overall, internationally, women have experienced important changes in the workforce over the years. However, women still have a way to go in achieving equality in employment in terms of equal pay and complete access to employment.

A deep embedded patriarchal authority is still keeping society on the designated track, as de jure discrimination has given way to de facto discrimination, and in essence, inequality, once obvious and accepted, is now hidden and protected in a most dangerous way. Since within society there is an a priori assumption of freedom and impartiality, the burden is high on the attackers of this universal opinion. Human inequality both encompasses gender inequality and conceals it, and although other types of discrimination exist apart from gender inequality, discrimination which is so blatant and open as to focus on one's gender is most persistent and threatening to society. Therefore, seeking out gender inequality and bringing it to the forefront of microscopic debate can only serve to advance all quests for equality.

Both legislation and the court system have made inroads into gender injustice, but there is not yet parity in salary or full access to employment for men and women anywhere in the world. It is important to have adequate legislation to influence conduct and outcomes, as well as an appropriate legal system to achieve favorable and enforceable results. By cooperating and learning from other similarly disadvantaged groups in the fight for equality of opportunity, more advances can be made in the fight for equal pay and equal access to employment. We will never totally correct the injustices of the past or of the present. However, with a greater appreciation of the gender issues, as well as a better understanding of the importance of adequate legislation, future endeavors in the field will help to improve the situation not only for women, but for all people.

Gender differences have historically been used to justify differences of treatment between male and female applicants and employees, on the basis of the inherent strength or ability to perform particular physical tasks, the potential need for women to take time off during pregnancy or to fulfill caring responsibilities, or the perceived 'appropriate gender roles', which may favor women staying at home raising families and men taking the responsibility as the primary bread-winners. Evidence internationally suggests that women continue to earn less than men for equivalent work. Women still confront the 'glass ceiling', and tend to be concentrated in particular sectors, where prospects for advancement tend to be more limited.

The situation of women in the work force is ever important: 1. Women now comprise an increasing share of the world's labor force, at least one third in all regions except for northern Africa and western Asia; 2. Self-employment, part-time work and home-based work have expanded opportunities for women's participation in the labor force, but are characterized by lack of security, lack of benefits and low income; 3. The informal sector is a larger source of employment for women than men, affording less stability; 4. More women than before are in the labor force throughout their reproductive years, though obstacles to combining family responsibilities with employment continue to persist; and 5. Women, especially younger women, experience more unemployment than men and for longer periods of time. In essence, too often, women remain at the lower end of a segregated labor market and continue to be concentrated in a few occupations, holding positions of little or no authority and receiving less pay than men.[4]

Generally, employment raises the status of women by allowing them to earn income and hence have more control over resources.[5] As such, women's participation in the labor force has increased in almost all regions of the world and several factors explain this, namely attitudes today toward the employment of women are more accepting; and new policies in some countries on family and childcare favor working women. These trends are positive. However, equality in the workforce is still a long way from reality. Women typically occupy lower-paid, lower-status jobs, and have higher unemployment rates than men. Further, the connection between gender and poverty has attracted more attention recently, because women's lack of social power and lack of resources can be mutually reinforcing. Overall, gender disparities are greatest in the poorest countries and regions, but promoting gender equality can contribute to greater prosperity and many governments now recognize that female education can foster economic growth.

Insufficient attention to gender analysis has meant that women's contributions and concerns remain too often ignored in economic structures, such as financial markets and institutions, labor markets, the economic and social infrastructures, and taxation and social security systems, as well as in families and households.[6] As a result, many policies and programs may continue to contribute to inequalities between men and women. Where progress has been made in integrating gender perspectives, program and policy effectiveness has also been enhanced.

However, it is important to note that women contribute to human development, not only through remunerated work but also through unremunerated work. Women still perform the great majority of unremunerated domestic work and community work, such as caring for children and older persons, protecting the environment, and providing voluntary assistance to vulnerable and disadvantaged individuals and groups. This work is often not measured in quantitative terms and not valued in national accounts. Women's contribution to development is seriously underestimated, and thus its social recognition is limited. It is hoped that the full visibility of the type, extent and distribution of this unremunerated work will also help to devise a better sharing of responsibilities within families and within societies.

Although some new employment opportunities have been created for women as a result of the globalization of the economy, there are also trends that have exacerbated inequalities between men and women. Globalization and economic integration can create pressures on the employment situation of women to adjust to new circumstances and to find new sources of employment as patterns of trade change. These trends have been characterized by low wages, little or no labor standards protection, poor working conditions particularly with regard to women's occupational health and safety, low skill levels, and a lack of job security and social security, in both the formal and informal sectors.

Women's unemployment is a serious and increasing problem in many countries and sectors. In countries that are undergoing fundamental political, economic and social transformation, the skills of women, if better utilized, could constitute a major contribution to the economic life overall. Further, lack of employment in the private sector and reductions in public service jobs have affected women disproportionately. In many cases, employment creation strategies have not paid sufficient attention to occupations and sectors where women predominate, nor have they adequately promoted the access of women to those occupations and sectors that are traditionally male.

For those women in paid work, many experience obstacles that prevent them from achieving their full potential. Attitudinal discrimination often hinders women from being progressively promoted. Additionally, there is still the experience of sexual harassment which is an affront to a worker's dignity and prevents women from making a contribution commensurate with their abilities. As well, the lack of a family-friendly work environment, including a lack of appropriate and affordable childcare and inflexible working hours, prevent women from achieving their full potential. In the private sector, including transnational and national enterprises, women continue to be largely absent from management and policy levels, denoting discriminatory hiring and promotion policies and practices.

The persistent unfavorable work environment as well as the limited number of employment opportunities available have led many women to seek alternatives. Women have increasingly become self-employed, and owners and managers of micro, small and medium-scale enterprises. The expansion of the informal sector, in many countries, and of self-organized and independent enterprises is in large part due to women, whose collaborative, self-help and traditional practices and initiatives in production and trade represent a vital economic resource. When they gain access to and control over capital and credit, technology and training, women can increase production, marketing and income for sustainable development.

Taking into account the fact that continuing inequalities and noticeable progress coexist, rethinking employment policies is necessary in order to integrate the gender perspective, not only to address any negative gender implications of current patterns of work and employment, but also to draw attention to a wider range of opportunities. To realize full equality between men and women in their contribution to the economy, active efforts are required for equal recognition and appreciation of the influence that both men's and women's work, experience, knowledge and values have in society. In addressing the economic potential and independence of women, before decisions are taken, an analysis should be made of the effects on both women and men. Governments and other actors need to promote an active and visible policy of mainstreaming a gender perspective into all policies and programs.[7]

The Human Development Report of the United Nations Development Programme (UNDP) concluded: 'In no society do women enjoy the same opportunities as men'.[8] In 2000, progress in the implementation of the 1995 Beijing Declaration and Platform for Action was reviewed by the special session of the United Nations General Assembly entitled 'Women 2000: gender equality, development and peace for the twenty-first century', known as Beijing +5. The event noted that 'even though significant positive developments can be identified, barriers remain and there is still the need to further implement the goals and commitments made in Beijing', and this is still true today.[9]

Gender relations structure the entire life cycle, from birth to old age, influencing access to resources and opportunities, and shaping life choices at every stage. The relevance of gender is both ongoing and cumulative, since the different circumstances that shape the lives of women and men in later years are the outcome of the many different opportunities, challenges and constraints that have gone before.

Through this book, it is clear that the legislative and legal systems are of primary importance in the fight against gender injustice and for gender justice. The study has shown: 1. Women overall have positively influenced legislation and the court process in the pursuit of equality; 2. Women have made some inroads in the labor market, but there is still not wage parity or equal access to employment; and 3. Laws have been enacted internationally on the issue of gender equality, but they must be enforced with zero tolerance.

Countries around the world have made important progress in the development of equal rights, most particularly in the right to equal pay and the right to access to employment for women. Gender rights legislation and court challenges are required, in order to better improve the situation of women in the workplace. The desire is for equal social rights for all. Therefore, the law needs to be enforced by way of the courts to achieve greater gender equality in an effort to modify historical attitudes toward women, so that Nations conform to certain standards. There should be real freedom to choose one's amount of participation in the work force, in the pursuit of flexibility as to a just remuneration and access to employment. This must be done so that men and women can truly be on more equal terms.

The central importance of equality legislation in order to bring about change is evident and indeed critical. Our very rights as human beings emanate from the word of the law and the interpretation given by the highest courts in the land. Therefore, it is imperative that the struggle for gender justice encompass the legal system. The concept of total equality has never truly existed, nor was it ever meant to be anything more than empty promises of change. Absolute equality is not sought in this book, nor is it realistic. However, in a feeling of mutual respect for individual differences, a better equality between the sexes is possible and desirable through society's laws and legal institutions.

The keys to the future are the implementation and development of the law, the deepening in understanding of specific legal issues relating to employment discrimination, and the raising of the level of awareness of legal rights and obligations. As well, there needs to be a full employment policy for the integration of women into the labor market, the reduction of barriers to women's access and participation in employment, the improvement in the quality of women's employment through education, training and management of resources, and the improvement in the status of women in society for a change of attitudes and a lasting progress.[10] In addition, a continuing exchange of experience and expertise needs to occur on the international front for mutual benefit among all groups in order to best serve the fight for gender equality. We must all strive to promote and improve the situation of women through networks of awareness, in the raising of initiatives, the dissemination of information and the provision of support for equality.

We must learn from other groups' experiences in the fight for equality. As such, in examining legislation, we should take into account the civil rights movement of the 1960s, and its advancements in racial rights and tolerance. Gender justice and its fight to at least achieve what racial justice has achieved in the laws and in the courts can only help to serve the female struggle. Therefore, in the struggle to secure equal rights for women, the consultation process must include input from other groups for strategic purposes in order to strengthen the cause. The process must be one of inclusion not exclusion.

It is realistic to say that inequality in general exists between the sexes, but especially inequality of opportunity within the labor force. This is to be expected, since women have occupied a major role in the employment sphere for a shorter time than men. In addition to this, laws have been enacted and courts have enforced them in a traditionally male dominant way. This again is to be expected, since women have occupied a major role in the legal sphere for a shorter time than men. However, women too need to be a rallying symbol of political and economic force, so that equality can become a reality.

Internationally, changes in public policy and the introduction of equality legislation have impacted on the evolution of the male-female wage differential. In addition, the differential has been affected by changes in the supply of and the demand for male and female labor, such that if a sector with a high concentration of female employment experiences a period of strong growth, this could increase the demand for female labor and put upward pressure on female wages.

Many employment practices that explicitly discriminate against women are still prevalent, however, with legal action suggesting some still exist which produce discriminatory outcomes for women. The impact of equal pay legislation will depend on the legislative provisions as well as the effectiveness of the legislation's enforcement. In general, it is expected that equal pay laws mandating equal pay for equal work within the same occupation and firm will have a relatively small effect on the gender pay gap, due to the considerable segregation of women by occupation, firm and industry.

The full and equal enjoyment of all human rights and fundamental freedoms by women should be a priority for all and is essential for the advancement of women. Equal rights of men and women are explicitly mentioned in the Preamble to the Charter of the United Nations, and all the major international human rights instruments include gender as one of the grounds upon which States may not discriminate. Unless the human rights of women, as defined by international human rights instruments, are fully recognized and effectively protected, applied, implemented and enforced in national law as well as in national practice in family, civil, penal, labor and commercial codes and administrative rules and regulations, they will exist in name only.[11]

It is evident that we are moving in the right direction, since some change has taken place. However, further change is necessary and plausible. By working on the very thing that controls and defines all of our lives, the law, further progress can be made.

Perhaps one day, there will be no need to have the 'Year of the Woman'. However, this day has not come, since it is fair to say that we are still in the 'Years of the Man'. Women's liberation is the longest revolution. Once again, the memorable words of the Rev. Martin Luther King Jr. in his struggle for civil rights can also be applied in the struggle for gender rights:

> I have a dream that one day every valley shall be exalted, every hill and mountain shall be made low, the rough places shall be made plain, and the crooked places shall be made straight and the glory of the Lord will be revealed and all flesh shall see it together. This is our hope....And when we allow freedom to ring, when we let it ring from every village and hamlet, from every state and city, we will be able to speed up that day when all of God's children...will be able to join hands and to sing in the words of the old Negro spiritual, 'Free at last, free at last; thank God Almighty, we are free at last'.[12]

Notes

1 Scott, Joan, *Feminism and History*, Oxford University Press, Oxford, 1996, p.153.
2 *Ibid.*, at p.167.
3 Scott, Hilda, *Working Your Way to the Bottom*, Pandora Press, London, 1984.
4 United Nations, *The World's Women 2000: Trends and Statistics*, 2000.
5 Population Reference Bureau, *Women of Our World,* 2002.
6 Department of Justice, Equality & Law Reform, *Developing Sectoral Strategies to Address Gender Pay Gaps*, 2003.
7 *Ibid.*
8 United Nations Division for the Advancement of Women, *Women 2000*, 2002.
9 *Ibid.*
10 Commission of the European Communities, *Promotion of Positive Action*, Brussels, p.4.
11 United Nations, *Beijing Declaration and Platform for Action, Fourth World Conference on Women.*
12 King Jr., Martin Luther, *March on Washington*, 1963.

References

Commission of the European Community (1995), *Equal Opportunities for Women and Men*, Brussels.
Commission of the European Communities, *Promotion of Positive Action*, Brussels.
Department of Justice (2003), Equality & Law Reform, *Developing Sectoral Strategies to Address Gender Pay Gaps.*
Jordan, Bill, 'The Reform of Social Security', *Administration*, 1986, p.208.
King Jr., Martin Luther, *March on Washington*, August 28, 1963.
Population Reference Bureau (2002), *Women of Our World.*
Scott, Hilda (1984), *Working Your Way to the Bottom*, Pandora Press, London.
Scott, Joan (1996), *Feminism and History*, Oxford University Press, Oxford.
United Nations, *Beijing Declaration and Platform for Action, Fourth World Conference on Women.*
United Nations (2000), *The World's Women 2000: Trends and Statistics.*
United Nations Division for the Advancement of Women (2002), *Women 2000.*

Bibliography

Abramson, Joan (1979), *Old Boys New Women*, Praeger, New York.

Acker, Joan (1989), *Doing Comparative Worth*, Temple University Press, Philadelphia.

Action Travail des Femmes v. Canadien National, 1984 CHRT.

Affirmative Action (Equal Employment Opportunity for Women) Act, Australia, 1986.

African Charter on Human and Peoples' Rights.

Ali, Suki (2000), *Global Feminist Politics*, Routledge, London.

American Constitution, 1776.

American Federation of State, County and Municipal Employees v. Washington, 770 F.2d. 1401 (1985).

American Nurses' Association v. State of Illinois, 783 F.2d. 716 (1986).

Andrew, Caroline (1988), *Life Spaces*, University of British Columbia Press, Vancouver.

Andry, Jacqueline Hunt, 'The Supreme Court Tightens the Reins on Heightened Scrutiny', *Loyola Law Review*, Vol. 35, 1989, p.267.

Ang-Lygate, Magdalene (1997), *Desperately Seeking Sisterhood*, Taylor & Francis, London.

Antoine, Louis (2000), *Ah les Femmes, Tribulations, Struggles and Triumphs*, Minerva, London.

Arendt, Hannah (1957), *Rahel Varnhagen*, Harcourt Brace Jovanovich, New York.

Arendt, Hannah (1959), *The Human Condition*, Doubleday, Garden City.

Argawal, Naresh, 'Pay Equity in Canada', *Labor Law Journal*, Vol.41, 1990, p.518.

Armstrong, Donald (1987), 'Canada-U.S. Free Trade and Canadian Culture', in A.R. Riggs and Tom Velk, *Canadian-American Free Trade: Historical, Political and Economic Dimensions*, The Institute for Research in Public Policy, Montreal.

Asimakopoulos, A. (1978), *An Introduction to Economic Theory: Microeconomics*, Oxford University Press, Don Mills.

Atkins, Susan (1984), *Women and the Law*, Blackwell, Oxford.

Axworthy, Lloyd (1988), 'Free Trade, The Costs for Canada', in A.R. Riggs and Tom Velk, *Canadian-American Free Trade: (The Sequel) Historical, Political and Economic Dimensions*, The Institute for Research on Public Policy, Montreal.

Bacchi, Carol Lee (1990), *Same Difference; Feminism and Sexual Difference*, Allen & Unwin, North Sydney.

Ballard v. United States, 329 U.S. 187 (1946).

Balthazar, Louis (1984), 'Quebec's Policies Toward the United States', in Alfred O. Hero, Jr. and Marcel Daneau, *Problems and Opportunities in the United States and Quebec Relations*, Westview Press, Boulder.

Barlow, Maude (1990), *Parcel of Rogues*, Key Porter Books, Toronto.

Basi v. Canadian National Railway (1984), 9 C.H.R.R.4. D/5029.

Baumeister, Andrea (2000), *Liberalism and the Politics of Difference*, Edinburgh University Press, Edinburgh.

Beijing Declaration.

Bhavnani, Kum-Kum (2001), *Feminism and Race*, Oxford University Press, Oxford.

Bill of Rights Act, New Zealand, 1990.

Blake v. Ministry of Correctional Services and Mimico Correctional Institute (1984), 5 C.H.R.R. D/2417 (Ontario).

Board of Trustees v. Sweeney, 439 U.S. 24 (1978).

Bock, Gisela and James, Susan (1992), *Beyond Equality and Difference, Citizens, Feminist Politics and Female Subjectivity*, Routledge, London.

Borchardt, Klaus-Dieter (1993), *The ABC of Community Law*, Official Publications of the European Communities, Luxembourg.

Bradwell v. State, 16 Wall. 130 (1873).

Braidotti, Rosi (2001), 'Becoming Women, Rethinking the Positivity of Difference', in Elisabeth Bronfen, *Feminist Consequences, Theory for the New Century*, Columbia University Press, New York.

Brecher, Irving (1987), 'The Free Trade Initiative, On Course or Off', in A.R. Riggs and Tom Velk, *Canadian-American Free Trade: Historical, Political and Economic Dimensions*, The Institute for Research in Public Policy, Montreal.

Brecher, Irving (1988), 'Free at Last', in A.R. Riggs and Tom Velk, *Canadian-American Free Trade: (The Sequel) Historical, Political and Economic Dimensions*, The Institute for Research on Public Policy, Montreal.

Brennan v. City Stores, 479 F.2d. 235 (1973).

Briskin, Linda (1993), *Women Challenging Unions, Feminism, Democracy and Militance*, University of Toronto Press, Toronto.

British North America Act, 1867.

Bronfen, Elisabeth (2001), *Feminist Consequences, Theory for the New Century*, Columbia University Press, New York.

Bullough, Vern L. (1973), *The Subordinate Sex*, University of Illinois Press, Urbana.

Cameron, Duncan and Watkins, Mel (1993), *Canada Under Free Trade*, James Lorimer & Co., Toronto.

Campbell, Bruce (1992), *We Need Free Trade Abrogation to Rebuild the Nation*, Canadian Centre for Policy Alternatives, Ottawa.

Campbell, Bruce (1993), *Free Trade, Destroyer of Jobs*, Canadian Centre for Policy Alternatives, Ottawa.

Canada Employment Equity Act, 1995.

Canada – United States Free Trade Agreement, 1989.

Canadian Advisory Council on the Status of Women (1992), *Feminist Guide to the Canadian Constitution*, Ottawa.

Canadian Bill of Rights, 1960.

Canadian Charter of Rights and Freedoms, 1982.

Canadian Human Rights Act, 1978.

Canadian Human Rights Commission (1991), *Equal Dollars Make Good Sense*, Ottawa.

Cassells, Peter, 'Can Europe Solve its Job Crisis?', *Administration*, Vol.40, N.1, 1992.

Cassin, René, *From the Ten Commandments to the Rights of Man*.

Catterall, Miriam (2000), *Marketing and Feminism*, Routledge, London.

Charles, Nickie (1996), *Practising Feminism*, Routledge, New York.

Charter of the United Nations.

Chartier, Armand (1984), 'Franco-Americans and Quebec', in Alfred O. Hero, Jr. and Marcel Daneau, *Problems and Opportunities in the United States and Quebec Relations*, Boulder: Westview Press, Boulder.

Chorney, Harold (1990), *City of Dreams*, Nelson Canada, Scarborough.

Clark, Lorenne (1979), 'Women and Locke: Who Owns the Apples in the Garden of Eden', in Lorenne M.G. Clark and Lynda Lange, *The Sexism of Social and Political Theory, Women and Reproduction from Plato to Nietzsche*, University of Toronto Press, Toronto.

Clark, Lorenne M.G. and Lange, Lynda (1979), *The Sexism of Social and Political Theory, Women and Reproduction from Plato to Nietzsche*, University of Toronto Press, Toronto.

Clayton, Susan and Crosby, Faye (1992), *Justice, Gender and Affirmative Action*, University of Michigan Press, Ann Arbour.

Cockburn, Cynthia (1991), *In the Way of Women, Men's Resistance to Sex Equality in Organizations*, ILR Press, Ithaca.

Cohen, Gary L. (1996), *Women Entrepreneurs*, Perspectives.

Coleman, Frank (1977), *Hobbes and America*, University of Toronto, Toronto.

Commission of the European Communities, *Equal Opportunity for Women and Men*, Brussels.

Commission of the European Communities, *Promotion of Positive Action*, Brussels.

Commission of the European Communities (1991), *The Position of Women on the Labour Market*, Brussels.

Commission of the European Communities (1992), *From Single Market to European Union*, Brussels.

Commission of the European Communities (1992), *Women's Information Service*, Brussels.

Commission of the European Communities (1993), *Equal Opportunities for Women in the Community*, Brussels.

Commission of the European Communities (1994), *Europe*, Brussels.

Commission of the European Communities (1995), *Employment in Europe*, Brussels.

Commission of the European Communities (1996), *Burden of Proof in Sex Discrimination Cases*, Brussels.

Commission of the European Communities (1996), *Serving the European Community*, Brussels.

Commission Recommendation 92/131/EEC of 27 November 1991 on the protection of the dignity of women and men at work [OJ L 049, 24/02/1992 P. 0001–0008].

Commonwealth of Australia, *Women 2002*.

Commonwealth Office, *Advancing the Commonwealth Agenda for Gender Equality into the New Millennium (2000-2005)*.

Commonwealth Office of the Status of Women, Australia, 2002.

Commonwealth Secretariat, *1995 Commonwealth Plan*.

Constitución Política de los Estados Unidos Mexicanos.

Constitution of South Africa.

Convention on the Elimination of all Forms of Discrimination Against Women.

Coppock, Vicki (1995), *The Illusions of Post Feminism*, Taylor & Francis, London.

Corning Glass Works v. Brennan, 417 U.S. 188 (1974).

Costa v. ENEL, [1964] CMLR 425.

Council Directive 75/117/EEC of 10 February 1975 on the approximation of the laws of the Member States relating to the application of the principle of equal pay for men and women [OJ L 045, 19/02/1975 P. 0019–0020].

Council Directive 76/207/EEC of 9 February 1976 on the implementation of the principle of equal treatment for men and women as regards access to employment, vocational training and promotion, and working conditions [OJ L 039, 14/02/1976 P. 0040–0042].

Council Directive 79/7/EEC of 19 December 1978 on the progressive implementation of the principle of equal treatment for men and women in matters of social security [OJ L 006, 10/01/1979 P. 0024–0025].

Council Directive 86/378/EEC of 24 July 1986 on the implementation of the principle of equal treatment for men and women in occupational social security schemes [OJ L 225, 12/08/1986 P. 0040–0042].

Council Directive 86/613/EEC of 11 December 1986 on the application of the principle of equal treatment between men and women engaged in an activity, including agriculture, in a self-employed capacity, and on the protection of self-employed women during pregnancy and motherhood [OJ L 359, 19/12/1986 P. 0056–0058].

Council Directive 92/85/EEC of 19 October 1992 on the introduction of measures to encourage improvements in the safety and health at work of pregnant workers and workers who have recently given birth or are breastfeeding [OJ L 348, 28/11/1992 P. 0001–0008].

Council Directive 93/104/EC of 23 November 1993 concerning certain aspects of the organization of working time [OJ L 307, 13/12/1993 P. 0018–0024].

Council Directive 96/34/EC of 3 June 1996 on the framework agreement on parental leave concluded by UNICE, CEEP and the ETUC [OJ L 145, 19/06/1996 P. 0004-0009 CONSLEG 96L0034 16/01/1998 11 P].

Council Directive 97/80/EC of 15 December 1997 on the burden of proof in cases of discrimination based on sex [OJ L 014, 20/01/1998 P. 0006–0008].

Council Directive 2000/78/EC of 27 November 2000 establishing a general framework for equal treatment in employment and occupation [OJ L 303, 02/12/2000 P. 0016–0022].

Council Recommendation 84/635/EEC of 13 December 1984 on the promotion of positive action for women [OJ L 331, 19/12/1984 P. 0034–0035].

Courchane, Marsha and Redish, Angela (1992), 'Women in the Labour Force, 1911-1986', in Robert Allen and Gideon Rosenbluth, *False Promises*, New Star Books, Vancouver.

Cox, Archibald (1967), *Civil Rights, The Constitution and the Court*, Harvard University Press, Cambridge.

Cox, Archibald (1976), *The Role of the Supreme Court in American Government*, Oxford University Press, New York.

Cox, Oliver (1970), *Caste, Class and Race*, Monthly Review Press, New York.

Craig v. Boren, 429 U.S. 190 (1976).

Creighton, Donald (1970), *The Empire of the St. Lawrence*, Macmillan, Toronto.

Crompton, Susan and Geran, Leslie (1995), *Women as Main Wage-Earners*, Perspectives.

Daltrop, Anne (1982), *Political Realities, Politics and the European Community*, Longman, New York.

Dandridge v. William (397 U.S. 471 (1970)).

D'Aquino, Thomas (1987), 'Truck and Trade with the Yankees, The Case for a Canada-U.S. Comprehensive Trade Agreement', in A.R. Riggs and Tom Velk, *Canadian-American Free Trade: Historical, Political and Economic Dimensions*, The Institute for Research on Public Policy, Montreal.

Davenport, Paul (1988), 'L'Economie Politique du Libre Echange, Un Survol', in A.R. Riggs and Tom Velk, *Canadian-American Free Trade: (The Sequel) Historical, Political and Economic Dimensions*, The Institute for Research on Public Policy, Montreal.

Davis, Lenwood (1969), *I Have A Dream*, Negro University Press, Westport.

Davis v. Passman, 442 U.S. 228 (1979).

Davis Gould, Elizabeth (1976), *The First Sex*, Putnam, New York.

DeBeauvoir, Simone (1974), *The Second Sex*, New York.

Delamont, Sara (2001), *Changing Women, Unchanged Men*, Open University Press, Buckingham.

Department of Justice, Equality & Law Reform (2003), *Developing Sectoral Strategies to Address Gender Pay Gaps*.

Dinsmore, John (1975), 'Elements d'une position du Québec dans les relations économiques avec les Etats-Unis', in *Choix*, Centre Québécois de Relations Internationales, Laval.

Directive 2002/73/EC of the European Parliament and of the Council of 23 September 2002 amending Council Directive 76/207/EEC on the implementation of the principle of equal treatment for men and women as regards access to employment, vocational training and promotion, and working conditions [OJ L 269, 05/10/2002 P. 0015–0020].

Disability Discrimination Act, Australia, 1992.

Disability Discrimination Act, Great Britain, 1995.

Discrimination (Employment and Occupation) Convention.

Department of Trade and Industry, Great Britain (2003), *Key Facts about Women in the Labour Market.*

Domestic Violence Act, New Zealand, 1995.

Donovan, Josephine (1993), *Feminist Theory*, Continuum, New York.

Doucet, Andrea (2001), 'Can Boys Grow into Mothers?, Maternal Thinking and Fathers' Reflections', in Andrea O'Reilly, *Mothers and Sons: Feminism, Masculinity and the Struggle to Raise Our Sons*, Routledge, London.

Duff, Andrew, Pinder, John and Pryce, Roy (1994), *Maastricht and Beyond*, Routledge, London.

Easterbrook, W.T. and Aitken, Hugh (1976), *Canadian Economic History*, Macmillan, Toronto.

Economic Commission for Africa (2002), *Africa's Population and Development Bulletin*, Addis Ababa.

Economic Commission for Africa (2002), *Economic Report on Africa.*

Elgin Marcy Reciprocity Treaty, 1854.

Ely, J. (1980), *Democracy and Distrust*, Harvard University Press, Cambridge.

Employment Act, Great Britain, 1989.

Employment Contracts Act, New Zealand, 1991.

Employment Equality Act, Ireland, 1998.

Employment Equity Act, South Africa, 1998.

Employment Relations Act, Great Britain, 1999.

Employment Rights Act, Great Britain, 1996.

Employment Tribunals (Interest on Awards in Discrimination Cases) Regulations, Great Britain, 1996.

Equal Opportunities Commission, *Code of Practice on Equal Pay.*

Equal Opportunities Commission (2003), *Facts About Women and Men in Great Britain.*

Equal Opportunities Commission (2003), *Facts About Women and Men in Scotland.*

Equal Opportunities Commission (2003), *Facts About Women and Men in Wales.*

Equal Opportunities Commission (2003), *Women and Men in Britain, Pay and Income.*

Equal Employment Opportunity Commission v. Sears Roebuck & Company, 839 F.2d 301 (1988).

Equal Pay Act 1970 (As amended), Great Britain.

Equal Pay Act (Northern Ireland) 1970.

Equal Pay (Complaints to Employment Tribunals) (Armed Forces) Regulations, Great Britain, 1997.

Equal Remuneration Convention (ILO No. 100).

Equal Status Act, Ireland, 2000.

Equality Commission for Northern Ireland, *Sex Discrimination and Equal Pay in Northern Ireland.*

European Charter of Fundamental Social Rights, 1989.

European Convention for the Protection of Human Rights and Fundamental Freedoms, 1950.

European Convention for the Protection of Human Rights and Fundamental Freedoms as amended by Protocol No. 11.
European Convention for the Protection of Human Rights and Fundamental Freedoms as amended by Protocol No. 12.
European Social Charter (revised), 1996.
Eurostat (1995), *Statistics*.
Eurostat (1996), *Statistics in Focus*.
Eurostat (2001), *Yearbook, 1989-1991, Statistical Guide to Europe*.
Evans, Judith (1995), *Feminist Theory Today*, Sage Publications, Thousand Oaks.
Evans, Mary (1997), *Introducing Contemporary Feminist Thought*, Polity Press, Cambridge.
Falardeau, Jean-Claude (1953), *Essays on Contemporary Quebec*, Les Presses Universitaires Laval, Québec.
Faludi, Susan (1992), *Backlash, The Undeclared War Against Women*, Vintage, London.
Faucher, Albert and Lamontagne, Maurice (1953), 'The History of Industrial Development', in Jean-Claude Falardeau, *Essays on Contemporary Quebec*, Les Presses Universitaires Laval, Québec.
Fawcett, Barbara (2000), *Practice and Research in Social Work, Postmodern Feminist Perspective*, Routledge, London.
Federalist Papers, 1787-1788.
Firestone, Shulamith (1971), *The Dialectic of Sex*, Jonathan Cape, London.
Flax, Jane (1992), 'Beyond Equality: Gender, Justice and Difference', in Gisela Bock and Susan James, *Beyond Equality and Difference, Citizens, Feminist Politics and Female Subjectivity*, Routledge, London.
Flynn, Padraig (1996), *Defining the Gender Contract*, Ireland.
Folch v. Canadian Airlines, 1992 CHRT.
Fox-Genovese, Elizabeth (1991), *Feminism Without Illusions*, University of North Carolina Press, Chapel Hill.
Fox-Genovese, Elizabeth (1995), *The Birth of American Feminism*, Brandywine Press, St. James.
Fox-Genovese, Elizabeth (1996), *Feminism Is Not the Story of My Life*, Doubleday, New York.
Freedman, Jane (2001), *Feminism*, Open University Press, Buckingham.
Free Trade Agreement of the Americas.
Fried, Morton (1967), *The Evolution of Political Society*, Random House, New York.
Friedan, Betty (1963), *The Feminine Mystique*, Penguin, Harmondsworth.
Friedan, Betty (1983), *The Second Stage*, Sphere Books, London.
Frontiero v. Richardson, 411 U.S. 677 (1973).
Fry, Earl (1987), 'Trends in Canada-U.S. Free Trade Discussions', in A.R. Riggs and Tom Welk, *Canadian-American Free Trade: Historical, Political and Economic Dimensions*, The Institute for Research in Public Policy, Montreal.
F.S. Royster Guano Co. v. Com of Virginia, 253 U.S. 412 (1920).
Fudge, Judy (1991), *Just Wages, Feminine Perspective of Pay Equity*, University of Toronto Press, Toronto.
Garside Allen, Christine (1979), 'Nietzsche's Ambivalence about Women', in Lorenne M.G. Clark and Lynda Lange, *The Sexism of Social and Political Theory, Women and Reproduction from Plato to Nietzsche*, University of Toronto Press, Toronto.
General Agreement on Tariffs and Trade.
Gerhart Barry, 'Gender Differences in Current and Starting Salaries', *Industrial and Labor Relations Review*, Vol.43, N.4, 1990, p.418.
Gerhart, Barry and El Cheich, Nabil, 'Earnings and Percentage Female', *Industrial Relations*, Vol.30, N.1, 1991, p.62.

Glennon, Lynda (1979), *Women and Dualism*, Longman, London.
Goesaert v. Cleary, 335 U.S. 464 (1948).
Gold, Michael (1983), *A Dialogue on Comparable Worth*, Cornell University Press, Ithaca.
Goshen, Erica, 'Structure of Female/Male Wage Differentials', *Journal of Human Resources*, Vol.26, Summer 1991, p.457.
Government of Australia, *Australia's Beijing Plus Five Action Plan 2001-2005.*
Government of Australia, *Implementation of the Beijing Platform for Action*, 2000.
Government of Canada (1993), *The North American Free Trade Agreement At A Glance*, Ottawa.
Government of Canada (2002), *NAFTA at Eight*, Department of Foreign Affairs, Ottawa.
Government of Quebec, Ministère des Affaires Internationales (1993), *Quebec and the North American Free Trade Agreement*, Québec.
Government of Quebec, Ministère des Affaires Internationales, de l'Immigration et des Communautés Culturelles du Québec (1994), *Commerce International du Québec, Etats-Unis, Jan-Juin, 1993-1994*, Quebec.
Government of Quebec, Ministère des Affaires Internationales, de l'Immigration et des Communautés Culturelles du Québec (1994), *Commerce International du Québec, Etats-Unis, 1992-1993*, Quebec.
Government of the United Kingdom (2002), *Equality in Practice.*
Grande Jensen, Pamela (1996), *Finding a New Feminism*, Rowman & Littlefield Publishers, Lanham.
Greer, Germaine (2000), *The Whole Woman*, Anchor, London.
Griffin Cohen, Marjorie (1987), *Free Trade and the Future of Women's Work, Manufacturing and Service Industries*, Garamond Press, Toronto.
Griggs v. Duke Power Co., 401 U.S. 424 (1971).
Guindon, Hubert (1988), *Quebec Society: Tradition, Modernity, and Nationhood*, University of Toronto Press, Toronto.
Gunther v. County of Washington, 452 U.S. 161 (1981).
Habermas, Jurgen (1998), *Between Facts and Norms*, MIT Press, Massachussetts.
Hamelin, Jean (1976), *Histoire du Québec*, Edisem, St. Hyacinthe.
Hamelin, Jean and Roby, Yves (1971), *Histoire Economique du Québec 1851-1896*, Fides, Montreal.
Hansen, Phillip (1993), *Hannah Arendt*, Stanford University Press, Stanford.
Harris, Richard (1988), 'Some Observations on the Canada-U.S. Free Trade Deal', in A.R. Riggs and Tom Velk, *Canadian-American Free Trade: (The Sequel) Historical, Political and Economic Dimensions*, The Institute for Research on Public Policy, Montreal.
Hayes, Bernadette, 'Female Intergenerational Occupational Mobility Within Northern Ireland and the Republic of Ireland', *British Journal of Sociology*, Vol.38, May 1987, p.66.
Hazledine, Tim (1987), 'What do Economists Know about Free Trade', in A.R. Riggs and Tom Velk, *Canadian-American Free Trade: Historical, Political and Economic Dimensions*, The Institute for Research in Public Policy, Montreal.
Health and Disability Commissioner Act 1994 and Code of Health & Disability Services Consumers' Rights, New Zealand.
Health and Safety at Work Act, Great Britain, 1974.
Hegel (1967), *The Philosophy of Right*, London.
Hero, Alfred and Balthazar, Louis (1988), *Contemporary Quebec and the United States 1960-1985*, University Press of America, Boston.
Hogan, Richard and LeVoir, John (1985), *Covenant of Love*, Doubleday & Co., New York.

Hollows, Joanne (2000), *Feminism, Femininity and Popular Culture*, Manchester University Press, Manchester.
Horkheimer, Max and Adorno, Theodor (1972), *Dialectic of Enlightenment*, Herder & Herder, New York.
Hoyt v. Florida, 368 U.S. 57 (1961).
Hughes, Patricia (1989), 'Fighting the Good Fight', in Angela Miles and Geraldine Finn, *Feminism*, Black Rose Books, Montreal.
Human Rights Act, Great Britain, 1998.
Human Rights Act, New Zealand, 1993.
Hume, David (1988), *Treatise of Human Nature*, Oxford.
Hurtig, Mel (1991), *The Betrayal of Canada*, Stoddart Publishing, Toronto.
Innis, Harold (1995), *Staples, Markets and Cultural Change*, McGill Queen's University Press, Montreal.
Interim Constitution of South Africa, Schedule 4.
International Convention on the Elimination of All Forms of Racial Discrimination.
International Covenant on Civil and Political Rights.
International Covenant on Economic, Social and Cultural Rights.
Internationale Handelsgesellschaft, [1970] ECR 1125, [1972] CMLR 255.
Irigaray, Luce (2000), *Democracy Begins Between Two*, Athlone Press, London.
Jackson, Pauline (1986), *Worlds Apart*, Ireland.
Jacoby, Russell (1975), *Social Amnesia*, Beacon Press, Boston.
Jacoby, Russell (1982), *The Last Intellectuals*, Basic Books, New York.
Jagentowicz Mills, Patricia (1979), 'Hegel and the Woman Question: Recognition and Intersubjectivity', in Lorenne M.G. Clark and Lynda Lange, *The Sexism of Social and Political Theory, Women and Reproduction from Plato to Nietzsche*, University of Toronto Press, Toronto.
Johnson v. Transportation Agency, 480 U.S. 616 (1987).
Jones, Robert, 'Agriculture in Lower Canada, 1792-1815', *The Canadian Historical Review*, Vol.27, 1946, p.33.
Jordan, Bill, 'The Reform of Social Security', *Administration*, 1986.
Jung, Anees (1997), *Breaking the Silence*, Penguin Books, New York.
Kahn v. Shevin, 416 U.S. 351 (1974).
Kahn, Peggy (1992), *Equal Value/Comparable Worth in the U.K. and the USA*, St. Martin's Press, New York.
Kanowitz, Leo (1969), *Women and the Law, The Unfinished Revolution*, University of New Mexico Press, Albuquerque.
Kanowitz, Leo, 'Benign Sex Discrimination: Its Troubles and Their Cure', *Hastings Law Journal*, Vol. 31, 1980, p.1379.
Kaufman, Bruce E. (1988), *How Labor Markets Work*, Lexington Books, Lexington.
Kelly, J.M. (1984), *The Irish Constitution*, Leinster Leader, Ireland.
Kennedy, President John .F.
King Jr., Dr. Martin Luther, March on Washington, August 28, 1963.
Kirchberg v. Feenstra, 450 U.S. 455 (1981).
Klarman, Michael, 'Interpretive History of Equal Protection', *Michigan Law Review*, Vol. 90, 1991, p.213.
Kokott, Juliane, 'European Communities, Equal Pay for Men and Women, DeFacto Discrimination', *American Journal of International Law*, Vol.86, N.2, 1991, p.348.
Kouba v. Allstate (691 F.2d. 873 (1982)).
Kremer, John, 'Attitudes Toward Women in Northern Ireland', *Journal of Social Psychology*, 127(5), 1987, p.531.

Labour Canada (1986), *Equal Pay for Work of Equal Value*, Ottawa.

Lahey, Kathleen (1989), 'Celebration and Struggle', in Angela Miles and Geraldine Finn, *Feminism*, Black Rose Books, Montreal.

Lange, Lynda (1979), 'Rousseau: Women and the General Will', in Lorenne M.G. Clark and Lynda Lange, *The Sexism of Social and Political Theory, Women and Reproduction from Plato to Nietzsche*, University of Toronto Press, Toronto.

Lange, Lynda (1979), 'The Function of Equal Education in Plato's Republic and Laws', in Lorenne M.G. Clark and Lynda Lange, *The Sexism of Social and Political Theory, Women and Reproduction from Plato to Nietzsche*, University of Toronto Press, Toronto.

Lasch, Christopher (1977), *Haven in a Heartless World, The Family Besieged*, Basic Books Inc., New York.

Lasch, Christopher (1979), *The Culture of Narcissism*, W.W.Norton & Co., New York.

Lasch, Christopher, 'The Revolt of the Elites, Have They Cancelled their Allegiance to America?', *Harper's*, November 1994.

Laun, Louis (1987), 'U.S.-Canada Free Trade Negotiations: Historical Opportunities', in A.R. Riggs and Tom Velk, *Canadian-American Free Trade: Historical, Political and Economic Dimensions*, The Institute for Research in Public Policy, Montreal.

Lavoie, Yolande (1981), *L'Emigration des Québécois aux Etats-Unis de 1840-1930*, Editeur Officielle du Québec.

Layton, Robert (1987), 'Why Canada Needs Free Trade', in A.R. Riggs and Tom Velk, *Canadian-American Free Trade: Historical, Political and Economic Dimensions*, The Institute for Research in Public Policy, Montreal.

Lee, Yong, 'Shaping Judicial Response to Gender Discrimination in Employment Compensation', *Public Administration Review*, Sept. 1989, p.420.

Ley del Seguro Social, Mexico.

Ley Federal de Trabajo, Mexico.

Lindsley v. Natural Carbonic Gas Co., 220 U.S. 61 (1911).

Lipsey, Richard (1987), 'Canada's Trade Options', in A.R. Riggs and Tom Velk, *Canadian-American Free Trade: Historical, Political and Economic Dimensions*, The Institute for Research in Public Policy, Montreal.

Lisée, Jean-Francois (1990), *Dans l'Oeil de L'Aigle*, Boreal, Montreal.

Little, J.I. (1989), *Nationalism, Capitalism and Colonization*, McGill Queen's University Press, Kingston.

Livingstone, David (1996), *Recast Dreams*, Garamond Press, Toronto.

Locke, John (1963), *Second Treatise*, New York.

Loewy, Arnold, 'Returned to the Pedestal the Supreme Court and Gender Classification Cases: 1980 Term', *North Carolina Law Review*, Vol. 60, 1981, p.87.

Lorde, Audre (1984), *Sister Outsider*, The Crossing Press, Freedom.

Lyon, Peyton (1987), 'CUFTA and Canadian Independence', in A.R. Riggs and Tom Velk, *Canadian-American Free Trade: Historical, Political and Economic Dimensions*, The Institute for Research in Public Policy, Montreal.

Maastricht Treaty, 1992.

Mackinnon, Catharine (1987), *Feminism Unmodified*, Harvard University Press, Cambridge.

Mackinnon, Catharine (1989), *Toward a Feminist Theory of the State*, Harvard University Press, Cambridge.

Mackinnon, Catharine (1993), *Only Words*, Harvard University Press, Cambridge.

MacLeod Burns, Steven (1979), 'The Humean Female', in Lorenne M.G. Clark and Lynda Lange, *The Sexism of Social and Political Theory, Women and Reproduction from Plato to Nietzsche*, University of Toronto Press, Toronto.

MacPherson, C.B. (1962), *The Political Theory of Possessive Individualism*, Clarendon Press, Oxford.

Magna Carta, 1215.

Maltz, Earl, 'Legislative Inputs and Gender-Based Discrimination in the Burger Court', *Michigan Law Review*, Vol. 90, 1992, p.1023.

Management of Health and Safety at Work Regulations, Great Britain, 1999.

Mandel, Michael (1989), *The Charter of Rights and the Legalization of Politics in Canada*, Wall & Thompson, Toronto.

Marbury v. Madison, 1 Cranch 137 (1803).

Marcil Lacoste, Louise, 'Hume's Method in Moral Reasoning', in Lorenne M.G. Clarke and Lynda Lange (1979), *The Sexism of Social and Political Theory, Women and Reproduction from Plato to Nietzsche*, University of Toronto Press, Toronto.

Marr, William and Paterson, Donald (1980), *Canada: An Economic History*, Gage, Toronto.

Marx, Karl (1955), *Communist Manifesto*, New York.

Masters, Donald (1963), *The Reciprocity Treaty of 1854*, McClelland & Stewart Ltd., London.

Maternity and Parental Leave Regulations, Great Britain, 1999.

McCarty, Claire, 'The International Aspects of Procedural Justice', *Labor Law Journal*, Vol.41, 1990, p.580.

McCullough v. Maryland, 4 Wheaton 415 (1819).

McDonnell Douglas Corp. v. Green, 411 U.S. 792 (1973).

McGowan v. Maryland, 366 U.S. 420 (1961).

McMahon, Gerard, 'Pay Inequality in the 1990s', *Administration*, Vol.40, 1992, p.97.

McPhail, Brenda (1985), *NAFTA Now*, University Press of America, Lanham.

McRobbie, Angela (2000), *Feminism and Youth Culture*, Macmillan, Basingstoke.

Meehan, Johanna (1995), *Feminists Read Habermas*, Routledge, New York.

Melvin, James (1986), *A Statement of Hope, The Essential Writings of Martin Luther King Jr.*, Harper & Co., Washington.

Merrett, Christopher (1996), *Free Trade, Neither Free Nor About Trade*, Black Rose Books, New York.

Metropolis Theatre Co. v. City of Chicago, 228 U.S. 61 (1913).

Mexican Investment Board (1994), *Mexico Your Partner for Growth, Regulatory Reform and Competition Policy, Setting the Incentives for an Efficient Economy*, Mexico.

Michael M v. Sonoma County Superior Court, 450 U.S. 464 (1981).

Miles, Angela (1989), 'Ideological Hegemony in Political Discourse', in Angela Miles and Geraldine Finn, *Feminism*, Black Rose Books, Montreal.

Mill, John Stuart and Taylor Mill, Harriett (1970), *Essays on Sex Equality*, University of Chicago Press, Chicago.

Minister of Industry (1997), *Canada Yearbook*.

Ministry of Women's Affairs, New Zealand, 1998.

Montgomery Bowker, Marjorie (1988), *On Guard For Thee*, Voyageur Publishing, Hull.

Murphy v. Miller Brewer Co., 307 F.Supp. 829 (1969).

Nader, Ralph (1993), *The Case Against Free Trade*, Earth Island Press, San Francisco.

National Minimum Wage Act, Great Britain, 1998.

National Minimum Wage Regulations, Great Britain, 1999.

Neufeld, E.P. (1987), 'Financial and Economic Dimensions of Free Trade', in A.R. Riggs and Tom Velk, *Canadian-American Free Trade: Historical, Political and Economic Dimensions*, The Institute for Research on Public Policy, Montreal.

Nicoll, William and Salmon, Trevor (1994), *Understanding the New European Community*.

Nietzsche, Friedrich (1966), *Beyond Good and Evil*, New York.

Nietzsche, Friedrich (1967), *Ecce Homo and the Genealogy of Morals*, New York.

Niles, Thomas (1987), 'Address', in A.R. Riggs and Tom Velk, *Canadian-American Free Trade: Historical, Political and Economic Dimensions*, The Institute for Research on Public Policy, Montreal.

North American Agreement on Labor Cooperation, 1994.

North American Free Trade Agreement, 1991.

North, Arthur (1964), *The Supreme Court, Judicial Process and Judicial Politics*, Appleton Century Crofts, New York.

Nussbaum, Martha (2000), *Women and Human Development*, Cambridge University Press, Cambridge.

O'Brien, Mary (1979), 'Reproducing Marxist Man', in Lorenne M.G. Clark and Lynda Lange, *The Sexism of Social and Political Theory, Women and Reproduction from Plato to Nietzsche*, University of Toronto Press, Toronto.

Occupational Pension Schemes (Equal Treatment) Regulations, Great Britain, 1995.

Oliver, Michael (1991), *The Passionate Debate*, Vehicule Press, Montreal.

Olivier, Christiane (1989), *Jocasta's Children, The Imprint of the Mother*, Routledge, London.

Ontario Human Rights Commission v. Simpsons-Sears Ltd., [1985] S.C.R. 536.

Optional Protocol to the Convention on the Elimination of All Forms of Discrimination against Women.

Optional Protocol to the International Covenant on Civil and Political Rights.

O'Reilly, Andrea (2001), *Mothers and Sons: Feminism, Masculinity and the Struggle to Raise Our Sons*, Routledge, London.

Orenstein, Peggy (2000), *Women on Work, Love, Children and Life*, Piatkus, London.

Orr v. Orr, 440 U.S. 268 (1979).

Papillon, Benoit (1987), 'Bankruptcy Law, Free Trade and Economic Adjustments, Preliminary Considerations', in A.R. Riggs and Tom Velk, *Canadian-American Free Trade: Historical, Political and Economic Dimensions*, The Institute for Research on Public Policy, Montreal.

Part-Time Workers Regulations, Great Britain, 2000.

Pease, Bob (2000), *Recreating Men, Postmodern Masculinity Politics*, Sage, London.

Pensions Act, Great Britain, 1995.

Pettman, Barrie (1975), *Equal Pay for Women*, MCB Books, Bradford.

Phillips v. Martin Marietta Corp., 400 U.S. 542 (1971)).

Piori, Michael (1980), *Dualism and Discontinuity in Industrial Societies*, Cambridge University Press, Cambridge.

Plato (1968), *Republic*, New York.

Pope John XXIII (1963), *Pacem in Terris*.

Pope John Paul II (1981), *Laborem Exercens*.

Pope John Paul II (1991), *Centesimus Annus*.

Population Reference Bureau (2002), *Women of Our World*.

Promotion of Equality and Prevention of Unfair Discrimination Act, 2000.

Protection from Harassment Act, Great Britain, 1997.

Protocol on the Rights of Women in Africa.

Protocol to the African Charter on Human and Peoples' Rights.

Pyle, Jean (1990), *The State and Women in the Economy*, State University of New York, Albany.

Race Relations Act, Great Britain, 1976.

Racial Discrimination Act, Australia, 1975.

Rado, Lisa (1997), *Modernism, Gender and Culture*, Garland Publishing, New York.

Raynauld, Andre (1987), 'Looking Outward Again', in A.R. Riggs and Tom Velk, *Canadian-American Free Trade: Historical, Political and Economic Dimensions*, The Institute for Research on Public Policy, Montreal.

Razack, Sherene (1991), *Canadian Feminism and the Law*, Second Story Press, Toronto.

Reed v. Reed, 404 U.S. 71 (1971).

Regina v. Oakes, [1986] 1 S.C.R. 103.

Research and Advocacy of the Hull House Association (1982), *Women in Poverty*, Report on a Conference about the Feminization of Poverty.

Reskin, Barbara and Roos, Patricia (1990), *Job Queues, Gender Queues*, Temple University Press, Philadelphia.

Riggs, A.R. and Velk, Tom (1987), *Canadian-American Free Trade: Historical, Political and Economic Dimensions*, The Institute for Research on Public Policy, Montreal.

Riggs, A.R. and Velk, Tom (1988), *Canadian-American Free Trade: (The Sequel) Historical, Political and Economic Dimensions*, The Institute for Research on Public Policy, Montreal.

Ritchie, Gordon (1988), 'The Free Trade Agreement', in A.R. Riggs and Tom Velk, *Canadian-American Free Trade: (The Sequel) Historical, Political and Economic Dimensions*, The Institute for Research on Public Policy, Montreal.

Rothblatt, Martine (1995), *The Apartheid of Sex*, Crown Publishers, New York.

Rotsker v. Goldberg, 453 U.S. 57 (1981).

Rousseau, Jean-Jacques (1969), *Emile*, New York.

Rousseau, Jean-Jacques (1973), *Discourse on the Origin of Inequality Among Men*, London.

San Antonio Independent School Division v. Rodriguez, 411 U.S. 1 (1973).

Sargeant, Georgia, 'Pay Equity: Lagging in Court, Gaining at the Bargaining Table', *Trial*, Vol.26, N.2, 1990, p.98.

Schlesinger v. Ballard, 419 U.S. 498 (1975).

Schwartz, Barry (1975), *Queuing and Waiting*, University of Chicago Press, Chicago.

Scott, Hilda (1984), *Working Your Way to the Bottom*, Pandora Press, London.

Scott, Joan (1988), *Gender and the Politics of History*, Columbia University Press, New York.

Scott, Joan (1996), *Feminism and History*, Oxford University Press, Oxford.

Sex Discrimination Act 1975 (As amended), Great Britain.

Sex Discrimination Act, Australia, 1984.

Sex Discrimination (Complaints to Employment Tribunals) (Armed Forces) Regulations, Great Britain, 1997.

Sex Discrimination (Northern Ireland) Order, 1976.

Sex Discrimination (Questions and Replies) Order, Great Britain, 1975.

Shakes v. Rex Pak Ltd. (1982), 3 C.H.R.R. D/1001.

Shuaib, Susan, 'Courtesy of Europe', *New Statesman & Society*, Dec. 1988, p.25.

Shultz v. Wheaton Glass, 421 F.2d. 259 (1970).

Skud, Tim (1988), 'Free Trade, What Now for the U.S.', in A.R. Riggs and Tom Velk, *Canadian-American Free Trade: (The Sequel) Historical, Political and Economic Dimensions*, The Institute for Research on Public Policy, Montreal.

Smith, Murray (1988), 'Free Trade and the European Experience', in A.R. Riggs and Tom Velk, *Canadian-American Free Trade: (The Sequel) Historical, Political and Economic Dimensions*, The Institute for Research on Public Policy, Montreal.

Snitow, Ann (1996), 'A Gender Diary', in Joan Wallach Scott, *Feminism and History*, Oxford University Press, Oxford.

Social Security Contributions and Benefits Act, Great Britain, 1992.

Soldatos, P (1988), 'Canada's Foreign Policy in Search of a Fourth Option: Continuity and Change in Orientation Towards the U.S.', in A.R. Riggs and Tom Velk (1988),

Canadian-American Free Trade: (The Sequel) Historical, Political and Economic Dimensions, The Institute for Research on Public Policy, Montreal.
Soreman, Elaine (1994), *Comparative Worth, Is It a Worthy Policy?*
South African Census (1996).
Spaulding v. University of Washington, 740 F.2d. 686 (1984).
Spencer, Anne (1987), *In a Man's World*, Tavistock Publishing, London.
Stanton v. Stanton, 421 U.S. 7 (1975).
Statistics Canada (1994), *Women in the Labor Force*.
Statistics Canada (1996), *Canada at a Glance*.
Statute of the International Court of Justice.
Statutory Maternity Pay (General) Regulations, Great Britain, 1986.
Statutory Maternity Pay (General) (Modification and Amendment) Regulations, Great Britain, 2000.
Sterba, James (2001), *Controversies in Feminism*, Rowman & Littlefield, Oxford.
Stevens, Paul (1987), Reciprocity 1911: The Canadian Perspective, in A.R. Riggs and Tom Velk, *Canadian-American Free Trade: Historical, Political and Economic Dimensions*, The Institute for Research on Public Policy, Montreal.
Stone, Frank (1987), 'Removing Barriers to Canada', in A.R. Riggs and Tom Velk, *Canadian-American Free Trade: Historical, Political and Economic Dimensions*, The Institute for Research on Public Policy, Montreal.
Surrey, David (1982), *Choice of Conscience Vietnam Era and Draft Resisters in Canada*, Praeger, New York.
Tawney, R.H. (1920), *The Acquisitive Society*, Harcourt, Brace & Co., New York.
Taylor v. Louisiana, 419 U.S. 522 (1975).
Teuling v. Bredrijfsvereniging, [1987] ECR 2497.
Thompson, Mark (1975), 'Le Syndicalisme Québecois dans le contexte Nord-Americain', in *Choix*, Centre Québécois de Relations Internationales, Laval.
Thompson, Denise (2001), *Radical Feminism Today*, Sage, London.
Tietjens Meyers, Diana (1993), *Kindred Matters, Rethinking the Philosophy of the Family*, Cornell University Press, Ithaca.
Tietjens Meyers, Diana (1997), *Feminists Rethink the Self*, Westview Press, Boulder.
Treaty of Amsterdam, 1997.
Treaty of Paris, 1951.
Treaty of Rome, 1957.
Twine, France (2001), *Feminism and Antiracism, International Struggles for Justice*, New York University Press, New York.
United Nations (1997), *Demographic Yearbook*.
United Nations (2000), *The World's Women 2000: Trends and Statistics*.
United Nations Development Program (1994), *Human Development Report*, Oxford University Press.
United Nations Division for the Advancement of Women (2002), *Women 2000*.
United Nations Women Watch, *Beijing+5 Process and Beyond*.
United Nations Women Watch, *Commitments of Governments to Implement the Beijing Platform for Action*.
United Nations, *Beijing Declaration and Platform for Action, Fourth World Conference on Women*.
United Nations Women Watch (2000), *Progress of the World's Women*.
United States Census Bureau (1997), *Statistical Abstract*.
United States Census Bureau (2000), *Women in the United States*.
United States Civil Rights Act, 1964.
United States Declaration of Independence, 1776.

United States Equal Pay Act, 1963.

Universal Declaration of Human Rights, 1948.

Van Lenning, Alkeline (1997), *Feminist Utopias in a Postmodern Era*, Tilburg University Press.

Velk, Tom and Riggs, A.R. (1987), 'The Men that Corrupted Everyburg, American Farmers and the Free Trade Initiative 1911', in A.R. Riggs and Tom Velk, *Canadian-American Free Trade: Historical, Political and Economic Dimensions*, The Institute for Research on Public Policy, Montreal.

Velk, Tom and Riggs, A.R. (1987), 'The Ongoing Debate Over Free Trade', in A.R. Riggs and Tom Velk, *Canadian-American Free Trade: Historical, Political and Economic Dimensions*, The Institute for Research on Public Policy, Montreal.

Violi, Patrizia (1992), 'Gender, Subjectivity and Language', in Gisela Bock and Susan James, *Beyond Equality and Difference, Citizens, Feminist Politics and Female Subjectivity*, Routledge, London.

Wallach Scott, Joan (1988), *Gender and the Politics of History*, Columbia University Press, New York.

Wallach Scott, Joan (1996), *Feminism and History*, Oxford University Press, Oxford.

Walsh, Brendan, 'Can Europe Solve its Job Crisis?', *Administration*, Vol.40, N.1, 1992.

Walter, Natasha (2000), *On the Move, Feminism for a New Generation*, Virago, London.

Warskett, Rosemary, 'Wage Solidarity and Equal Value: Or Gender and Class in the Structuring of Work Place Hierarchies', *Studies in Political Economy* 32, 1990.

Warskett, Rosemary (1991), 'Political Power, Technical Disputes, and Unequal Pay: A Federal Case', in Judy Fudge, *Just Wages, Feminine Perspective of Pay Equity*, University of Toronto Press, Toronto.

Warskett, Rosemary (1993), 'Can a Disappearing Pie Be Shared Equally?: Unions, Women, and Wage Fairness, in Linda Briskin, *Women Challenging Unions: Feminism, Democracy and Militancy*, University of Toronto Press, Toronto.

Washington v. Davis, 426 U.S. 229 (1976).

Watkins, Mel, *Alternatives to Free Trade*, Centre for Policy Alternatives, Ottawa.

Watkins, Mel (1989), 'The Political Economy of Growth', in Wallace Clement and Glen Williams, *The New Canadian Political Economy*, McGill-Queen's University Press, Kingston.

Watson, William, 'The Draft Agreement, Cohabitation Worth a Try', in A.R. Riggs and Tom Velk (1988), *Canadian-American Free Trade: (The Sequel) Historical, Political and Economic Dimensions*, The Institute for Research on Public Policy, Montreal.

Weisberg, D. Kelly (1982), *Women and the Law*, Schenkman, Cambridge.

Whelehan, Imelda (2000), *Overload, Popular Culture and the Future of Feminism*, Women's, London.

White, Gerry, 'Report of the Revision Group on the Treatment of Households in the Social Welfare Code', *Administration*, Vol.40, N.3, 1992.

White, Randall (1988), *Fur Trade to Free Trade: Putting the Canada-U.S. Trade Agreement in Historical Perspective*, Dundurn Press, Toronto.

Wickham, James (1986), *Industrializing Work and Unemployment*, Ireland.

Wigle, Randall (1987), 'The Received Wisdom of the Canada-U.S. Free Trade, Qualifications', in A.R. Riggs and Tom Welk, *Canadian-American Free Trade: Historical, Political and Economic Dimensions*, The Institute for Research in Public Policy, Montreal.

Wollstonecraft, Mary (1792), *Vindication of the Rights of Women*, Source Book Press, London.

Women and Equality Unit (2002), *Key indicators of women's position in Britain*.

Working Time Regulations, Great Britain, 1998.
Workplace Relations Act, 1996, Australia.
Wyatt, Addie, *Public Policy Today: Its Effect on Poor Women*.
Yohalem, Alice (1979), *The Careers of Professional Women*, Allanheld Osmun & Co., Montclair.
Young, Robert (1987), 'Canada-U.S. Free Trade, Economic Realities and Political Choices', in A.R. Riggs and Tom Velk, *Canadian-American Free Trade: Historical, Political and Economic Dimensions*, The Institute for Research on Public Policy, Montreal.

Index